DETROIT REMAINS

DETROIT REMAINS

Archaeology and Community Histories of Six Legendary Places

KRYSTA RYZEWSKI

THE UNIVERSITY OF ALABAMA PRESS

TUSCALOOSA

The University of Alabama Press
Tuscaloosa, Alabama 35487-0380
uapress.ua.edu

Copyright © 2022 by the University of Alabama Press
All rights reserved.

Inquiries about reproducing material from this work should be addressed to the
University of Alabama Press.

Typeface: Scala Pro, Avenir

Cover image: *Detroit 1967* by Jack Ward, Gordon Park,
Detroit, site of the July 1967 uprising; photograph courtesy of Krysta Ryzewski
Cover design: David Nees

Cataloging-in-Publication data is available from the Library of Congress.
ISBN: 978-0-8173-2104-8 (cloth)
ISBN: 978-0-8173-6028-3 (paper)
E-ISBN: 978-0-8173-9373-1

In memory of
Richard A. Gould, archaeologist and storyteller extraordinaire, and
Jeri Lynn Pajor, Detroit's first rock 'n' roll archaeologist

CONTENTS

ACKNOWLEDGMENTS

Dozens of people contributed to the research and collaborations featured in *Detroit Remains*. Most of them have long-term connections with the area and personal experiences with Detroit's struggles. All share a deep appreciation for the ways in which the city's history can be told, and its heritage appreciated, from the perspective of historical archaeology.

First and foremost, I owe my deepest gratitude to those archaeologists who participated as members of the fieldwork and research teams on more than one of the *Detroit Remains* projects. This core group includes Don Adzigian, Bridget Bennane, Lorin Brace, Brendan Doucet, Samantha Ellens, Jeri Pajor, and Athena Zissis. They were integral to the success of these projects. Without their dedication in the field, this book would not have been possible. I am thankful to them for their continued commitment to Detroit and to its archaeology. They have helped chart new courses for recognizing the histories of the city's marginalized communities and for promoting Detroit's rich cultural heritage.

I am fortunate to be part of a supportive and energetic community of scholars at Wayne State University. In the Department of Anthropology, my home base, I am especially indebted to my faculty colleagues Tamara Bray and Yuson Jung, who willingly read and commented on drafts of this manuscript. I also thank Tom Killion and Andrea Sankar, who invited me to speak about these projects in their classes; Julie Lesnik and Jessica Robbins, who helped me brainstorm ideas for the book's structure and tone; and Stephen Chrisomalis, for his shared enthusiasm for archaeology and for supporting the graduate students who worked with me in his capacity as director of graduate studies. Uzma Khan and Debra Mazur provided invaluable administrative support, becoming experts in finding deals on five-gallon buckets, tarps, and shovels in the process. Katharine Blatchford assisted with digitizing maps and plans. I am also appreciative of my colleagues Sangeetha Gopalakrishnan, Alina Klin, Laura Kline, Julie Koehler, Jennifer Hart, and Karen Marrero, who have encouraged this research as it emerged during the course of various digital humanities projects, working groups, and conferences. Dean Wayne Raskind and Dean Stephanie Hartwell of the College of Liberal Arts and Sciences provided resources and enthusiasm. Funding for the completion of this book was provided by the Arts and Humanities Research Program, Office of the Vice President for Research, Wayne State University.

Beyond Wayne State I owe thanks to John F. Cherry, who provided constructive comments on the manuscript's first draft. Several colleagues invited me to present lectures about the projects in *Detroit Remains* at their universities in recent years. It was through these talks and the conversations afterward that I honed the framework for the book. Thanks to Susan Hyatt and Paul Mullins (IUPUI), Andy Roddick (McMaster), Matt Reilly (City College New York), Meredith Chesson and Ian Kuijt (Notre Dame), Sue Alcock (University of Michigan), Tim Scarlett and Don Lafreniere (Michigan Tech), and Chris Rodning (Tulane). I am also grateful to Rebecca Graff and Lorin Brace for co-organizing sessions with me at the Society for Historical Archaeology meetings in Boston and New Orleans that focused on topics within this book, to photographer and history buff Eileen Krugel (my aunt), who assisted me with image edits, and to my eagle-eyed proofreader, Leah Jones.

At Tommy's Detroit Bar and Grill, the site of Little Harry speakeasy, I owe sincere thanks to Tom Burelle and Marion Christiansen, who took a chance on archaeology and gave my team the first opportunity to hone our collaborative archaeology skills at a legendary Detroit site. Thanks also to Lucy Kaiser. In addition to the archaeologists listed at the outset, the project team included section leaders Brenna Moloney and Shawn Fields, and contributions from field crew members and researchers Paul Carlson, Catherine Devereaux, Elspeth Geiger, Ken Krutcher, Jaroslava Pallas, Graham Sheckels, and Michael Vandro. I am also grateful to Katie Korth, who provided archival research and production assistance on the NEH-funded digital story we produced about the speakeasy as part of the Ethnic Layers of Detroit project. Former Preservation Detroit president Melanie Markowicz supported event programming and publicity efforts. Detroit historian Mickey Lyons shared her expertise on Prohibition legislation. Arthur and Gina Horwitz played essential roles in connecting the project with the Jewish community and media nationally. Jacqueline Ogus, Bruce Finsilver, Marina Nelson, Carol Woodruff, Pam Steinmetz, and Michael Whiteman, who are descendants of the building's prior owners, Harry Weitzman and Harry Bianchini, provided invaluable insights into these two noteworthy Prohibition-era entrepreneurs.

The Ransom Gillis house project would not have been possible without a serendipitous Uber pickup by Jennifer Ruud, then of Preservation Detroit. Thanks also to Amy Elliott Bragg, former president of Preservation

Detroit, and Steve McBride, executive director of Pewabic Pottery for partnering their organizations with me on the project. We enjoyed the opportunity to work with the Rehab Addict production team and Nicole Curtis, and I appreciate the adjustments they made to their filming schedule to accommodate our archaeology project. I also thank Bedrock Detroit, who granted us permission to work on the site. Thanks to the archaeologists named above, as well as field crew members Eric Boulis, Kaitlin Deslatte, Mark Jazayeri, Lydia Rennalls, Kimberly Shay, and Susan Villerot. Stacy Tchorzynski from the Michigan State Historic Preservation Office helped me with access to Brush Park's archaeological site file research, author John Kossik assisted with historical information, and Pewabic archivist Anne Dennis located photos of Stable Studio.

The Blue Bird Inn project was a collaboration with Carleton Gholz of the Detroit Sound Conservancy. The immense energy and commitment he has devoted to protecting Detroit's music heritage are unmatched in the city's preservation advocacy scene. I am grateful to him for his willingness to work with me over the past five years, to include archaeology in the Detroit Sound Conservancy's vision and planning process, and for furnishing important feedback on a draft of the Blue Bird chapter. Lorin Brace and Samantha Ellens led the first archaeological survey crew inside the Blue Bird, and I am also thankful to Lorin for sharing his thesis data with me. In addition to those already mentioned, thanks to field crew members Chris Papalis and Sarah Beste. Rob McCallum shared firsthand accounts of his visit to the Blue Bird as well as the *Metro Times* article he wrote about it.

The surveys at Gordon Park involved students from Wayne State University, who make up an important and diverse group of local stakeholders from Detroit and its suburbs. In addition to those already listed, I thank Luke Buzo, Bailee Earl, Paula Henderson, Ashlee Jed, and Elizabeth Reidman. Marlowe Stoudamire, an early victim of the COVID-19 pandemic in Detroit, is remembered here for his contributions to the historical marker's language. Thanks also to Kevin Mueller for sharing his photographs of the park, and to artist Jack Ward for granting his permission to use the image of his monument on the book's cover.

The Grande Ballroom project took years to execute. In the time leading up to it I enjoyed countless hours of conversations with archaeology graduate student Jeri Pajor about her memories of attending concerts there in the 1960s. Jeri gave me valuable comments on an earlier draft of this chapter and connected me with former concertgoer Michael Bolan. Jeri passed away suddenly in May 2020, days after the Wayne State Department of

Anthropology conferred on her a master's degree. I hope to honor her passion for Detroit's history and archaeology with this book. Our work at the Grande Ballroom was made possible by Leo Early, who orchestrated access to the building and coordinated contacts with other stakeholders, including Roger Manela and Reverend Lamont Smith of the Chapel Hill Missionary Baptist Church. In addition to the archaeologists named previously, I thank Beau Kromberg for his participation in the Grande survey.

Our work at the Halleck Street log cabin was possible because of a tip I received from Joe Goeddeke, an environmental inspector for the state of Michigan. I thank him for his vigilance and willingness to reach out to me. The log cabin project was a collaboration with the Hamtramck Historical Museum and would not have achieved the level of potency and visibility that it did without the involvement of museum director Greg Kowalski. Thanks also to Hamtramck Historical Museum Board members Joe Kochut, Tom Cervanek, and Cindy Cervanek for participating in the project. In Hamtramck we received support from Mayor Karen Majewski, the Hamtramck City Council, and City Clerk August Gitschlag. Melissa Arrowsmith from the Michigan Historic Preservation Network provided an important voice from the Detroit preservation community, as did Marion Christiansen. Local reporters Neal Rubin, Roop Raj, and Jill Washburn produced thorough coverage of the controversy. Those involved with the survey, excavation, open day, and artifact processing included Hannon Hylkema, Misty Jackson, Kelsey Jorgensen, Megan McCullen, Andrew McKinney, Malik Pasha, Luke Pickrahn, David Pitawanakwat, Carly Slank, Samantha Spolarich, Kazimir Ryzewski, Hannelore Willeck, and other archaeologists listed above. Special thanks to Misty Jackson for joining forces with me and bringing the federal funding loopholes to the attention of the State Historic Preservation Review Board. Dean Anderson, state archaeologist of Michigan, provided guidance on state and federal blight management policies. Tim Bennett pointed me to earlier maps of the area, Zachary Merrill conducted dendrochronology analysis, and the Conference of Michigan Archaeology recognized the value of the work with its Outreach Award.

For their assistance with archival research and historic images, I thank the librarians and staff at the Detroit Public Library (Burton Historical Collection), Walter P. Reuther Library at Wayne State University, Bentley Library at the University of Michigan, the Detroit Historical Society, Grosscup Museum of Anthropology at Wayne State University, Detroit Sound Conservancy, Hamtramck Historical Museum, Hamtramck City Hall, and the Wayne County Register of Deeds.

I wanted to write a book that would be accessible and maybe even enjoyable to read. While I worked to minimize jargon and distill theoretical debates, I had my undergraduate students, the local residents I connected with during our various projects, and my family in mind. Fortunately, Wendi Schnaufer, my editor at the University of Alabama Press, enthusiastically supported my vision. I thank her for facilitating the book's smooth review and publication process and for championing Detroit. I also thank the anonymous reviewers who took the time to provide me with insightful feedback that I used to improve my final manuscript.

Finally, I owe my ability to conduct and complete this work to my energetic and devoted family at Quad K Ranch: Kaitlin, Kazimir (5), and Kamille (1). Having to complete this manuscript as Michigan descended into the COVID-19 lockdown meant that I gained the company of two junior editorial assistants. While I take full responsibility for any oversights and factual errors, they may have contributed a couple of typos.

INTRODUCTION

Detroit Remains
The Legendary Heritage of an Iconic City

What makes a place legendary? A place—whether an entire city, neighborhood, building, or park—accrues legendary status because of its memorable associations with compelling events and people. Archaeologists, no matter where in the world they work, are routinely confronted by narratives about places whose significance is attached to heroes, ghosts, criminals, disasters, or, of course, long-lost treasures. These stories run the gamut from verifiable historical accounts to fanciful myths.

Detroit, Michigan, is replete with colorful tales about its tumultuous past. Many of these stories boast ties to physical places in the postindustrial city: Prohibition-era speakeasies, secret tunnels for Underground Railroad travelers, vacant automobile factories, Native American burial mounds, once-popular music venues, and haunted historic buildings. Other stories reference unsolved mysteries. In fact, the most common question onlookers ask when they visit archaeological excavations in Detroit is whether diggers are searching for the body of Jimmy Hoffa, the notorious labor union leader and convicted criminal who vanished in 1975.

Fortunately, archaeologists are equipped with the tools and techniques to sift fact from fiction when they examine places that feature prominently in the public imagination. Archaeology is the discipline that studies the human past through material remains. The key words in this definition are *material* and *human*. Material remains are tangible things made or altered by humans. They range in size from microscopic domesticated plant remains to portable objects, written records, buildings, monuments, cemeteries, and road systems (and everything in between). When archaeologists speak of the human past, they refer to the entirety of human history—the period beginning about 200,000 years ago, when our species, *Homo sapiens*, first emerged, up to the present. In practice, archaeologists tend to focus their research on particular periods within this timeframe: millennia, centuries, or even decades. This book is an example of historical archaeology, a particular subfield of archaeology. Historical archaeology is concerned with the study of the relatively recent past, beginning in North America around AD 1500 (the early modern era) and extending into the present. This period encompasses the emergence of global capitalism and the unprecedented expansion of industries, cities, and social inequalities that accompanied it.

Archaeologists may be sticklers for referencing accurate historic and scientific details, but they are also the first to admit that their data are always fragmentary. They will never know for sure what happened at a particular place in time because they cannot recover a complete picture of its past from broken bits of trash, decaying buildings, subjective written records, or fading memories. Although archaeologists enlist as many sources of information as possible in their efforts to reconstruct past activities, there will always be gaps for creative interpretations to fill in. This is why archaeologists never issue a final verdict on a site or an artifact's meaning. They recognize that the things they excavate and the buildings or landscapes they document are not static or fixed in time. Rather, the meanings of things and places change as new discoveries and circumstances emerge. This interpretive process is visible in Detroit, where engagements with archaeological remains and historic structures reflect present-day interests in economic recovery, civil rights–era heritage, and resident immigrant communities.

Detroit's recent history of industrialization and urban renewal bears similarities to the transformative experiences that shaped many North American cities. While the city's historical processes may not be especially unique, Detroit has nonetheless succeeded in capturing public imagination internationally. Detroit is captivating and iconic because of its epic successes and failures. Residents' creative energies revolutionized manufacturing industries, automotive technology, and music. The magnitude of these accomplishments, their importance in the lives of people worldwide, and their loss at the hands of economic downturn cast Detroit as a textbook example of urban failure. The extent to which these achievements and losses are evident in extant material remains is revealed in this book through the lens of archaeology.

Detroit Remains presents archaeologically based narratives about six legendary places in the city. The case studies span a period of unprecedented industrial growth, decline, and revitalization between the late nineteenth century and the present. They foreground the processes of community-involved and collaborative archaeological research and detail how these interventions connect legendary places in the city with underrepresented communities and their histories. I present each of the six sites against the backdrops of Detroit's current struggles, the city's legacy of grassroots political activism, and its future-oriented recovery efforts. The sites include Little Harry speakeasy, the Ransom Gillis house, the Blue Bird Inn jazz club, Gordon Park, the Grande Ballroom, and the Halleck Street log cabin (Figure I.1). Throughout this book, connections run deep between archaeology, heritage, politics, historic preservation, and storytelling.

OBJECTIVES AND SCOPE

Detroit Remains has four objectives. First, its case studies demonstrate the benefits of an applied archaeological approach for assembling and recounting, from a material standpoint, some of the rich place-based community histories that survive in the city, even when traces of these pasts are no longer immediately visible aboveground. Instead of perpetuating the myth that Detroit lies in ruins, I focus on what remains of the city's past in the present. Each case study reflects on how various traces of the city's iconic entrepreneurial, musical, industrial, and activist heritage persist within the context of the city's present-day struggles. I also mobilize the case studies to consider how the preservation of these remains (or the lack thereof) fits within the city's fast-moving revitalization plans.

Second, I use archaeological findings to foreground the cultural expressions, social relationships, and material remains associated with Detroit's

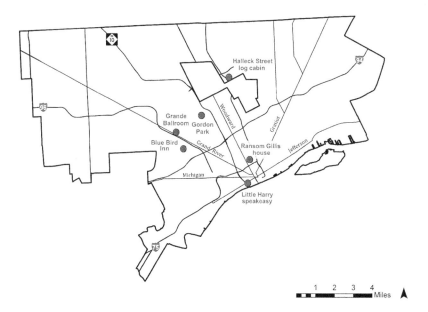

Figure I.1. Map of Detroit showing main arterial roads, freeways, and the six archaeological sites discussed in *Detroit Remains*. (Katharine Blatchford and Krysta Ryzewski)

underrepresented communities, past and present. These groups include: low-income residents displaced by mid-twentieth-century urban renewal efforts; Jewish entrepreneurs; African American jazz musicians and small business owners; female artists; counterculture-era rock musicians and their fans; civil rights–era activists; Prohibition-era criminals; newcomers during the Great Migration (ca. 1915–1970); and recent immigrant communities. Understanding the connections of these people in relation to specific places requires a historical anthropological reflection on the complex processes of community formation in a fast-changing urban setting. This perspective considers how communities are constituted as well as how they intersect and disband over time in response to various sociopolitical and geographic circumstances.

Third, of particular value to my historical archaeology colleagues, I present archaeological scholarship that is rooted in collaborative, community-involved, and public-facing initiatives. In each chapter I describe and evaluate the processes, results, challenges, and afterlives of the associated participatory projects. The stories in *Detroit Remains* demonstrate how community histories resonate with and empower present-day stakeholder groups.

Finally, *Detroit Remains* serves a broader practical purpose by providing extensive and previously unpublished historical and archaeological details about the six case study sites. It is my hope that this information will serve as the basis for future preservation, education, and advocacy initiatives led by local communities, nonprofits, or scholars. It may also lay the foundation for securing future funding and the scaling up of sustainable community-involved archaeology and preservation projects in Detroit and beyond.

Readers who are new to historical archaeology may find themselves wondering at some points in this book where the familiar stuff of archaeology is—the large-scale excavations, awe-inspiring artifacts, and robust scientific data sets. It is present, rest assured, albeit in more diverse forms and combinations than might be expected. One of the distinct advantages of historical archaeology is that there is an abundance of different types of evidence available to study. Not only do historical archaeologists have access to excavated artifacts, but the relatively recent sites and topics they study also tend to be associated with troves of documentary sources (textual and visual) as well as oral histories (e.g., personal memories and folklore). As a result, some of the most impressive scholarly contributions result from the combination of mundane textual details and artifact data; these findings have the potential to convey significant information about the forgotten or unspoken daily experiences of people whose stories tend not to appear in history books.

As I discuss further in chapter 1, historical archaeologists consider all of their sources of evidence, whether written documents or portable objects, to be forms of material culture. They examine these sources critically and attempt to understand them anthropologically in relation to the contexts within which they were produced, used, and either discarded or preserved. Each source of information provides a different scale of resolution about the people and processes associated with archaeological study sites.[1] Historical archaeologists blend these multiple types of evidence into responsible, interpretive narratives that recognize the complexities of how people negotiated their positions in society relative to the distinct interpersonal, sociopolitical, and environmental circumstances of their time.

In the remainder of this introductory chapter, I set the stage for the book's case studies by providing a brief summary of Detroit that reflects on its legendary status, key transformative moments, and present-day situation. I also explain why archaeology has a vital role in telling community-based histories before I conclude by charting the course for the rest of the book.

LEGENDARY DETROIT

Detroit's legendary associations vary in terms of their scope and scale.[2] The positive and negative ways in which they are woven into conversations about the city have a powerful influence in shaping narratives about its rich history and cultural heritage.

When we celebrate Detroit as the Motor City—the birthplace of the automobile and the city that put the world on wheels—we use "legendary" as an adjective to describe a transformative, world-changing invention and the famous places associated with it. We recognize the historical accomplishments that occurred at Henry Ford's Piquette Avenue and Highland Park plants, especially the company's introduction of revolutionary assembly-line production and the five-dollar-per-day wage during the first two decades of the 1900s.

Detroit's legendary reputation as a place of innovation extends to its music scene too. Its distinct Motown sound of the 1960s and its status as the birthplace of techno music in the 1980s are associated with the entrepreneurial genius of Berry Gordy Jr. and Motown's signature musicians as well as techno artists and producers ranging from Juan Atkins to Jeff Mills.[3] These genealogies are rooted, respectively, in Studio A at Motown Records and Submerge Records on the city's east side. In these cases, the city's legendary music heritage invites pride in the industry's connections to particular places.

It is also common to construe Detroit in a negative light by perpetuating myths whose details are disconnected from facts. Media portrayals of Detroit over the past decade seize on images of ruins to recast the city as a place that is infamous worldwide for its unprecedented blight, crime, and abandonment. Owing to decades of economic downturn, foreclosures, and social upheaval, over 78,000 decaying structures create a scarred landscape of modern, untimely ruins.[4] Reporters, urban explorers, and artists routinely collect and circulate photographs of decaying buildings and open swaths of land where houses used to stand. These images are broadcast in the media and across the internet as metaphors for a deteriorating modern society. Such messaging has damaging consequences, especially locally, for how the city's history, people, and heritage are portrayed and understood.

Like many cities, Detroit also has its fair share of fantastic urban legends tied to specific buildings and landscape features. Urban legends are stories of popular tradition that are collectively invented, embellished, and remembered. Two favorite topics of urban legend in Detroit involve Prohibition-era alcohol smuggling (bootlegging) and Underground Railroad sites.[5] Both subjects require place-based connections in their reliance on hidden spaces—basement rooms, tunnels, secret passageways, and hideouts. But because these accounts revolve around covert activities in which participants were less likely to leave behind material traces, physical sites associated with them are challenging to locate and verify. Nevertheless, these subjects offer the perfect ingredients for urban legends, evocative elements of resilience, danger, and secrecy that make legendary stories fascinating and memorable.

Detroit's legendary stories share two themes. First, they feature stories of people who were, in some measure, creative and entrepreneurial risk-takers—whether they were Prohibition-era Purple Gang mobsters or pioneering bebop jazz musicians. Second, they reside in the public's collective memory and tend to be transmitted in informal settings. Archaeologists who work on sites associated with legendary histories must strike a careful balance to engage the many communities of people whose interests their work serves.[6] On the one hand, it is archaeologists' responsibility to employ the discipline's methods to create historically and scientifically grounded stories; on the other hand, because they will never reconstruct a full picture of what happened in the past, archaeologists must also leave room for creative interpretations.

DETROIT IN THE TWENTY-FIRST CENTURY: RUINATION AND THE MYTH OF A DEAD CITY

Over the course of the past two decades Detroit has become the poster child for urban decay in the United States as it experienced a dramatic and seemingly rapid downturn from a thriving global manufacturing center in the twentieth century, emblematic of upward mobility and progress, to a bankrupt city riddled with blight and mismanagement. These stark contrasts position Detroit as a poignant metaphor for the collapse of neoliberal capitalism, urban planning, and American industrial strength.[7] The city's struggles, illustrated by jarring images of ruined buildings, vistas of empty fields where tightly packed neighborhoods used to stand, and grim demographic statistics stoke anxieties about the future of this iconic city, and, more generally, the fate of comparable American cities. Detroit is far from the only industrial city to suffer from disinvestment, blight, and out-migration in recent years. Dozens of major cities and postindustrial towns across the United States (e.g., Cleveland, St. Louis, Buffalo) are experiencing similar upheavals. In Michigan alone, areas of Flint, Pontiac, and Saginaw mirror the postapocalyptic landscape so often essentialized as the hallmark of contemporary Detroit. Yet these places do not capture public imagination with the same intensity as Detroit, and so they tend to receive far less attention from media, politicians, and scholars. American studies scholar Jerry Herron suggests that Detroit garners more coverage than other struggling cities because it is the most representative city in the United States; this distinction is what sustains it as a national, if not international, focal point for conversations about the consequences of deindustrialization in urban centers.[8]

There is no question that the scale of Detroit's physical losses, among its built environment, infrastructure, and population base, is unprecedented within the context of American history. My intention here is not to speculate about the root causes of Detroit's hardships but rather to focus on the facts and figures of Detroit's recent losses to highlight some of the associated material remains and social relationships that may be examined archaeologically.[9] These details provide an important backdrop for the archaeological case studies that appear in the following chapters.

Detroit is a sprawling 139-square-mile city. Within its borders the cities of Boston, San Francisco, and Manhattan could fit comfortably with room to spare.[10] At its peak in 1950, the city housed 1.86 million residents; as of 2018 there were 673,000 people living in Detroit. The city has lost nearly two-thirds of its population (64%) over the past seventy years.[11] During the first two decades of the twenty-first century, the decline of residents accelerated, especially in the wake of the 2008 mortgage and foreclosure crises. By January 2014, city officials estimated that Detroit was losing 1,000 people per month. In his 2018 State of the City address, Mayor Mike Duggan underscored the scale of this population loss by displaying a chart of the ten largest cities in Michigan. Detroit topped the list, and Grand Rapids secured the third spot with its population of 196,000. The second-place ranking was not assigned to a city. Instead, it was occupied by the 244,000 "Detroiters Who Left"—those who moved out of the city in the decade between 2004 and 2014. In other words, the second highest population group in the state of Michigan is currently made up of former Detroit residents. Placing this loss in a broader national context, Duggan argued that the financial and services crisis facing twenty-first-century Detroit has been more devastating to the city's ability to function and rebuild than Hurricane Katrina was to New Orleans in 2005. Between 2004 and 2014 New Orleans lost 17% of its population; Detroit lost 26%.[12] There now exists a substantial Detroit diaspora who maintain close ties to the city but live beyond its borders, mainly in the Metro Detroit suburbs.[13]

As Detroit's residents and businesses exited the city over the course of the past seventy years, few newcomers moved in to reoccupy buildings that the exodus left behind. In its wake, the out-migration left a landscape saturated by "untimely" modern ruins.[14] Blight did not discriminate according to neighborhood or building type; it affected all manner of structures across the city: churches, schools, theaters, shops, hospitals, and homes. It ravaged industrial giants, like the hulking remains of the Packard Automotive Plant, spread across 40 acres on the city's east side. The skeleton of the eighteen-story Michigan Central Train Depot in Corktown, a "must-have" ruin photograph, became the most recognizable and symbolic image of the city's economic collapse (Figure I.2).[15] Until their demolition in 2014, the fourteen-story towers of the Brewster-Douglass housing projects stood empty, covered in graffiti and hovering over the Chrysler Freeway at the entrance to downtown Detroit. In between these monumental ruins spanned thousands of blocks of empty early twentieth-century detached homes, built for the Great Migration–era automotive industry workers whose labor elevated Detroit to the status of a global manufacturing powerhouse.

By 2014 there were 78,506 unoccupied buildings in Detroit, over half of which were slated for demolition by the city.[16] Upwards of 20,000 vacant lots also fell under the city's managerial purview. In total, of the 380,000 parcels of land in Detroit, almost one-third suffered from some degree of neglect and ruin.[17] As I discuss in the case study of the Halleck Street

Figure I.2. Michigan Central Train Depot in 2012 when it was in a state of decay and one of the city's most popular sites for ruin photographers. (Krysta Ryzewski)

log cabin in chapter 7, numerous strategies have been proposed and employed by government entities and private investors alike to manage Detroit's blight. As of 2020, there have been few uncontroversial successes.

Various attempts to restructure city services, curtail debts, and mitigate blight in the early 2000s failed due in large part to widespread corruption and government mismanagement. In September 2008 Mayor Kwame Kilpatrick resigned from his position after being convicted of obstruction of justice and perjury. His conviction was part of a far-reaching corruption racket among city government officials that spanned the entirety of his six-year mayoral tenure. Five years later, in 2013, Kilpatrick was found guilty of another twenty-four felony counts, including bribery and fraud, for which he received a twenty-eight-year prison sentence.[18] That same year, Detroit's city government realized that it could no longer function on its own. Operating with a $327 million budget deficit, the city deprived local residents of reliable municipal services with potentially deadly consequences; they cut funding to public transportation, schools, and even basic emergency services. At the start of 2013 the city had no more than ten working ambulances to serve its population of almost 700,000; police response times to priority emergency calls averaged fifty minutes, and one-third of the Fire Department's stations were shuttered.[19] In an effort to overhaul the city's management, Governor Rick Snyder stripped authority from elected city officials and placed bankruptcy lawyer Kevyn Orr in charge of all city resources and finances. Orr promptly enacted austerity measures that involved cutting pensions and medical benefits of city employees and raising costs for basic services, including access to water. These actions placed the city's debt burden directly on its residents—83% of whom were African American and 40% of whom lived below the poverty level.[20] Nevertheless, Detroit was in such a dire state that the emergency manager's reductions to services and programs resulted in no immediate improvements to the city's crime rate, infrastructure, public transportation system, schools, or unemployment.[21] On June 18, 2013, under the emergency manager's leadership, Detroit filed the largest-ever municipal bankruptcy in United States history.[22]

It should come as no surprise, then, that efforts to protect and work with Detroit's tangible heritage—its historic buildings, archaeological sites, and collections in museums—were not a priority among public officials during the financial crises (nor should their funding have trumped residents' needs for access to essential resources). But rather than falling out of focus, Detroit's cultural resources found themselves in the crosshairs of economic strategies that the state and city devised to cut costs and generate revenue. The state of Michigan made the first move in 2011 when they deincentivized developers' investment in historic buildings by withdrawing the statewide historic preservation tax credit, which awarded developers a credit of up to 25% on every dollar spent on qualifying rehabilitation expenses.[23] By deincentivizing the adaptive reuse of historic buildings in downtown Detroit, redevelopment slowed, leaving dozens of buildings unoccupied.

Two years later, in 2013, Detroit's emergency manager, Kevyn Orr, with the support of Governor Snyder, suggested that the city's cultural resources were assets that could be monetized and sold to pay off its creditors. In a controversial move, Orr proposed the sale of collections from the city-owned Detroit Institute of Arts (DIA).[24] At one point Orr's plan involved monetizing a half billion dollars' worth of the museum's collections, including paintings and sculptures by Degas, Rembrandt, and Picasso.[25] During the ensuing controversy and negotiations, corporate and government officials openly conflated the collections' cultural significance with economic value, pitting artworks and the social welfare of Detroiters against one another. As Derek Donnelly, managing director of the Financial Guaranty Insurance Company, put it, "The DIA or art is not an *essential asset* and especially not one that is essential to the delivery of services in the city."[26] Facing both the liquidation of its artworks by creditors and vociferous opposition to the proposal from the international art, archaeological, and historic preservation communities, the DIA entered into negotiations with state and city creditors. The resulting passage of the so-called Grand Bargain ultimately prevented the loss of the museum's collections after the DIA agreed to participate in the city's restructuring plan. In the Grand Bargain the DIA committed $100 million to city pensioners, and in return, they acquired independence from city ownership.[27]

The notion that Detroit's cultural worth, historic resources, and physical remains are expendable and nonessential components of civic identity contributes to the discourse of Detroit as a "dead" city, a sentiment that was especially prevalent during the bankruptcy process.[28] Descriptions of Detroit's collapse abounded in national and international media accounts. Among the most sensational were stories published by the UK-based *Daily Mail*. One July 2011 headline read: "From Motown to Ghost Town: How the Once Mighty Detroit Is Heading Down a Long, Slow Road to Ruin."[29] Detroit, the reporter commented, "wallows in decline." Other *Daily Mail* stories emphasized emptiness and decay with headlines like "Derelict Detroit" (2012) and "Left to Rot: 40,000 Abandoned and Empty Buildings" (2014).[30] Scholars have also been guilty of perpetuating the myths of a lifeless, postapocalyptic city by publishing works like "The Last Days of Detroit" or by asserting that Detroit is "posturban," no longer qualified to be a city.[31]

To be fair, given the extent of Detroit's blight it has become relatively easy to issue damning verdicts of the city's viability through the widespread circulation of ruin photographs. Urban explorers, artists, and reporters flock to Detroit to collect aesthetic imagery of postindustrial decay. While their voyeuristic and opportunistic images can be striking works of art and reflections on postmodern conditions, their value is limited beyond these privileged realms. On the whole, this genre of imagery disengages from the city's pervasive issues of race and economic inequality. Such disengagement is especially damaging at a time when ongoing processes of gentrification, local impacts of the COVID-19 pandemic, and widespread protests against police brutality in the wake of George Floyd's murder are magnifying socioeconomic and racial disparities.

Detroit's ruin photographs rarely include people. Featured buildings are often disconnected from their surrounding environments. Historical information is almost always absent. There is never an acknowledgment of particular illegal activities or tragic incidents that may have taken place within the photographed spaces (e.g., arsons, drug consumption, sexual assault, deaths). Nor is there a recognition of how many of the spaces are not completely abandoned but instead continue to be used for alternative purposes by new transient populations.[32] Some artists and archaeologists argue that such images should be left to speak for themselves, but in Detroit these photographs continue to silence and render invisible the most vulnerable people and neighborhoods in the city who deserve recognition.[33] The vast majority of ruin photographs are of little service to the social welfare, heritage preservation, or revitalization efforts in Detroit (nor are most intended to be). They are, as art historian Dora Apel concludes, "a source of demoralization and embarrassment" for the people of Detroit who live among distressed buildings.[34]

DETROIT LOOKS TO THE FUTURE

Over the past decade urban planners have created a citywide land-use plan that has become the basis for a number of privately and publicly funded revitalization initiatives. The privately funded Detroit Future City strategic framework and land-use plan was released in 2012 as a colorfully illustrated 761-page book; a follow-up seventy-seven-page executive summary was produced in 2017.[35] The strategic framework was the culmination of a two-year process of community outreach undertaken by the Detroit Works Project, initiated by then-mayor Dave Bing.

The Detroit Future City framework aligns with the strategic renewal and rightsizing goals of its precursor, the Detroit Works Project. Data from this project and the broader Detroit Future City framework have inspired current developers to propose revitalization and building campaigns that redirect resources from poorer and less-populated neighborhoods to the downtown economic core of the city (e.g., 7.2 SQ MI, Olympia Entertainment).[36] Geographer Sara Safransky warned in 2017 that the Detroit Future City framework had the potential to inspire large-scale land grabs by major developers in downtown areas, eliminating opportunities for valuable property ownership among the city's majority African American population and treating the areas as blank slates for building initiatives.[37] As my discussion of the Ransom Gillis house and the Brush Park neighborhood reveals in chapter 3, her predictions have come to fruition.

Although the revitalization efforts currently unfolding in Detroit are future-oriented, they also aim to distance the next-generation city from the challenges of its past. In the process of future-making, planners and developers are paying only minimal attention to the documentation and preservation of historical and archaeological resources in the areas under rapid redevelopment. Preservationists and archaeologists working in the city recognize that present future-making efforts have direct implications on which community-based histories will be included in narratives for generations to come. As the following case studies demonstrate, many of us have taken grassroots approaches to ensuring that the remains of Detroit's past are not lost and forgotten, and that one community-based history is not privileged over another.

LANDMARK HISTORICAL EVENTS IN TWENTIETH-CENTURY DETROIT

It is important for readers to be aware of some of the major demographic transformations and historic events in Detroit during the late nineteenth and twentieth centuries. These circumstances structure the unstable scaffold that supports contemporary Detroit.

Detroit, from the mid-nineteenth-century onward, was shaped by the contours of industrial capitalism that propelled it from a regional port city with a population of 45,619 in 1860 to the global center of automobile manufacturing with a population just shy of one million in 1920. Detroit's industrial base was already well established by the time automobile production began during the first decade of the 1900s. In the decades prior, the city's manufacturers were among the United States' leading producers of cast iron stoves, pharmaceuticals, ships, cigars, and upright pianos. The twentieth-century automobile industry succeeded, in part, because of its ability to fit into an established economic system and manufacturing infrastructure. However, the large-scale automotive industry ushered in an entirely new population of residents who, in turn, transformed the cultural dynamics of the city and the conditions of industrial labor in their workplaces.

Detroit grew at breakneck speed during the first decades of the twentieth century, accelerated by Henry Ford's introduction of the five-dollar-per-day wage in 1914. By 1920, Detroit was the fourth largest city in the United States. The prosperous automotive industry ushered in waves of job-seeking foreign-born immigrants and migrants from other parts of the United States. Polish immigrants comprised the largest group of foreign-born arrivals, while the most substantial base of American-born newcomers were African Americans, most of whom were descended from previously enslaved laborers. Their arrival in Detroit as part of the Great Migration was an effort to escape the oppressive conditions of the American South. By 1950, African Americans comprised 16% of Detroit's population.[38]

Detroit's population more than doubled every decade between 1900 and 1930. City officials scrambled to meet residents' needs with adequate housing, infrastructure, and other municipal services. Then, and in the decades to follow, the city's efforts were contentious, inequitable, and short-sighted. City managers built racially segregated public housing complexes, restricted Jews from participation in government and social organizations, prevented African Americans from purchasing homes in White neighborhoods, and enacted aggressive urban renewal campaigns that targeted poor, minority neighborhoods for demolition. Within the deeply segregated city, marginalized Detroiters created tight-knit communities with thriving businesses, entertainment venues, informal economies, and pseudo-governmental organizations in areas like Paradise Valley, Black Bottom, Virginia Park, and the West Side. From these resilient communities came the city's legendary twentieth-century music, which included the genres of swing, bebop jazz, polka, Motown, and rock 'n' roll. Even these most celebratory notes of Detroit's twentieth-century history emerged from places with a constant undercurrent of social discord.

Deep-seated prejudice, resentment, and frustration instigated major conflicts between residents in 1943 and 1967. On June 20, 1943, a racially motivated riot erupted at Belle Isle between more than two hundred Detroiters.[39] The violence spanned three days and involved groups of White and Black individuals who vandalized property, overturned cars, and attacked one another. Thirty-four residents were killed, and about seven hundred were injured.[40] The conflict was partly a result of tensions over the city's housing crisis, which reached an all-time high after the city proposed to build a public housing project for Black residents in a White neighborhood. It was also instigated by the ongoing opposition among a number of White autoworkers to the inclusion of Black laborers in the wartime assembly lines. Industrial production in America's "Arsenal of Democracy" suffered as White workers initiated slowdowns in protest.

On July 23, 1967, a police raid of an after-hours blind pig (illegal bar) in the African American neighborhood of Virginia Park ignited simmering tensions and resulted in five days of looting, arson, and violence across the city. At the time, the July 1967 uprising was the most destructive and deadly episode of civic unrest in the United States. Forty-three people were killed and nearly 1,200 injured. The fires damaged more than 1,600 buildings and eradicated entire commercial and residential areas across the city. Ultimately, it would take the arrival of 7,000 federal troops to suppress the violence.

The 1967 uprising is often touted as the starting point for Detroit's twentieth-century economic downturn and population loss. This claim, which places the city's African American population as the root cause of the city's misfortunes, is inaccurate. Numerous scholars have demonstrated how Detroit began to experience economic strains much earlier, in the immediate post–World War II years.[41] In 1950, when Detroit was at its peak population of 1.8 million, manufacturers began to downsize their workforces, first cutting the least skilled laborers, who were largely African American. Rising unemployment and continued housing shortages drove residents who could afford to relocate out of the city. In the decade between 1950 and 1960 the city lost a fifth of its population, which, at the time, was predominately White. Although Detroit's so-called White flight was well under way before the 1967 unrest, in its immediate aftermath, between 1967 and 1969, 173,000 White residents moved to the suburbs.[42]

The circumstances of the uprising exacerbated previous socioeconomic issues and caused lasting changes to the city's demographics and landscape. In the coming decades, the loss of revenue from residential and business taxes, coupled with the decline in manufacturing jobs, resulted in the steady reduction of city services, an increase in unemployment and poverty, and widespread vacancy. Today, it is not uncommon to hear Detroiters who lived in the city during the 1960s and 1970s talk about themselves as survivors. Indeed, decades of loss and unfulfilled promises have left devastating scars on the city's landscape and even deeper psychological traumas in the minds of those who remember and continue to hope for a safer, more vibrant city.

Over the course of the past century, countless subtle and overt attempts by politicians, corporate managers, and others to silence Detroit's nonelite residents have failed due in large part to residents' longstanding commitment to solidarity and their willingness to engage in collective action. Beginning with the establishment of labor unions and civic organizations in the early decades of the Great Migration, including the United Automobile Workers (UAW) and the Detroit Urban League, Detroit's working-class and minority communities have been vocal advocates for equitable labor conditions, civil rights, and other social welfare issues (Figure I.3).

Activism and activist causes in Detroit have rarely been exclusive to one particular ethnic or interest group. Indeed, two of Detroit's most prominent labor and civil rights activists were James "Jimmy" and Grace Lee Boggs, an interracial Afro-Chinese couple. He was an autoworker and she was a PhD-holding pragmatist philosopher. Their extensive writings and engagement work, spanning from the 1950s through the early 2000s, instilled the spirit of collective action that still thrives in Detroit today. Their work also inspires the types of engaged heritage-based interventions that many practitioners undertake in the city (see chapters 1 and 5). In this book readers will encounter the contributions of locally based activist politicians,

Figure I.3. Martin Luther King Jr. leads the Walk to Freedom down Woodward Avenue in Detroit on June 23, 1963. With more than 125,000 participants, it was the largest civil rights march in US history at the time. (Walter P. Reuther Library, Archives of Labor and Urban Affairs, Wayne State University)

musicians, philosophers, pastors, labor union organizers, students, neighborhood associations, and artists, among others. It is impossible to appreciate Detroit's heritage without accounting for these active voices and their roles in championing equitable courses for the city's future.

CASE STUDIES

The six case studies in *Detroit Remains* use a historical archaeological approach to construct stories about people and places that are underrecognized in the city's histories. Each of the case studies is based on a problem-oriented research project. The sources that I cite to construct them are academic and archival. I integrate data from a wide range of archaeological, historical, and anthropological sources, including excavated objects, but also buildings, historical maps, primary archival records, photographs, modern materials, and oral histories. I also move beyond the confines of archaeological literature to flesh out the site narratives with scholarship from other fields: urban studies, history, cultural anthropology, African American studies, geography, music history, architecture, philosophy, and popular culture studies.

With the exception of chapter 1, which provides a scholarly discussion of historical archaeology and community-involved practice, each of the book's chapters focuses on a particular place within the city where I have undertaken collaborative archaeological research projects since 2013. These projects involved university students, partners from nonprofit organizations, local volunteers, and numerous other stakeholders. Archaeology is not a neutral scientific observer in these stories. Instead, I orient archaeology as a practice that assumes political standpoints, accepts social responsibility, and adopts activist positions.

Little Harry Speakeasy

Chapter 2 is a case where archaeology was used to examine a prominent urban legend and to create an alternative historical narrative about Little Harry, a Prohibition-era speakeasy with possible ties to the notorious Purple Gang, located in the basement of a modern bar in downtown Detroit.[43] In the process of research we confirmed the existence of the speakeasy, unearthed new historical insights, and connected with descendants of Detroit's Jewish underworld. This case study highlights the intersections between archaeology, a local business, and unconventional stakeholder communities. It also demonstrates the contributions of archaeological findings to interpreting place-based histories and engaging with urban legends.

Ransom Gillis House

Chapter 3 contrasts a developer-funded historic rehabilitation project at the Ransom Gillis house (a Victorian mansion in the Brush Park neighborhood) with an archaeological approach to the property's social history and built environment.[44] Archaeological investigations trace the evolution of the Ransom Gillis house's property in ways that call attention to its creative, entrepreneurial, and personal histories. The Ransom Gillis property was the site of the first incarnation of the Pewabic Pottery, the scene of a conflict during the 1943 race riot, and, eventually, one of the city's epic ruins. The chapter's archaeological interpretations extend into the present in order to illustrate the historical trajectories and material remains of blight and urban renewal processes. They also provide the basis for evaluating how Brush Park's nineteenth-century heritage has been leveraged by various planning efforts over the past several decades in the name of civic improvement and historic preservation.

Blue Bird Inn Jazz Club

Chapter 4 highlights the power of collaborative grassroots preservation efforts in Detroit by recounting the recovery, analysis, and afterlives of materials collected from the legendary mid-twentieth-century Blue Bird Inn jazz club on the city's West Side.[45] The Blue Bird Inn is the first historic site in Detroit associated with African American property owners to be researched by archaeologists. During the survey and excavations of the property, archaeologists uncovered mundane portable objects and a cache of over 2,000 managerial and accounting documents dating to the beginning of the club's bebop heyday in the late 1940s. These small finds and paper records illustrate the inner workings of the prominent Black-owned business and its networks around the city, including in the neighborhood of Paradise Valley, which was soon thereafter demolished by urban renewal projects. Other objects recovered during the survey project, including the small stage on which legendary musicians like Charlie Parker and Miles Davis once performed, have become vehicles for creative and imaginative heritage preservation efforts by the site's owner, and this project's collaborator, the Detroit Sound Conservancy.

Gordon Park

Chapter 5 focuses on Gordon Park, a public plaza that stands on top of the flashpoint site of Detroit's 1967 uprising. This case study applies archaeological techniques to examine the processes of forgetting, remembering, and commemorating connections between the site and the uprising. These processes were materialized at the park by the layout of space, physical objects, landscape architecture, and artistic interventions. The chapter first documents the gradual shift of the park from a forlorn, neglected place to a community-curated space over the course of fifty-one years between 1976 and early 2017. Then it reflects on the park's complete transformation by the city of Detroit into a neighborhood center in mid-2017, in coordination with the uprising's fiftieth anniversary.

Grande Ballroom

Chapter 6 features another place associated with Detroit's rich musical heritage. This case study combines archaeological, historical, and oral history sources to depict the Grande Ballroom as a space of evolving twentieth-century popular music, a venue of activism, and a site of willful neglect and ruination over the span of its nearly century-long existence. The ballroom was initially a fixture of Detroit's Jewish community when it was built in 1928, but it is fondly remembered today as the epicenter of Detroit's counterculture scene between 1966 and 1972, when it showcased pioneering rock musicians and was the forum for prominent activist groups, including the White Panther Party. This case study considers how the power of material remains, living memories, and sensory experiences may be mobilized into creative preservation alternatives. It also recounts points of contention among stakeholders who have mixed feelings about preserving a building and history that some perceive to be irretrievable because of its state of decay; others argue that the venue's significance lies not in the ballroom's physical remains but in the ephemeral musical experiences of the counterculture era. Of the six sites featured in *Detroit Remains*, the Grande Ballroom is the only site that currently has an official federal preservation designation.

The Halleck Street Log Cabin

Chapter 7 presents the case of the Halleck Street log cabin, a chance discovery in a blighted Great Migration–era neighborhood that became the centerpiece of an enthusiastic community-led restoration and educational project—until it met an untimely and sudden demolition at the hands of the city of Detroit in 2019. This chapter recounts the archaeological investigations of the late nineteenth-century log cabin in the context of the city's blight removal campaign, with close attention to the political and future-oriented dimensions of heritage efforts in the city. It also details the process of advocacy that unfolded during the project as collaborators identified significant loopholes in a federally funded blight removal program that adversely affect the identification and preservation of poor, working-class historic resources in postindustrial cities. Our creative approaches to presenting the log cabin's heritage and investigating its archaeological remains demonstrate the resilient and renewable afterlives of the archaeological record and community-based histories.[46]

There are many remarkable and surprising connections between the people, places, and materials featured in the following six chapters. In highlighting the relationships between seemingly disparate actors, the *Detroit Remains* case studies underscore how the city's past and present communities do not exist in isolation but instead are tightly interwoven into its urban fabric.

CHAPTER ONE

Historical Archaeology and Community-Based Research in Detroit

In Detroit there are hundreds of documented archaeological sites ranging in age from thousands of years to just a few decades old. The six sites featured in the following chapters occupy the more recent end of this spectrum. I pieced together stories about these places by applying methodological and theoretical approaches from historical and contemporary archaeology—two specializations within the wider discipline of archaeology.[1] There exists considerable overlap between historical and contemporary archaeological practices in Detroit, especially since both enlist similar sources of data and share priorities of collaborative, politically engaged public scholarship. Rather than dwell on the finer academic distinctions between these two specializations, I position this book's case studies within a broad conception of historical archaeology that includes the time frames of the recent past and present.[2]

This chapter provides an overview of the archaeological scholarship that I used to inform the design of the community-involved and collaborative research projects featured in the following case studies. I begin by briefly defining the scope of historical archaeology. I then summarize the history of the field's development in Detroit, highlighting important contributions my predecessors made over the past sixty years to our present-day practices of urban historical archaeology, cultural resource management, and collaborative archaeology. As I segue into a discussion of public archaeology and community-involved research, I first call attention to some of the gaps and challenges facing historical archaeology in Detroit, most notably the lack of archaeological engagements with the city's historically marginalized communities and contingent social issues. I then review relevant archaeological scholarship and align it with the civic engagement and social justice aims that were central to the projects in my case studies. I conclude the chapter by establishing the pragmatic orientation of the archaeology in *Detroit Remains*.

HISTORICAL ARCHAEOLOGY

In the central Great Lakes region historical archaeologists focus on sites whose ages span from about four hundred years old to the present.[3] This time frame begins with European arrival and expansion in the region and coincides with the emergence of capitalism during the modern era. Historical archaeology therefore uses material remains as the basis for examining the transformative processes of modernity—industrialization, commercialization, mass immigration, and urbanization. It studies the physical effects of these processes in various circumstances, including social organization, labor, interpersonal relationships, economic disparities, and built environments.

Historical archaeologists apply a suite of methods to material culture and human-modified landscapes in order to examine historically situated social issues at a variety of scales, from households to entire regions. During fieldwork archaeologists often recover artifacts by excavating sites systematically; they also map material evidence of past human activities in situ as part of landscape surveys or standing building documentations. Once archaeological fieldwork is complete, the lengthy process of interpretation begins. This involves performing rigorous laboratory analysis, conducting historical research in archives, collecting oral histories, and continuing consultations with relevant stakeholders (i.e., local residents, descendants, avocational archaeologists, heritage professionals, educators, and others invested in the history or preservation of a site). To link materials to their wider sociohistorical contexts and broader theoretical issues, historical archaeologists consult a vast range of primary archival sources, including historical maps, photographs, government records, business accounts, personal correspondence, newspaper reports, digital media, and oral histories. An important distinction is to be made between conventional historical research and the anthropological approach to documentary records that historical archaeologists undertake. As discussed in the introductory chapter, historical archaeologists consider written records to be artifacts or sources of material culture in their own right, and so they approach these sources with a critical eye toward understanding the inherent biases and underlying concerns with which they were compiled.[4] The interpretations historical archaeologists produce from contextual analyses of material culture may be mobilized for a number of scholarly, professional, and public purposes—including narrative storytelling.

HISTORICAL ARCHAEOLOGY'S POWER AND PURPOSE

Skeptics might question whether the information historical archaeologists generate adds anything new to information present in historical documents or recounted in the memories of living people. They may critique artifact-derived accounts as handmaidens to history, whose utility is limited to filling gaps in archival sources or providing tangible accompaniments to known social histories. Fortunately, most historical archaeologists avoid the pitfalls of producing such supplementary historical appendixes by emphasizing the nuances of material culture in particular sociohistorical contexts and by considering the broader intellectual and practical outcomes of their projects. Archaeologists recognize that there exists a materially evident disparity between what people say they do (or what historical records detail) and how people actually behave in private settings. They also consider how people in the past made decisions that may have been either knowingly or unconsciously shaped by political and economic constraints.

Historical archaeologists often interpret material culture with the purpose of gaining access to the intimate, everyday lives of populations whose accomplishments tend to be overlooked by dominant historical narratives. Such insights may elicit information about individual or small-group decisions that were enacted locally. Historical archaeology's greatest intellectual power, however, lies in its ability to connect people's localized behaviors to broader systemic pressures and circumstances that inspired, limited, or even prescribed their decisions. In Detroit, I examine how local residents collectively respond to systemic inequalities maintained by certain political, economic, or social orders, such as race-based segregation, class-based discrimination, and inequitable resource allocation. Such a multiscalar focus moves historical archaeology's relevance beyond the specificity of local situations to far-reaching engagements with the causes and consequences of sociohistorical phenomena.[5]

Archaeological research has many practical applications beyond the contributions it might make to historical studies and social theory. As demonstrated by the case studies in the following chapters, archaeological findings are often involved in historic preservation initiatives. They may also inform the management strategies of heritage sites, incentivize sustainable development, and dictate the course of building or infrastructure construction. In instances where archaeological findings intersect with sites of "dark heritage"—places with contested histories of conflict or trauma—archaeology may be a vehicle for constructive, therapeutic dialogues that invite communities to acknowledge and talk about past and present injustices.[6] Examples of reconciliation involving archaeology include collaborative projects at the Mount Pleasant Indian Boarding School in Michigan between Sarah Surface-Evans and the Saginaw Chippewa Tribe; studies on Japanese American internment camps by Bonnie Clark and Ann Amanti in Colorado and Stacey Camp in Idaho; Laura

McAtackney's work on commemoration and "The Troubles" in East Belfast, Northern Ireland; and the case study of Gordon Park, the flashpoint for Detroit's 1967 uprising, in this book.[7]

Historical archaeological projects may also result in efforts of civic engagement and political action that aim to inform and advocate for change in existing governmental policies about social welfare, cultural resources, or budgetary allocations, among other issues. Rachael Kiddey's archaeological collaborations with the homeless communities of Bristol and York, England; Sarah Mallet and Dan Hicks's study of forced migration via the Calais "Jungle" refugee camp; and the discussion of the Halleck Street log cabin in chapter 7 are three such examples.[8] As archaeologist Barbara Little contends, historical archaeology has the ability to affect communities by employing a practice that is "active and empowering," one that conceives of archaeology as a more fluid, transparent, and unpredictable social science.[9]

Finally, perhaps one of the most poignant contributions of historical archaeology to contemporary cities like Detroit is the capacity for an archaeological site to function as what archaeologist Gabriel Moshenska calls an "arena of memory."[10] Moshenska's scholarship on World War II–era bombing sites in London, Cheryl LaRoche and Michael Blakey's work on the African Burial Ground in New York City, Shannon Lee Dawdy's evaluation of Post-Katrina New Orleans, and the Grande Ballroom (chapter 6) and the Blue Bird Inn jazz club in Detroit (chapter 4) each showcase examples of publicly situated, sociopolitical spaces that invite people to create, negotiate, and contest place-based memories.[11]

In terms of its public-facing concerns and broader impacts, historical archaeology has much in common with the wider field of critical heritage studies. Drawing on an interdisciplinary suite of methods from geography, anthropology, sociology, history, ecology, and other fields, heritage practitioners situate the past in the present by generating interpretations of places that foreground specific cultural meanings and social values.[12] Heritage, of course, is an amorphous term, and in the context of Detroit it can be difficult to point to a factory, neighborhood, monument, or even a vacant lot that cannot somehow be construed as a culturally meaningful illustration of the city's historical layers. Arguably, the capacity of heritage to accommodate such a vast range of places, stories, materials, and intangible histories is one of its greatest strengths. This openness encourages the creation of narratives that are flexible, relevant, and available for renegotiation in the present and future.

The fluidity of cultural heritage approaches, and their ability to desegregate colonialist, racist, and other legacies in the present, is sometimes positioned in opposition to the efforts of preservationists to restore or re-habilitate historic buildings, monuments, or sites. Such critiques promote the perceived tendencies of historic preservationists to create conservative and static interpretations of places that are fixed to a certain point in time. As the case study of the Ransom Gillis house (chapter 3) illustrates, historic preservation efforts and more dynamic cultural heritage approaches need not be framed in oppositional terms. While there may be limitations to creating representative and inclusive histories of buildings, some of the historic preservation efforts in Detroit are not mutually exclusive of creative and socially aware interpretations of the built environment, or the archaeological remains associated with them.

When archaeologists apply their findings to contemporary situations they assume the heavy responsibility of acting as stewards—caretakers and advocates of the past. This role is a fundamental component of professional practice; in fact, stewardship is the first principal in the Code of Ethics of the Society for American Archaeology, the largest professional organization in the discipline. As caretakers, archaeologists have a responsibility to contribute to conversations about preserving and protecting cultural resources. In the following chapters I demonstrate the importance of stewardship in Detroit, but I also argue that being a steward is not equivalent to assuming the role of a first responder whose primary concern is to rescue endangered archaeological sites or resources before they disappear. Archaeologists Sara Perry and Sarah May rightly caution against this sort of first-responder mentality. Not only does this mindset perpetuate the archaeologist-as-savior complex, but, they argue, the depiction of archaeological recoveries as urgent charity or rescue missions tends to underestimate the renewability and survivability of the archaeological record.[13] While this is certainly a valid point, there are some settings where archaeologists work that are in the midst of major loss-inducing crises that are causing fast-moving or unquantifiable damage to cultural resources. In these cases archaeologists have demonstrated how it is possible to conduct mindful recoveries when under pressure from time constraints or dangerous situations. Examples include Hurricane Maria on Puerto Rico, the impacts of ongoing volcanic eruptions on the Caribbean island of Montserrat, and, of course, the large-scale blight and rapid demolition efforts under way in Detroit (chapters 3 and 7).[14] Although such instances tend to involve rescue and recovery priorities, archaeologists who work in these settings coordinate closely with local heritage agencies, governments, and community groups to ensure that significant sites and their remains are recovered, documented, and creatively interpreted for the educational and cultural benefit of present and future generations.

A SHORT HISTORY OF HISTORICAL ARCHAEOLOGY IN DETROIT

The year 2020 marked the sixtieth anniversary of the first professional urban historical archaeological excavations in Detroit. With the vast majority of Detroit's archaeological research published in local outlets or housed in unpublished "gray literature" (e.g., reports, memos, notes), the reputation of the city's twentieth-century archaeologists as pioneers in the development of urban historical archaeology and in the professionalization of the field internationally is underappreciated. Nevertheless, seven decades of historical archaeological projects in Detroit have produced information from hundreds of sites about the city's history. In the process, these projects established a legacy of collaborative, public-facing urban research—what we might now call public or community archaeology—long before such terms were in widespread use.

The history of historical archaeology in Detroit begins with the late Arnold Pilling, who was a professor of anthropology at Wayne State University for much of his forty-year career. Pilling arrived at Wayne State from Berkeley, California, in 1957, and he immediately established the first institutionally based historical archaeology projects in Detroit. His first initiative, during the fall of 1957, was the Detroit and Wayne County Survey Project. In close collaboration with local museums, the Wayne County medical examiner, and nonprofessional archaeology groups, Pilling's team canvassed archival and newspaper accounts for mention of historic and prehistoric sites. They then used this information to create a map of known and possible archaeological site locations in Detroit. This base map of cultural resources informed numerous development-related archaeological projects in Detroit and the surrounding metropolitan region in the decades to come.

During the 1960s Pilling earned the nickname "Skyscraper Archaeologist" because of the numerous excavations he led at construction sites in downtown Detroit. The first professional archaeological excavations in the city to be explicitly focused on the recovery of historic-period remains took place in 1960 at the site of the future Michigan Consolidated Gas Company building (designed by architect Minoru Yamasaki).[15] The site's location along the Detroit River, at the northwest corner of Woodward and Jefferson Avenues, coincided with the area of the first European settlement in the city in the early eighteenth century (Figure 1.1).[16] The excavations took place under a contract agreement between the Gas Company and

Figure 1.1. Stratigraphic profile of the leatherworking shop site (ca. 1850) and the foundations of the Norton Hotel, unearthed during the first historical archaeological excavations in Detroit at the Michigan Consolidated Gas Company site, 1960. The then-new *Spirit of Detroit* statue is visible in the background. View from northeast corner of Jefferson and Woodward Avenues. (Grosscup Museum of Anthropology Archives, Wayne State University)

Wayne State University.[17] This is one of the first examples of professional urban contract archaeology in the United States.

During the spring of 1960, Pilling and a team of men, made up of his students and local avocational volunteers from the Michigan Archaeological Society, excavated several early nineteenth-century features at the Gas Company site. In a controversial mandate, against which Pilling vehemently protested, women were barred from working on the site; the Gas Company alleged that their presence would distract workers and compromise site safety.[18] Nonetheless, Pilling's crew located thousands of extremely well-preserved artifacts from an early nineteenth-century leatherworkers shop and adjacent building features. The assemblages included personal and architectural objects: an 1837 Mexican silver dollar, brass candlestick holders, and a brass padlock, the last of which was painstakingly conserved. The quantity and quality of finds were also significant because they disproved a common argument of the time, which alleged that urban growth over the course of the nineteenth and twentieth centuries had eradicated any archaeological traces of earlier settlements. Instead, Pilling's work at the Gas Company and other sites in downtown Detroit proved that intact archaeological deposits survived with considerable integrity beneath heavily modified contemporary urban surfaces.

The success of the Michigan Consolidated Gas Company project brought about a number of other skyscraper archaeology recoveries during the 1960s. One of the most notable was Pilling's second excavation project between 1962 and 1965 on the remains of Fort Lernoult. Constructed under British command during the winter of 1778–1779, remnants of the fort remained well preserved ten feet below the surface of the Detroit Bank and Trust building's construction site. Thick clay deposits native to downtown Detroit's geology provided excellent preservation of the wooden palisades and timbers. The project's archaeologists documented seventeen stages of modifications made to the fort when it was in use between 1778 and 1827 (Figure 1.2).

Like the Gas Company project, the excavations of Fort Lernoult generated considerable public interest. In both instances Pilling and his institutional partners made efforts to connect the relevance of historical archaeology to Detroit's contemporary population. During the Gas Company project, onlookers were invited to become a designated, card-carrying "Sidewalk Superintendent." Superintendents were encouraged to "make full use of sidewalk observation facilities at the site of construction of our new building . . . with complete authority to scrutinize, supervise, philosophize and eulogize" the work of the archaeologists and contractors below (Figure 1.3).[19]

At Fort Lernoult, Pilling and the bank officials held public events and media presentations. In one such event Pilling is pictured in the trenches holding four-year-old Donald F. Morgan, a descendant of one of the fort's eighteenth-century soldiers, Captain Moses Porter. The Detroit Bank and Trust vice president, Charles Hewitt, is pictured passing the boy a wooden nail from the fort's palisade that Pilling's team excavated (Figure 1.4).

The year 1967 was emblematic both for Detroit's history and for the field of historical archaeology. In Detroit this was the year when tensions reached a boiling point in July and a violent five-day uprising devastated the city (chapter 5). On a more positive note, 1967 saw the founding of

Figure 1.2. Excavations of Fort Lernoult's palisade remains at the construction site of the Detroit Bank and Trust Building in downtown Detroit, 1962. (Grosscup Museum of Anthropology Archives, Wayne State University)

Figure 1.3. Sidewalk Superintendent membership card given by the Michigan Consolidated Gas Company to onlookers of the excavations led by Wayne State University archaeologist Arnold Pilling. Card enclosed in a letter to archaeologist Arnold Arnoldy, February 7, 1961. (Grosscup Museum of Anthropology Archives, Wayne State University)

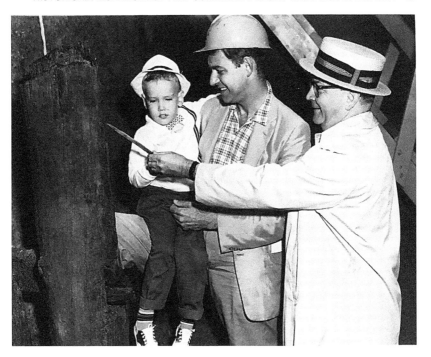

Figure 1.4. Archaeologist Arnold Pilling (*center*) and Charles Hewitt, executive vice president of the Detroit Bank and Trust Company (*right*), present four-year-old Donald F. Morgan with a wooden nail recovered from the remains of Fort Lernoult by archaeologists in 1962. (Grosscup Museum of Anthropology Archives, Wayne State University)

the Society for Historical Archaeology (SHA), the preeminent professional organization in this field. Pilling was a founding member of the SHA and served as its first secretary/treasurer. It is perhaps unsurprising, therefore, that in 1967 Detroit the practice of historical archaeology and the era's social justice and civil rights causes converged.

Pilling and his collaborators adjusted the focus of their work in ways that intersected with relevant social issues of the time. In 1967 Pilling was a collaborator on the Fitzgerald Project, a community-based research initiative organized by Bill Bunge, a Wayne State University geography professor and "radical cartographer."[20] The Fitzgerald Project studied one square mile of Detroit, the Fitzgerald neighborhood, with the intention of mapping and addressing issues of racial inequity through material remains, oral histories, and physical landscape features. Pilling's contribution to the Fitzgerald Project was the application of what he called a "saturation oral history approach."[21] In his interviews of long-term residents, Pilling recorded their memories about the Native Americans who lived in the vicinity, along the modern city's northernmost outskirts, in the early twentieth century. Pilling asked residents to recall the neighborhood's farming days and to describe their encounters with any Native American artifacts they recovered during plowing or planting activities. Some residents produced personal artifact collections for Pilling to document and identified their findspots; others elaborated on their indigenous family histories. Through the combination of oral histories and artifact-based descriptions, Pilling was able to identify the location of thirteen archaeological sites within the one-square-mile area of Fitzgerald, some of which were associated with historic-period Native American artifact remains. The Fitzgerald Project marks a turning point for urban historical archaeological practice in its adoption of a community-engaged, problem-oriented approach.[22]

During the 1960s Detroit's landscape was in the process of radical trans-formations at the hands of large-scale, federally funded urban renewal proj-ects. Slum clearance initiatives spurred by interstate highway construction programs and civic revitalization schemes radically altered the social orga-nization of the city, displacing tens of thousands of residents and erasing entire neighborhoods in the process. Within this climate emerged the Na-tional Historic Preservation Act of 1966 (NHPA). The provisions set out by Section 106 of the NHPA legally required the investigation and mitigation of historic and archaeological resources in advance of federally funded con-struction projects. They also established procedures for the protection of historic resources via the National Register of Historic Places. The NHPA thereafter formed the basis for historic preservation initiatives and the de-velopment of the cultural resource management (CRM) industry nation-wide. Although university-based archaeologists continued to conduct con-tract (or developer-funded) archaeology and academic research projects in the city, private CRM firms, like Commonwealth Cultural Resource Group and Great Lakes Research Associates, eventually subsumed most archaeo-logical recovery efforts in Detroit by the late 1970s. Archaeologists including C. Stephan Demeter, Mark Branstner, and Karen Krebs and other students of Wayne State University spearheaded many of Detroit's archaeological re-covery operations from the late 1970s through the 1990s.

Even in the absence of a comprehensive database, over the past seven de-cades historical archaeology projects in Detroit have recovered millions of artifacts from dozens of major excavations.[23] Many of these site locations are now buried underneath prominent landmarks in the city: the People Mover stations, Millender Center, Hart Plaza, Renaissance Center, Roosevelt Park, Aretha Franklin (Chene) Park, and Eastern Market, to name just a few. As of 2020, archaeologists have documented 106 sites in the four-square-mile riverfront area of downtown Detroit (Figure 1.5). These materials provide unparalleled insights into the circumstances of rapid industrial growth and urban expansion of the city following the devastating fire of 1805.[24]

Detroit's historical archaeologists have made significant contributions to the specialization of urban historical archaeology as it is now practiced nationally and internationally. They introduced systematic survey methods to archaeological practice in urban settings. As early as the 1950s, their projects developed and applied the methods of archival research, artifact analysis, and oral histories into project design and interpretations. Beginning in 1960, their projects established the groundwork for contract-based archaeology; by the time the CRM industry emerged over a decade later, there was already a well-established precedent for developer-funded archaeology in the city. Detroit's first-generation professional archaeologists also conducted public-facing and collaborative archaeological projects, working closely with locally based cultural organizations, city

Figure 1.5. Archaeologists under the direction of C. Stephan Demeter excavated twenty-six privy and midden features from a nine-city-block area in 1973–1974 in advance of the Renaissance Center's construction along the Detroit riverfront. Archaeologists Kent Taylor, Steve Demeter, and Charles Orser Jr. are pictured excavating in Sector G. (Grosscup Museum of Anthropology Archives, Wayne State University)

government, and community stakeholders. Through their recognition of the value of archaeology to local communities, these predecessors worked to make the stories that historical archaeology tells relevant and meaningful to the city and its stakeholders. The success of their initiatives and the continued positivity of Detroiters toward historical archaeology today has enabled new community-involved initiatives, like the Unearthing Detroit Project, to flourish in the twenty-first century.[25]

URBAN ERASURES

With the accomplishments of Detroit's twentieth-century historical archaeologists in mind, it is necessary to point out a major shortcoming in the practice of historical archaeology in Detroit—the lack of identified archaeological sites associated with the city's twentieth-century immigrant and migrant communities, most notably the African Americans who first arrived in substantial numbers during the Great Migration of the 1910s and 1920s. Today Detroit has the highest percentage of African American residents (nearly 83%) among cities of its size in the United States. But there exists minimal historical connections between the city's hundreds of documented archaeological sites and these residents. In fact, there are fewer than a handful of archaeological sites in the city of 139 square miles that recognize associations with past African American occupants or other early twentieth-century immigrant communities (e.g., Jewish, Polish, Hungarian, Middle Eastern). I offer three explanations for this disparity.

The first explanation centers on the city's aggressive urban renewal campaigns, which spanned four decades, beginning in the 1930s. In response to a rapidly growing population, the city targeted, planned, and demolished the physical traces of African American and other modest, ethnic neighborhoods, without much regard for displaced communities' futures. During the 1930s, 90% of Detroit's Black population lived within the adjacent neighborhoods of Paradise Valley and Black Bottom on the city's near east side. African Americans' residency was restricted to these congested neighborhoods because the city's housing market remained segregated into the 1960s and there existed few welcoming options elsewhere. As a result, Paradise Valley and Black Bottom grew into two of the most prosperous Black business and entertainment districts in the country (see chapter 4). Nevertheless, in 1933, when the federally managed Public Works Administration awarded Detroit funding for the city's first slum clearance and low-income public housing program, they targeted Black Bottom. Five years later a section of the Brewster-Douglass homes, the first federally funded housing projects for African Americans in the United States, was completed to house displaced Black Bottom residents. Twelve years later, in 1950, Detroit launched its full-scale urban renewal plan. Within the first six years of the campaign the city cleared seven districts and 7,357 dwellings. In the years to come, another 9,000 dwellings were removed during the course of federal interstate highway construction.[26]

Urban renewal programs were not the only mechanism involved in erasing the physical traces of Detroit's marginalized communities. The second explanation for the lack of investigations into these twentieth-century communities rests at the hands of archaeologists and historic preservationists, who have perpetuated the oversight through the standards of their practices. With deep roots in developer-funded and contract archaeology projects, much of the historical archaeological work in Detroit over the past sixty years was practiced with an eye toward establishing temporal and cultural "significance"—in the language of historic preservation and Section 106 of the National Historic Preservation Act (see chapter 7).

In his 1989 paper on the evolution of Detroit's cultural resource management assessment strategies, archaeologist Mark Branstner explains how Detroit-based practitioners assigned sensitivity and significance to known or potential sites during the dozens of projects that took place during the 1970s and 1980s.[27] Some of these projects involved excavations, while many others gathered information on historical land-use patterns and locations of archaeological sites. As Branstner explains, during their cultural resource assessments archaeologists assigned sites values of "high," "medium," or "low" based on the assumption that a site's significance correlated to its age; in other words, the older the site, the more important it was for archaeologists to examine (Table 1.1).

Branstner and his colleagues debated the need to assign values to more recent sites. They ultimately concluded that the advent of insurance atlases and indoor plumbing in the 1880s (i.e., the presumed disappearance of outdoor privies) reduced the significance of archaeological remains from then onward. They established the date of 1890 as a cutoff for assigning archaeological sensitivity and significance to sites. A few years later, following excavations of a working-class community at the Stroh's Brewery site, local archaeologists revised the terminal date for site significance to 1900 to take into consideration the city's delay in providing sanitation services to working-class neighborhoods. The cutoff date of 1900 was never formally enshrined in law or policy, but it is still in widespread use in Michigan today.[28] The obvious consequence of this convention is that it excludes the entirety of twentieth-century sites from being considered

Table 1.1. Archaeological value determinations based on categories of temporal and historical significance

Archaeological value	Dates	Historical periods
High	1701–1837	French and British Colonial Territorial
Medium	1838–1853	Early Statehood Urbanization
Low	1854–1900	Urban Growth Industrialization
Not assessed	Post–1900	Automobile Age Great Migration Deindustrialization

Source: After Mark C. Branstner, "Historical Archaeology in Detroit: The Evolution of an Urban Management Strategy" (paper presented to the Symposium on Ohio Valley Urban and Historic Archaeology, Cincinnati, Ohio, March 17, 1989; on file with the State Historic Preservation Office, Lansing, Michigan, ER-890283).

archaeologically significant and from receiving recognition in the Section 106 review process. The excluded time frame begins with the advent of the automobile and includes the Great Migration, when the majority of African American newcomers arrived in the city. The subtext of this arbitrary boundary enforcement is that archaeological remains associated with African American and other marginalized ethnic communities are less important and do not merit preservation or mitigation.

Finally, I suggest that a shortage of twentieth-century archaeological sites associated with the city's most marginalized or underrepresented communities exists because archaeologists have not been approaching the sites and associated stakeholder communities with the appropriate questions or project frameworks in mind. Archaeologists have examined the conditions of working-class inequality, predominately among Irish and Irish Americans in mid to late nineteenth-century Detroit, at the sites of the Workers Row House in Corktown and Stroh's Brewery on the east side, as well as the multiethnic working-class community at turn-of-the twentieth-century Roosevelt Park in Corktown.[29] Yet they have not extended their studies beyond the initial decades of the twentieth century, or focused explicitly on communities who routinely faced overt discrimination during the so-called Automobile Age. If one purpose of historical archaeology is, as archeologists John Roby and Maria Starzmann suggest, "to uncover how people are made vulnerable in the first place and to explain the mechanism used to render power largely invisible," then historical archaeologists in Detroit still have much work to do.[30] Furthermore, historical archaeology will have limited effectiveness as an action-oriented and emancipatory practice unless, as LouAnn Wurst and other scholars argue, its studies address the persistent structural inequalities that constitute and reinforce social differences in places like Detroit.[31]

I intend for the case studies in the following chapters to make some initial inroads toward addressing these systemic issues in Detroit and to affect changes in historical archaeological and heritage practices, both locally and in comparable settings elsewhere. As a first step toward creating a more diverse and inclusive historical archaeology of Detroit, I argue that it is necessary to recognize how power is exercised in the city's communities: how it has been stripped from its twentieth- and twenty-first-century residents, but also how residents acquired alternative sources of power by establishing creative and illicit informal economies, most of which still operated within the city's capitalist system. It is especially the case that Detroit's Black history—and by extension, its archaeology— is predominately focused on what has been lost at the hands of White power structures, erased by urban renewal, destroyed by conflicts like the 1967 uprising, and neglected by absentee landlords. In the following case studies, I hope to move beyond these prevailing racially divisive narratives of loss and focus on what survives in places that might seem to be unconventional locales for archaeological research—jazz rooms, contemporary neighborhoods, and community parks.[32]

To conduct historical archaeology in Detroit in a way that is relevant to present-day communities and mindful of past circumstances, I argue that practitioners have a responsibility to engage the city's history and legacy of racism, segregation, and class-based inequality. In the previous generation of historical archaeological scholarship, as Charles Orser critiques, many archaeologists chose to sidestep race by focusing on ethnicity, a term of collective or self-ascribed identity that seemed to be a safety net for avoiding the controversial dimensions of race-based discrimination and marginalization.[33] Times have changed. In today's Detroit, and in other American cities for that matter, it would be counterproductive to undertake any academic or community-involved historical archaeological research in the city without acknowledging how these issues shape the present and color interpretations of the past.[34]

Detroit's twentieth-century histories are replete with different vectors of oppression based on economic inequality, racially based segregation, ethnic discrimination, labor exploitation, and gender exclusion. Historical archaeologists working within this time frame operate at the intersection of these circumstances. As Maria Franklin and others discuss, historical archaeologists have tended to focus on one axis of oppression at the expense of others, thereby creating interpretations that do not capture the complexities among intersecting experiences of subjugation and resilience. Following the work of archaeologists Paul Mullins, Laurie Wilkie, and Teresa Singleton, Franklin endorses a practice of historical archaeology informed by Black feminist perspectives that entails the simultaneous examination of different facets of injustice and exclusion.[35] Whitney Battle-Baptiste's scholarship provides a methodological tool kit to the perspectives Franklin outlines, offering archaeologists the framework for examining intersecting issues of race, class, gender, and other social dynamics in the settings where they work.[36] By adopting the intersectional basis of Black feminist archaeology through applied and community-involved archaeology in Detroit, I anticipate that the following case studies will be in a position, as Mullins notes, to recognize the impact of racial and other inequitable social situations on the landscape in ways that would be otherwise irresponsible and impossible to ignore.[37]

PUBLIC ARCHAEOLOGY AND COMMUNITY-INVOLVED RESEARCH

The involvement of stakeholder communities in all stages of archaeological research is a practice that goes by many names in anthropological and archaeological circles: community archaeology, public archaeology, community-based participatory research, and collaborative archaeology. Some scholars have attempted to make distinctions between these different methods, while others have defined subtypes of practice for the purpose of acknowledging the various settings and objectives of community-involved archaeology. Gabriel Moshenska and Chiara Bonacchi, for example, identify seven distinct forms of public archaeology, ranging from popular archaeology to archaeology done by or with the public.[38] For the most part, however, the terms *public archaeology* and *community archaeology* can be used interchangeably; participatory and collaborative research practices typically provide the basis for the projects that operate within their remits. The projects featured in *Detroit Remains* were community-based, participatory, and public-facing, and their aims were oriented toward collective action.

As was the case in Detroit, public archaeology coincided with the professionalization of the field between the 1960s and 1980s.[39] But as

Moshenska and others note, it was not until the 1990s that community-involved and collaborative research began to incorporate the robust, participatory methods, theoretical orientations, and action-oriented outcomes that are now recognized as commonplace in public archaeology.[40] In 2004, at the turn of the twenty-first century, anthropologist Louise Lamphere observed that, on the whole, anthropology (archaeology's parent discipline), was in the midst of a transformative "sea change" with regard to how practitioners were prioritizing community involvement in their research projects.[41] Carol McDavid and other archaeologists who were swept up by these currents promoted community-involved archaeology as multivocal, democratic, and open processes.[42]

The decentering of archaeologists' power and the desire to include the perspectives of stakeholder communities into archaeological projects were two of the initial motivators behind the increased popularity of public archaeology projects in the early 2000s. With the evolution and expansion of community-involved projects, archaeologists realized the potential of public archaeology to expand the reach and impact of their work beyond the confines of academia. As historical archaeology's visibility increased, Barbara Little observes, so too did its roles in outreach, in education, in cultural resource management, and for addressing social problems in communities.[43]

At their best, public and community-involved archaeology projects are attuned to the desires, concerns, capabilities, and constraints of participant and stakeholder communities. As archaeologist Anna Agbe-Davies cautions, this mindfulness requires recognizing that communities—at any scale—are not homogeneous or static.[44] In reality, there is no singular "public" or "community." The people who are involved in collaborative archaeology projects may identify themselves with multiple communities; they may have competing goals, opposing political viewpoints, different historical interests, and varying levels of investment or involvement in a project as it progresses.[45] My approach to community-involved archaeology operates optimally within a flexible concept of community. It recognizes the many "publics" among stakeholders and attempts to understand how archaeological work might best fit with and contribute to them.[46]

In practice, community-involved archaeology involves organizing archaeological research as a participatory process in which stakeholders associated with the places archaeologists study are involved in designing and contributing to research efforts (to the extent that they are willing and able). These individuals contribute an equal, if not greater, voice to the scope of study, recovery of information, and presentation of findings.

Their presence and participation ensures that archaeological interpretations are appreciative and respectful of particular community values and histories.[47] Such collaborative practices redistribute archaeologists' positions of power and authority, and introduce negotiation, unpredictability, feedback, and even disagreement into the scientific research process.[48]

In many cases of participatory research, archaeologists invite community members to collaborate with them at all stages of research, including the project planning processes, excavations, lab work, presentations, and publications. One of the pioneering examples of this process in an urban setting was coordinated in 1999 by Paul Mullins, between his home institution, Indiana University–Purdue University of Indianapolis (IUPUI), and members of the Near Westside African American community.[49] The Near Westside neighborhood of Indianapolis, once located along the western edge of campus, was demolished during the 1960s as the university expanded its footprint to accommodate new parking lots and facilities. Mullins and his community partners employed archaeology to relocate and reclaim the neighborhood's community histories. Through excavations, public events, and educational initiatives, they used physical remains, memories, and historical records as the means to establish the "symbolic proprietorship of spaces" where remnants of African American heritage were intentionally erased.

Another influential example of urban, community-involved research is David Gadsby and Robert Chidester's Hampden Community Archaeology Project in the Hampden neighborhood of Baltimore, a participatory research program that examined the gentrifying neighborhood's working-class heritage sites.[50] By involving members of the long-standing working-class residential community in data recovery and interpretative processes, the archaeologists and local community partners effectively repopulated the neighborhood's working-class history through public programming and dissemination of their findings. In this instance, the combination of archaeology with community consultation produced democratized narratives about the neighborhood's past for the benefit of residents in the present and future.[51]

In some iterations of community-involved archaeological practice, archaeologists intentionally take a secondary or backseat role. Instead of establishing a framework for a project in which community members are then invited to participate, they facilitate actions that lead participants to engage with heritage sites on their own terms. This approach is evident in archaeologist Teresa Singleton's work. In her experience, permitting stakeholders and descendant communities to set the research agenda exposed the desire among African American collaborators to approach issues that focused more on understanding the African diaspora through celebratory aspects of their heritage—those associated with contributions to society, rather than designing projects that foregrounded slavery, violence, and other frameworks of oppression.[52] In North America similar consultative and agenda-setting collaborative approaches have been undertaken between archaeologists and Native American groups with work that concerns indigenous histories and archaeological sites.[53] In these cases, as archaeologist Sara Gonzalez and others demonstrate, the benefits of community-based participatory research extend well beyond scholars and academic institutions to affect broader educational, heritage management, and community history initiatives.[54] Community archaeology is, as Agbe-Davies puts it, an accountable, "community-serving" practice.[55]

ACTION-ORIENTED ARCHAEOLOGY

Regardless of terminology, public archaeology and its affiliate practices encourage participation and civic engagement in ways that have the potential to make archaeological research more inclusive and action-oriented.[56] For some, the conception of public archaeology extends far enough to encompass action-oriented aims. Archaeologist Jay Stottman, for example, draws a distinction between public archaeology and activist archaeology, arguing that the former is based on collaborations that have locally specific impacts, while the latter projects are designed to be agenda-oriented and affect systemic change.[57]

The situation in Detroit does not readily lend itself to such a neat distinction between public and activist archaeology because its community-involved archaeology projects are well integrated with activist and social justice aims. Here, archaeologists and their public stakeholders (whether or not they are collaborators on projects) work and live among poignant circumstances that are impossible to ignore and that they want to see change in ways that acknowledge the city's diverse heritage. In some cases, as Wurst notes, archaeologists enter into public archaeology projects without a vision for the types of change a project might promote or the role archaeology might play in such an advocacy process.[58] But in Detroit, there already exists a shared sense of social consciousness among both archaeologists and the communities with whom they work.

As discussed at the end of this chapter, Detroit's communities share a heritage that is deeply rooted in social justice causes; they are familiar and comfortable with processes of collective action. Borrowing from Wurst's description of collective action, Detroiters have, over the course of the twentieth century, forged "a sense of commonality in the struggle against capitalism despite real differences among them" by implementing mechanisms for citizenship, solidarity, and belonging despite constant attempts by city officials, competing groups, and conditions of blight to deprive them of basic services, shelter, job security, and recognition of their history.[59] With respect to the city's recent history, it is nearly impossible to separate archaeology projects or other heritage-based initiatives from processes or outcomes that engage issues of race, inequality, politics, and access. Of course, the production of action-oriented outcomes is a gradual, often contentious process, but the connections that historical archaeology provides to place-based histories is a welcome contribution.

In conducting historical archaeological and public-oriented projects, Detroit's contemporary circumstances push archaeologists into unconventional arenas of practice. In some cases, archaeological methods are improvised in response to the constraints of time, resources, or adverse physical settings. Some of these creative, grassroots engagements coincide with recent notions of punk archaeology, which encourages archaeologists to approach familiar places and histories in ways that respond to unconventional settings and invite social critique in and of the present.[60]

In other instances public archaeology's process and outputs are applied in creative or advocational ways, often in the service of broader social justice or political causes (see the discussions of the Blue Bird Inn jazz club and the Halleck Street log cabin in chapters 4 and 7).[61] Barbara Little and Paul Shackel's positioning of archaeology as a tool of civic engagement is the intellectual foundation for my approach to the case studies in *Detroit Remains*.[62] Little and Shackel adopted their working definition of civic engagement from the University of Maryland's Coalition for Civic Engagement and Leadership.[63] In this definition, civic engagement is conceived of as a practice that acts on a heightened sense of responsibility to communities. The process of engagement requires civic sensitivity and partaking in efforts to build societies that benefit the common good. Empowered citizens (including archaeologists) exhibit agency to enact positive change by undertaking the following actions: "developing empathy, promoting social justice, active participation in public life, public problem solving, community service, working through controversy with civility, recognizing human diversity, learning from others, and developing informed perspectives on social issues."[64] This strategy for archaeologically based civic engagement locates archaeology's authority in its ability to create factually based, scientifically and historically rooted stories that can be employed to address issues of common concern and prompt communities to take action.[65]

As the following case studies illustrate, community-involved archaeology projects have a tendency to extend the duration of our projects well beyond the time when fieldwork or lab work finishes. Community-involved projects rarely end; they have afterlives that may be more affecting and far-reaching than the initial acts of archaeological recovery and analysis might ever be. And for this reason, I underscore the advantages of slow and locally based historical archaeology in Detroit and other urban settings, where practitioners are able to be present, invested in the longer term outcomes of their work, and involved in ongoing conversations about how their findings might continue to benefit communities in conventional and imaginative ways.

POINTS OF CAUTION AND CRITIQUE

It is worth recognizing three major points of caution involved in conducting community archaeology in Detroit and elsewhere. First, there is a tendency, when archaeologists write or talk about community-involved research, to focus on the happy endings and high points of collaborations. Rarely do they expose the nitty-gritty details, roadblocks, and failures they often encounter in their attempts to align our work with various stakeholders and the general public. The net loss of glossing over the hard work of community-involved archaeology is that archaeologists tend to reproduce similar structures and outcomes of collaborative projects in different settings. As archaeologist Christopher Matthews argues, in these cases, public archaeology can come across as self-congratulatory and simplistic; practitioners may struggle to produce outcomes that are novel and impressive.[66] Similarly, Barbara Little notes that a great deal of public archaeology risks "falling into the trap of gullible sentimentality, where a naïve desire to do good replaces critical analysis of substance, means, and ends."[67]

A second challenge that practitioners of community-involved archaeology face is the tendency to construct uncritical and monolithic notions of the public, past and present, who our work claims to represent or serve. Archaeologist Anne Pyburn cautions scholars about the pitfalls of failing to define and understand communities who are the focus of our public-oriented work and who collaborate with archaeologists in conducting research.[68] In particular, she notes that uncritical approaches tend to treat people as if they are part of single, static communities. She also identifies the tendency of scholars to create imaginary communities that have no correlation to either historical or present-day groups. Following Pyburn's charge, I articulate differences and overlaps between communities of descendants, local residents, powerful officials, and other stakeholders throughout the following case studies. In the process, I employ a longitudinal (diachronic) archaeological approach in telling stories of communities. This long-term focus allows me to articulate what Agbe-Davies calls the "contours of community," the processes by which Detroit's communities formed and transformed over time—and what these changes mean for understanding community heritage sites in the city today.[69]

Last, the most important issue that all community-involved archaeology practitioners must contend with is ethical practice. As archaeologist Rachael Kiddey argues, the information historical archaeologists produce tends to be intimately related to living populations and interpretations of it may resurrect sensitive histories, political issues, or sentiments that will have adverse effects on stakeholders.[70] Therefore, community-involved projects demand strong awareness of the possible negative impacts they might have on those who our collaborative work intends to serve.[71] This ethical awareness, Little suggests, requires historical archaeologists to be self-aware about their political agendas, ensuring that their work does not simply support the status quo.[72] Ethical practice must be a foremost concern when dealing with populations, like contemporary Detroiters, who cope with the effects of psychological and physical trauma as a result of decades-long experiences with catastrophic losses, social upheaval, mass conflicts, political abuse, and economic distress.

PRAGMATISM AND THE PRACTICAL APPLICATIONS OF ARCHAEOLOGY

The following case studies detail the processes and outcomes of collaborative and public-facing urban archaeology projects in light of their historical and contemporary contexts of collective action. They position archaeology as discipline that matters. My emphasis on the practical contributions and action-oriented consequences of archaeological research is rooted in Detroit's own school of pragmatist thought and action. Pragmatism is an American-based philosophy that gained popularity in the early twentieth century through the scholarship of William James, Charles Sanders Peirce, George Herbert Mead, and John Dewey, among others. Over the past two decades archaeologists have increasingly framed their work in relation to pragmatist philosophies. With pragmatism's emphasis on accounting for the contexts of historical phenomena, directing attention to the consequences of research for living populations, and identifying the practical applications of archaeological knowledge, perhaps the only real surprise in archaeologists' move toward the philosophy is how long it took me and my colleagues to explicitly engage with it.[73]

To be fair, historical archaeological thinking was not especially concerned with public-oriented notions of civic engagement, collective action, or other practical outcomes for much of the twentieth century. Public archaeology emerged in response to, what Pyburn says, was the "arrogant refusal of mainstream practitioners to acknowledge that all archaeology is and should be treated as public archaeology."[74] As she recalls, public archaeology was initially viewed by the field's leading scholars as an initiative to be done beyond and apart from "real" scientific, hypothesis-driven archaeology.[75] Fortunately, community-involved archaeology has now developed to the point that it is increasingly intertwined with mainstream archaeology, particularly in the scope of historical archaeological projects. Most practitioners of historical archaeology no longer treat archaeology as an objective science that is divorced from sociohistorical contexts and living populations.[76] The notion that rigorous scientific archaeology requires conducting fieldwork or lab work outside of the public gaze is also an artifact of twentieth-century archaeological thought. The title and scope of a recent coauthored publication by seven North American archaeologists, whose diverse expertise ranges from the fourteenth-century settlements at Mesa Verde, Colorado, to the remains of student life on the campus of Michigan State University, amplifies the prime position that action-oriented public archaeology occupies in the present and future directions of the discipline: "The Future of American Archaeology: Engage the Voting Public or Kiss Your Research Goodbye!"[77]

Long before archaeologists caught on, Detroit's twentieth-century social justice movements had deep roots in pragmatist philosophy and collective action, owing in large part to the academic training of Grace (Chin) Lee Boggs. Born in 1915 to Chinese immigrants and married to James Boggs, one of the most highly regarded radical Black philosophers of the twentieth century, Grace Lee was a student of pragmatism from the 1930s, as a sixteen-year-old undergraduate at Barnard College, onward. In 1940 she received her doctorate in philosophy from Bryn Mawr College after completing a dissertation on the work of George Herbert Mead. Despite her widely recognized intellect, there existed few opportunities for women, much less minority women, to obtain university-level faculty positions in philosophy programs during the 1940s. She went on to apply the theoretical insights from Mead and other pragmatist philosophers to her work with the Socialist Workers Party and, later, to various civil rights and social justice causes in Chicago and Detroit, including issues of fair housing, segregation, and poverty.[78]

Arriving in Detroit in 1953, Grace Lee and James Boggs initiated six decades' worth of place-based activism and theoretical writing, advising, and collaborating with the era's most prominent political activists and civil rights figures, including C. L. R. James, Rev. Martin Luther King Jr., and Malcolm X. As two of the most influential radical philosophers in twentieth-century Detroit, the Boggses' pragmatic approaches to collective action and social justice advocacy influences my work here, much as it continues to inspire community-based revitalization and heritage interpretation efforts among many other groups who live and work in the city. It provides a means to conceptualize connections to social issues beyond the immediate sites archaeologists study in ways, as Charles Orser suggests, that emphasize thinking about the "unity of the diverse" over dwelling on differences.[79]

The narratives in the following chapters illustrate the potential impacts that archaeologically derived community histories have for stakeholders and for the city of Detroit's present and future heritage-based initiatives. They contribute to histories of collective action and connect to the legacies of Detroiters' activism through present-day civic engagement initiatives. In the course of the following accounts, I attend to the successes and the shortcomings of various collaborative efforts, emphasize different points of engagement, and recognize the broader political agendas of my research projects.

Finally, I do not contend that a book of historical archaeological stories about Detroit will change how the city functions or how local communities think about themselves. Nor do I intend for my approach to community-involved archaeology in Detroit to act as a manifesto for best archaeological practices in other parts of the world. Instead, I simply aim for this book to present engaged, place-based heritage narratives derived from archaeological investigations that are in conversation with the interests of local stakeholders and address deep-rooted systemic issues.

CHAPTER TWO

Little Harry Speakeasy
Detroit's Underworld Resurfaces

From its brilliant art deco skyscrapers to its hidden underground speakeasies, Detroit was a city of excess during the 1920s. Fueled by the prosperous new automotive industry, Detroiters embraced the decade's indulgent and carefree spirit with gusto.[1] Prohibition may have been in place, restricting the manufacture and consumption of alcohol, but as thirsty Detroiters saw it, the rigid state and national laws were made to be broken. On any given night music, dancing, gambling, and booze filled unsanctioned speakeasies, or blind pigs, throughout the city. As one local newspaper reporter described the scene in Detroit on New Year's Day 1924, "It was drink, drink, drink everywhere."[2] The dilemma facing revelers was not where they might find a forbidden beverage, but rather which of the poorly disguised speakeasies to visit.

Detroiters' flagrant disregard for Prohibition laws frustrated the few officials who attempted to curtail the city's illicit alcohol industry and the vast network of criminal activity associated with it. "Detroit is the wettest city I have been assigned to," complained A. B. Stroup, the federal enforcement officer assigned to crack down on the city's violators. Stroup's efforts to eliminate alcohol from Detroit during the 1920s were futile because he failed to secure cooperation from local authorities. Elected officials and local police were largely indifferent about squashing the profitable smuggling routes that coursed through the city.[3] Bootlegging arrests and speakeasy raids were not worth the hassle, officials argued, because the undercover surveillance on which they relied was too difficult to prosecute in court. Local police officers were also reluctant to enforce the laws because many of them reaped advantages from the underground economy, either as speakeasy patrons or financial beneficiaries of trafficking operations.

The resulting lawlessness of Prohibition-era Detroit bred the notorious Purple Gang, a ragtag group of Jews of Eastern European descent who had been raised along Hastings Street on the city's lower east side. The Purples controlled the city's bootlegging activities and an extensive regional distribution network throughout the 1920s. Their stronghold on Detroit's alcohol traffic exasperated Officer Stroup to the point that he eventually quit his job in a fit of fury. On November 3, 1925, Stroup penned a resignation letter to his federal supervisor, venting his frustrations with the fast-and-loose city. Excerpts of his outraged message appeared in newspapers nationwide the next day. "There is something radically wrong with law enforcement in Detroit," he began, "I can say without hesitation that nowhere else is the law so openly violated as it is here."[4]

It was simply too convenient for Detroiters to defy Prohibition laws. With the midsized city of Windsor, Ontario, located directly across the Detroit River, bootleggers had quick access to a steady supply of Canadian-made alcohol. Ontario had its own Prohibition laws in effect between 1916 and 1927 (the Ontario Temperance Act), but unlike their American counterparts, Canadians were still permitted to manufacture alcohol for export. As a result of this exception, it is estimated that 70% of all liquor to enter into the United States during Prohibition came across the Detroit River from Ontario (Figure 2.1).[5]

Today, a century later, the success and notoriety of Prohibition-era Detroit's illicit economy and its operators are still prominent fixtures

Figure 2.1. Rumrunners landing a shipment of alcohol that was smuggled across the Detroit River from Canada to downtown Detroit, April 1, 1929. (Walter P. Reuther Library, Archives of Labor and Urban Affairs, Wayne State University)

in local historical narratives. This chapter presents the results of an investigation that applied archaeological techniques to the identification of a speakeasy—and its legendary operations—in the basement of Tommy's Detroit Bar and Grill. It recounts the process and outcomes of the Speakeasy Archaeology Project, a collaborative initiative focused on recovering the speakeasy's physical remains and its criminal associations. It also discusses archaeology's role in constructing a place-based historical narrative whose details existed in three intertwined, and sometimes conflicting, sources of information: physical traces (buildings and portable artifacts), archival records, and the local imagination (memories and lore transmitted across generations of storytellers). After describing the process of identifying the speakeasy, I consider how our interpretations of its remains were received by different audiences with various degrees of enthusiasm and skepticism, and why there continues to be such widespread interest in the criminal heritage of the Prohibition era.

SPEAKEASY LORE

Tommy's Detroit Bar and Grill is a cozy but lively sports bar and restaurant located at 624 Third Avenue in downtown Detroit, just two blocks north of the Detroit River. For most of its history the nineteenth-century brick building housed saloons, bars, and restaurants. In the early 2000s Tom Burelle, the bar's current manager, met an elderly man who was then in his late eighties. The man, a bar regular, regaled Burelle with stories about an alleged Prohibition-era speakeasy that, he claimed, once existed in the basement of Tommy's Bar underneath the building's front room. He recalled visiting the speakeasy with his father as a young boy of about ten years old, sometime in the late 1920s or early 1930s. Drawing from his childhood memories, the man recounted details about the underground bar, clandestine access to it, and its clientele with varying degrees of specificity.

In the following years, the legendary speakeasy became a popular topic of barstool conversation. Speculative stories about the building's eventful past captivated bar staff and patrons. The possible presence of a speakeasy was enough to inspire theories about the bar's associations with other clandestine activities—notorious gangsters, smuggling, and even supernatural forces. Urban legends about the Tommy's Bar building and its patrons seemed to spawn and feed off one another. There were the dead bodies—victims of the Purple Gang, perhaps—buried in the heaping pile of dirt concealed by the basement stairwell. There was a black-and-white photograph of Al Capone taken on one of his many visits to Detroit, posing outside of a nondescript brick building that *might just be* Tommy's Bar. There were the ghostly encounters—the pushes, taps, cold breaths of air, apparitions, and mysteriously moved objects—that Burelle and his staff reported experiencing on numerous occasions. And, of course, with the historic building's position in between an antebellum church and the Detroit River, there were tales of a forgotten passageway used by fugitives from slavery as they traveled from the Underground Railroad stop at the next-door Fort Street Presbyterian Church to the Detroit River crossing to Canada. As a local history buff with a desire to preserve the building, Burelle was keen to explore and, if possible, verify the speakeasy and its role within Detroit's history.

Burelle befriended local preservationist and educator Marion Christiansen, who, at the time, organized themed tours of the city's historic buildings for Preservation Detroit—the nonprofit organization that champions the city's historic preservation causes. Christiansen was excited by the prospects of incorporating the remains of an extant speakeasy into Preservation Detroit's tours. Her expertise was especially useful for gathering information about the property's owners and associated businesses during the Prohibition era. In 2013 Christiansen and Burelle approached me with an invitation to investigate whether a speakeasy once existed in the basement of Tommy's Bar. Christiansen had already compiled a convincing body of circumstantial historical evidence that, I thought, made the site worthwhile for further investigation. This was a community-guided project from the outset. Christiansen and Burelle—a historic preservation professional and a small business owner—initiated the investigations, and, during the summer of 2013, I designed the Speakeasy Archaeology Project in collaboration with them. I brought to the project the tools of historical archaeology: systematic survey, mapping, photo documentation, archival research, and even a bit of excavation.

In what follows I recount the findings of the Speakeasy Archaeology Project, the demystification of an urban legend or two, interactions with an unusual descendant community, and the contributions archaeology made to a small business in the process. To establish the historical context for the speakeasy's archaeological investigation, I begin with a historical overview of Prohibition and Detroit's criminal underworld during the 1920s and 1930s. I then introduce the scope of the Speakeasy Archaeology Project and its setting at Tommy's Bar. From there, I present our findings about the speakeasy based on three sources of information—archival documents, oral histories, and archaeologically recovered data (i.e., objects and building information).[6] To interpret these findings in light of the characters and events of the time, I descend into the Prohibition-era underworld. Finally, I reflect on archaeology's role in constructing a historical narrative about the speakeasy. This reflection considers reasons for the persistence of the speakeasy's legendary status in the imaginations of people today.

PROHIBITION AND THE PURPLE GANG

On May 1, 1918, when Michigan's statewide Prohibition laws went into effect, Detroit became the first major city in the United States to outlaw the sale of alcohol. Eighteen months earlier, in November 1916, Michiganders had cast their votes in favor of statewide Prohibition. The statewide ban on the manufacture and consumption of alcohol was the culmination of decades' worth of contentious efforts by temperance crusaders to restrict Michiganders' intake of alcohol through the passage of constitutional amendments and licensing laws. Debates raged in the preceding years between rural and urban residents over whether limits on alcohol should be enacted statewide or on a county-by-county basis (i.e., Home Rule). Rural residents, the moral and political force behind the temperance movement, set their sights on "wet" urban areas, especially Detroit, to make their case for statewide Prohibition. With more than 6,000 saloons and, according to historian Mickey Lyons, an "epidemic of alcoholism," Detroit was a textbook study on the evils of debauchery.[7] Lobbyists from the Anti-Saloon League and the Washingtonian Society used incidents from Detroit to grab lawmakers' attention and to stoke animosity between the so-called Wets and Drys. Sensational newspaper headlines reported heated confrontations between teetotalling vigilantes and Detroit's saloonkeepers, including those by the notorious hatchet-wielding Carrie Nation and her followers in the Women's Christian Temperance Union.[8]

Throughout 1917, in the interim between the 1916 Prohibition vote and the enactment of the law in 1918, the Michigan state legislature passed a series of acts that specified further restrictions on the sale and importation of liquor (Damon Act), granted law enforcement agencies increased search and seizure authority (Wiley Act), and suppressed the proliferation of speakeasys, or "blind pigs" (Amon Act).[9] Detroiters, who had voted overwhelmingly against Prohibition, were unmoved by the criminal misdemeanor charges that violation of these acts carried. Instead, they exploited the fact that the state legislation did not prohibit individuals from consuming or possessing alcohol in the privacy of their homes. Once Prohibition restrictions were in place in 1918, local residents relied on the steady stream of illicit suppliers to restock their home bars. Meanwhile, the city's thriving saloon scene took their activities out of sight and, in the case of the speakeasy at Tommy's Bar, underground.

In January 1919 the US Congress ratified the Eighteenth Amendment to the Constitution, the Volstead Act.[10] Initially, President Woodrow Wilson vetoed the federal Prohibition act, but Congress overrode his ruling on October 28, 1919. The United States went dry at midnight on January 17, 1920, nearly two years after Michigan's Prohibition began. Thirteen years later, Michigan would become the first state to ratify the Twenty-First Amendment, which eliminated nationwide Prohibition restrictions on December 5, 1933.

In the face of Prohibition restrictions, the Purple Gang wasted no time organizing international smuggling operations across the Detroit River.[11] In Ontario, the syndicate invested heavily in Canadian distilleries; in Detroit, they enlisted affiliates to ferry alcohol across the river.[12] From their base in Detroit, the Purple Gangsters monopolized the profitable illicit liquor manufacturing industry and product distribution throughout the 1920s.[13]

Trafficking, or rum-running, as it was called at the time, was a year-round affair. Smugglers devised bold tactics to transport booze across the Detroit River.[14] Their inventive techniques involved underground tunnel systems, railroad cars, hidden compartments in automobiles, and speedboats. Once the alcohol arrived in Detroit, it entered into the Purples' extensive distribution network, which served local clients throughout Michigan and Ohio as well as regional affiliates in Indianapolis, St. Louis, and Chicago.[15] To manage such a complex trafficking operation, the forty to fifty men in the Purple Gang coordinated a massive system of suppliers and distributors. Historian Robert Rockaway estimates that the Purples' illicit operations involved around 50,000 people and grossed over $215 million annually.[16] At the start of the Great Depression, profits from liquor trafficking amounted to Detroit's second-largest industry, surpassed only by automobile manufacturing.[17]

The Purple Gang's rise and fall coincided with Michigan's Prohibition era between 1918 and 1933. Throughout southeastern Michigan, the Purples ran blind pigs, established gambling houses, and operated cutting mills, where they diluted imported liquor prior to distribution. Locally, they maintained control over Detroit's alcohol-fueled underworld with a combination of bribery, racketeering, extortion, and ruthless violence, including over five hundred murders, according to police estimates.[18] Speakeasy operators who were not directly affiliated with the gang were required to pay a "protection fee" to them. The Purples allowed compliant operators to stay open without interference; those who refused to pay were tipped off to the police or roughed up by gang members.

Although most Purple Gangsters were Jewish, their misdeeds were not representative of the character of the city's larger Jewish community. By 1920, Jews constituted 35,000 (3.4%) of Detroit's nearly one million residents; their numbers were only slightly smaller than the city's African American population of 40,838 (4%).[19] Despite their success in establishing respectable businesses and institutions in the city, Detroit's Jews were actively marginalized during the 1920s by discriminatory civic policies that barred them from becoming officeholders and from membership in social clubs. They were further denigrated by Henry Ford's nationwide anti-Semitic propaganda campaigns, which he promoted in his controversial four-volume booklet *The International Jew*. Ford also used his weekly newspaper, the *Dearborn Independent*, to air his personal grievances against Jews, blaming them for all manner of social and economic problems.[20] The Purple Gang's notoriety coincided with Ford's negative publicity, further damaging the reputation of Detroit's Jewish community in the public eye. Among the local Jewish community, the gang's criminal activities were a great source of shame.

Toward the end of Prohibition, in 1933, the *Detroit Free Press* published a retrospective on the operation of speakeasies in the city over the course of the preceding decade. In the initial years of Prohibition, a *Free Press* reporter estimated that there were 7,000 blind pigs operating in the city. At the height of the Purple Gang's influence in 1928, there were an astounding 25,000. Some city blocks, the reporter alleged, were home to over one hundred speakeasies; this was the case on Second Avenue in downtown Detroit, just one street east of Tommy's Bar. At the end of Prohibition, following the demise of the Purple Gang's stronghold on the region's illicit alcohol trade, 7,500 blind pigs remained.[21] Of course, it is impossible to verify these numbers; they reference illegal operations that leave no trace in official directories of city businesses or census records. But even a conservative approach to the city's underground scene could reasonably assume that, at any point during Prohibition, there were thousands of speakeasies in operation across Detroit. It is perhaps unsurprising, then, that there exists such widespread public interest in locating and verifying these venues; they offer a tangible connection with a chapter in Detroit's defiant, bootstrapping history.

Tens of thousands of structures may have disappeared from the city's landscape since the 1920s due to urban renewal, construction, and blight removal campaigns, yet today it seems that every local resident knows a

story about Prohibition-era Detroit that is somehow rooted in extant physical remains. With a century now passed since Prohibition, none of these
accounts are firsthand memories; they are instead local folklore, stories
passed between generations, with details forgotten or embellished along
the way. The most common stories describe the remnants of speakeasies housed in the back rooms or basements of restaurants, businesses, or
homes. Others recall the whereabouts of secret tunnels, canals, or load-
ing docks the Purple Gang used to traffic liquor from Canada. The most
captivating reminiscences connect specific places to the scenes of Purple
Gang crimes: the murder of radio host Jerry Buckley at the LaSalle Hotel,
the Collingwood and Milaflores Massacres, Al Capone's visits to Detroit,
raids on the bar and gambling rooms at the fashionable Blossom Heath
Inn, a favorite gang hangout.[22] These stories thrive, in part, because the
passage of time has created a safe space where morbid fascinations with
past crimes and violence may be indulged in without any of the serious
repercussions that loose-lipped storytellers would have faced just a few
generations ago. Indeed, as personal memories of Prohibition-era Detroit
have faded, the danger and defiance of the Purple Gang—for better and
worse—have become sources of pride, fascination, and popular history,
including among present-day Jewish communities.

As an archaeologist driven by scientific and humanistic research questions, I could be inclined to write off the majority of these Prohibition-era
accounts as the stuff of fanciful myth and urban legend, unlikely to leave
physical remnants in the archaeological record of standing historic buildings or buried soil deposits. I could choose to critique these stories for
their tendency to glorify the history of a bloodthirsty gang, whose mur-
derous approach to business deeply affected the city's Jewish community
and its reputation at the time. Or, as I do here, I might first take a step
back, look at the surviving physical, documentary, and personal evidence,
and consider the real possibility that there are more than a few nuggets of
truth buried within these colorful stories.

TOMMY'S DETROIT BAR AND GRILL

Tommy's Bar is the lone bastion of another era, a stalwart survivor among
a sea of asphalt parking lots that cover the remnants of a once-thriving
residential, industrial, and commercial district. A narrow twenty-foot alleyway separates Tommy's from the backside of the enormous Fort Street
Presbyterian Church. First built in 1855, at least a decade before the earliest brick iteration of Tommy's, the church casts a tall shadow over the
bar every afternoon. Access to ambient, natural lighting is not important

to the patrons of Tommy's though, nor has it been for some time, as the building's windowless architecture suggests.

From the street Tommy's Bar appears to be a compact two-story, square-shaped building (Figure 2.2). A one-story extension to the 3,369-square-foot building is totally obscured from the sidewalk view.[23] Beneath the roofline's understated geometric-motif brickwork, two windows flank a semicircular opening to a second story. A striped awning hangs over the first story frontage, covering the bar's only ground floor window and the thick metal door through which patrons enter. Crossing from the vestibule entryway into the bar's front room is like entering a cave. Inside, the glare of overhanging TVs and the neon jukebox (playing a heavy rotation of classic rock and Motown) is blinding by comparison with the rest of the dimly lit room. The front room's architecture creates the effect of a tunnel, its oak walls covered with ice hockey and baseball memorabilia curve upward toward a low ceiling. A sturdy, dark wooden bar protrudes out from the wall, leaving just a narrow passageway between it and the cluster of tables and chairs along the northern perimeter of the room.

The square-shaped front room is configured much the same today as it was a century ago. It occupies just under 495 square feet of the building's footprint. It stands atop a six-foot-deep basement. In back of the front bar room, the building transitions into a one-story rectangular addition with no underlying basement. The addition extends to the rear of the building, and its brick architecture shows evidence of numerous modifications that owners made to it over time (Figure 2.3). Today, this ground floor addition houses a more spacious dining area, a pool table, restrooms, and a kitchen.

When local sports teams are in town, the bar is packed with customers. Otherwise, it is a laid back, no-frills hangout where friendly staff, regulars, and patrons sit around swapping stories and sharing news over food and drinks. The tight quarters do not afford much privacy, and the front room is an especially compact space conducive to socializing. The manager, Tom "Tommy" Burelle, always occupies the same seat at the corner of the bar. From his perch he chats with customers, files paperwork, phones in orders, and monitors pedestrian traffic and parking lot security cameras. It was from these barstool conversations between Burelle and his customers that the Speakeasy Archaeology Project originated.

THE SPEAKEASY ARCHAEOLOGY PROJECT

The first step of the Speakeasy Archaeology Project involved identifying everyone's interests, roles, and responsibilities. It was a straightforward and uncontroversial process. My team of archaeologists established a set

Figure 2.2. Tommy's Detroit Bar and Grill, the former location of Little Harry speakeasy, in 2013. The front two stories of the building were extended to the current frontage in the late 1880s. The owners made several additions to the back of the structure in subsequent decades. (Krysta Ryzewski)

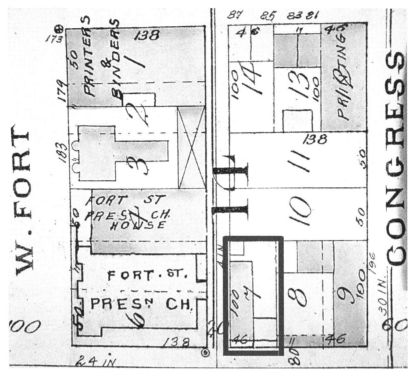

Figure 2.3. Present-day Tommy's Detroit Bar and Grill building (outlined by dark rectangle) and environs in 1918. The rectangular brick building is shaded red, and the wooden outhouse and adjacent one-story building are colored yellow. The adjacent wooden building first appears on the Baist Real Estate map of 1915. (Baist Real Estate map, 1918)

of research questions about the speakeasy and planned to document the exterior and interior of the building using archaeological methods. We would also undertake extensive archival research on primary source historical records and conduct oral history interviews. Marion Christiansen, the Preservation Detroit board member and tour guide, would take the lead on public interpretation and preservation efforts. Our groups would collaborate to publicize the outcomes of the archaeological project. Christiansen would then work with our survey team to coordinate a series of events through Preservation Detroit that showcased our findings. Burelle facilitated the logistics of access to the bar and provided the space for outreach events. His initial role was one of support, but eventually he would come to be the major player in the project in the aftermath of the archaeological documentation and public outreach efforts, as the bar became a regular destination for groups of tourists, history buffs, and ghost hunters, among others.

My archaeological survey team included seventeen participants. Half of the team members were current anthropology undergraduate and graduate students from Wayne State University. The remainder were a mixture of students from other departments (Geology, Engineering), universities (Eastern Michigan University, University of Michigan, and University of Minnesota), and local residents whose expertise in education, history, photography, and electrical engineering would wind up making important contributions to the speakeasy's interpretation. The fieldwork process spanned three months, from July to September 2013. It involved on-site work several days per week and concurrent research in the laboratory and in local archival repositories.

When the project began, we had only minimal information about the building's history—mostly details conveyed to us in conversations. There was no prior archive-based historical or archaeological research conducted on the property (although there were photographs from a prior visit by a Preservation Detroit associate). Our best, and only, description of the alleged speakeasy came via Burelle from the elderly man who frequented Tommy's Bar in the early 2000s. The man's memories were specific in their descriptions of the more sensational elements and sufficiently vague about mundane details, as childhood recollections tend to be. There were three unwavering facts in the man's telling and retelling of the speakeasy story. First, he recalled entering the speakeasy from an underground tunnel. This tunnel, he insisted, ran underneath Third Avenue and then ended at the entrance to the basement room. His recollections failed to mention where, exactly, he entered the tunnel from aboveground; nevertheless, the existence of the tunnel was a matter of fact. Second, he remembered that the speakeasy was a small, underground room. Decorative wood paneling covered the bare stone and brick walls, formalizing the social space. Finally, he recalled that patrons of the speakeasy came to gamble and drink; a few tables fit into the small room to accommodate these activities. The underground room was not a space where alcohol was cut, packaged, or stored; it was an active place for socializing and drinking. The man's childhood memories offered no recollections of the speakeasy's name, the Purple Gang's involvement with it, or any notable raids or incidents that took place there.

To organize our approach to the archaeological survey we began by posing a simple research question: was there a Prohibition-era speakeasy in Tommy's Bar? From there, we set out a series of subquestions. If there was indeed a speakeasy in the bar, where was it? How was it accessed? What did it look like? What, if any, material evidence recovered from it might help us to identify the activities that took place there? Who was responsible for running the speakeasy? Was it associated with the Purple Gang?

Based on the lack of historical and archaeological information about the Tommy's Bar building and the alleged speakeasy, we established two research priorities at the outset of the project. First, we prioritized research in various archives with the purpose of gathering primary sources that detailed the building's construction history and its past owners. Second, we planned to conduct a thorough and comprehensive archaeological survey of the Tommy's Bar building, inside and out, to document the architectural changes made to the building over the course of its history and to discern which, if any, of them may have related to the existence of a Prohibition-era speakeasy. To tackle these dual aims, I divided our archaeological survey team into two task groups: one focused on archival research, and one conducted the archaeological survey.[24] I now turn to a summary based on the team's archival research findings about the building's history and owners. Then, I will detail the archaeological survey results and discuss connections between these two sources of information and the speakeasy in the basement of Tommy's Bar.[25]

A SALOON FOR THE AGES

For the majority of its 150-year existence, the building at 624 Third Avenue that now houses Tommy's Bar operated as a saloon.[26] The first mention of a bar (and restaurant) within the building appears in city records from 1892. Soon thereafter, from 1893, it is listed as either the Andrew Healey Saloon or Whelan's Saloon.[27] Over the next forty years, until the end of Prohibition in 1933, the bar's ownership and management changed hands, back and forth, between six different proprietors; some were close-knit associates, some were in debt to each other.[28] Managers promoted the bar's offerings according to the trends of the times, sometimes advertising its resident restaurant, other times its soda fountain, billiards, or barbershop.[29] Regardless of the featured business, the availability of alcohol on the premises of 624 Third Avenue was a constant.

When thirty-three-year-old Andrew Healey purchased the building in 1893 he acquired a one-story brick building with two rooms.[30] The front of the building was set back about fifteen feet from the street, and there was a lean-to attached to its backside. In the northeast corner of the small backyard there was a shed and another 10-by-10-foot outbuilding, probably an outhouse.

Just nine years earlier, when the property appeared on the 1884 Sanborn insurance map, it was dwarfed by the adjacent Murphy Iron Works, whose foundry, cupola, machine shop, and flask platform then consumed the remainder of the block leading toward West Congress Street.[31] That year the Michigan Central Railroad Depot opened two blocks to the south, on the southwest corner of Third Avenue and West Jefferson.[32] The terminal and its traffic accelerated the area's transformation from an elite residential neighborhood to the north, distinguished by ornate gothic mansions lining West Fort Street (one block north of the bar) and the monumental Fort Street Presbyterian Church (next door), to a center of heavy industry and manufacturing. To the south along Third Avenue, between the bar building and the railroad depot, stood the Murphy Iron Works, Detroit Casket Company, two boiler shops, the Detroit Lead Pipe Works, and the Western Hotel. Along the narrow cobblestone thoroughfare of Third Avenue, the building that would soon become Andrew Healey's Saloon in 1893 stood as a fulcrum between these two residential and industrial worlds.[33]

Healey's establishment of the saloon was well timed, perhaps even strategic. In 1893, directly across the street, on the southwest corner of West Fort and Third Avenue, a second railroad terminal opened, Fort Street Union Station.[34] The new passenger train service delivered a steady influx of transient travelers to the area; some arriving for short-term business or pleasure, others searching for employment opportunities. The Fort Street station dealt the final blow to the adjacent neighborhood of palatial homes and their high-society residents—the Algers, Lothrops, and Delanos, among others. Longtime residents publicly lamented the passing of the former Fort Street West social center.[35] Soon, homeowners and landlords began to convert their old mansions into rooming houses and hotels to accommodate the city's new arrivals.

Historic Sanborn and Baist Real Estate maps of the property illustrate how Andrew Healey quickly capitalized on the saloon's prime location and the appetites of train travelers (Figure 2.4). The insurance maps, created by the Sanborn Map Company for 12,000 US cities in the nineteenth and twentieth centuries, depict the dimensions, materials, and configuration of all buildings and infrastructure on individual property parcels. The 1897 Sanborn map confirms that Healey added a second story to the building and extended its frontage and the facade that exists today to the sidewalk. Subsequent map data detail how, in the following decades, he made at least four structural modifications to the back of the building, adding brick extensions to elongate it. As the building expanded, so too did Healey's commercial ventures within it.[36] At one point, in 1898 and 1899, no fewer than five businesses operated under the same roof: John W. Geir's Restaurant, William Owen's Barbershop, William Holly's

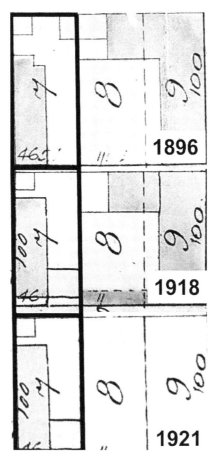

Figure 2.4. Changes in the speakeasy property's buildings between 1896, when Andrew Healey's saloon operated there, through the beginning of Prohibition, when the restaurant and other business operations were managed by Louis Gianotti. (Baist Real Estate maps of 1896, 1918, and 1921)

Cigar Manufacturing company, the Union Athletic Club, and the saloon—then managed by Patrick Whelan.

Toward the end of Healey's ownership of the saloon, in 1915, he constructed a new one-story structure on the same narrow parcel of land as the saloon. The wooden building appears on Baist and Sanborn maps from 1915 through the 1920s, where it is depicted as adjoining the saloon's south wall.[37] But it disappears from city maps and directory records by the 1940s. Although no photographs or descriptions of the wooden building survive, its existence during the Prohibition era played an important role in our investigations.

When Prohibition began in Michigan in 1918, Healey listed the saloon as a soda fountain in the Detroit City Directory; whether the switch was actually made inside the building remains unknown.[38] Whatever the case, Healey stepped back from the building's management during the Prohibition era. By 1920 he transferred its ownership to his associate Louis Gianotti, a twenty-seven-year-old Italian immigrant. Gianotti operated an Italian restaurant out of the building's ground floor along with his wife, Anita Nebiolo, who worked there as a waitress.[39] Curiously, Gianotti also identified himself as a Saloon Keeper in the 1920 census, an occupation that suggests a dual purpose for the Italian restaurant.[40] The transfer of the building between Healey and Gianotti is a critical moment in the story of the speakeasy because it coincides with the increase of blind pigs and Purple Gang–related bootlegging activities in Detroit during the early years of Prohibition.

According to historic maps, from the street level, the only notable changes Gianotti made to the property were a small addition to the back of the building and the installation of a chimney to the ten-foot-square outbuilding in the building's backyard. Added by 1921, three years into Prohibition, the new chimney suggests that the outbuilding's function was upgraded or changed to accommodate some sort of heating operation, the identity of which would become a focus of our archaeological excavations.

For the majority of the Prohibition era, explicit mention of the building at 624 Third Avenue as well as its businesses or proprietors, is conspicuously absent from maps, photographs, and media accounts. However, circumstantial evidence gathered during our research of property records, biographical research, and oral histories details the tangled web of proprietors who managed the building's businesses during the 1920s and early 1930s and their questionable affiliations with Detroit's underworld.

During Prohibition, the building's ownership changed hands four times between Gianotti and two different Harrys—Harry Weitzman and Harry Bianchini. The first and most notable transfer occurred in 1927, between Gianotti and noted "tough guy" Harry Weitzman.[41] Oral historical accounts suggest that Weitzman acquired the building as payment for a gambling debt that Gianotti owed him.[42]

Harry Weitzman was an entrepreneur whose business ventures trod a fine line between underworld and mainstream clientele. A second-generation American of Russian Jewish heritage, Weitzman lived among and attended school with the members of the Purple Gang on Detroit's lower east side. Though he certainly knew the gang's members, he was careful to avoid associations with them in public. No records exist to suggest that Weitzman was a formal member of the Purple Gang. Nevertheless, our research revealed how his fortunes rather curiously paralleled the growth of the Purple Gang's stronghold on Detroit's economy. Fueled by winnings from his gambling habit and support from patrons in his local networks, Weitzman's business ventures expanded in scope and reputation rather quickly, from pedaling scalped baseball tickets and selling pawned diamonds and furs in the late 1910s to operating as an insurance bondsman and property owner by the mid-1920s.[43] By 1927, when he acquired the property at 624 Third Avenue, he was a well-established real estate investor with an extensive business network that included old friends from the Jewish east side community as well as the city's high-profile lawyers and architects.[44] He is perhaps best characterized as someone who provided a supporting role for the Purple Gang, a position that helped them sustain, and perhaps mask, their criminal activities during Prohibition.

Weitzman owned the building at 624 Third Avenue from 1927 until 1930, a period that spanned the heyday of speakeasies in Detroit and Purple Gang activity.[45] No records detail the type of legitimate businesses that operated within 624 Third Avenue during Weitzman's ownership, although it is possible that Gianotti continued to maintain a restaurant on the ground floor.

Perhaps sensing the crackdown of Purple Gang activities as a sign of changing times, Weitzman sold the building in 1930 back to Louis Gianotti, who operated Cuneo Restaurant there until 1937.[46] At one point in 1932, Gianotti fell behind on his tax payments, and the IRS placed a lien on the building. Its ownership was then transferred to his associate, Italian businessman Harry Bianchini, for a short period between 1932 and 1933. Bianchini owned the building at the end of Prohibition, but soon thereafter he transferred its title back to Louis Gianotti. Bianchini went on to pursue grander plans of opening a high-end restaurant in 1934—Little Harry—on Jefferson Avenue, two miles to the east. Meanwhile, Gianotti struggled to adjust to post-Prohibition regulations on alcohol service. After Prohibition ended in 1933, the city required restaurant and saloon proprietors to purchase a license to serve alcohol. Those who were accustomed to serving alcohol under the radar during Prohibition were resistant to the new fees. Many saloonkeepers, including Gianotti, ignored them. Gianotti's attempt to flout the regulations placed on the bar's alcohol distribution in 1934 was unsuccessful, and he was duly fined twenty-five dollars by the city.[47]

None of the historic maps, city directory records, or land deeds hint at the existence of a speakeasy at 624 Third Avenue during Prohibition. This is an unsurprising finding. We did not expect an illegal establishment to appear on maps, in advertisements, or in print. So imagine our amazement when one of the project researchers was flipping through the pages of Philip Mason's popular history of Prohibition, *Rumrunning and the Roaring Twenties*, and stumbled across a photograph of a membership card from a speakeasy at 624 Third Avenue![48] The speakeasy's name, "Little Harry," is boldly printed in the center of the card. On the bottom right corner appears an address and further information to assist patrons in locating it: "624 Third Street, Opposite Union Depot," and on the bottom left corner—a phone number, "CLifford 3871"! There also appears a faint trace of the name "Helen Berkheimer" written on the front side, above the Little Harry name. Covering the backside is the bold signature of "George B. Schaffer." We located no further information about either individual during the course of our research, but based on comparisons with membership cards from other Detroit speakeasys, we surmised that George B. Schaffer may have either been a patron of Little Harry or perhaps its manager. We had assumed that the speakeasy's operators would have made every effort to obscure its existence, but the guest card proved us wrong (Figure 2.5).

We then learned that the Detroit Historical Society's collections contain dozens of similar speakeasy guest cards bearing names, addresses, and contact info for Prohibition-era establishments throughout the city. These cards were issued by speakeasy operators to trusted clientele, who, in turn, brandished them to gain entry. For our research team, the guest card was the "smoking gun"; it confirmed that there was certainly a speakeasy somewhere on the premises of 624 Third Avenue and that it was named for someone called Harry. The location of the speakeasy and its possible association with either Harry Weitzman or Harry Bianchini is a matter of archaeological investigation and interpretation, to which I now turn.

Figure 2.5. Membership card used to gain admission to the Little Harry speakeasy, late 1920s. The name "Helen Berkheimer" is written in faded ink in the upper left corner. A signature on the back reads "George B. Shaffer." There are no accounts of these individuals in association with the building's occupancy or ownership history. (Detroit Historical Society)

SEARCHING FOR THE SPEAKEASY

Prior to our archaeological survey, the one source of information we had about the speakeasy's location came from the elderly patron of Tommy's Bar. According to his childhood memories, the speakeasy was a small wood-paneled room housed in the building's basement. It was accessed by a tunnel that ran underneath Third Avenue. At the interior end of the tunnel there was a vestibule, bounded by doors on both sides. A guard stood in the vestibule and admitted approved guests into the underground bar room. There, patrons gathered to drink, socialize, and gamble.

At the time of our survey in 2013 there survived no visible remnants of the tunnel entrance at the street level. We accessed the building's basement and the alleged speakeasy from inside the bar and restaurant. On the ground floor of Tommy's, in the far corner of the front room, there is a narrow doorway and staircase leading down to the basement. The staircase runs along the building's northern wall and terminates in a cramped storage area with a low-hanging six-foot-two-inch ceiling and just enough space for one person to maneuver among the stacked cases of beer and soft drinks (Figure 2.6).

During Prohibition, inspectors would be fooled into thinking this compact storage area at the bottom of the staircase was the extent of the basement. They would not have been able to see the eighteen-foot-long hallway that runs along the basement's south wall and connects to the speakeasy room at the front of the building because the storage area was completely walled in at the time. Thin wooden panels, painted a pale green, hung on the storage area's walls and unified the space so it looked like a self-contained room. But the storage area's south wall was a decoy built to conceal the hallway leading to the speakeasy room (see Figure 2.6). This false wall no longer exists, but remnants of where it was once attached to the floor and ceiling do. It is likely that the false wall was movable, or perhaps had a hidden door in it, so that staff from the business on the ground floor could access the speakeasy from inside the building.

Between the storage area at the bottom of the staircase and the speakeasy room at the opposite end of the basement stands another mysterious architectural feature—a 162 square foot enclosure. There are no indications in the enclosure's floor-to-ceiling brick walls that there was ever any doorway leading to its interior. Instead, missing baseboards along the basement staircase revealed that the enclosure conceals a mound of dirt that extends to within inches of the ceiling and fills the entire enclosure

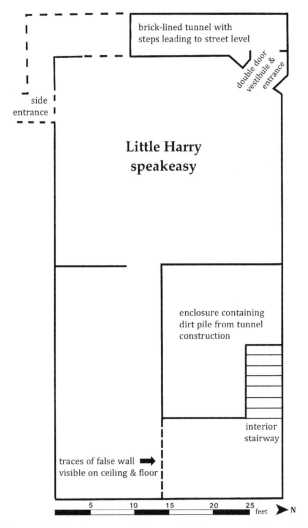

brick-lined tunnel with
steps leading to street level

double door
vestibule &
entrance

side
entrance

**Little Harry
speakeasy**

enclosure containing
dirt pile from tunnel
construction

interior
stairway

traces of false wall ➡
visible on ceiling & floor

5   10   15   20   25
                        feet   ➤ N

Figure 2.6. Plan map showing the present-day layout of the basement of Tommy's Detroit Bar and Grill and the remnant features of the speakeasy documented within it during the archaeological survey. (Krysta Ryzewski)

(Figure 2.7). The mound and the brick walls surrounding it would have functioned as a convenient sound barrier between the basement speakeasy and the restaurant operations upstairs.

The staff and present-day patrons of Tommy's Bar were aware of the unusual enclosure, and they often speculated about the bodies of Purple Gang enemies, criminal evidence, or other treasures that might be buried within it. During the archaeological investigations we used soil augers to probe the dirt mound for datable artifacts. To the disappointment of the bar's patrons, we extracted no evidence of grizzly criminal activities. We did, however, recover fragments of machine-made, embossed bottles that date to the first third of the twentieth century. The bottles' positions at the base of the mound and their manufacturing dates suggest that the enclosure was constructed during the Prohibition era.

Figure 2.7. Interior stairway leading down to the basement from the barroom of Tommy's Detroit Bar and Grill. The missing planks reveal a formerly concealed six-foot-high dirt pile that is enclosed by floor-to-ceiling brick walls on all sides. (Krysta Ryzewski)

Our documentation of the enclosure raised questions about how and why such a massive pile of dirt was transported to the basement of the bar in the first place. It would have been extremely difficult to maneuver inconspicuously what amounted to 1,050 cubic feet of dirt through the upstairs restaurant and down the narrow staircase. Where did the dirt come from? Was the enclosure purpose-built to conceal it?

The answer to these questions stood in the opposite end of the basement, in the speakeasy room. At the end of the narrow hallway once obscured by the pale green decoy wall is a square-shaped room of 455 square feet. Just slightly smaller than the front room of Tommy's Bar above it on the ground floor, this section of the basement was originally constructed in the 1890s when Andrew Healey extended the front half of the building to align with the sidewalk frontage. During Prohibition, this room was Little Harry speakeasy.

In the northwest corner of the speakeasy room still stands a wood-framed entryway (Figure 2.8). It is positioned diagonally, at a 140 degree angle to the building's west wall. The doorway leads into a vestibule that is about three feet deep and three-and-a-half feet wide. On the other side of the vestibule is a second wooden doorframe with hinges where a door between the speakeasy and its primary access point—the tunnel—once hung.

The discovery of the tunnel confirmed that the basement speakeasy room was indeed accessed by an underground entrance; in this case, a brick-lined tunnel with a wooden flight of stairs that originated at the street level. Underground, the tunnel runs for almost fifteen feet and is three feet wide; it is difficult to discern what its original height would have been.

One point of divergence between the tunnel's physical remains and the oral history is that the extant tunnel runs parallel to the building's frontage; it only extends underneath the sidewalk. By contrast, in his childhood recollections, the bar patron recalled that he entered the underground speakeasy from a tunnel that ran underneath the street and across Third Avenue. To test the possibility that the tunnel may have turned toward the street, we removed bricks from its wall and probed the soil behind them with boring tools and video scopes. Our investigations determined that there was no further extension of that tunnel underneath the street; no connector between the basement and the 7,000-gallon cistern in the middle of Third Avenue or with the railroad culverts that sat exposed nearby in the 1940s, as some theories suggested.[49]

When we first encountered the tunnel it was completely filled with debris (Figure 2.9). After it was sealed from the street level, the tunnel

Figure 2.8. Vestibule and doorway at the end of the hidden tunnel that led from the street level to the basement speakeasy. View from the speakeasy room. (Krysta Ryzewski)

became a convenient receptacle for decades' worth of trash deposited by successive generations of restaurant owners and employees. The fill created a sloped but otherwise undisturbed vertical stratigraphy, with debris from the present-day bar at the surface and layered deposits of older materials underneath. We approached the removal of the tunnel's trash with the methods of archaeological excavation, carefully extracting more recent objects from the topmost layers and working our way down to the older objects nearer the base of the tunnel, noting the depths and location of particular finds along the way. We removed all manner of loose

Figure 2.9. Excavation of eighty years' worth of debris from the underground tunnel. (Krysta Ryzewski)

architectural and infrastructural materials from the tunnel—bricks, nails, electric wiring, and copper tubing. There were broken bottles, bits of barstools, and tattered floormats. The occasional rodent bone and rat trap were mixed in. The most interesting and perhaps informative artifacts came from the bottom of the tunnel deposit. From the lowermost level, the first to be filled in, we collected embossed beverage bottles whose manufacturing technology and markings date them to the 1930s at the latest, and the 1880s at the earliest (Figure 2.10). We also recovered remnants of electrical fuse sockets and fuse bulbs, one of which was identified as a Royal Crystal glass top fuse. This type of fuse was produced by the Royal Electric Company in Chelsea, Massachusetts, during the 1920s.[50] Based on datable artifacts from the bottommost layer of the tunnel, we concluded that the first round of trash was deposited there sometime in the 1930s, suggesting that the building's owners—perhaps Louis Gianotti or Harry Bianchini—dismantled the speakeasy and capped it from above with sidewalk pavement around the time that Prohibition ended in 1933.

Once we cleared the tunnel of debris, we were able to measure it, calculate its dimensions, and make a better estimation about how patrons accessed it. The surviving area of the tunnel comprises just forty-eight and a half square feet. Estimating the height of the original tunnel at six feet,

Figure 2.10. Artifacts recovered from the speakeasy tunnel include (*clockwise from top left*) a wrench; light bulb sockets and electrical wiring; alcohol bottles with manufacturing technology and makers' marks dating to the first third of the twentieth century; a bottle base embossed with the initials of G. Norris & Co., a Detroit-based bottling company in operation between 1885 and 1900; and a Royal Crystal glass fuse produced by the Royal Electric Company during the 1920s. (Krysta Ryzewski)

builders would have removed 315 cubic feet of dirt to make the extant portion of the tunnel (Figure 2.11).

It seems most likely that the dirt pile housed within the basement's brick enclosure came from the excavations of the tunnel. Perhaps workers dug the tunnel from the inside of the basement, upward to the street level. The dirt from the tunnel could have been easily scooped inward and transported across the basement without attracting attention aboveground. Intriguingly, the measurements of the tunnel's volume (315 cubic feet) did not match the volume of dirt enclosed within the brick room (1,050 cubic feet). The puzzling disparity between the volume of the tunnel chamber and the much greater amount of dirt in the brick enclosure suggested that another void, perhaps a secondary passageway or room, existed in another part of the basement.

After we had an idea about how the speakeasy was accessed and constructed, we shifted our focus to documenting any surviving traces of Prohibition-era activity within the single twenty-one-by-twenty-three-foot room that served as Little Harry speakeasy. We carefully examined the four walls, ceiling, and floors to collect information about the room and to compare with the surviving oral history. Three findings were particularly noteworthy. First, we located horizontal wooden beams inserted into the upper and lower surface of the brick walls around the entire room. The beams matched the height and width of the bricks. Remnants of nail holes

Figure 2.11. Excavations of the speakeasy tunnel revealed five wooden stairs leading to a bricked-up ceiling and wall. The tunnel is supported by a series of horizontal wooden support beams. In the foreground one beam has a cutout to accommodate a door. (Krysta Ryzewski)

were visible in the beams at regularly spaced intervals. We concluded that these wooden beams likely served as supports for hanging wood paneled walls. A second notable find was electrical wiring running along the ceiling of the speakeasy room. With the help of an electrical engineer who was volunteering on the project's survey team, we determined that the speakeasy room operated on a wiring and circuit system that was separate from the upstairs business. The remnants of this system matched the fuse and sockets recovered during the excavations of the tunnel debris. The third discovery was that the speakeasy did not extend beyond the one small room. The bar's owner and staff speculated that the speakeasy would have been larger than the 455 square foot basement space, perhaps extending underground beyond the current basement walls. To test this theory, we removed bricks from two of the walls and probed the soil behind them. We identified no additional voids or rooms. This conclusion was disappointing to some of the project's stakeholders, whose fantasies of speakeasy experiences differed from the physical reality. Nevertheless, from our archaeological survey of the basement space of Tommy's Bar, we concluded that the speakeasy was housed in one small room that was decorated with wood-paneled walls. It had its own electrical system, and the covert room was accessed from the outside via a tunnel.

OUTDOOR CLUES AND URBAN LEGENDS

We next moved our archaeological investigations outdoors. Along the exterior perimeter we documented the many modifications owners had made to the building over the course of its occupation. Our intention was to identify any architectural changes that might coincide with the speakeasy's operation. Differences between the sequential phases of building construction were visible in surviving wall seams and contrasts in brick and other building materials. Modifications to the building on the sides and rear of the building included cement or brick patches over nine windows, two ground-level doors, three smaller windows or vents, and one basement-level door. Unlike the other building modifications, which remained sturdy, we observed that one patch at the top of the current basement level was crumbling. Located along the south wall and near the building's northwest corner, this patch revealed another possible access point to the underground speakeasy. With the owner's permission, we removed the cement patch from the wall. Behind it was a wooden doorframe; its top extended about a foot above the modern ground surface (Figure 2.12). Probing into the doorway, we discovered a void at least two feet deep. The entryway aligned with the south wall of the speakeasy.

We returned to the basement to search for evidence of the access point along the interior walls, but our efforts to locate further architectural evidence of it were hampered by the placement of the building's modern heating and cooling system. Nevertheless, our video and soil probes from the exterior suggested that the doorway led to a passageway along the western and southern walls. Although we were unable to calculate the size

Figure 2.12. Another underground access point to the basement speakeasy along the south wall of the building. This entryway would have been accessible from the interior of the one-story wooden building that stood adjacent to the brick building between 1915 and ca. 1933. (Krysta Ryzewski)

of the passageway, the dirt removed during its construction would have certainly contributed to the size of the mound within the enclosure.

The discovery of the second entryway raised new questions about how the speakeasy was accessed from the street level. We returned to the historic maps of the property and noted the presence of the one-story wooden building on the adjacent lot (622 Third Avenue, which had the same owners as the speakeasy). No photographs survive of this wooden building, but maps indicate that its northern wall touched the southern wall of the speakeasy building at 624 Third Avenue, and that it stood for the duration of Prohibition. Based on this information, we realized that it may have been possible to enter the basement speakeasy from a passageway that began inside the next door building. This short underground journey may have disoriented patrons and, perhaps, given them the impression that they were traveling underneath the street.

The final part of our archaeological investigation involved conducting excavations outdoors, in the backyard of the building, at the location where the ten-foot-square outbuilding once stood. By 1950 the outbuilding was demolished, but maps from the 1920s and earlier indicate that it remained intact and relatively undisturbed—except for the addition of an iron chimney in 1921—for the duration of its existence. The excavations were designed to address two questions. First, we wanted to understand how the building's function changed over time. We speculated that it could have been the location of an outhouse in the saloon's early years before it was adapted for other uses—perhaps related to Prohibition-era activities—in the 1920s. Second, we intended to address our partners' theories that the outbuilding disguised (yet another) tunnel that connected the bar building to the basement of the neighboring Fort Street Presbyterian Church.

During the 1850s and 1860s, Fort Street Presbyterian Church was an important stop on the Underground Railroad. Some of our collaborators and stakeholders claimed, contrary to information in city records and on maps, that the brick iterations of the Tommy's Bar building existed prior to the Civil War and that people escaping from slavery could have passed through it en route to the Detroit River crossing. Interestingly, these speculative histories had many of the same structural elements as the speakeasy stories, especially in their reference to a brick-lined tunnel running under the street and secret rooms in the bar's basement. Both sets of stories pose challenges for archaeologists and historians because they are associated with ephemeral and illicit activities that were intentionally designed to leave behind minimal physical traces.[51] Nonetheless, such speculations remain important to understanding and interpreting the power of certain places in the collective imagination. As Rebecca Graff, James Delle, and other archaeologists who conduct research on Underground Railroad sites observe, these sites and the social myths attached to them serve important roles in preserving collective memories, commemorating the resiliency of African Americans, and recognizing the struggle involved in the transit process—whether or not there exists tangible historical archaeological evidence between the site and these activities.[52]

Based on our historical background research and our survey of the bar's basement, we already knew that there was almost certainly not a direct connection between the current brick iteration of the Tommy's Bar building and Underground Railroad traffic from the Fort Street Presbyterian Church. The brick building that houses Tommy's Bar was not constructed until at least the late 1860s or 1870s, after emancipation. There were, however, earlier nineteenth-century wooden dwellings that stood on the site of the brick bar building prior to the 1860s; faint images of these structures appear in the background of historic photographs on display inside Fort Street Church. We therefore approached the excavations with open minds, recognizing that the earlier nineteenth-century wooden dwellings may have played a supportive role in the Underground Railroad.

In total, we recovered over three hundred artifacts from the excavations of the outbuilding, the basement tunnel, and the dirt pile inside the enclosed brick room. The majority of these artifacts came from the outbuilding excavations. They included all manner of refuse, including broken dishes from the various restaurants housed within the building, pig and cow bones from entrees served there, bottle caps, iron nails, a child's plastic hair barrette, and dozens of broken beer, alcohol, soda pop, and cosmetic bottle remains. The dishes included fragments of ironstone and Warwick restaurant-ware plates from the early 1930s. The majority of the datable bottles were produced after 1930. Excavations revealed no evidence of a tunnel or any other type of passageway underneath the outbuilding. Nor did they locate remains of the earlier wooden buildings that once stood in the vicinity. But there was an indication that the outbuilding may have once been used as a space to process and/or store alcohol. During the excavations we uncovered iron hoops surrounding a decayed, buried wooden hogshead barrel. From this find, we entertained the possibility that perhaps a stove was added to the outbuilding in the early 1920s to fuel a distilling or cutting process that may have been taking place within it. It is unlikely that the speakeasy would have relied exclusively on alcohol processed on site, but the ability to have access to a steady supply—even before the speakeasy was established—would have kept the saloon and speakeasy businesses running smoothly.

WHO WAS LITTLE HARRY?

Based on the historical archaeological evidence, the physical remains inside and outside the Tommy's Detroit Bar and Grill building, and archival records, we were able to answer our first research question with confidence. Yes, there was a speakeasy in the basement of 624 Third Avenue that operated during Prohibition; it was called Little Harry. At the

conclusion of our survey and excavations, though, we still could not answer our question about whether the speakeasy was associated with the
Purple Gang. To do so we needed to dig deeper into biographies, historic
media accounts, and living memories.

Our starting point for making connections with the Purple Gang was
to return to the speakeasy membership card that our team located during
the process of archival research. If we could identify the "Harry" who was
the namesake of the speakeasy, then we might try to trace the extent of
his underworld connections. There were two options: Harry Bianchini or
Harry Weitzman.

Harry Bianchini owned the building for just over a year between 1932
and 1933. Bianchini initially acquired the building from fellow Italian immigrant Louis Gianotti after the US Internal Revenue Service placed a
tax lien on it in 1932. Bianchini's ownership of 624 Third Avenue lasted
through the end of Prohibition in 1933, but not long beyond it. In May of
that year, in preparation for the end of the Prohibition laws, Detroit police
superintendent John P. Smith ordered his officers to close the city's estimated 7,500 speakeasies once and for all. Police officers were to first issue
a warning to proprietors, allowing them the opportunity to close down the
operations on their own terms. If they resisted, officers were to employ
their "iron fist" method—the ax squad—to destroy speakeasy furnishings.
After the speakeasies ceased operations, police were instructed to "maintain a twenty-four-hour-a-day vigil there to see that [they] remain closed."[53]
The hundreds of speakeasies lining Second Avenue, one block away from
the Little Harry speakeasy, were the first to go. By mid-1933 there was no
longer a need or incentive to operate a clandestine blind pig in the basement of 624 Third Avenue; with the purchase of a liquor license, alcohol
could once again be served legally in the upstairs Cuneo Restaurant. Bianchini moved his business interests across town, where he brought the
speakeasy's name aboveground with the establishment of his new restaurant, Little Harry's, on East Jefferson.[54]

Did Harry Bianchini operate Little Harry speakeasy in the basement of
the Tommy's Bar building in 1932–1933, and was he connected with the
Purple Gang? At first glance, Bianchini seems to be the obvious bridge
between the city's two "Little Harry" institutions—the Prohibition-era
speakeasy and the famous Little Harry's Restaurant, which remained a
popular eatery until it closed in 1990.[55] Local urban legends recount how
Little Harry's Restaurant was a hangout for Purple Gang members, but
the connections are tenuous. First, by 1934, the Purple Gang was all but
defunct as a result of their own internal conflicts.[56] A handful of Jewish

gangsters remained in the news in the following years, and they may have frequented Little Harry's Restaurant, but the notorious gang's reputation and control over the Detroit underworld was greatly diminished by the time the restaurant opened. By the mid-1930s, members of the city's Italian immigrant community assumed control over the underworld.

It is not unreasonable to suggest that Bianchini at least knew about the existence of the Little Harry speakeasy at 624 Third Avenue, or even continued to operate it in the final year of Prohibition. As a prominent restauranteur, he was probably also familiar with clientele who were Purple Gang members. But if he had business or social connections to them that extended beyond the relationship of food and drinks service, they remain well hidden. There is no evidence to suggest that Bianchini was connected to the Purple Gang or that he operated as an affiliate of the next-generation Italian American gangsters. Harry Weitzman, by contrast, had direct ties to the city's Jewish underworld, an eye for opportunistic business ventures, and deep pockets.

When forty-three-year-old Weitzman acquired 624 Third Avenue from Louis Gianotti in 1927, the Purple Gang's bootlegging activities were at their height, as was the proliferation of speakeasies in the city. During his three-year ownership of the building, a subsidiary gang of the Purples— the Third Avenue Navy (a.k.a. the Little Jewish Navy)—were responsible for smuggling alcohol from Canada to a dock located just two blocks away to the south of the Little Harry speakeasy. In September 1931, just months after Weitzman sold his ownership stake in 624 Third Avenue, three of the Third Avenue Navy members were violently murdered by the Purple Gang in apartment 211 at Collingwood Manor. The event that became known as the Collingwood Massacre dried up the conduit of alcohol on Third Avenue.[57]

Like many of the Purple Gang members, Weitzman was a second-generation American of Russian Jewish heritage. He was quite wealthy by 1927, owing to a decade's worth of gambling winnings and risky business ventures. Each winter he sailed with his wife and three children to Miami, where they enjoyed the comforts of their vacation home. Weitzman's wealth was a measure of his ability to enter, profit from, and exit business ventures at opportune moments. These ventures—fur and jewelry sales, bail bonds, real estate, speakeasies—both profited from and supported the local Jewish business community, including its underworld.

Weitzman's investment in entertainment venues during Prohibition is well documented. At the same time that he owned the Tommy's Bar building at 624 Third Avenue, Weitzman was operating at least one other speakeasy, Deutches Haus, on 9149 Lyon Street, which in 1928 the *Detroit Free Press* reported was padlocked for liquor violations.[58] On the opposite end of the entertainment spectrum, in 1927 Weitzman commissioned acclaimed local architect Charles N. Agree to build the magnificent Moorish art deco–style Grande Ballroom, whose second-story 5,000-square foot dance floor was touted as the largest hardwood dance floor in the country (see chapter 6). Weitzman cemented his legacy on the building by molding the initials of his three children's first names—Clement, Dorothy, and Seymour—under each of the building's second-story window frames. Following its opening in 1928, the Grande Ballroom remained a popular gathering spot for the city's society functions, Jewish community, and, some say, Purple Gang members.

Given the circumstances of the late 1920s and Weitzman's role in the city's entertainment and business enterprises, it seems most likely that the Little Harry speakeasy was Weitzman's namesake, and that it began under his ownership of 624 Third Avenue. Weitzman would have seen an opportunity to capitalize on the building's central location by running a speakeasy across from the Fort Street train depot and along the smuggling routes of the Third Avenue Navy. The historical archaeological evidence that our research compiled supports this interpretation.

Weitzman's connections to the Purple Gang remain suitably fuzzy. There are no media accounts, arrest records, or other evidence to suggest that he was a member of the Purple Gang. Nevertheless, his social and familial networks hint that his ties to the gang were stronger than records detail.

In the course of collecting oral histories about the speakeasy, several of Weitzman's family members reached out to me, eager to share their family histories and lore.[59] They recalled that Harry Weitzman was a "tough guy" whose education was limited to grade school. Despite his lack of formal education, his sharp-witted sense of humor, persuasive negotiating skills, and loyal family ties generated considerable success in his business ventures. In their oral history interviews, Weitzman's descendants recalled how he conducted business with members of the Purple Gang under the guise of his Detroit Bonding and Insurance Agency. Profits from this agency and other commercial operations allowed Weitzman to enjoy a life of luxury. A chauffer named Mitchell drove him daily from his spacious home in the upscale Boston Edison neighborhood to various business meetings, and then on to an assortment of gambling parlors, high-end restaurants, or to his own box at the 8 Mile horse racing track.[60]

Weitzman had allies in the local media and law enforcement who may have ensured that his shady business dealings evaded scrutiny, police investigations, or news coverage. The *Detroit News*, located less than a block from the Little Harry speakeasy, seemed to have ignored the activities that took place within eyeshot. Conveniently, the city's lead prosecuting attorney, who also defended Purple Gang leader Abe Bernstein, was Harry's nephew, Lewis J. Weitzman.

DESCENDANT COMMUNITIES AND DARK HERITAGE

What began as a local collaborative archaeology project quickly grew into a story of national interest, with a community of stakeholders interested in the criminal heritage of the speakeasy that extended far beyond Michigan. Whether or not the Little Harry speakeasy had direct ties to the Purple Gang hardly seemed to matter; the mere possibility that it *could have* attracted the media's attention and captured public interest. Local television stations and newspapers, who learned about the Speakeasy Archaeology Project through word of mouth and our social media postings, broadcast stories about the excavations.[61] They focused on the intrigue of the gangsters, ghostly hauntings, hidden tunnels, and illicit activities. The media coverage, especially a story by the *Jewish News*—an outlet that directly connects nationally with the Jewish American community—triggered an influx of community contacts and oral histories about the Jewish underworld, Prohibition-era Detroit, and speakeasies in the area.

Archaeologists who conduct community-involved research are accustomed to working with descendants of residents and other local stakeholders who share personal connections with the sites they study. Sometimes these relationships involve full-on collaborations, from the start through the completion of projects. Other times, they involve consultations or oral history interviews in which information is shared about the site's history or archaeological remains. In either scenario, it tends to be the case that these conversations are based on the premise that we, as researchers, respect and appreciate the accomplishments of the preceding generations of occupants at a site. Rarely do we, or the descendants, draw attention to past occupants' failures or shortcomings in our conversations, much less their dark, criminal activities. In the wake of media coverage, I was surprised to receive an influx of messages from relatives of Harry Weitzman and Harry Bianchini, and Purple Gang members, who were eager to share uncensored accounts of their relatives' involvement in Prohibition-era Detroit. In the years that followed, I met, exchanged emails, and held phone conversations with relatives as far away as North Carolina, where ninety-year-old Jackie Hill (née Jacquelyn Weitzman), the niece of Harry Weitzman lives, and California, where Marina Nelson, Harry's first cousin thrice removed, researches the Weitzman family's checkered past. Their accounts are the basis for many of the aforementioned details about the Little Harry speakeasy's operation and owners.

In all of my conversations with people who were connected to the Purple Gang or the Weitzman family, they stressed how deeply ashamed the Jewish community of the 1920s was of the gangsters' activities during Prohibition. The retelling of a Prohibition-era story through the Speakeasy Archaeology Project was, for the families tied to the Purple Gang and the Little Harry speakeasy operators, an opportunity to acknowledge a dark period in Jewish American history. But the retelling was also a means for recognizing, without glorifying gang violence and criminal activity, the extent to which Detroit's Jewish community shaped the city during its most prosperous years.

THE NEXT CHAPTER OF THE SPEAKEASY PROJECT

The survey and excavation activities of the Speakeasy Archaeology Project ended in early September 2013. At that point, we handed off the planning of public events showcasing our findings to our partner Marion Christiansen, then of Preservation Detroit. Some archaeologists might call this next period the aftermath of the project, but that would imply that the process of research and dissemination was over. It was not; this was a process of slow, community-involved archaeology.[62] The real impacts and lasting contributions of the Speakeasy Archaeology Project, the afterlives of the survey and excavations, were really just beginning. The next chapter followed a trajectory over which, by design and intent, I had a decreasing amount of control.

In the case of the Speakeasy Archaeology Project our community-involved collaborations and partnership roles were relatively straightforward and staged according to different parts of the project's workload: documentation and research, public outreach, and curation of the speakeasy site. Everyone from the archaeologists to the bar's owner had a specific role to play; some roles overlapped, but for the most part, each of us had the latitude to pursue our priorities as we wished. Fortunately, we were able to avoid disagreements or competing agendas because the three of us who were the lead collaborators on the project—myself, preservationist and educator Marion Christiansen, and bar owner Tom Burelle—shared common priorities and outlooks on how the speakeasy's story might be told.

The next chapter of the Speakeasy Archaeology Project began with a 1920s-themed party, hosted at Tommy's Bar on December 5, 2013, on the eightieth anniversary of the repeal of Prohibition. The event, coordinated by Christiansen, was a fundraiser benefit for Preservation Detroit, and tickets to it sold out within a few hours. Two hundred attendees, dressed in flapper costumes and zoot suits, packed the bar to enjoy guided tours of the basement speakeasy by our archaeology team and to view the interpretive posters and artifacts we put on display for the event.

The success of the first public event generated a buzz among local tour operators, which, in Detroit, are dominated by unique, experience-based and themed bus tours. One such tour, led by the Detroit Experience Factory, involves a pub crawl to Prohibition-era bars; the speakeasy at Tommy's Bar, the only one to be verified archaeologically, became a necessary stop on the circuit. Similarly, local meet-up groups, including the popular Detroit Drunken Historical Society, began to gather at the bar. Prior to the archaeological project, Tommy's Bar was a sports bar. Afterward, the bar increasingly attracted history buffs, whose pilgrimages to the speakeasy were a boon to the local business. At first the bar's owner was excited about the influx of new customers. But eventually, the bar became such a popular tour stop that the stream of visitors strained the small staff, and Burelle had to scale back the number of group visits to the speakeasy by bar-hopping history buffs and ghost hunters.

Over the past seven years, the findings from the speakeasy project have continued to generate media attention in blog posts, newspaper reports, and television series; they have become part of the local lore in their own right. Some stories feature the speakeasy's history and archaeology, as was the case of the PBS-like Dig Detroit series produced by Kevin Walsh. Others make imaginative connections between archaeology and ghosts, as in the Sci-Fi channel's ghost hunters' attempts to detect electromagnetic fields in the basement and to use ground-penetrating radar in an effort to find the "tunnel under the street" that archaeologists may have missed.

THERE *MUST* BE MORE TO THE STORY

Nowadays the stories about the speakeasy and its history tend to vary depending on who is telling them. On any night of the week a visitor may walk into Tommy's Bar and, depending on the staff behind the counter, they will hear a different story about the building's ghosts, the Purple Gang, the speakeasy, or the archaeology project. No two stories are exactly the same, nor do they tend to highlight our archaeological findings. As heritage scholar John Lennon notes, this variability in how the bar's past is portrayed to patrons is a result of different priorities and interactions; the speakeasy's history has become a space where the quest for historical accuracy is not always the goal of the storyteller.[63] Nevertheless, elements of the speakeasy's story, whether verified or not, continue to occupy an evocative place in the imagination of visitors and scholars alike, who, as archaeologist Rebecca Graff contends, are seeking a "personal connection to the narrative[s] via the built environment and aided by archaeological research."[64]

In the end, the historical narrative that archaeologists constructed about Little Harry speakeasy did not become an authoritative account that trumped all other imaginings of the space (nor was that our aim). The fact that there still remains a mixture of verified and speculative details in the public accounts of the speakeasy's history does not, however, diminish archaeology's contributions. It would be impossible to tell this particular story about the speakeasy without including archaeologically recovered information. The most distinguishing features of Little Harry speakeasy are its material remains and the ways in which they are woven into its historical narrative—the tunnel, subtle architectural features of the basement, objects that date to the Prohibition era, and the speakeasy membership card. These provide clear, tangible connections with the Prohibition era that illuminate the speakeasy experience and bond local stakeholders to its narrative and to Tommy's Bar.

The widespread attention that the Speakeasy Archaeology Project's findings received raises questions about why the public is so utterly fascinated by criminal heritage and the Prohibition-era history in Detroit. There is irony in this fascination. Contemporary Detroit is plagued by its associations with violent crime, drug trafficking, and rampant corruption, yet somehow parallel acts from a century ago have achieved a revered, mythological, and uncontroversial heritage value. In this case, the presence of the speakeasy and its potential connections with the Purple Gang elevated the profile of Tommy's Bar to a must-visit historical site. For some stakeholders, the tangible connections that archaeology provides with criminal activity are perhaps the closest they will ever come to breaking the law; a visit to Tommy's is a thrilling occasion to explore the underworld from a safe distance. For others, the significance is more personal. The mythological status of Jewish gangsters, and the effects that their illicit economy had on shaping the city during Prohibition, serve meaningful ideological ends, especially among the Jewish American population who have ties to Detroit. Although the vast majority of Jews moved beyond the city limits generations ago, there still exists a sizable, engaged Detroit Jewish diaspora (in local suburbs and nationally) who seek to articulate their community's role in the city's historical development. For these stakeholders, the speakeasy connects with issues of belonging in a city where they no longer live. By recognizing Prohibition-era heritage as it is manifested by Little Harry speakeasy, Jewish communities have an opportunity to assert their long-standing roots in Detroit, demonstrate their continued investment in the city, and contribute to its historical narratives.

There are many parts of the Little Harry speakeasy story that remain incomplete. There are also historically and archaeologically verified details that the project partners remain skeptical about, such as the construction date of the brick building, the size of the speakeasy room, and the location of the tunnel. In these instances our findings do not align with their knowledge or expectations. This dissonance is not a deterrent to future investigations; in fact, the Speakeasy Archaeology Project's partners want to do *more* archaeology because, they argue, there *could* be another speakeasy room beyond the back wall, a second tunnel under the alleyway, or artifacts that might connect more explicitly to criminal activities. They are happy with the results so far but not fully satisfied that the whole story has been recovered archaeologically. For those who care most about the history of Tommy's Bar, there *must* be more to the story. Maybe there is. But as an archaeologist, I doubt that it will ever be possible to achieve a full understanding of the speakeasy's operations. No matter how many archaeological investigations take place, there will always be missing pieces to the puzzle. And so, perhaps it is appropriate to end by thinking of the Little Harry speakeasy as what archaeologist April Beisaw calls an "archaeological ghost story," where some of the missing details cannot be fleshed out with historical facts; they are best explored and discovered by visitors' imaginations.[65]

CHAPTER THREE

Ransom Gillis House
Archaeology and the Long Century of Urban Renewal in Brush Park

On a cold, gray Thursday in March 2012, I stood with a dozen students from my Urban Archaeology class in the middle of a grassy field in Brush Park, the Midtown neighborhood just north of downtown Detroit. We held copies of Sanborn insurance maps depicting the rows of ornate Victorian and Gothic Revival mansions that had once lined the twenty-four blocks of Brush Park a century ago, when the area was home to the most desirable addresses for Detroit's blue blood elites (Figure 3.1).[1] Gusty winds kept pulling the maps from our hands, making it difficult for us to identify the few standing remains of the bygone era.[2] It was as if Mother Nature did not want us to look beyond the sweeping landscape of absence and ruination that stood before us.

Figure 3.1. Wayne State University students stand in an empty field in Brush Park studying Sanborn maps that depict the rows of mansions that once stood there during the late nineteenth century, March 2012. (Krysta Ryzewski)

We positioned ourselves on Alfred Street, a short residential road bounded by Brush Park's main thoroughfares, John R Street and Brush Street. In 1897 there were eleven mansions on the south side of Alfred; none survived in 2012. Across the street four unoccupied brick homes stood in various states of decay. The most derelict of them—the Ransom Gillis house—clung to life on the northeast corner of Alfred and John R. The two-and-a-half-story Venetian Gothic home's chimney leaned to one side. Boards covered its windows and doors. A corner turret, barely attached to the building's second story, lunged forward, supported underneath by only a slim metal rod. Even though there were faint traces of intermittent maintenance, a decade-old asphalt roof and a recent chain-link fence, the house looked exhausted by the ravages of a difficult life. It seemed ready to surrender.

To the north and south of Alfred Street the derelict scene repeated itself block after block; occasional remnants of stately Victorian homes punctuated the area's open fields. Only a handful of the buildings were occupied. Most residents struggled to maintain the structures, although a couple had invested substantial funds to restore the architectural features of their homes to their nineteenth-century splendor. On the whole, the Brush Park residential community was quiet, piecemeal, and riddled with blight.

On the day of our visit Brush Park was eerily silent. Few cars passed along the side streets. A wild pheasant ran through the overgrown lots. The Brush Park landscape in 2012 echoed former resident Russell Mc-Lauchlin's mournful description of Alfred Street and its environs. McLauchlin was born and raised on Alfred Street but left the area as a young adult. Thirty years later, he returned to visit the area as a middle-aged man. In the wake of his visit, overwhelmed by feelings of nostalgia and loss, McLauchlin was inspired to chronicle his experiences in the book *Alfred Street*, a romanticized historical retrospective of Brush Park.[3] In it, he describes Alfred Street's untimely transformation from a wealthy neighborhood into a "desolate . . . scene of poverty and chopfallen gloom . . . with dismal structures." He mourns the disappearance of the extravagant homes, manicured streetscapes, and genteel residents preserved in his childhood memories. In the course of a generation, he lamented, Brush Park had become a "blighted area in bitter need of paint and repair."[4] McLauchlin's accounts of the neighborhood's blight could have been referring to the same landscape we experienced in 2012, but, in fact, his encounter with the area's decline was actually based on another time—sixty-six years earlier—during his visit to Brush Park in 1946.

McLauchlin's decades-old observations underscore how blight and decay in Brush Park are neither recent nor objective phenomena. Historical and archaeological sources further demonstrate how blight is a gradual and uneven process that unfolded alongside the city's rapid growth, decline, and urban renewal, during a span of time considerably longer than the neighborhood's distinguished late nineteenth-century heyday.

Over the past two decades Brush Park has become a favorite destination for visitors seeking raw and authentic experiences with the "ruins of Detroit."[5] Scholars, urban explorers, and photographers have flocked to the neighborhood to gaze on the contemporary ruptured landscape and contemplate the systemic global failures that its decay seems to represent. In their focus on present-day ruins, few, if any, engaged with the remains of Brush Park's deeper human history. As a result, prevailing narratives deliver a verdict of lifelessness to the neighborhood. One damaging consequence of this portrayal is that it sidelines the histories of the twentieth-century communities who resided in Brush Park as it transitioned from an elite to a working-class neighborhood. These resilient residents left their own imprints on the area, but most traces of them have been rendered invisible by images of ruination and by Brush Park's contemporary developer-funded revitalization projects. With Brush Park cast as a place of irretrievable ruins—or in designer speak, a blank slate—developers are in the midst of converting the area into City Modern, a new, futuristic community.

In just eight short years, since my class visit to the area in 2012, Brush Park and the Ransom Gillis house have been completely transformed by privately funded construction projects in ways that are both beneficial and detrimental to recognizing the area's historical legacy and urban renewal heritage (Figure 3.2). While the pace and scale of changes in the neighborhood are striking, Brush Park's dramatic metamorphosis over the course of the past century is not unique. Its transformations mirror the historical trajectories of countless other neighborhoods in cities across the United States that have been similarly reconfigured by circumstances of industrial prosperity, urban renewal, blight, and gentrification. Brush Park differs from its urban counterparts though because of its staggering quantity of deteriorating physical remains—homes, outbuildings, parks, and infrastructure. The neighborhood provides an exceptionally rich base of material and historical evidence for examining urban transformations from an archaeological perspective.

This chapter is a case study in the historical archaeology of urbanization and in the politics surrounding the relationship between heritage and urban renewal. It tells three intertwined stories. First, I use findings from

Figure 3.2. Changes to the Ransom Gillis house in the twenty-first century as viewed from John R Street. (Krysta Ryzewski)

archival and archaeological research to present a comprehensive life history of the Ransom Gillis house and to chart how its changes over time parallel Brush Park and Detroit's industrial and social transformations of the past 150 years. Second, I detail the unique process of conducting the Ransom Gillis house investigations as part of a collaborative, developer-funded rehabilitation project. The partners and stakeholders involved in the project included a major corporation, a television network's production team, local nonprofit arts and preservation groups, students, and volunteers. Third, I consider the divergent outcomes of archaeology and historic preservation efforts at the Ransom Gillis house.[6] I reflect on how Brush Park's heritage has been leveraged by different interest groups to reposition the Ransom Gillis house and the neighborhood within contemporary Detroit. I conclude the chapter by situating Brush Park's urban renewal heritage within a longer term trajectory of blight designation and revitalization efforts to reveal long-term urban land management issues and to identify competing future-oriented agendas between archaeologists, historic preservationists, residents, and developers.[7]

RANSOM GILLIS'S SHORT STAY

One would be forgiven for assuming that the Ransom Gillis house is named for a famous occupant. In fact, the house's history and significance have very little to do with its namesake. Ransom Gillis was a dry goods merchant during the last quarter of the nineteenth century. In 1872 he and four partners established Edson, Moore & Co. Wholesale Dealers, located on Jefferson Avenue at the southwest corner of Bates.[8] Their business grew quickly, profiting from its advantageous position along the city's main commercial thoroughfare and proximity to Detroit's riverfront. Gillis never ranked among the city's wealthiest entrepreneurs or political elite, but his successful business secured him a place in Detroit's upper echelon and afforded him access to one of the city's most exclusive social institutions, the Old Michigan Club. There, he socialized in the company of influential men, and with their support he secured reputable leadership positions, including as a board member of Grace Hospital and the Lake St. Clair Fishing and Shooting Club.

Ransom Gillis purchased the property at 63 Alfred Street in Brush Park to escape the increasing industrialization of the downtown riverfront neighborhood where he lived.[9] From the time of Detroit's initial European occupation in 1701 through the early nineteenth century, the city's oldest Euro-American families inhabited ribbon farms along the Detroit River. These so-called private claims were long, narrow strips of land that extended northward from the waterfront (where most residents lived), across the Jefferson Avenue commercial corridor, and up to two miles inland into the agricultural fields that once covered present-day Midtown. Following the opening of the Erie Canal in 1825 and subsequent improvements in steamship transportation, manufacturing industries and immigrants flocked to Detroit. Their arrival altered the configuration of the long-standing private claims. To accommodate the new manufacturers and their laborers, property owners in the riverfront neighborhoods converted their single-family homes into rooming houses and boardinghouses. They also began subdividing individual ribbon farms, selling parcels from them to investors and developers. By the 1860s overcrowded conditions caused the deterioration of the downtown riverfront neighborhoods. The Potomac Quarter on the east side, near Gillis's wholesale business, became a notorious, squalid, crime-ridden slum.[10] Like many other merchants and businessmen who then lived near the riverfront, Gillis escaped the fray by relocating to the city's hinterlands. Two miles to the north, Detroit's upper echelon converted agricultural land from the Brush Farm private claim into Brush Park, a new, exclusive neighborhood distinguished by its Victorian mansions and wealthy residents. Brush Park's initial building campaign peaked in the 1880s (Figure 3.3).

Gillis invested in Brush Park in 1876, hiring local architects Henry T. Brush and George D. Mason to construct the house at 63 Alfred (the home was Mason's first design project). Brush and Mason introduced Venetian Gothic architecture to Detroit through the home's decorative elements, which were designed in the style of the then-popular Arts and Crafts movement. At a cost of $12,000 ($287,000 in today's money), the architects designed a robust 4,800-square-foot home using orange-red common brick. Builders accented the brick with tile and stone detailing and added a third story mansard roof tiled with gray slate and wrought iron cresting. An elaborate decorative chimney stood along the west elevation and was attached to the home's most distinctive feature, a turret with a conical roof, positioned

Figure 3.3. George S. Frost house at 86 Edmund Place and its stately neighbors, one block north of Alfred Street, 1890. (Courtesy of the Burton Historical Collection, Detroit Public Library)

at the building's southwest corner.[11] Standing on the northeast corner of Alfred and John R, the home was a prominent feature of the neighborhood's landscape; it was optimally situated to convey the prestige of its owners to those passing along the main thoroughfare of John R Street.[12]

It took two years for builders to complete the house at 63 Alfred. In 1878 Gillis and his wife Helen moved in. Two years later, they moved out. Whether the corner lot lost its appeal, or whether they had other plans from the outset is unknown. In 1880 the Gillis's moved next door to 69 Alfred, where they lived for thirty-four years until 1914.[13] At no point during Gillis's lifetime was either residence referred to as the Ransom Gillis house. This association was attached to the property at 63 Alfred by historic preservationists decades later in an effort to elevate the home's significance by connecting it to a particular individual and point in time. The few years that Gillis spent building the house and living there would eventually have a disproportionate effect on decisions to restore the home and shape narratives about its history.

PRESERVATION NIGHTMARE, ARCHAEOLOGICAL DREAM

By 2015, when our archaeology project began, the city of Detroit had been the owner of the Ransom Gillis house for fourteen years. When the city purchased the home through eminent domain in 2001 it was in shambles; the roof was gone, the corner turret's top half was missing, and brick walls crumbled inward. Thick vegetation blanketed the building from bottom to top, totally obscuring its few surviving architectural features. It was the city's intention to demolish the Ransom Gillis house. One obstacle stood in its way: football.

Located within walking distance of Ford Field, the Detroit Lions' National Football League stadium, city officials considered the house an eyesore that would send the wrong message about Detroit to the 100,000 visitors and potential investors who would be attending the 2006 Super Bowl XL (the National Football League's championship game). In preparation for the one-day sporting event, Mayor Kwame Kilpatrick embarked on an aggressive cleanup and demolition campaign of the derelict downtown and Midtown buildings that stood closest to the stadium. The city tore down iconic vacant structures, like the Donovan Building (former Motown Records headquarters), and concealed other vacant properties with tarpaulins, many of which were decorated with advertisements that exaggerated the buildings' future development prospects.[14] To demolish the Ransom Gillis house in time for the Super Bowl, the city would have to mitigate a host of environmental concerns—lead paint, asbestos, and soil contamination—at a cost well in excess of the $329,560 they paid to acquire the property in 2001.[15] It was not worth the time or investment, they concluded. Instead, the city decided to "mothball" the property, adding a new asphalt roof, wall supports, and boarding to stabilize the house from further decay.[16] They cut back the vegetation, erected a chain-link fence, and hung a sign whose language referenced vague plans for the property's redevelopment in the near future. If the Ransom Gillis house could not be demolished, city officials figured, at least it could be made to look like a work in progress.[17]

No progress came. In the years after the Super Bowl the city descended into bankruptcy. Mayor Kwame Kilpatrick assumed a new post, in federal prison, after being convicted of twenty-four corruption-related felonies, and an epidemic of blight expanded across the city (see chapter 7). It would take a decade for Brush Park's fortunes to change at the hands of billionaire real estate mogul Dan Gilbert, founder of Quicken Loans (the United States' second largest mortgage lender). In the early 2010s, Gilbert purchased and reactivated nearly three dozen empty or struggling office buildings in downtown Detroit, breathing new life into the low-occupancy city center through private investment and management. By 2015, Bedrock, Gilbert's real estate company, began to extend its gaze beyond downtown to Brush Park, purchasing 8.4 acres of properties, including the Ransom Gillis house in preparation for undertaking Detroit's largest-scale mixed-use development in decades. The new buildings and streetscapes within this section of Brush Park are soon to be part of a developmental ecosystem called City Modern. The City Modern project involves constructing over four hundred new housing units, restoring five historic houses, and opening thirty new retail spaces among the area's carefully manicured "European street scene."[18] The Ransom Gillis house was the initiative's first rehabilitation project; its restoration was choreographed to be the anchor of the ruins-to-prosperity narrative that City Modern was designed to instantiate.

In May 2015, shortly after Gilbert and the Brush Park Development Corporation launched the City Modern project, they announced plans to renovate the Ransom Gillis house under the direction of Nicole Curtis.[19] In addition to her background leading historic property restoration projects in Michigan, Curtis was also the host of the top-rated television show *Rehab Addict* on the cable networks HGTV and DIY. The entire process of renovating the Ransom Gillis house was to be aired in an eight-part series of *Rehab Addict* in November, just seven months later.

My colleagues at Preservation Detroit and I first heard about the renovation plans during the winter of 2014, two years after I visited the site with my Urban Archaeology class. We shared mutual interests in the property's history and archaeology, and we agreed to partner on an excavation project there. We then began the slow process of making contact with various officials and stakeholders with the intention of learning more about the renovation process and gaining access to the site in order to conduct an archaeological survey of the backyard before heavy equipment arrived. It was a circuitous and frustrating process. City officials referred us to public relations staff at Quicken Loans. They passed us along to contacts at Bedrock, who, in turn, suggested that decisions about access were in the hands of the HGTV network. It was unclear among the various stakeholders who had the authority to consult with us or grant us permission to work on the site.

In the process of designing our approach to the site and securing permissions, we partnered with Pewabic Pottery, whose founder Mary Chase Perry Stratton operated a studio in the former stable behind the Ransom Gillis house in the early 1900s. Together, we formed a team of three collaborating institutions: Wayne State University, Preservation Detroit, and Pewabic Pottery. By May 2015, when the local media announced the renovation plans for the house, we had made little progress toward gaining access to the site. Like many parts of the archaeological process, it would take a serendipitous moment, a chance encounter, to bring our project to fruition. One evening in May, Jennifer Ruud, a Preservation Detroit board member and collaborator on the project, was moonlighting as an Uber driver when she picked up the HGTV production crew. They were in town to plan the filming for the Ransom Gillis house renovations. Ruud seized the opportunity to pitch our proposal to her captive audience, and they immediately expressed interest in it. As producers, they were most enthusiastic about the production value that an ongoing archaeological excavation would add to the episodes. We, on the other hand, had no desire to be filmed as part of the television series, but as we were to learn, this was not going to be a community-involved or collaborative archaeology project conducted on our terms.

The planning process proceeded in fits and spurts from May until August 2015. After Ruud's initial meeting with the television production team, we incorporated HGTV producers into all stages of our planning process; they became integral collaborators on the project and intermediaries between us and Gilbert's supervisory organizations. The Ransom Gillis house renovation was a developer-funded project, a cornerstone of the much larger City Modern plan, and so its messaging was carefully controlled in the local and national media. In order to work on the heavily guarded site, each member of our team was required to sign a nondisclosure agreement. It stated that Quicken Loans maintained control over all messaging and media related to the project until the *Rehab Addict* episodes aired on HGTV later that year. This meant that even though our work was highly visible to all passersby and appeared in local media coverage, we were not allowed to talk about it or share information in any form for several months. The restrictions also meant that we were forbidden from consulting with any local stakeholder or community groups during the course of the excavations, as we were accustomed to doing. We were uncomfortable with this disconnection but still committed to recovering a more inclusive history of the property, and so we embraced the idea that we might introduce ways to connect with stakeholders in another phase of the project.

To ensure the possibility of broader participation in the future, we established a memorandum of understanding (MOU) with HGTV and Quicken Loans. The MOU stated that we would have the authority to publicize and disseminate the results of our excavations and related research in perpetuity, after the episodes aired. We also established an agreement for the ownership of the artifacts, which were to be curated at the

Grosscup Museum of Anthropology at Wayne State University. Gilbert's companies would have unlimited access to objects for display in their properties according to the museum's standard loan procedures. After a long wait, extended by production delays and weather, we finally began excavations at the Ransom Gillis house on August 7, 2015. Our excavation team of fifteen included one partner from Pewabic Pottery, three Preservation Detroit members, two local residents with prior fieldwork experience, and nine Wayne State University students and staff.

Our archaeological interests diverged from those of the historic preservationists and developers who led the house renovation project. Those professionals were strictly concerned with the house's origins and its future marketing potential as a historic building restored to its nineteenth-century origins. On its own, the house offered very limited possibilities for archaeological analysis. Over the decades it was altered many times and suffered from neglect and vandalism to the point where the structure was barely intact in 2005. Initially, we conceived of our archaeological project with specific aims in mind, to identify and examine the remnants of the Pewabic Pottery's Stable Studio. Once the project was underway, however, we reoriented our work. Rather than focusing on a particular moment in time or a single occupancy of the house, we chose to investigate the entire 142-year history of the Ransom Gillis property through its archaeological remains. We then planned to interpret our findings within the context of Brush Park's complex history of urban renewal.[20] Our excavations focused on the property's backyard, which contained intact buried traces of activities that took place in and around different outbuildings—a stable, sheds, outhouse, and restaurant.[21] Artifacts connected to these places had the potential to provide us with information about the operation of the home, the quality of life within it, and changes to its household composition throughout the course of its occupancy. The excavated artifacts also provided us with clues about the conditions of the Brush Park neighborhood and the urban community's dramatic transformations during the course of the twentieth century.

THE FIRST PEWABIC POTTERY

Most backyards in Detroit and elsewhere are not associated with major historical figures, technological innovations, or pioneering works of art. They are the domain of the mundane, everyday tasks, often performed by supporting members of a household. In these spaces out-of-sight activities too routine to merit documentation take place—hanging laundry, emptying trash, feeding animals, playing games, gardening, or fixing cars.

The backyard of the Ransom Gillis house, at least at one point in its history, was a notable exception. There, in a converted two-story stable, Mary Chase Perry operated the first iteration of the Pewabic Pottery studio between 1903 and 1906 (Figure 3.4).[22]

Histories of the Ransom Gillis house recognize the significance of the Pewabic Pottery studio on the property. A cultural resource survey of Brush Park conducted in 1996 also designated the backyard as an area of high archaeological potential on account of the likelihood that excavations might uncover remains associated with the pottery studio.[23] This connection, between the Ransom Gillis house, the Pewabic Pottery studio, and the potential that remains of it survived archaeologically, is what initially attracted us to the site. We were excited about locating evidence of pottery-making in an urban domestic setting, a rare occurrence in twentieth-century North America. Even rarer still would be the ability to link the creative and technological processes of pottery production, including successes, failures, experiments, and innovations, with a particular craftsperson. The connection between the Pewabic Pottery's Stable Studio in the backyard of the Ransom Gillis house with artist/ceramicist Mary Chase Perry offered a tantalizing opportunity to explore these relationships in the archaeological record.

Mary Chase Perry was born in 1867 in the industrial town of Hancock, in Michigan's Upper Peninsula. By the time she was a teenager, Perry's family relocated to Detroit (via Ann Arbor), where they lived among well-heeled neighbors in one of Brush Park's elegant brick homes on Edmund Place, just one block north of Alfred Street. As a young adult Perry received formal art training, learning how to paint china from Franz A. Bischoff at the Detroit Museum of Art (present-day Detroit Institute of Arts). She then studied ceramics under Louis Rebisso at the Art School of Cincinnati. At the age of twenty-six, in 1893, Perry and three other women shared a studio on West Adams Avenue in Detroit. There Perry mastered the process of overglaze decorations, experimented with mixing new glazes, taught classes on china painting, and prepared publications about her techniques.[24]

The distinctive iridescent glaze that would make Pewabic pottery world famous was the product of a neighborly collaboration between Perry and fellow Brush Park resident Horace J. Caulkins. Like Perry, Caulkins shared a passion for experimenting with new technologies and manufacturing processes. His desire to boost his dental supply business motivated him to invent a kiln called the Revelation, a portable, high-heat oven designed, initially, to fire dental enamel. Perry observed the kiln at work

Figure 3.4. Mary Chase Perry (Stratton) inside the Stable Studio at 63 Alfred Street, 1905. (Pewabic Pottery Archives)

and had a different revelation—she could use it to fire her glazed pottery vessels. Perry and Caulkins became business partners; she acted as the spokesperson for the Revelation kiln and he adapted it to suit pottery production. Soon he was assisting with her fast-growing business operations, including her first exhibit at the 1893 World's Fair in Chicago. Their partnership gave Perry the freedom to spend years conducting research and carefully controlled experiments on clay composition, heat treatments, and glaze colorants in her quest to develop her signature glazes.

In 1903 Perry and Caulkins cofounded the pottery, later naming it Pewabic in 1905 in reference to the copper mine in Michigan's Upper Peninsula where Perry's father once worked.[25] In October 1903, during one of her strolls through Brush Park, Perry noticed that the stable behind the Ransom Gillis house was empty. The Fox family who resided in the home at the time had recently replaced their horse-drawn carriage with an automobile.[26] Perry summoned her courage and asked homeowner Alanson Fox permission to operate her pottery studio out of his stable. He agreed to lease her the building at a rate of eight dollars per month. This was a perfectly affordable sum for Perry, whose decorative Arts and Crafts–style vases, jars, and tiles were in increasingly high demand. As soon as the Stable Studio was up and running, she received a major order from Chicago-based Burley and Company requesting $1,000 worth of bowls and lamps.[27] This would be the first of Perry's prominent commissions, which included installations at several state and national landmarks: the Guardian Building in Detroit; the Detroit Public Library; the State Capitol Building in Lincoln, Nebraska; and the National Shrine of the Immaculate Conception in Washington, DC.

Perry modified the stable to accommodate pottery production, attaching a kiln to the chimney and installing mills to grind her glazes (Figure 3.5). These were changes that might be identifiable archaeologically, if parts of the building survived intact (aboveground or below). Perry fulfilled the Pewabic Pottery's orders with a skeletal staff of two: Julius Albus, an assistant, and Joseph Heerich, a potter. Heerich was an immigrant trained in the potteries of Alsace-Lorraine. By day he cleaned Pullman train cars at Michigan Central Railroad Depot on Third Avenue (see chapter 2). Each night during production runs, he spent three hours at the Stable Studio using his kick wheel to throw pots based on Perry's sketches.[28] The vessels then hardened overnight and Perry would spend the following day applying decorative trim and glazes to them on her own. Perry fiercely guarded the composition of her signature iridescent green Pewabic glaze, taking its recipe to the grave with her in 1961.

Figure 3.5. Ransom Gillis carriage house when it was in use as the Pewabic Pottery's Stable Studio. Vessels in various stages of production are visible in the window. (Pewabic Pottery Archives)

During the three years that Pewabic Pottery operated in the backyard of the Ransom Gillis house, the Stable Studio was as much a workshop as a gathering place for high-society patrons of the arts. Perry regularly hosted tea parties, classes, and other events to showcase her work. Guests, ranging from local Brush Park housewives to her mentor Charles Lang Freer, gathered among the crowded shelves of pottery in various stages of completion, reveling in the energy of her creative environment.[29] In 1907 Perry and Caulkins relocated the Pewabic Pottery to a much larger, purpose-built production complex on East Jefferson, where it remains active today. Perry's distinguished career would continue for another half century before her death at the age of ninety-four. The backyard stable, however, met a much earlier demise. It was demolished in 1935 after being converted in the 1910s and 1920s into an auto repair shop and filling station.[30]

EXCAVATING STABLE STUDIO . . . OR NOT

We knew from historic maps of the Ransom Gillis house property exactly where the stable once stood. From these maps we calculated the dimensions of the stable and the position of the alleyway. We also used clues from old photographs of the Stable Studio to guide our placement of excavation units in an area that aligned with the former building's perimeter. By excavating along the walls of the former stable, we hoped to locate refuse, firing wasters, or castoffs from the pottery production process, and maybe even traces of the building's structural foundation, buried deep beneath the modern backyard's surface.

At the beginning of the excavations, when our focus was on locating remains of the Pewabic Pottery studio, we placed three units (Units 1, 2, and 3) in the vicinity of the former exterior perimeter of the stable building. We placed a fourth unit (Unit 4) in the middle of the backyard, four meters away from the back of the house (Figure 3.6). In Unit 4 we hoped to locate traces of outbuildings and trash deposits associated with the nineteenth-century occupants of the Ransom Gillis house.[31]

At the risk of spoiling the end of a good story, our excavations recovered no artifacts that definitively related to Perry's activities inside the pottery studio. This was disappointing for all of us, especially our collaborator from Pewabic Pottery, who patiently screened soil in the hot August sun while searching for elusive fragments of Perry's handiwork. We knew from the property records that the backyard stable and other outbuildings were heavily modified and eventually demolished over the course of the twentieth century, but we did not know whether these alterations had altogether erased belowground traces of them. Based on our experience excavating other twentieth-century domestic sites in Detroit, we were hopeful that when the stable was demolished, its foundation had been simply covered over by new construction. It had not.

We came up short on locating remains of Perry's pottery production inside Stable Studio, but we did recover 1,286 artifacts from the four one-by-one-meter excavation units, including architectural remains of the Stable Studio building: broken slate roof tiles, iron nails, and brick fragments.

These artifacts, and the layered soil deposits (strata) from which they were recovered, illustrated how drastically the backyard had been modified since the late nineteenth century. Each of the excavation units had four distinct soil layers, but in all but one layer, historic and modern materials were mixed together.[32] This commingling of materials from different time periods signaled to us that most of the backyard's older archaeological remains had been disturbed and disassociated from their original depositional contexts by various construction and demolition projects over the

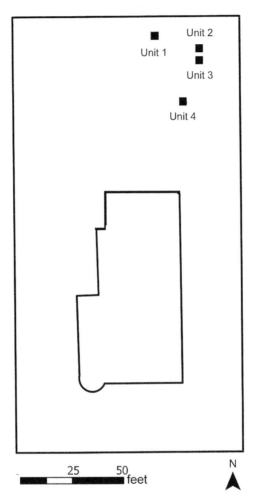

Figure 3.6. Plan map of the Ransom Gillis house and property denoting location of the 2015 excavation units. (Krysta Ryzewski)

years. In other words, it was impossible to make specific ties between individual soil deposits and distinct periods or episodes of the site's occupational history. Nevertheless, the overall assemblage of historic artifacts that we recovered from these mixed soil layers did provide valuable information about the activities residents engaged in during the entirety of the site's occupation. In order to make sense of these finds in relation to the history of the house and its occupants, we realigned our research orientation from a quest for the Pewabic Pottery studio to a more general focus on the Ransom Gillis house's 142-year social history.

Along the former perimeter of the stable, from Units 1, 2, and 3, we recovered an assemblage of pottery fragments. Later, during our laboratory analysis of the finds, we dated the vessels' manufacture to the mid to late nineteenth century. These fragments were therefore likely associated with the first period of Ransom Gillis house residents. The variety of pottery types in the assemblage included whiteware, yellowware, ironstone, stoneware, redware and Rockinghamware. Although most of the pottery we recovered was undecorated, the fragments came from several different vessel forms—teacups and saucers, plates, bowls, chamber pots, and storage containers. Within the assemblage there were also pottery sherds bearing makers' marks. From these diagnostic clues we were able to obtain precise information about their date and origin of manufacture (Figure 3.7).

The diagnostic sherds included a portion of a blue transfer-printed plate with Canton-style motif, a whiteware plate with a flow blue-decorated border, and a flow purple transfer-printed plate. The flow purple plate had a makers' mark on its underside that identified its manufacturer as the T. J. & J. Mayer pottery in Longport, Burslem, England; the Mayer pottery produced flow purple plates between 1842 and 1855. Another undecorated ironstone plate bore the mark of the G. Wooliscroft pottery in Staffordshire, England, and a production run number that we dated precisely to October 1852. These early manufacturing dates indicated that some of the pottery used in the Ransom Gillis house would have been several decades old by the time the house was first occupied in 1878. In addition to this disparity, we were also intrigued by the fact that the excavated pottery assemblage contained relatively few decorated wares, no examples of matching dishware sets, and only four porcelain vessels (porcelain is considered a more refined, expensive ware). This is not to say that higher-end wares were absent within the Ransom Gillis house. It may well have been the case that, if they existed, they were treated with more care and therefore did not find their way into the trash as frequently as the lower-quality and utilitarian vessels. But if the archaeological evidence is somewhat representative of the diversity of pottery types and vessels used in Ransom Gillis house during its initial decades of occupation, then it may indicate that the families who lived within the single-family mansion were more frugal and less ostentatious than the grand architecture of the nineteenth-century home might otherwise convey.

In addition to pottery, we recovered hundreds of artifacts from the excavation units that provided details about the material dimensions of the property's other uses as a rooming house, auto mechanic, filling station, and restaurant (Figure 3.8). From the third-deepest level of Unit 1 we

Figure 3.7. Artifacts recovered from the 2015 excavations of the Ransom Gillis house include painted wallpaper, porcelain AC Champion Ignition Company spark plug, white Prosser button, green beer bottle base, amber whiskey flask finish, slate roof tiles, and a variety of pottery. The pottery varieties include blue transfer-printed whiteware, ironstone, flow purple whiteware, a red transfer-printed whiteware chamber pot handle, porcelain, yellowware, annular-banded industrial slipware, and both redware and stoneware (*not pictured*). Two flatware sherds displayed makers' marks on their undersides (*second row, from left*): a whiteware plate with flow purple decoration manufactured at the T. J. & J. Mayer pottery in Burslem, England (1842–1855), and an ironstone plate manufactured by the G. Wooliscroft Pottery in Staffordshire, England (October 1852). (Krysta Ryzewski)

recovered a porcelain AC Champion Ignition Company spark plug case. Produced in Flint, Michigan, in the late 1920s and 1930s, this particular spark plug was common in Ford vehicles; its manufacture date pairs it with the period during which an auto mechanic operated out of the former Stable Studio. In the uppermost soil levels of the adjacent Unit 2, we excavated intact gray brick fragments stamped with their manufacturer's label: Royal Gray, from the Staso Mill in Darlington, Pennsylvania. These bricks were remnants of the walls of the long, rectangular restaurant that stood along the northwest corner of the original Ransom Gillis house lot from the 1940s until it was demolished in 2005. We also recovered hundreds of bottle glass fragments from trash deposits related to the restaurant as well as backyard consumption of alcohol and soda pop throughout the twentieth century.

Unit 4, located closest to the rear entry of the Ransom Gillis house, contained the only undisturbed soil deposit of our excavations. The fourth (and deepest) layer of the deposit was twenty-five centimeters thick and contained butchered bones from cuts of beef and pork, square-cut nails (predating the late 1880s), a four-holed ceramic Prosser button

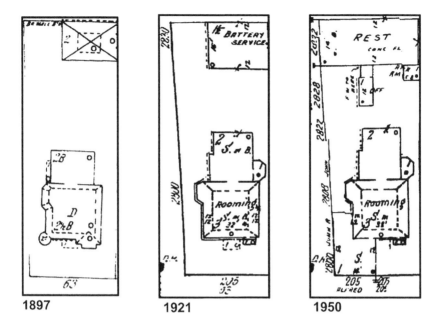

1897   **1921**   **1950**

Figure 3.8. Changing configurations of the Ransom Gillis house and its backyard outbuildings as depicted by Sanborn insurance maps in 1897, 1921, and 1950. (Krysta Ryzewski)

(manufactured post-1840), a Faber pencil lead (post-1861), fragments of mold-made bottle glass, and a chamber pot handle with a red transfer-printed geometric design (ca. 1880–1890). Since all of the temporally diagnostic objects had manufacturing dates squarely within the nineteenth century, we associated this deposit with one of the first families to reside in the Ransom Gillis house.

Within the same undisturbed level of Unit 4 we encountered remnants of a posthole with fragments of the original wooden post in it. The round post had a diameter of eighteen centimeters. Based on its position relative to the house, it was likely a support for a lean-to or other outbuilding in the nineteenth century. Perhaps it covered a trash receptacle for the servants who worked in the home's basement kitchen at the time, or, it may have been part of an outhouse. City records indicate that lateral sewer lines were installed in the alleyway behind the home in 1871, meaning that indoor plumbing would have been available to residents when the house was first occupied in 1878. But the recovery of two chamber pot handles from our excavations suggests that at least some of the home's residents continued to rely on older relief habits despite the available modern alternatives.[33] As was the case with Russell McLauch-lin's childhood home just two doors down, the existence of indoor plumb-ing did not preclude the continued use of outdoor privies (with surface tanks). McLauchlin's parents kept a backyard privy for servants to use well into the 1890s.[34]

Overall, our excavations produced an assemblage of artifacts and strati-graphic data that allowed us to view the Ransom Gillis property as rep-resentative of Brush Park and Detroit's urbanization from the late nine-teenth century through the early 2000s. We may not have recovered intact, exhibition-worthy artifacts, but the fragments that we did unearth were tangible connections to previously undocumented social and land-use his-tories that illuminated the local experiences of the long century of urban transformations, to which I now turn.

A MICROCOSM OF DETROIT'S RISE, FALL, AND RECOVERY

To understand the 63 Alfred Street property in the context of Brush Park's and Detroit's urbanization, it is useful to divide the history of the Ransom Gillis house into four periods that correspond to the dwelling's use as: (1) a single-family mansion between 1878 and 1916; (2) a rooming house from 1916 to 1973; (3) an unoccupied structure between 1973 and 2015; and (4) a renovated duplex from 2015 to the present.

A Gilded Age Mansion (1878–1916)

The Ransom Gillis house was a single-family mansion for thirty-eight years between 1878 and 1916, a period that coincided with Brush Park's Gilded Age. This was the era when the grandiose homes lining the neigh-borhood's gridded streets enclosed an insular community of a well-heeled and exclusively White subsect of Detroit's upper class. It is the period that designers and developers aim to connect with in property renovations. It is a time whose passage historians recount with forlorn nostalgia. A long-term archaeological perspective, however, portrays this first period as an abridged history, comprising only a quarter of the Ransom Gillis proper-ty's life story.

Four prominent local families owned and lived at 63 Alfred Street be-tween 1878 and 1916. All of the families who resided in the house during this period were listed in the *Detroit Blue Book*, the city's society directory. The first three families, Gillis (1878–1880), Stinchfield (1880–1888), and Fox (1888–1909), amassed their fortunes as merchants and entrepreneurs in the Great Lakes region.[35] Ransom Gillis operated a wholesale business, managing the sale of dry goods that arrived at Detroit from ports along the

Great Lakes. Charles Stinchfield and Alanson J. Fox were leaders of the most profitable industry in Detroit at the turn of the twentieth century: lumber.

Alanson J. Fox moved to Detroit from upstate New York with his wife Cornelia and three children in 1888 to strengthen his connections to the northern Michigan lumber industry. At the time he was president of the Chicago Lumbering Company in the Upper Peninsula town of Manistique. In the wake of Chicago's great fire of 1871, the city turned to Michigan for the lumber it needed to rebuild. Fox formed his company in response to these regional demands, becoming rich off of Chicago's reconstruction. Despite the fact that Detroit was 380 miles southeast of Manistique, Fox's lumbering operations were so well connected to Detroit via the transit networks of Lake Huron and Lake Michigan that it made sense for him to run the business out of his home office at 63 Alfred Street. The fourth family to own the Ransom Gillis house during the Gilded Age (1909–1919) was headed by the Reverend Maurice Penfield Fikes, pastor at the nearby Woodward Avenue Baptist Church.

If there was a high point of the property's Gilded Age occupancy, it would be associated with the Fox rather than the Gillis family. During the two decades of Fox ownership, 63 Alfred Street became a fixture of the local arts scene. The Foxes were avid patrons of the arts, and they organized a social club, the Tuesday Musicale, whose membership gathered at the home on a weekly basis to enjoy lectures by artists and recitals by musicians.[36] To accommodate more spacious entertaining and living arrangements, Alanson Fox built an addition to the back of the house.

Alanson Fox is often given sole credit for fostering Mary Chase Perry's Pewabic Pottery, since he granted her a lease to the property's stable. His connection to Perry was short-lived, though; he died within months of leasing the property to her in 1903.[37] It was his widow Cornelia who would accommodate and promote Perry's business for the next three years, hosting Perry's first pottery exhibit in the Stable Studio in October 1904.[38] Perry and Cornelia Fox both moved off the property in 1906, and Fox then leased the home to fellow society member James H. Drake and his family.[39]

At any point during the Gilded Age an average of seven people lived in the Ransom Gillis house: two parents, between two and three children, and two live-in servants.[40] Spread across the three floors of the Ransom Gillis house (including the basement kitchen) and its backyard, the residents would have enjoyed rather spacious living arrangements.

This degree of privacy and comfort would be unimaginable for the dozens of itinerant laborers who would soon occupy the house during its next phase of occupation.

A Rooming House in the Automobile Age (1916–1973)

The second and longest period in the history of the Ransom Gillis house spans the fifty-seven years between 1916 and 1973, a time when the single-family home was converted into a rooming house.[41] During this period Detroit's automotive industry expanded rapidly, attracting influxes of newcomers to the city.

Between 1900 and 1920 Detroit's population quadrupled from 285,000 to nearly one million. New arrivals relocated from foreign countries and other regions of the United States to fill readily available manufacturing jobs as well as service positions that supported the fast-growing city. These demographic changes spelled the end of the neighborhood as Ransom Gillis and his gentlemen successors knew it. The combination of migrants and the expanding automotive industry completely altered the sociocultural fabric of the city, disrupting the carefully maintained cohesion and exclusivity of upper-class Brush Park in the process.

The influx of new arrivals to Detroit created an acute housing shortage. City officials and developers scrambled to expand access to basic services and transit systems, but they simply could not build new accommodations fast enough to meet the needs of the growing population. Instead, local residents and investors took matters into their own hands, transforming single family homes into unregulated boardinghouses. The aging mansions of Brush Park and West Fort Street were optimal for conversion because of their size and proximity to downtown employers. Transformations to Brush Park began around 1910, one house at a time, and accelerated quickly thereafter as the older blue blood generation passed on or relocated to newer upscale neighborhoods, such as Boston Edison and Indian Village. In 1910 the first Brush Park rooming house appeared on Alfred Street six doors east of the Ransom Gillis house; seventeen people from eleven different families lived there.[42] Reverend Fike, then-owner of the Ransom Gillis house, was among the local residents who profited from the housing shortage; by 1916 he was renting rooms to itinerant laborers like Harry E. Vrooman, a factory manager.[43] Within the space of four years, by 1920, the Ransom Gillis house and the majority of homes in the Brush Park neighborhood were fully converted into rooming houses.

Bertha Noeske, the daughter of German immigrants, purchased the

Ransom Gillis house from the Fikes in 1919 with the intention of running it as a rooming house, her second in the neighborhood. The 1920 census shows a culturally diverse household of thirty-five boarders crowded into newly subdivided rooms within the house. They were a motley crew of hopefuls, ten men and twenty-five women ranging in age from three to fifty. There were three different families, a single widowed mother from Florida (Claudette Nayden and her three-year-old daughter Phyllis) as well as two divorcees and a number of single lodgers. All of the boarders were White; the majority (seventeen) were born in Michigan, two were immigrants from Hungary, and others came from New York, Kansas, Ohio, and Canada. They were employed in low-wage service or manufacturing jobs, and their occupations included bookkeeper, elevator operator, factory timekeeper, railroad fireman, telephone operator, waitress, theater actor, and trained nurse. None lived in the boardinghouse for more than a couple of years.[44]

Noeske continued to own the rooming house ten years later, but Andrew Rich and his wife Eva, both Canadian immigrants, managed it. By 1930, Detroit was a totally different place than it had been a decade earlier. The city boasted a prosperous automotive economy, and its demographics were diversified by waves of new African American migrants from the American South as well as immigrants arriving from foreign countries, especially the Middle East and eastern Europe. To some degree the population of the Ransom Gillis rooming house in 1930 reflected these economic and demographic shifts in its mixture of foreign and domestic residents. Notably, however, the rooming house managers did not appear to rent to African American boarders, despite the fact that the adjacent neighborhoods of Paradise Valley and Black Bottom were experiencing acute housing shortages as Black migrants from southern states sought housing in the deeply segregated city. Of the twenty-four residents at the Ransom Gillis house in 1930 (twelve White men and twelve women), there were three Chaldean Syrian immigrants (Frank Elias and Mary and Les Anitiony). Lenard Shaw came from Afghanistan, the Fukalek family were recent migrants from Missouri, and Odelle Wallace was born in Alabama. The majority of male boarders worked in the automotive industry, while the women and other men performed service and manual labor as waitresses, a chef, tailor, foundry blacksmith, and shoemaker.[45] With such a congested living situation inside the rooming house during the 1920s and 1930s, it is reasonable to assume that the residents made regular use of the property's limited backyard space, leaving trash and accidental deposits in their wake. It is impossible, however, to make direct associations between the dozens, if not hundreds, of boarders who occupied the house during these decades and the artifacts we excavated that date to this period.

With the onset of the Great Depression, even with income from two dozen boarders, Bertha Noeske struggled to maintain the Ransom Gillis house. She leased the stable and former pottery studio to the proprietor of an auto repair shop and filling station, but the property's upkeep eventually became too expensive and in 1935 she demolished the stable and sold the back half of the parcel. After its sale, the former backyard then became the site of a newly built restaurant at 2832 John R. Unfortunately for Noeske, the proceeds from the land sale did not alleviate her financial debts, and in 1936 she was forced to surrender the Ransom Gillis house when the Detroit Savings Bank foreclosed on it.[46]

The final chapter in the occupancy of the Ransom Gillis house coincides with its ownership by Chaldean immigrants John and Amina Essa during a period in which the Brush Park neighborhood became an area notable for its crime, conflict, and blight.[47] After leasing the house from the city in 1938, John Essa and his twenty-three-year-old daughter Anna converted part of its ground floor to a grocery store, adding a storefront extension to the building's southwest corner.[48] Four years later in 1942, when John's four sons were serving with American troops in World War II, he and his wife Amina purchased the property.[49] The Essas continued to operate the building as a rooming house. In 1940 thirty-six White residents from a variety of foreign and nonlocal backgrounds rented rooms in the house. The attached grocery store served Brush Park residents as well as the increasing number of low-income African American residents who then lived nearby, especially at the Brewster Douglass housing projects two blocks away, at the junction of Paradise Valley and Black Bottom.[50]

During the Essas' ownership, the Ransom Gillis house bore witness to the city's racial tensions and conflicts. Over the course of a three-day period in 1943, beginning on June 20, racially motivated riots erupted in pockets across the city, leaving thirty-four dead and hundreds injured. White mobs terrorized Black residents, flipping their cars, vandalizing property, and assaulting them; Black residents defended themselves. The violence was a response to increased competition for jobs and housing, caused in part by the arrival of a second Great Migration wave of over 400,000 newcomers from southern states to wartime Detroit. A news photograph taken during one of the local clashes shows a burning car, overturned by a gang of White rioters in John R street, directly across from the Essas' grocery store. The Ransom Gillis house looms in the background of the chaotic scene.[51] Just three years after the violence, former resident

Russell McLauchlin would return to his childhood neighborhood and describe Alfred Street as an area of "chopfallen gloom" plagued by blight, poverty, and desolation.[52]

By the 1950s, two generations into the use of the Ransom Gillis house as a rooming house, city officials categorized Brush Park as a slum. Disinvestment in local manufacturing industries and simmering social tensions were contributing to Detroit's economic decline, labor struggles, and deindustrialization. City residents began to out-migrate, relocating to the suburbs in search of more stable living arrangements. The effects of the city's boom-to-bust transformation during this period are visible in modifications made to the Ransom Gillis house, the composition of its residents, and the complete metamorphosis of the surrounding Brush Park neighborhood.

Despite the exodus of middle- and upper-class residents from the city, Detroit's housing crisis for working-class and minority residents continued through the 1950s and into the 1960s, as discriminatory lending practices and segregated districting restricted African Americans' access to affordable housing.[53] The Essas responded to the housing shortage in 1955 by illegally subdividing the space within the Ransom Gillis house, converting the prior nine apartments into fourteen units, for which they charged fifteen dollars a week. When city officials identified this code violation, they declared the Essas slumlords, brought them to court, and fined them $200, a substantial sum at the time.[54] In the early 1960s, as the neighborhood succumbed to crime, vandalism, and vacancies, the Essas abandoned the store and rooming house. The Ransom Gillis house would never again be occupied in the twentieth century.[55] Six years after the 1967 uprising, which destroyed over 2,000 buildings across Detroit, the Essas sold the Ransom Gillis property to the Woodward East Development group.[56] Then the house entered into a period of prolonged neglect.

An Unoccupied House (1973–2015)

The third period of the life history of the Ransom Gillis house, from 1973 to 2015, occupies one-third of the property's existence. During this time the Ransom Gillis house sat unoccupied and deteriorating, caught in the cross-currents of bureaucracy, competing revitalization agendas, and development schemes. This phase of the house's history is the most underexamined, yet its story reveals the aspirations and shortcomings of grassroots rehabilitation efforts, preservationists' interventions, city-led urban renewal campaigns, and developers' ambitions. Archaeological remains of the Ransom Gillis property provide tangible connections to the circumstances of neglect and underscore how its blight was not a consequence of residential carelessness but rather an artifact of civic management decisions aligned with future-oriented agendas.

Long before Dan Gilbert's enterprises arrived in Brush Park, efforts to revitalize the neighborhood and the Ransom Gillis house alternated leadership between community groups, the city of Detroit, and local residents. Three of the most notable initiatives include the rehabilitation scheme by the community-based nonprofit Woodward East Renaissance Inc. between 1968 and 1977, the private acquisition of the property in the mid-1980s, and a city-led development project in the mid to late 1990s.

In the wake of the 1967 citywide uprising, local resident Edith Woodbury formed Woodward East Renaissance Inc., a nonprofit organization of Brush Park residents who banded together to save the neighborhood's houses from being destroyed, vandalized, and occupied by drug dealers.[57] The group's vision was to keep the Brush Park community intact through the creation of low- and middle-income housing as well as recreational sites, for the benefit of neighborhood residents and occupants of the nearby Brewster Douglass public housing complex. Initially, Woodward East planned to demolish all of the homes in the area and create a new Brush Park from scratch. Head city planner Charles Blessing intervened, arguing that Brush Park was one of Detroit's "few really legitimate historic districts."[58] He convinced the group to spare the sturdiest of the 150 Victorian homes that then survived in the neighborhood. Blessing organized a task force to identify which homes in the twenty-four-block area merited preservation. He next arranged for the salvageable historic homes to be boarded up for protection, since the city's Common Council routinely ordered the demolition of unsecured vacant homes.[59] Woodward East and the city's Community and Economic Development Department/Bicentennial Commission were then awarded $2 million in public and private grants between 1973 and 1977 to purchase and renovate parts of seventeen homes, including the Ransom Gillis house. Woodward East's preservation plan, spearheaded by Woodbury and supported by city officials, was expected to be completed in four years.

The push to rehabilitate Victorian homes in Brush Park coincided with the rise of the national historic preservation movement, and the local initiative marked one of the first formal preservation efforts in the city.[60] Charles Blessing coupled Woodward East's fundraising efforts with a request to list Brush Park as a local historic district in 1973. Years later, in 1980, it received federal designation as the Brush Park Historic District on the National Register of Historic Places.[61] Blessing and local preservationists were optimistic that the revitalization efforts in Brush Park would set a standard of practice that old neighborhoods across the country might follow.

Unfortunately, no amount of preservation protections could forestall the disastrous outcome of the Woodward East project. By 1977 Woodward East was ensnared in what Anthony Brioc, president of a rival Brush Park community group, called "a situation of scandalous proportions."[62] After four years and $2 million worth of block grant investments, the project's work stopped abruptly. Funds were exhausted, yet the city and Woodward East had only produced "shabby" repair work to the exteriors of twelve houses. No homes were fully rehabilitated, and no new housing was available.[63] Years of investigations by journalists and lawyers never determined exactly what happened to the mismanaged redevelopment funds.[64] After the funding ran out, the Ransom Gillis house fell back into the city's hands.

In the aftermath of the Woodward East scandal, the city took a more circumspect approach to developing Brush Park. In 1981 Detroit's Community and Economic Development Department (CEDD) commissioned the preparation of a land use history and archaeological sensitivity survey for a 100+ acre redevelopment parcel within Brush Park.[65] The resulting assessment by archaeologists John Gram and David Barton identified high and moderate archaeological sensitivity areas in three of the four survey zones within Brush Park, including the area of the Ransom Gillis house, where they recommended further investigations.[66] The proposed CEDD development did not come to fruition, and so the city did not issue a contract for further archaeological investigations of the property.

Three years later, with development plans on hold, the city decided to rid itself of twenty Victorian houses within Brush Park. In January 1984 the city auctioned off the first six homes, including the Ransom Gillis house. Billed as a "Handyman's Dream," bids on the house began at $1,000, but bidders had to prove that they had the means to fund between $100,000 and $200,000 worth of required renovations.[67] Douglas Kuykendall and his sister Ernestine Rooks purchased the Ransom Gillis house for $1,000.[68]

It would take almost two years for Kuykendall and Rooks to obtain the deed to the Ransom Gillis house on November 13, 1985. An exposé published nine months earlier in February 1985 by *Detroit Free Press* reporter Rick Ratliff accused the city of failing to uphold their end of the auction sales. None of the properties purchased by members of the public during the January 1984 auctions had yet been deeded to purchasers. The city was intentionally dragging its feet, Ratliff alleged. In the meantime, the Ransom Gillis house and three hundred other homes in the neighborhood sat vacant and decaying.[69] The auction would begin a seventeen-year battle between owners Kuykendall and Rooks and city officials. Each party blamed the other for the demolition by neglect of the Ransom Gillis house. The owners claimed the city delayed and stonewalled building permit applications, while the city denied permits on the basis of the property's progressive deterioration. In the end, the restoration of the Ransom Gillis house proved to be an insurmountable obstacle for both parties.

In the midst of this struggle, in 1995 mayor Dennis Archer's administration announced an ambitious development plan to build seven hundred condominiums in Brush Park. There was no room for the old in this vision of a new Detroit neighborhood, so Archer planned for "the Mother of All Moves," the relocation of five nineteenth-century Victorian mansions to Alfred Street and Woodward Avenue. The plan was to repopulate the Victorian streetscape by relocating homes from other parts of the neighborhood to Alfred Street, which would keep the Ransom Gillis house in place.[70] To prepare for the project, the city hired archaeologist Mark Branstner in 1996 to conduct a cultural resource management study that determined the location of potential archaeological sites in the project area. Among other recommendations, Branstner identified the Ransom Gillis house property as an important archaeological resource because of its association with the Pewabic Pottery; he recommended that excavations be undertaken at the site of the former Stable Studio as part of the redevelopment project.[71]

Two years later, the city hired archaeologist C. Stephan Demeter to carry out Phase II excavations based on Branstner's recommendations.[72] But, like so many of the ambitious development plans that came before, Mayor Archer's condominium project stalled. In the years between the archaeological surveys by Branstner and Demeter, the Brush Park development site was truncated to exclude the condominium and mansion relocation projects. Instead, plans were scaled down to focus only on the construction of a senior housing complex along Alfred Street between Brush and Beaubien. The Ransom Gillis house was no longer in the scope of the development plan, so archaeological investigations were not undertaken on the property.

In 2000, when the National Football League selected Detroit to host Super Bowl XL, the city returned full circle to pursue the same plan for the Ransom Gillis house as was proposed by Woodward East Renaissance Inc. in 1973, demolition. Their pathway to demolishing the eyesore began in 2001 with the acquisition of the house from Kuykendall and Rooks via eminent domain. As discussed previously, city officials ultimately decided, due to the high costs of remediation, to mothball the house instead of removing it.

DEVELOPER-FUNDED PRESERVATION AND COLLABORATIVE ARCHAEOLOGY

This account ends with the current phase of the Ransom Gillis house's history, from the renovations in 2015 to the present. Here, I recap the outcomes of the restoration efforts and their intersections with our collaborative archaeology project.

As a preservation-oriented home rehabilitator, Nicole Curtis faced an uphill battle in her efforts to restore the Ransom Gillis house. No architectural drawings and few nineteenth-century photographs survived of the building. With the exception of the central staircase banister, one of the fireplaces, and a handful of decorative tiles, all of the interior's original architectural features had been lost over the course of the century as the building was subdivided into a rooming house and, later, when it was left open to decay and scrapping. The brick walls were bare, windows were missing, ornately carved wood and plaster molding was long ago removed or rotted. Curtis and her team decided to restore the house so that its exterior facade and elements of its interior design were consistent with the house's appearance in 1878, when it was first occupied by Ransom Gillis and his family. They conducted extensive comparative research on the few extant nineteenth-century houses in Brush Park and other buildings constructed by Henry T. Brush and George D. Mason to inform the period-specific design elements of the restoration. Curtis also consulted with our archaeology team, questioning us about thicknesses of historic window glass and designs on the late nineteenth-century pottery we were recovering. The process Curtis used to reassemble and redesign the Ransom Gillis house by evaluating contemporary materials and placing the house within the context of the vestiges of the nineteenth-century neighborhood was, perhaps unconsciously, quite archaeological. By September 2015 the exterior of the Ransom Gillis house was returned to a diligent approximation of what the structure looked like in 1878. The interior, by contrast, contained elements that referenced the nineteenth century within an otherwise twenty-first-century design aesthetic. During the renovations, the house was subdivided into a duplex, and its two new condominium units sold for over $300,000 apiece.

Since few of the artifacts we recovered dated exactly to 1878 or to the immediate surrounding years, they were not relevant to informing the house's redesign. Curtis, however, deemed the connection between the Pewabic Pottery and the house's history as a unique attraction that added value to the property. As a result of personal connections made on site between our partner Steve McBride, executive director of Pewabic Pottery, and the contractors, Curtis's team commissioned the Pewabic Pottery to create a decorative tile installation for the renovated home's entryway. The center tile bears an outline of the house, its distinctive turret, and a title recognizing the home's namesake, Ransom Gillis.

Throughout the process of the rehabilitation project, a construction crew descended on the property daily and worked around the clock to re-build the house within the tight time frame that the television produc-tion team's filming schedule required. When Curtis was inside the house to consult with contractors or to lend a hand, a gaggle of cameramen, lighting specialists, and producers followed close by. Everyone carried on working as if the film crew was invisible. The same buzz surrounded our archaeological excavations (Figure 3.9). For the duration of the exca-vations some of us wore microphones and gave occasional interviews to producers when we encountered an interesting find. When Curtis vis-ited with our archaeology team, the film crew followed. We shot (and re-shot) artifact discoveries, discussions about the finds, and activities that seemed to make for good TV viewing, especially shaking screens and emptying buckets.

The design team's decision to restore the house to its Gilded Age glory conveniently sidestepped the challenge of integrating aspects of its storied past that would potentially detract economic value and positive messaging from its role as the cornerstone of the new City Modern development.[73] In the media coverage and real estate listings, there was no mention of the house's history as a rooming house, or its working-class, immigrant residents. The rioting of 1943 that took place across the street, the Syrian entrepreneurs who converted the house into a grocery store, or the local residents who tried, but failed, to renovate the property with their own funds and elbow grease were omitted from the story of the new Ransom Gillis house.

Our excavations at the Ransom Gillis house were constrained from the outset by developer and media restrictions; this was not a collabora-tive archaeology project on familiar community-involved terms. When the

Figure 3.9. Wayne State archaeologists excavate in the area of the stable during renovations of the Ransom Gillis house in 2015. (Krysta Ryzewski)

episodes of *Rehab Addict* aired in November 2015, they reached an audience of millions (ninety-six million households subscribe to HGTV/DIY). We realized then that our work was engaging a far greater segment of the American public than we would ever be able to recruit through our own local efforts and professional networks. The disconnect between our archaeological findings and the restoration of the Ransom Gillis house to its 1878 appearance did not seem to matter to the *Rehab Addict* audience (Figure 3.10). Nor did it matter to the producers that we did not find any glamorous remains from inside the Pewabic Pottery studio. The problem-solving process of archaeology and the insights it provided about the people whose histories aligned with the image of the nineteenth-century Ransom Gillis house were of greater interest.

The public intrigue about the archaeological discoveries and rehabbers' decision-making process extended to Curtis's work too. In November, shortly after the *Rehab Addict* episodes aired, HGTV hosted a day-long event at the Ransom Gillis house, inviting the public to visit the restored

Figure 3.10. Ransom Gillis house from Alfred Street following the completion of renovations in 2015. (Krysta Ryzewski)

space and learn about its history, architecture, and archaeology. On the morning of the tour hundreds of visitors queued around the block, clamoring for a glimpse inside.[74] Over 2,000 local residents toured the house during the day-long event.

CITY MODERN

One year later, in 2016, Dan Gilbert's Bedrock Real Estate broke ground in Brush Park for the new housing units at the core of their City Modern development. At an estimated cost of $100 million, Bedrock pledged to build a variety of multiuse buildings and mixed income dwellings in order to revitalize a segment of the neighborhood, including Alfred Street (Figure 3.11).

With the century-long history of Brush Park's various urban renewal efforts in mind, there was widespread skepticism about the ambitious plan. But unlike previous city-led initiatives, Gilbert's plans to transform Brush Park progressed because they were backed with substantial funds from private investors. Presently, City Modern includes 405 newly constructed apartments, townhomes, and carriage houses and five historic homes across an 8.4 acre area. The aesthetic of the City Modern development is distinctively future-oriented. The project capitalizes on Detroit's 2016 designation as a UNESCO City of Design to justify its ultramodern aesthetic—spartan, geometric buildings with green roofs and minimal ornamentation. These new buildings do not connect in any way with the distinctive architectural heritage of Brush Park. They instead reflect a conscious design decision to disassociate the neighborhood's future from its checkered past.

During the City Modern groundbreaking ceremony Mayor Mike Duggan praised the developers for their promise to create "an area of downtown Detroit where there is room for everybody."[75] Whether this promise of inclusivity comes to fruition remains to be seen. In April 2019 Bedrock completed The Flats, a fifty-four-unit affordable senior living complex at 124 Alfred Street, proclaiming it as a victory for their affordable housing plan. Meanwhile, the overwhelming majority of new properties in City Modern are listed for sale at prices ranging from $425,000 to $761,000. Over a dozen units sold before they were even constructed. It will be worthwhile to observe how this new residential community takes shape as Brush Park enters into its next phase of existence.[76]

WHOSE BRUSH PARK?

Even with its nineteenth-century facade restored, the Ransom Gillis house is, in anthropologist Ann Stoler's words, a place of "unfinished histories."[77] So too, is Brush Park and the City Modern. As this archaeological case study illustrates, the Ransom Gillis house was never a static dwelling, and Brush Park was never an innocent witness to the city's urban transformations and social pressures.[78] These places and their remains tell the ongoing story of Detroit's tangled encounters with urban renewal from a materially based vantage point.

Our archaeological investigations of the Ransom Gillis house and its situation within Brush Park demonstrates how tangible heritage in Detroit has been, and continues to be, leveraged and edited in the name of development. An equally important takeaway is the revelation that there exist irreconcilable differences between archaeologists and their efforts to record the multiple dimensions of places like the Ransom Gillis house and Brush Park, and developers and their inclinations to fix places to those

Figure 3.11. Ransom Gillis house among the City Modern's new housing units on Alfred Street, 2020. (Krysta Ryzewski)

particular points in time that will be most attractive to potential investors (i.e., profitable). This tension between inclusion and exclusion is an unavoidable reality in cities like Detroit, but its existence need not drive a wedge between archaeologists and developers or prevent them from seeking middle ground. Although I am critical of the civic disregard for Brush Park's history and archaeology, and the lack of investment by developers in preserving the area's historic architecture, I would categorize the Ransom Gillis project as a successful, mutually beneficial undertaking between archaeologists and developers. In the end, both parties achieved their goals through a process of negotiation and collaboration. It was never our intention to slow development in the name of archaeological site preservation; the Ransom Gillis house and its backyard remains did not have the makings of an intact, well-preserved archaeological site. Nor did we intend to be involved in the house's restoration process. For our team, the purpose of engaging with the archaeology of the Ransom Gillis house, and of Brush Park, was a matter of both intellectual concern and stewardship. It was an effort to recover historical information from significant but poorly documented archaeological features before they were destroyed by construction activities. The information that we gathered from the excavated materials as well as from subsequent archival research, produced insights into a site and neighborhood associated with Detroit's underrepresented residents and its long saga of blight and revitalization efforts.[79]

The archaeological findings added alternative perspectives that counter the persistent longing for the nineteenth-century good old days, a sentiment that still prevails in the public perception of Brush Park's history. While the contemporary revitalization projects underway there purport to champion the neighborhood's historical roots, our archaeological approach suggests otherwise. As archaeologist Lynn Meskell notes in reference to revitalization efforts elsewhere, Brush Park's developers remain disconnected from the neighborhood's century-long, multiethnic cultural heritage in a way that risks further "marginalizing the bearers of heritage themselves."[80] In this case, historical archaeology was a tool for both drawing attention to the lasting material and historical legacies of inequitable urban renewal practices and for advocating for the recognition of marginalized communities' voices in historic preservation processes.

CHAPTER FOUR

Blue Bird Inn
Jazz Archaeology of the Great Migration Era

One Friday night late in the summer of 1948, September 10 to be exact, pianist Phil Hill and his jazz combo took to the stage at the Blue Bird Inn for the first time. The trio, rounded out by vibraphonist Abe Woodley and drummer Art Mardigan, performed a new style of fast-paced improvisational jazz. The music featured unexpected chord changes, syncopated rhythms, complex harmonies, and passing references to melodies.[1] This was not the mainstream swing jazz that patrons of the Jewish-run Grande Ballroom or the Black-owned 606 Horseshoe Bar in Detroit's Paradise Valley danced to at the time. It was bebop, an emergent genre of progressive jazz pioneered by the next generation of African American musicians. There was no dancing; audiences simply sat and listened as the musicians played their instruments in conversation with one another.[2]

Within three weeks of the Phil Hill combo's Blue Bird debut, local music reporters touted the club as one of the city's new modern jazz hot spots. Progressive jazz fans flocked to the small 2,000-square-foot bar and restaurant at 5021 Tireman Avenue in the city's old West Side neighborhood to witness the bebop revolution for themselves.

From September 1948 through 1949, the Phil Hill combo was the Blue Bird's house band. During their performances the combo huddled together on a compact *u*-shaped stage that stood three feet off the ground. From this modest perch the musicians entertained crowds of over one hundred people, who, on the bar's busiest Friday and Saturday nights, filled every seat in the jazz room.[3] Patrons listened from a row of booths along the wall, small tables in the center of the room, and stools at the long bar. Neighborhood kids, too young to enter the Blue Bird, peered in from the back doorway. *Detroit Tribune* reporter Robert Allen Beatty witnessed one of the combo's first performances at the Blue Bird in September and was left awestruck. In his subsequent review, "Blue Bird Rocks," he marveled, "How a man can play the wildest of songs so soothing and nice is more than I can understand. With Phil Hill that is just the way it works, he has the 'wildest' little band on the West Side of Woodward Avenue, but it's still the soothingest [*sic*] music that is played today."[4]

Bebop acts during the 1940s and 1950s elevated the Blue Bird Inn to a legendary status as one of the most respected jazz music venues in the Midwest. At a time when Detroit's population was at its all-time peak of 1.8 million, the Blue Bird developed a reputation as the West Side's hippest bar largely because the Dubois and Eddins families who managed it created a welcoming environment for uninhibited musical expression. The club's promise of artistic freedom attracted younger performers who were tired of playing the commercial swing jazz standards at downtown bars and ballrooms. By the mid-1950s, the Blue Bird was a regular stop for locally and nationally acclaimed musicians: Wardell Gray; Charlie Parker; John Coltrane; Cannonball Adderley; Miles Davis; Tate Houston; Frank Foster; Billy Mitchell; Pistol Allen; Yusef Lateef; and Hank, Elvin, and Thad Jones, among others.[5] These performers played as featured acts but just as often used the stage as a space for creative experimentation during their late-night jam sessions.

The reason why it is possible to detail the Blue Bird's transformation from a neighborhood bar into a pioneer of Detroit's bebop jazz scene is because of objects gathered during an archaeological survey of the club in 2015 and the subsequent identification of historical archival sources related to them. These materials include a cache of over 2,000 bookkeeping and accounting documents, portable artifacts recovered during the building's archaeological survey and excavations, and the u-shaped stage (Figure 4.1).

There are countless stories to be told about the Blue Bird Inn's contributions to Detroit's musical heritage, but this case study is not focused on the legendary musicians who played the Blue Bird because that is not the direction in which the archaeological finds lead.[6] Here I use the investigative methods of historical archaeology to tell the story of a Black-owned business in midcentury Detroit. With a special focus on the bar's operation during 1948 and 1949, I combine archaeological data and archival sources to reveal the Blue Bird's management practices and the bar's relationships with other Great Migration–era entertainment venues, business networks, and communities in Detroit. While the Blue Bird's progressive jazz may have emerged as an anticapitalist alternative and a sonic resistance to mainstream popular music, historical and archaeological remains confirm that the club's well-organized business operations were certainly not improvisational or dependent on informal economic relationships (see Little Harry speakeasy, chapter 2). Instead, archaeologically recovered materials depict the Blue Bird as a thriving business whose success reflected the managers' reliable connections with local commercial markets, national brand-name consumer trends, and customers.

Figure 4.1. The document cache recovered from the vestibule ceiling of the Blue Bird Inn included neatly bundled stacks of receipts and records, organized into piles by day. (Krysta Ryzewski)

BLUE BIRD INN ARCHAEOLOGICAL SURVEY

The idea to conduct an archaeological survey at the Blue Bird Inn began with a digital storytelling project I created for my Urban Archaeology class at Wayne State University in 2014. One of the objectives of the assignment was to teach students how to tell the stories of significant historic sites and cultural contributions in Detroit using language and media that were accessible to nonacademic audiences. We adopted methods from the digital humanities and developed the "Making Music in Detroit" project. Students created short videos about places in Detroit associated with the city's world-famous music heritage.[7] Each video was tied to a specific place so that people viewing the videos on YouTube might be able to visit the site, either virtually or in person.[8] The class produced twenty-four place-based stories about different genres of music: jazz, techno, Motown, and rock 'n' roll. Several of the sites featured in stories were long ago demolished, like the Motown Records Headquarters in the Donovan Building, and so some corresponding videos were paired with empty lots. Other structures, like the Eastown Theatre and the Brewster Douglass homes, were present when the students made their digital stories but demolished shortly thereafter. The majority of the stories, however, depicted buildings in various states of disrepair and neglect. Their physical condition underscored Detroit's poor recognition and preservation of places associated with its rich musical heritage. The Blue Bird Inn was one of these buildings.

In the process of researching sites for the "Making Music in Detroit" digital stories, I connected with Carleton Gholz, founder and executive director of the Detroit Sound Conservancy (DSC). Established in 2012, the DSC is a nonprofit grassroots heritage preservation organization whose mission is to "create programs and provide leadership in the preservation of musical heritage in a spirit of partnership and celebration."[9] Our mutual interests in the Blue Bird's history, music heritage, and preservation converged, and we began to explore the possibility of including an archaeological survey in the DSC's plan to visit the Blue Bird and assess its potential for preservation. At the time, the Blue Bird was suffering from negligence by an absentee owner whose sole contribution to the building's upkeep was to spray paint a "For Sale" price of $3,000 on the building's facade. The owner's treatment of the building was just one episode in a decade-long process of abandonment, during which the building's title passed between a handful of absentee owners. In the interim, scrappers gutted the club's furnishings and infrastructure, removing almost every trace of the club's interior layout and decor. The building was on the brink of demolition by neglect.

Given the deteriorating state of the Blue Bird, Gholz was initially skeptical that there would be useful information for archaeologists to record and collect. I was eager to prove otherwise. My colleagues and I had recently completed a survey of AIR Studios on the Caribbean island of Montserrat; this project, as well as work by other archaeologists on contemporary music-related sites, proved to be productive in gathering the mundane but revealing remnants of entertainment and music-making venues.[10] After I made a case for applying the same techniques at the Blue Bird Inn, the

DSC invited my students and me to undertake an archaeological survey and documentation of the property. First though, they needed to secure access to the building.

It took a year for the DSC to locate the Blue Bird's absentee owner and gain permissions to enter and investigate the building. Over the course of several cold days in April 2015, the archaeological team conducted a survey and test excavations in the building's interior and back lot. The seven-member survey team consisted of Wayne State University graduate and undergraduate students, faculty, and one local volunteer. Given the constraints to access and the limited time available for completing the work, it was important that all of the survey team had prior archaeological or building documentation experience; they had to be able to work quickly and independently.[11] At the same time, Gholz led a team from the DSC in assessing the building's integrity and the condition of the stage, the only surviving furnishing inside the bar. His group included people with expertise in music performance, journalism, production, and construction.

My archaeological team designed the survey with two objectives in mind. First, we planned to examine the interior of the club systematically using a variety of recording methods (photography, mapping, scale drawings). We intended for the survey results to document previously unrecorded aspects of the Blue Bird experience, to inspire further research into places of music-making, and to inform the DSC's future plans to rehabilitate the building. Second, we aimed to recover any traces of portable objects or other material culture left inside or buried outside of the club, especially from its mid-twentieth-century heyday. Our expectation was that these objects might inform us about particular experiences of leisure, entertainment, and music-making at the Blue Bird. To achieve this objective, the team recovered objects inside the club and dug two excavation units in the property's back lot.

When the archaeological survey team first entered the narrow, one-room jazz club they encountered darkness. The building's electricity was cut off and boards covered the windows. Struggling to adjust their eyes to the dark space, the first few people who walked into the cavernous room paid no attention to the pile of trash strewn on the floor of the front vestibule. But one torn piece of paper with cursive handwriting caught archaeologist Athena Zissis's eye. An experienced surveyor, Zissis carefully scanned the ground for clues as she approached the building. She picked up the fragment of lined paper and saw a date of 1948 written in its corner. Zissis then noticed old receipts and notes scattered among the modern debris. She cast her flashlight around the vestibule and paused when it illuminated the ceiling. A stack of documents hung over the edge of a missing ceiling tile. Lorin Brace, one of the archaeologists leading the survey crew, grabbed a ladder and peered into a void between the dropped ceiling and the building's roof. There he discovered a cache of over 2,000 documents, organized in neatly stacked piles. The long-forgotten collection of receipts, pay ledgers, checks, and other managerial paperwork detailed the Blue Bird's business transactions during 1948 and 1949. The survey had barely begun and there were already new angles about the club's history to investigate.

This chapter's account of the Blue Bird's inner workings is inspired foremost by the people and places listed in this archaeologically recovered document cache. Details within these documents permitted specific inquiries during the subsequent research process. Credit is first owed to Lorin Brace, who created the initial inventory of the documents and analyzed aspects of the records for his master's essay in 2016.[12] Here I provide a finer-grained analysis of the documents in tandem with both portable artifacts recovered during the survey and information collected from other archival sources, especially census data, newspaper reports, and firsthand accounts, in order to reconstruct the operations of a Black-owned business during the post–World War II era of the Great Migration.

My account begins with a brief overview of Detroit's popular music scene in the late 1940s and the Blue Bird's situation within it. I next draw on archaeological and archival finds to illustrate how musical entertainment was managed and consumed at the club. Building from the information in the recovered document cache, I shift away from the Blue Bird's musicians to focus on the club staff's managerial practices, business connections, and customer experiences. After detailing the results of the Blue Bird Inn's archaeological analysis, I conclude with a discussion of the various heritage and future-making efforts that have taken place since 2015 involving the club's material remains: portable artifacts, the stage, and the building.

THE WEST SIDE NEIGHBORHOOD DURING THE GREAT MIGRATION ERA

Aside from its bright blue facade, the Blue Bird Inn occupies an unremarkable building (Figure 4.2). Its one-story, unadorned rectangular frontage blends in with adjacent businesses along the once-bustling commercial corridor of Tireman Avenue. City records indicate that Jewish businessman Jacob Molin received a permit to build a one-story brick store at 5021 Tireman in April 1926. This building may have replaced or

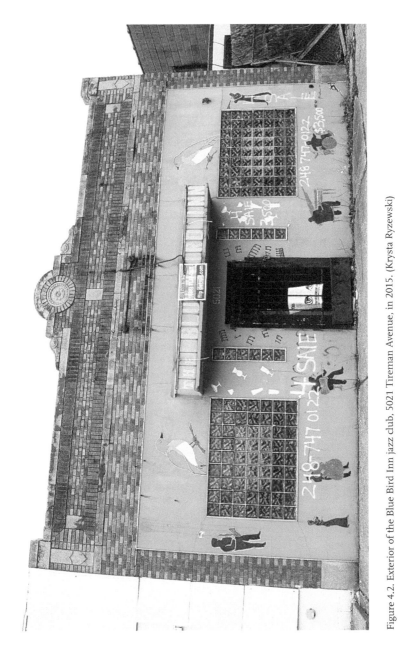

Figure 4.2. Exterior of the Blue Bird Inn jazz club, 5021 Tireman Avenue, in 2015. (Krysta Ryzewski)

expended on an earlier structure that is depicted on a 1917 Sanborn Fire Insurance map of the property.[13] From 1926 onward Molin's building was home to a series of small businesses, restaurants, and bars that were central gathering places for the West Side neighborhood's African American community.

Beginning in the mid-late 1910s, with the expansion of automobile manufacturing and the end of World War I, Detroit's African American population expanded rapidly as newcomers from southern states relocated to the city in large numbers. Detroit's Great Migration took place between 1915 and 1970, when an estimated six million people fled the oppressive conditions of the Jim Crow–era South to resettle in northern cities in the Midwest and Northeast.[14] In Detroit, the African American population grew from 5,741 residents in 1910 to 660,428 in 1970.[15] This demographic shift ushered in dramatic transformations to the city's living conditions, culture, labor economy, and society (see chapter 3).

In the 1930s the vast majority of Detroit's 120,000 African Americans lived in one of five neighborhoods: the lower east side areas of Paradise Valley and Black Bottom, and smaller enclaves in the West Side, Conant Gardens, and 8 Mile-Wyoming (although see chapter 7).[16] By the time that the Blue Bird started to advertise bebop jazz in 1948, the surrounding West Side neighborhood was home to 140,000 (47%) of the city's 300,000 African Americans, making it the second-largest community of Black residents in the city. The West Side was not, however, an exclusively Black neighborhood. Tireman Avenue was the dividing line between two strictly segregated districts. On the all-White north side, residents were buffered by restrictive housing covenants that prohibited Black Detroiters from renting or purchasing properties. African American residents, like the Dubois family, who managed the Blue Bird during the 1940s, lived south of Tireman.

William Dubois and his wife Pinkie acquired the building at 5021 Tireman and converted it into a bar and restaurant in August 1937.[17] William's contributions to the emergent jazz club were short-lived though. The bar's first exposure in the media came not from the musicians who played there, but rather from accounts of William's gruesome murder on November 17, 1937, at the hands of his thirty-two-year-old son Robert "Buddy" Dubois. According to news reports, Buddy confronted his father inside the bar and shot him five times in retaliation for assaulting his mother, Pinkie. Four months later a jury swiftly convicted him of murder, and Judge Christopher E. Stein sentenced him to serve a life term in prison. While in prison, Buddy's two sisters Gertrude (Dubois) Bulkley and LaJean

Dubois assisted Pinkie with the bar's day-to-day logistical operations. La-Jean's husband, Harry Black, served as the club's general manager and organized its entertainment.[18] By the spring of 1938, under their leadership, the bar featured weekend jazz performances, Thursday night jam sessions, drinks, dining, and swing dancing.[19] After Buddy was released from prison in 1946 on the basis of a self-defense appeal, he joined his sisters as a co-owner and manager of the bar. He is credited with introducing modern jazz acts to the bar in 1948.[20]

DETROIT'S MUSIC SCENE IN THE 1940S

During the interwar decades the adjacent lower east side neighborhoods of Paradise Valley and Black Bottom were home to the majority of Detroit's African American population. Hastings Street was the central artery of both neighborhoods, and most of the city's Black-owned businesses operated in its vicinity. In 1938 the city's Housing Commission designated Black Bottom a slum and began the process of clearing the neighborhood for urban renewal initiatives.[21] Paradise Valley remained the commercial center for Detroit's Black business community and one of the city's premier entertainment districts until it too was cleared in the name of urban renewal during the 1950s and 1960s.[22]

In the 1940s Detroiters of all backgrounds flocked to Paradise Valley clubs like Club Three Sixes, Stan's Turf Bar, and Avalon to enjoy evenings of fine dining and musical performances.[23] Kermit G. Bailer, a Detroiter and former Tuskegee airman, described Paradise Valley of the 1940s as "a thrilling place to be."[24] The Chitlin' Circuit, a national network of entertainment venues that welcomed African American musicians during the era of segregation, regularly brought popular mainstream bands like Lionel Hampton and Count Basie to perform at the Paradise Theatre and other high-profile neighborhood venues.[25] At the Masonic Temple, one of the city's largest auditoriums, fans paid to hear Duke Ellington, Sarah Vaughan, and Ella Fitzgerald—the first lady of swing—perform.[26] When Detroiters rang in the New Year on January 1, 1948, the most popular clubs in the city were Frolic Show Bar, Chesterfield Lounge, El Sino, Parrot Lounge, Club Three Sixes, and the Royal Blue Bar. The Three Sixes, Paradise Valley's largest entertainment venue (on 666 East Adams), boasted seating for 750 people, steak dinners, gambling, and a stage large enough to accommodate fifteen-piece swing bands and ten chorus girls.[27]

By the end of the decade, as a result of encroaching urban renewal and postwar economic stagnation, night life gradually moved out of Paradise Valley and off the Chitlin' Circuit to uptown areas, in what is now the Midtown neighborhood, in the vicinity of Canfield and John R Streets. There, venues like the Flame Show Bar and Frolic Show Bar featured Black musicians and, eventually, showcased bebop jazz.

In the African American neighborhoods beyond the city center, especially the West Side and 8 Mile-Wyoming, Black-owned jazz rooms flourished during 1948 and 1949. At the Blue Bird Inn and Bakers Keyboard Lounge, Detroiters enjoyed local sensations like Candy Johnson, Jimmy Caldwell, and Guy Lombardo. Jazz rooms thrived because of the talent they attracted, their devoted customer base, and the publicity they received from Detroit's Black-centered music industry, both on the radio and in local record shops. As music historian Mark Anthony Neal recounts, in many American cities during the late 1940s, as commercial music production increased alongside radio and TV programming, radio stations replaced live broadcasts of instrumental jazz performances with prerecorded vocal jazz and R&B songs, featuring the likes of Louis Jordan and Frank Sinatra.[28] In most cases, the increasing commercialization and mainstreaming of popular music excluded from the airwaves the emergent progressive or bebop jazz, and by extension, the talented Black musicians who performed it. Detroit was an exception.

During the late 1940s local radio programs in Detroit regularly featured the latest trends in modern jazz. Upon his visit to the city in September 1949, popular Chicago DJ Sid McCoy remarked to the *Michigan Chronicle*, Detroit's Black weekly newspaper, that the city was "about the most fertile field for Negro radio and video talent in the US."[29] At the time, at least two local radio stations featured regular jazz shows hosted by Black disc jockeys. Bob Murphy's show aired on WJBK on Saturday afternoons, and WJLB's Lloyd Richards hosted the weekly *Interracial Goodwill Hour*, which was especially popular with progressive jazz music fans.[30] By the end of 1949, three Black disc jockeys hosted jazz broadcasts on Detroit radio stations. Listeners enjoyed shows by Ernie Durham, Jerry Hemphill, and especially Leroy G. White, who hosted daily broadcasts of *Rockin' with LeRoy* on WJLB.[31] During their shows, Detroit's jazz DJs promoted upcoming performances at local venues (including the Blue Bird), discussed musicians and current music trends, and advertised record shops where listeners could purchase the music aired on their programs.

Detroit's recording industry also prospered during the 1940s, despite the wartime vinyl shortages that otherwise limited Black musicians across the United States from cutting albums with major commercial studios.[32] Inventive local merchants and producers devised their own homespun mechanisms to record and distribute blues, R&B, and jazz albums by

Black artists. Joe Von Battle's Record Shop at 3530 Hastings Street in Paradise Valley was, from 1945, the epicenter for such music circulation. Joe's Record Shop billed itself in the *Michigan Chronicle* as the "Largest outlet of Race records in the world." In 1948 Battle boasted an inventory of 25,000 records.[33] The shop also housed recording equipment that Battle made available to local artists.

The year after Joe's Record Shop opened, Idessa Malone, an enterprising thirty-three-year-old woman, convinced Battle to let her operate a progressive jazz advertising and record distribution business out of the store's back room. Malone was acting on a hunch she had in 1946, one based on her familiarity with Black music in New York and Detroit as well as conversations with alto saxophonist Earl Bostic and his wife Hildegarde. She predicted that jazz music was approaching a transformative moment and that bebop combos would soon dominate the genre. From Battle's back room, she represented New York City's Gotham Records in Detroit and founded the Idessa Malone Record Distributor Company. Her business expanded quickly, and within months she moved into her own headquarters at 606 East Vernor. There she bought and sold progressive jazz records by the thousands, introducing Detroiters to hits like Earl Bostic's "845 Stomp," and the most popular bebop songs of 1948, "Don't Blame Me," "Bird's Nest," "This Is Always," and "Dewey Square."

According to the *Michigan Chronicle*, Malone was "a woman that has nothing but determination and a facile tongue."[34] In actuality, she was a shrewd and visionary entrepreneur who, by 1948, ran the only Black-owned record distributing company in the Midwest. She would soon thereafter establish her own record production labels as well.[35] Malone is to be credited for disseminating, and even commercializing, bebop locally, while also boosting Detroit musicians' exposure on the national stage.[36] Together, Malone, Battle, local disc jockeys, and Detroit's Black-run newspapers cultivated the fertile grounds for the new style of modern, bebop jazz that dominated the city's music scene by 1950.

BEBOP'S EMERGENCE AT THE BLUE BIRD

Bebop's arrival at the Blue Bird Inn is well illustrated by the document cache that the archaeology team recovered during the 2015 survey, especially by a payroll ledger book that spans the period from March 5, 1948, through the end of the year. Entries in the ledger's columns record the weekly payments to musicians and employees (Figure 4.3).

In addition to the bar's twenty-four employees, the payroll ledger lists payments to two band leaders—Jimmie [sic] Caldwell and Phil Hill, whose roles are indicated by annotation "Band" written in pencil next to their names. The first payment to musicians, issued to Jimmy Caldwell and his band, was recorded on July 23, 1948. Given that the checks and supply orders in the document cache were cosigned by Gertrude (Dubois) Bulkley and LaJean Dubois, it is likely that the sisters also managed the bar's payroll accounts. Although we know that the bar hired musicians prior to this date, the new inclusion of band-related expenses into the managers' payroll system midway through 1948 signals the start of more formal, careful accounting practices that the Dubois siblings would continue to employ over the next few years.

Jimmy Caldwell was a saxophonist and leader of a quartet known for their fast-moving interpretations of popular swing and bebop tunes. In the months before Caldwell and his band appeared at the Blue Bird, they played regularly at the Royal Blue club in Paradise Valley. In one *Michigan Chronicle* story, Royal Blue owner Max Rott praised the band for providing "lovers of music an opportunity to hear their favorite selections" in a friendly atmosphere, and for rejuvenating his bar at 8401 Russell Street

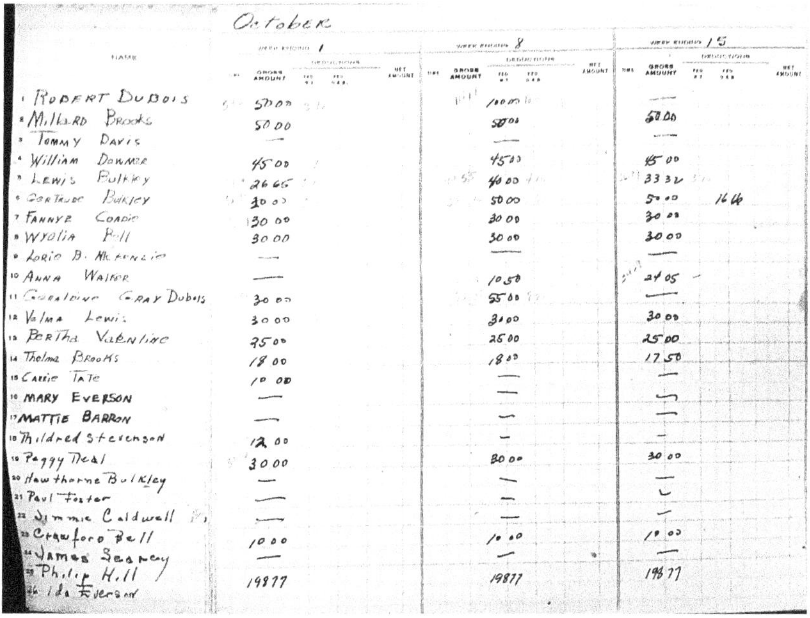

October

Name	Week ending 1 Gross amount	Week ending 8 Gross amount	Week ending 15 Gross amount
1 Robert Dubois	50 00	100 00	—
2 Millard Brooks	50 00	50 00	50 00
3 Tommy Davis	—	—	—
4 William Downer	45 00	45 00	45 00
5 Lewis Bulkley	26 66	40 00	33 32
6 Gertrude Bulkley	30 00	50 00	50 00
7 Fannye Condie	30 00	30 00	30 00
8 Wyolia Bell	30 00	30 00	30 00
9 Lorie B. McKenzie	—	—	—
10 Anna Walker	—	10 50	24 05
11 Geraldine Gray Dubois	30 00	55 00	—
12 Velma Lewis	30 00	30 00	30 00
13 Bertha Valentine	25 00	25 00	25 00
14 Thelma Brooks	18 00	18 00	17 50
15 Carrie Tate	10 00	—	—
16 Mary Everson	—	—	—
17 Mattie Barron	—	—	—
18 Mildred Stevenson	12 00	—	—
19 Peggy Neal	30 00	30 00	30 00
20 Hawthorne Bulkley	—	—	—
21 Paul Foster	—	—	—
22 Jimmie Caldwell	—	—	—
23 Crawford Bell	10 00	10 00	10 00
24 James Searcy	—	—	—
25 Philip Hill	198 77	198 77	198 77
26 Ida Everson			

Figure 4.3. Payroll ledger from October 1948 includes weekly wages for managers, servers, kitchen staff, and musicians. As can be seen, by October 1, Phil Hill (*second from bottom*) and his combo replaced Jimmy Caldwell (*fifth from bottom*, misspelled as "Jimmie") as the Blue Bird's house band. (Krysta Ryzewski)

into a popular night spot.[37] While at the Royal Blue, Caldwell's band performed mainstream swing music. Months later, during their headline act at Club Vogue, they began to feature bebop instrumentals.[38] By the time Buddy Dubois booked Caldwell to play the Blue Bird Inn during the summer of 1948, his versatile combo was well known among local audiences. Caldwell's reputation seems to have been enough to draw patrons to the Blue Bird; no advertisements for the band's performances appear in local newspapers during their two month gig.

Jimmy Caldwell and his combo played four nights a week at the Blue Bird, from mid-July until the week of September 10. According to the payroll ledger, the band's total pay averaged $134.70 per week (ranging between $114.70 and $179.60). If equally split between the four band members, as was customary, each performer in Caldwell's combo earned between seven and eleven dollars per show. At the time, the typical weekly pay for assembly men working in Detroit's automotive plants was sixty dollars per week ($1.50/hour).[39] If supplemented by other performances or part-time work, the twenty-eight to forty-four dollars that Caldwell's musicians took home for four nights' worth of work would have been a livable wage.

Phil Hill's combo replaced Jimmy Caldwell and his band during the week of September 10, 1948. That Friday night Buddy Dubois, the bar's entertainment manager, paid Hill and his two bandmates $41.40 for a performance ($13.80 per person). Phil Hill was a relative veteran of the Detroit jazz scene by the time of his first Blue Bird performance, having played piano in local groups for the previous nine years. Perhaps because of his local notoriety, or because of the new genre of music his combo played, the Dubois siblings were willing to pay Phil Hill's band considerably more than they paid Caldwell.

The payroll ledger lists weekly payments to Hill's band from September 10 through December 31, 1948.[40] Over the course of these four months the Duboises' investment in Hill's performances steadily increased. During September they paid the band up to $165.60 per week. As the club's popularity skyrocketed in October, Dubois increased their weekly pay to $198.77. By the end of that month, several reviews praising Hill's performances at the Blue Bird had appeared in local Black newspapers. On October 23 the *Michigan Chronicle*'s "Stemmin' with Steve" column labeled Hill's combo as "one of the most exciting in the city" and promoted the Blue Bird as the "who's who" hangout on Friday nights.[41] By the end of November the Duboises paid Hill's combo $240.17 weekly; at one point, during the first week of December, they earned $313.77. If the Hill combo continued to play as a trio during these initial months as the house band, then the performers were earning between fourteen and twenty-six dollars for each of their four evening performances between Thursday and Sunday ($56–$104 per week). It should be noted, however, that Hill often invited additional musicians to play with the group. By 1949, the combo was performing as a quartet, having added bassist Jimmy Richardson to its regular lineup.[42] The Dubois siblings nevertheless doubled their investment in the Blue Bird Inn's musical talent with the addition of the Phil Hill combo as their house band. The figures in the payroll ledger clearly reflect their commitment to the city's bebop jazz scene. In fact, the cost of hiring musicians was the Blue Bird's largest expense during 1948 and 1949. Other business receipts and cash ledgers found in the document cache corroborate that this was a wise and fruitful business strategy.

The Duboises' investment in bebop jazz was a risky, if not controversial, move within the context of Detroit's music scene. In 1948 Detroit jazz was in the midst of what some called a "musical war" between the genres of swing and bebop.[43] Modernist bebop, with its complicated rhythms, chord progressions, and improvisations, was an unpredictable counterpart to the standardized melody-forward songs performed by orchestral swing musicians. Bebop was not easily packaged into commercial recordings and sound bites. It pushed back against the standards, upturning the conventions of popular jazz music. Some jazz musicians, like Carl Stewart, publicly derided the new genre, and Phil Hill's performances at the Blue Bird, as "jerky and ragged" music that was being "forced upon listeners."[44] Others disagreed and saw bebop as the savior of Detroit's stagnating scene. Five months before the Hill combo debuted at the Blue Bird, local music critic Roy Stephens bemoaned the "tired" state of Detroit jazz. In his *Michigan Chronicle* column, he asked why, in a wealthy city that was home to more than 2,000 musicians, the performers offered little more "than trite Gillespie-isms, 12 bar blues (in B-flat usually), insipid 'originals' and ridiculous showmanship antics."[45] He complained that "real jazz" was difficult to find and enjoy. The Blue Bird Inn's embrace of bebop was a response to Stephens's plea.

Phil Hill's group continued to draw crowds to the Blue Bird well into its second year as the venue's house band, an eternity in the music world. Reviews from March 1949 report that the night spot's patrons found "the group's easy-moving instrumentals a fertile source of enjoyment."[46] Bebop performances may have been panned by some critics as "an excuse to wear horn-rimmed glasses, a beret, and goatee," but a well-groomed younger set of Detroiters found a welcoming home among kindred spirits at the Blue Bird, where its bartenders Millard Brooks and Buddy Dubois were both recently voted as "best dressed" among the city's most dapper men.[47] The Blue Bird of 1948 and 1949 was a bar for musicians and music lovers. Patrons came to hear Phil Hill's combo perform bebop numbers like "Billie's Bounce" and "Salt Peanuts" as well as standards like "Don't Blame Me" and "The Man I Love."[48] The Blue Bird's staff and performers made no apologies for raising the club's standards of respectability and creativity.

A THRIVING BLACK-OWNED BUSINESS IN SEGREGATED DETROIT

Bebop transformed the Blue Bird into the "nerve center" of Detroit's modern jazz scene in 1948 and 1949.[49] Talented musicians attracted clientele to the club and entertained them, but it was the Dubois family and their staff who maintained the underlying rhythm of the Blue Bird by managing its day-to-day operations. Archaeological finds and archival records reveal insightful details about the people who ran the Blue Bird offstage. These data illuminate the different positions Black entrepreneurs and laborers occupied in Detroit's midcentury social and business networks.

The Dubois siblings ran the Blue Bird Inn between 1937 and 1953 as a tight-knit family business. Like two-thirds of the city's Black population in 1948, siblings Buddy, Gertrude, and LaJean and their parents, Pinkie and the late William Dubois, were all born outside of Detroit.[50] Census records indicate that the family relocated from Selma, Alabama, in the mid-1920s as part of the Great Migration of southern African American families northward. Gertrude, LaJean, Lonnie, and Buddy, who were in their early to mid-twenties at the time, took jobs in Detroit as a waitress, hairdresser, chauffeur, and, in Buddy's case, as a machinist in a local automotive factory. Their father William also worked as a laborer and machine operator in a local Ford automotive plant until he saved enough money to open his first restaurant at 5113 Tireman in 1935.[51] By 1930, the family accumulated the means to purchase a two-story home at 6534 Whitewood, just one-half block south of the Blue Bird Inn. There, the adult Dubois children lived together in a household of eight to ten people, with their parents, spouses, and other family members through the 1940s.[52]

The Dubois family's experience as Black homeowners in Detroit was atypical for African Americans during the Great Migration era. Housing options for new arrivals to Detroit were extremely limited, especially for Black families who were restricted to renting or purchasing homes in one of the city's few African American neighborhoods. These circumstances

forced most lower-income African American migrants to live in inade-
quate apartments within subdivided homes in the already overcrowded
districts of Paradise Valley and Black Bottom.[53] In late 1944, the *Michigan
Chronicle* reported that over half of all dwelling units occupied by African
Americans in Detroit were substandard.[54]

The West Side neighborhood where the Dubois family lived was a
working- and lower-middle-class enclave characterized by detached single-
family and multifamily homes. Though the neighborhood's residents had
better financial means and more spacious living arrangements than their
counterparts in Black Bottom and Paradise Valley, they were not immune
to the discriminatory, race-based segregation policies that limited Black
residents' ability to live and conduct businesses freely in the city. The Dubois family home and the Blue Bird Inn were positioned within steps of
the boundary between the West Side's Black and White sectors. From this
invisible dividing line, they witnessed one of the country's most contentious race-based housing disputes of the 1940s when, in 1944, Orsel and
Minnie McGhee, a middle-class African American couple, purchased a
home on Seebaldt two blocks north of Tireman in the White area of the
neighborhood. The McGhees's White neighbors attempted to evict them
on the basis of an existing restrictive housing covenant, but they refused
to relocate and instead took the matter to court.[55] In 1948, during Phil
Hill's run at the Blue Bird, the United States Supreme Court issued the
Shelley v. Kraemer decision in favor of the McGhees. The Court's decision
ruled that racially restrictive covenants were not enforceable by state or local courts.[56]

The Duboises would have been acutely aware of the systemic discrimination and racist hostility that plagued Detroit during the 1940s. In February 1942, violent protests had erupted at the site of the 200-unit Sojourner
Truth Housing Project, a complex constructed in a White neighborhood to
house Black defense workers. Mayor Edward Jefferies mobilized the Michigan National Guard to ensure the safety of Black families as they moved
into the residences.[57] One year later, in June 1943, rioting broke out across
the city over the course of three days, injuring nearly seven hundred people and killing thirty four.[58] The violence was instigated by disenfranchised White factory workers who protested the promotion of Black laborers to higher ranking manufacturing jobs. Black Detroiters fought back in
protest against the systemic inequalities they faced in access to housing,
services, and wartime rations.[59]

During the interwar and wartime decades of the Great Migration city
officials and local residents leveraged restrictive covenants and property

ownership as mechanisms for protecting space, wealth, and power for the benefit of White Detroiters. As legal scholar and critical race theorist Cheryl Harris argues, this overt manipulation of property rights and access "played a critical role in establishing and maintaining racial and economic subordination."[60] Pervasive across the United States, this pattern was evident locally in 1940s Detroit, especially in places where Black and White families lived within the bounds of the same neighborhood (e.g., the West Side, Virginia Park, and 8 Mile-Wyoming). The Dubois family's ownership of their own home and business may have been among the first cracks in the gradual dismantling of Detroit's segregated property market, but the strides Black residents made in securing housing, owning land, and operating profitable businesses during the 1930s and 1940s were increasingly beset by interference from other oppressive entities, especially law enforcement.

As Detroit's neighborhoods and entertainment venues became more integrated, tensions between police and local residents enveloped the West Side neighborhood, affecting both the managers and clientele of the Blue Bird Inn. Records confirm that as the Blue Bird Inn became more prosperous, the club's managers were increasingly scrutinized by local and federal police agencies. In 1950 Gertrude Bulkley and LaJean Dubois were issued a stiff $200 fine and fifteen-day liquor license suspension for serving alcohol to a minor.[61] The following year, Detroit police and federal agents conducted a narcotics raid on the Blue Bird. They charged the sisters with permitting the sale of drugs between the club's employees and its customers. The Dubois sisters, along with their brother Buddy, were subsequently indicted by a federal grand jury, and the bar was temporarily shuttered.[62] Clarence Eddins, who purchased the Blue Bird from the Dubois family in 1953, complained about frequent harassment by the city's White police force during the bar's 1950s heyday.[63] Nevertheless, the Dubois family (and later Clarence Eddins) strived to maintain the environment of musicians, staff, and Black and White clientele inside the Blue Bird as a harmonious and integrated venue. As Eddins recalled, "The music was too good. The crowds too hip for true animosity."[64] It was within this climate that the Dubois family established their profitable business, developing the Blue Bird Inn into a highly regarded anchor for Detroit's jazz music scene.

STAFF AND SERVICE

During 1948 and 1949 the Blue Bird was open seven days a week. Music was the main attraction on Thursday through Sunday nights, but in the days and hours in between, the Blue Bird was a popular neighborhood spot for dining and socializing. The Dubois family ran the Blue Bird with an all African American staff made up of a reliable base of family members in senior and supervisory positions and a more fluid rotation of cooks and service staff.[65] According to the archaeologically recovered ledgers, the family spent an average of $2,054 per month on staff wages, which amounted to about 18% of the club's monthly operating costs.[66]

Of the twenty-four employees listed in the 1948 payroll ledger, at least five were related to the Dubois siblings by blood or marriage. These relatives, who held the full-time managerial positions, received the highest wages. Buddy Dubois and Gertrude (Dubois) Bulkley each earned fifty dollars per week for managing the bar. Gertrude's eventual husband Lewis earned forty dollars per week for serving as the bar's porter. The next highest paid employees were the club's two bartenders, Millard Brooks and William Downer. Each worked steadily throughout 1948, receiving an average of fifty and forty-five dollars per week respectively.

The Dubois family organized the Blue Bird's labor system along gender lines. Men held most of the positions that required prolonged face-to-face interactions with customers (bartender, porter, music manager), while women occupied positions as waitresses and cooks. Over the course of 1948, the Dubois family employed seven women in the kitchen. Most worked continuously and in pairs throughout the period covered by the payroll ledger. The cooks included Fannye Coadie, Bertha Valentine, Mary Everson, and Thelma Brooks; they earned between fifteen and thirty dollars per week. The Blue Bird's waitresses, Peggy Neal, Mary Everson, and Mattie Barron, worked for wages averaging twelve dollars per week, plus tips.

In the kitchen the cooks prepared a variety of food that was popular among Detroiters at the time. Newspaper advertisements during the 1940s promoted the Blue Bird as a destination for American *and* Chinese-inspired food, including chop suey (an Americanized entrée) and chow mein (a generic Chinese noodle dish). These novel dishes had gained popularity in the postwar years as American servicemen returned from postings in the Pacific and Detroit's downtown Chinatown thrived.[67] The cooks also prepared special holiday dinners throughout the 1940s, especially on Thanksgiving, when they served traditional turkey and duck entrees.[68]

These glimpses of the Blue Bird's meal offerings come from brief mentions in the media. By contrast, archaeologically recovered food remains and archival documents vastly expand information about the Blue Bird customers' tastes and the kitchen's operations. During the 2015 survey of the Blue Bird Inn the archaeology team excavated a one-meter-square unit outside of the bar's back door. There they recovered thirty-one butchered animal bones discarded from the kitchen during the 1940s and early 1950s. Of these bone fragments one was identifiable as belonging to a chicken, and the other thirty were associated with the beef, veal, and pork dishes prepared in the Blue Bird's kitchen.[69]

The document cache recovered from the Blue Bird's vestibule ceiling provided an invaluable context for interpreting these excavated faunal remains. It included nearly 1,900 documents detailing daily transactions with food vendors, wholesalers, markets, and suppliers. Most notable are the 490 receipts spanning an eight-week period between May and June of 1949 and 1,402 checks cosigned by LaJean Dubois and Gertrude Bulkley, issuing payment for various supplies and services between July 1948 and May 1949. These records detail the array of the food on offer at the Blue Bird. Fish and chicken were the most frequently purchased products from local markets. The Dubois sisters coordinated near-daily deliveries of freshly butchered chicken from two or three different vendors. A typical day's order might include five springers (chicken) from Gillow Poultry for $4.95, and 100 springers plus seasoning and oysters for $13.76 from Kyptyk Wholesale Grocery (both vendors were located in the city's open-air Western Market).[70] Jaffee's also provided regular deliveries of seasonal, freshwater fish. For the weekend crowds, receipts and cash ledgers suggest that the kitchen offered a variety of specials, and that patrons purchased the most meals on Sundays. One receipt lists the purchase from Western Market of a large quantity of T-bone and flank steaks, ham, ribs, veal chops, and pork chops for a weekend dinner service in May 1949.[71]

BEHIND THE BAR

One of the most important files in the document cache is a Cash Ledger, a notebook summarizing the bar's daily expenses for the entire year of 1949. The ledger book, along with receipts and excavated artifacts, permits a specific reconstruction of customers' experiences at the Blue Bird (Figure 4.4).

Account records and artifacts from the Blue Bird indicate that beer drinking was the most popular activity among the bar's patrons. This is an unsurprising finding, and probably would have been a foregone conclusion even in the absence of material and archival evidence. Yet the survival of this information is important because it conveys how the Blue Bird and its customers participated in the local market for alcoholic beverages, how leisurely beverage consumption was an integral part of the bar's social experience, and how maintaining a reliable flow of food and drink required the Dubois sisters to navigate a complex network of suppliers.

Throughout 1949 the Cash Ledger entries record beer purchases by patrons occurring at more than twice the rate of food, and over three times the rate of liquor sales. During a typical three week period between January 1 and 21, 1949, the Blue Bird sold $7,657.25 worth of food and drink. Nearly 58% ($4,419.17) of the sales came from beer. Liquor sales, by contrast, amounted to 17% of the bar's cash intake ($1,310.45), and food comprised 25% ($1,972.39).[72]

To quench the thirst of its patrons, receipts detail how the Dubois sisters placed weekly orders with eleven different beer distributors across Detroit, ensuring a ready supply for the weekend rush. On the bar's slowest days, Tuesdays and Wednesdays, deliveries arrived from national producers, Anheuser-Busch and Pabst; from local breweries, Goebel, Altes, Stroh's, and E&B; and from wholesale distributors Better Brands and Commonwealth. A typical weekday delivery order contained fifty-four cases of beer from Stroh's (with two dozen bottles in each case), forty-five cases from Pfeiffer, seventeen cases from Goebel, and two-and-a-half barrels of Friar's Ale from E&B.[73] This was the intake for a bar with a maximum capacity of 125. In his analysis of beer sales recorded in the Blue Bird's check stubs and receipts Lorin Brace determined that the vast majority—81%—of beer purchased between August 1948 and April 1949 was

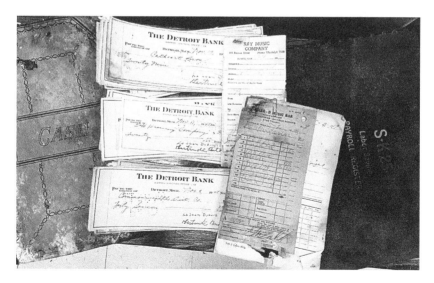

Figure 4.4. Records from the document cache include a cash ledger, receipts from local vendors, cashed checks, bills, and a payroll ledger. (Krysta Ryzewski)

produced at one of four local Detroit breweries: Stroh's (accounting for 25% of sales during the period), Goebel (22%), Pfeiffer (16%), and E&B Brewing's Friar's Ale (14%).[74] The popularity of these brands at the Blue Bird, and beer drinking in general, is corroborated by the recovery of sixty-five amber-colored beer bottle fragments during the outdoor excavations and a dozen metal beer bottle caps from a posthole at the former location of the bar counter inside the building.[75]

According to purchase records, the bartenders dispensed a steady supply of nonalcoholic drinks too, especially Coca-Cola and locally produced Vernor's Ginger Ale. They also kept a variety of juices on hand, to combine with liquor and serve as stand-alone drinks. The Dubois sisters relied upon Bireley's Orangeade Company for deliveries of orange, grape, grapefruit, tomato, and berry juices as well as a beverage called "the chocolate drink."[76] To pair with the drinks, the bar sold Kar-Nut peanuts and Wolverine potato chips.[77]

During the Blue Bird's quieter hours a television and jukebox provided entertainment. Receipts for repairs made by jukebox distributor Ray Music Company (based in Paradise Valley) and the Merit Radio and Television Company indicate that both pieces of novelty technology were operational in 1948 and 1949. A vacuum tube from a late 1940s model television was also recovered during the back-lot excavations, further confirming the TV's presence during the Dubois family's period of management (Figure 4.5).[78] At the time, only one million Americans owned televisions, and individual stations were just beginning to organize regular programming; 1948 saw the creation of the national networks ABC and CBS and the first nightly newscasts.[79] The fact that the Blue Bird owners promoted its television in advertisements suggests that some customers came to the bar to watch sports or news coverage. Meanwhile, the jukebox played an equally important role in disseminating information to customers. Managers carefully selected the latest jazz music recordings for it, ensuring that patrons were exposed to and appreciated the club's signature musical genre.[80]

The strong relationship between the Blue Bird's proprietors and local Black neighborhood residents is perhaps best illustrated by an unexpected find in the archaeologically recovered accounting records—evidence of informal banking transactions. In the late 1940s banks operated discriminatory lending policies, restricting Black Detroiters from receiving loans and financing for businesses. These exclusive policies cultivated a general mistrust among the Black community in financial institutions.[81] Some residents of the West Side's Black community avoided banks and instead cashed their weekly paychecks or withdrew pre-payday loans from trusted

Figure 4.5. Artifacts recovered from the indoor survey include floor and wall tiles, drink stirrers, straws, a four-leaf clover good luck charm, and a toy plastic spider. From the backlot excavations archaeologists recovered butchered cow bones (*bottom left*), a broken fork (*top right*), and a vacuum tube from late 1940s television (*top right*). (Krysta Ryzewski)

local businesses who had ready supplies of cash on hand.[82] The repository of 1,402 checks and the cash ledger recovered from our archaeological survey records 174 instances of "checks cashed" during the ten-month period between July 1948 and May 1949. According to these records, Gertrude Bulkley and LaJean Dubois typically conducted banking transactions at the bar for customers on Mondays, Wednesdays, and Fridays. These days may have corresponded to the paydays for local residents, the majority of whom worked at one of several nearby manufacturing plants: the Lincoln Motors Livernois Plant, the Kelsey-Hayes Wheel Plant, or the River Rouge Plant in Southwest Detroit (the largest employer of African Americans in Detroit).[83] The Dubois sisters cashed between four and twenty-six checks for customers per banking day. Over the course of ten months, these transactions comprised 12.5% of all checking traffic at the Blue Bird and amounted to $378,147.21, a tremendous sum at the time (almost four million dollars in 2020).[84] The banking services that the Blue Bird managers provided may not have been legal, but the Dubois sisters nevertheless structured these informal economic exchanges and kept careful records of the transactions as if they were bank clerks. After a round of in-house banking, the Dubois sisters visited a local branch of the Detroit Bank to deposit customers' checks into the bar's business accounts.

DETROIT'S BLACK BUSINESS NETWORKS AND LOCAL TASTES

Archaeological evidence reveals that the Dubois family ran the Blue Bird as a tightly organized business. Documents from the cache detail how they kept fastidious accounts of daily purchases and wage payments. They also paid all of their utility bills, taxes, loans, and license fees on time. Often their record keeping was redundant, with the same figures and transactions cross-referenced between different types of documents (e.g., check stubs and daily expenditure reports). After either LaJean Dubois or Gertrude Bulkley rectified the daily expenditures she bundled each day's accounting paperwork together and arranged them into neat piles, fastened with paper clips, exactly as they were found by archaeologists in the vestibule ceiling. The sisters' careful accounting and purchasing decisions ensured that the Blue Bird Inn was a profitable enterprise in the late 1940s. For each period reported in the cash ledger, the bar netted a profit of at least $1,000. In the time frame of May and June 1949, for example, they netted a handsome profit of $1,465.57 after all expenses were paid (i.e., $15,462.80 in 2020 dollars).[85]

The Dubois family operated in two different business worlds: within Detroit's Black business community and among larger regional outlets that provided commercially branded products. They made all of their supply and service-based purchases in 1948 and 1949 from merchants who operated out of Detroit, with the exception of one nut distributor, Kar-Nut, which was based in the neighboring city of Ferndale.

The Blue Bird's accounting records detail transactions with fifty-eight different businesses, ranging from beer distributors to laundry services.[86] In most cases the Duboises were loyal customers of the wholesalers, distributors, and businesses who provided the bar with regular supplies and maintenance services. From the documentary records, it is possible to reconstruct the extent to which they maintained connections with the Black business and entrepreneurial communities within Detroit's Black neighborhoods through their business practices. Over one-third (33%) of the businesses the Duboises contracted with on a regular basis were Black-owned or Black-operated companies located in the neighborhoods of Paradise Valley and the West Side. For their immediate needs, such as ice, bread, and produce, the Duboises frequented the West Side's Mello-D Music Shop (for ice cubes), Continental Bakery, and Vic's Market. All of these businesses were located within walking distance on Tireman Avenue, and the Duboises procured supplies from them almost every day.

In Paradise Valley, the Duboises frequented eight businesses, including the Supreme Linen & Laundry Company at 700 East Alexandrine and the Paradise Valley Distributing Company at 2467 St. Antoine.[87] There was no shortage of suppliers for the Duboises to purchase from in Paradise

Valley, a district that was already home to 350 Black-owned businesses by 1920.[88] Supreme Linen supplied the Blue Bird with clean aprons, towels, and table cloths.[89] Its affable owner Fred Allen had gradually built his business into one of Detroit's largest commercial laundries by purchasing old trucks, which he then converted into delivery vehicles.[90] The laundry service appears in the list of Black-serving businesses published in the 1949 *Negro Motorist's Green Book*, a nationwide travel guide that promoted businesses where Black tourists would be accommodated without "running into difficulties or embarrassments."[91]

The Blue Bird also relied on the Paradise Valley Beer Distributing Company to stock the bar with a steady supply of Friar's Ale and Clix Malt Liquor. Grady and Reuben Ray initially ran the distributing company out of a garage behind the famous Turf Bar on 514 Beacon Avenue, delivering supplies to local bars and restaurants with two old milk trucks. Within three years, by 1942, the company grossed one million dollars and boasted an all-Black workforce. Advertisements billed the Rays' business as Detroit's first and "only Negro beer distributor" and emphasized how the company contributed to the local Black community's strength by "building employment for Negro youth."[92] In supplying the Blue Bird Inn, the Dubois siblings apparently made strategic decisions to maintain connections with particular vendors. By purchasing from Black-owned businesses, the Dubois family endorsed the circulation of money among Black Detroiters, ensuring a measure of economic control and stability for their community as well as Paradise Valley and West Side businesses.

As much as they supported local Black-owned businesses, the Duboises were also consumers who sought top quality meats and nationally recognizable brands for their customers' enjoyment. For their daily meat and dairy purchases, they relied on the city's largest open-air market for access to wholesalers, butchers, and farm vendors, Western Market, which stood at the corner of Michigan Avenue and Eighteenth Street until it was demolished for freeway construction in 1965. The Dubois family made the majority of their other purchases (53%) from thirty-one vendors located downtown in the city's commercial warehouse and manufacturing districts. These vendors included the Blue Bird's suppliers of regionally and nationally recognizable brand name products like Stroh's Beer, Anheuser-Busch, and Coca-Cola. These mass-produced beverages offered customers the assurance of a standardized, reliable product, ensuring consumer confidence in the quality of the Blue Bird's offerings. As archaeologist Paul Mullins notes, in the post–World War II years, Americans embraced a contemporary consumer culture rooted in material consumption and reinforced through mass media. African American consumer culture, he asserts, reflected a desire to "equitably participate in consumer space[s]," which were not bound by systemic inequalities in ways that other facets of their daily experience were.[93] The decisions that the Dubois siblings exercised in supplying the Blue Bird, and the purchases their customers made at the bar, express their ability to move freely between multiple consumer spaces, some of which catered specifically to the local Black community, but others that served consumers on regional and national scales.

AFTER THE SHOW: MUSICAL MEMORIES KEEP THE BLUE BIRD ALIVE

The Dubois family and the musicians of Phil Hill's combo set the stage for the Blue Bird's continued success in the 1950s and the venue's legendary aftermath in the decades to come. Beginning in 1953 Clarence Eddins and his wife Mary took over the club's ownership and operation. They updated the bebop lineups with a new house band, the Billy Mitchell Quintet (featuring Elvin and Thad Jones), and they reorganized the bar, moving the stage from the front of the room to the back wall and adorning it with a glittering backdrop painted with a fan of red, yellow, and blue triangles.[94] Music historians associate Eddins's management of the bar in the 1950s with the Blue Bird's live music heyday. During this period, Miles Davis, John Coltrane, Cannonball Adderley, and many others dazzled audiences with memorable performances (Figure 4.6).

Gradually, by the late 1950s, the vibrancy of the local jazz scene was usurped by the rise of national touring acts.[95] Clarence Eddins ended the bar's regular live music performances in the early 1970s. By that point, the city and the West Side neighborhood were entering into a prolonged period of decline, accelerated by the uprising of 1967, which caused considerable damage to the infrastructure of the surrounding neighborhoods (though not to the Blue Bird itself; see chapter 5). In the following decades, residents and businesses departed the West Side neighborhood, leaving behind unoccupied buildings in the heart of the once vibrant community. Many of these well-built structures, including the Dubois family's house at 6534 Whitewood, succumbed to arson and city-led demolitions by the early 2000s.

The Blue Bird Inn almost met a similar fate. If not for a persistent, lingering nostalgia that kept the Blue Bird's accomplishments alive in the memories of musicians, former patrons, and journalists, it may have vanished unnoticed. As *Detroit News* reporter Jim Dulzo put it in 1992, the Blue Bird's ghost of soulful bebop was "slightly louder than memory."[96]

Figure 4.6. Performance at the Blue Bird Inn in 1961 featuring (*left to right*) Joe Henderson, Pepper Adams, Barry Harris, Ali Jackson, and Roy Brooks. (pepperadams.com)

Shortly after live music left the Blue Bird's stage, talk of preserving and revitalizing the club began.[97] In 1980 Detroiters Barbara and Ken Cox founded the Society of the Culturally Concerned to support emerging African American musicians. They promoted Detroit's music heritage among the city's politicians and its artist community, and they gathered support from United States congressional representative John Conyers, a longtime jazz aficionado. Representative Conyers championed the addition of the club to the National Register of Historic Places. Initial steps were taken to draft a proposal, but the nomination process was not completed.[98] The next two decades marked an interregnum for the Blue Bird as various attempts to elevate sites associated with Detroit's African American music heritage, including plans to resuscitate the Blue Bird, emerged and fizzled. One such effort, mobilized by former Blue Bird house band members and staff, involved organizing annual reunions in downtown's Greektown district. For one reunion performance, musician Thad Jones wrote "5021 Tireman" in tribute to the Blue Bird; it appeared on pianist Tommy Flanagan's 1990 album *Beyond the Bluebird*, which also featured a tribute track called "Bluebird."[99]

By the time Clarence Eddins passed away in 1992 the Blue Bird's clientele had diminished to a few neighborhood regulars and older patrons who came in to reminisce about the bar's heyday. Clarence's wife, Mary Eddins, decided against selling the bar because, as she confessed to one local reporter, she had "too many memories" to let it go.[100] But nostalgia was not enough to keep the bar in business. For various reasons, the musicians and patrons who treasured memories about the Blue Bird's past did not come to its rescue. By 2001, Mary was unable to pay the $367.91 property tax bill owed on the Blue Bird, and the Wayne County Treasurer's Office issued a certificate of forfeiture, the first step in a foreclosure process. With the help of a neighborhood resident, Mary was able to resolve the outstanding bill and redeem the property, but she was only able to hold onto it for three more years. On March 1, 2004, the Blue Bird again faced foreclosure, and the property was transferred from Eddins's ownership to the county.[101] Over the next fifteen years, the Blue Bird Inn passed through a series of at least five owners (including the county and city), none of whom maintained the building or envisioned a future for it.

THE BLUE BIRD TAKES FLIGHT: ASSEMBLING, DISMANTLING, AND CIRCULATING REMAINS

For the vast majority of its history, from the 1960s through the early 2000s, the Blue Bird Inn has grappled with the realities of economic and population decline in Detroit while simultaneously maintaining its status as a place of creativity and hope. By the time the archaeology survey team entered the building with the DSC in 2015 the building's future looked grim. Everyone approached the survey with a mindset that it could well be the last chance they would have to access the decrepit building (Figure 4.7). The combined pressures of time, uncertainty, and lack of structural integrity guided the team to take pragmatic and creative approaches to the Blue Bird's physical remains. It was agreed that if the stage, the documents, and the other portable objects were to survive for the benefit of future research or creative interventions, they had to be removed from the building.

Upon completion of the survey, the archaeology team took the recovered artifacts and document cache back to the Grosscup Museum of Anthropology at Wayne State University. There, students and faculty inventoried the collection and placed it into the museum's holdings. The assemblage then became the focal point for various research projects and exhibit content. It also provided the evidentiary basis for adding the property to the statewide inventory of archaeological sites; in this list the Blue Bird is recorded as site 20WN1201. It was during the process of examining

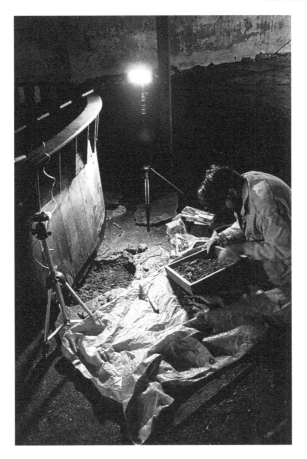

Figure 4.7. Lorin Brace, part of the Wayne State archaeology team, sifts soil excavated from a hole in the ground next to the Blue Bird's stage, 2015. (Courtesy of Don Adzigian)

other listings on the statewide inventory that I realized the Blue Bird Inn was the first site in Detroit exclusively associated with African American owners to be investigated archaeologically. The fact that it took until 2015 for archaeologists to focus on a site of Black heritage in a city where 83% of its residents are African American is astounding and, frankly, distressing.

During the survey the archaeology team documented the extant stage along the Blue Bird's back wall. While they worked a couple of jazz musicians from Wayne State University's music program performed on the stage in tribute to the Blue Bird's bebop ancestors (Figure 4.8).

The archaeologists and musicians who participated in the survey thought of the stage as an architectural feature permanently attached to

Figure 4.8. Interior of the Blue Bird Inn, from the front door, 2015. The archaeology survey team enjoys an impromptu performance by Wayne State University music students on the historic stage. (Courtesy of Don Adzigian)

the building's floor and wall; perhaps the scrappers did too, and that is why they had left it as the only untouched furnishing inside the bar. Our colleagues from the DSC imagined otherwise. In the months after the survey, as the building continued to exist in ownership limbo, DSC's director, Carleton Gholz, hatched a plan to salvage the stage and to restore it as a mobile performance site. The building's owner, who had little interest in the building's past or future, granted Gholz permission to extract the stage and for the DSC to assume ownership of it. In 2016, Gholz returned to the Blue Bird with a team made up of volunteers and archaeologists to systematically dismantle the stage and remove it off site to Detroit's College of Creative Studies, where it was then painstakingly conserved and restored (Figure 4.9).[102]

In the case of the Blue Bird Inn it is difficult to know when, or if, the archaeology project's work ended and when the next chapter of preservation, education, and economic development efforts began. The entire project,

Figure 4.9. Removal of the Blue Bird Inn stage by Wayne State archaeologists and members of the Detroit Sound Conservancy, 2016. (© 2016, Detroit Sound Conservancy/detroitsound.org)

and its aftermath, has been a case of creative, improvisational "jazz archaeology" in terms of its procedures and topical focus. Within a year and a half of the initial 2015 archaeological survey the Blue Bird Inn still existed, but not just on Tireman Avenue. Its remains had diffused across the city to at least three venues. The Blue Bird building still stood on Tireman, the Wayne State anthropology museum housed the document cache and portable artifacts, and the DSC managed the reconstructed stage.

Of all the remains recovered from the Blue Bird, it was the least mobile object, the stage, that would transmit the venue's material presence and musical legacy worldwide. Beginning in 2017 the DSC developed programming to reactivate the stage in various settings. In Detroit, the stage traveled to the Detroit Public Library and the Museum of Contemporary Art Detroit, among other destinations (Figure 4.10). The DSC invited musicians ranging from local middle school choirs to famous jazz artists to perform on it. In April 2017, the Saint-Étienne Biennale invited the DSC to exhibit the stage in France following Detroit's designation as the first UNESCO City of Design in the United States.[103] Since its return from France, the Blue Bird stage has featured prominently in festivals and exhibits, including in Toronto and at the Detroit Historical Museum.

The recovery of the stage was more than a rescue operation; it was a deliberate, thoughtful disassembly and reactivation of a legendary

Figure 4.10. Restored Blue Bird Inn stage on exhibit at the Detroit Public Library, August 2017. (Krysta Ryzewski)

performance space. By assuming the role of a mobile object of material culture and performance, the stage has, perhaps counterintuitively, added a level of stability and certainty to the Blue Bird's future in the face of the building's neglect. It is not just an artifact of the Blue Bird Inn, but an active site of Detroit's musical heritage. It is an object to be shared by all who love and appreciate music and Detroit's creative legacy. This might seem like a tidy spot to end the story, with a glimmer of hope in the face of the building's potential loss. But as its history demonstrates, the end of the Blue Bird has never been inevitable. There is yet another act on the place-keeping horizon, it seems.[104]

THE FUTURE OF THE BLUE BIRD INN AND COMMUNITY-INVOLVED CONTEMPORARY ARCHAEOLOGY

In 2018 the DSC received a $35,000 planning grant from the Kresge Foundation to purchase the Blue Bird Inn and initiate the process of restoring the building. The DSC's proposal involves stabilizing the building, securing its preservation status, and developing the building as the nonprofit's headquarters and archives.[105] As a first step to securing its status as a site of national heritage, on December 7, 2020, the city of Detroit designated the Blue Bird as a local historic district.

Eventually, the DSC intends for the Blue Bird Inn to become a space for music education and research. This long-term plan involves reinstalling the stage and reuniting the archaeological collections with the Blue Bird, adding them to the DSC's on-site archive. The new Blue Bird will also operate as a performance space, and possibly a bar, if that is what the local West Side community desires. In 2020, there were still many financial and logistical obstacles for the DSC to overcome to achieve the club's restoration, but their process of community-based collaborations and consultations, among people who the DSC calls "place keepers," was well underway (Figure 4.11).[106] All involved are hopeful that the Blue Bird will anchor the revitalization of the beleaguered yet resilient West Side neighborhood.

One surprise finding to emerge from the survey, results, and aftermath of the Blue Bird's archaeological investigations is that the project received criticism from some of our professional archaeology colleagues. Critics dismissed the validity of the Blue Bird Inn as an archaeological site because of its age and because the contemporary research time frame differed in scope from more conventional archaeological inquiries. It was too young to be considered a site worthy of study, they argued, especially if they could remember sitting in clubs like the Blue Bird listening to bebop

Figure 4.11. Musicians, descendants of past bar employees, archaeologists, historians, and neighbors gather at the Blue Bird Inn for a community day celebration, 2019. (© 2019, Detroit Sound Conservancy/detroitsound.org)

with a cold drink in hand. Our archaeological findings simply paired more stuff to the social histories that they experienced firsthand.

Such suggestions that our work with contemporary remains was not rigorous or relevant enough to fit within disciplinary standards are flawed. At a time when all other initiatives focused on reviving the Blue Bird had broken down completely, archaeological interventions refreshed conversations about the venue's significance. The elements of archaeological practice—its scientific methodology, careful attention to detail, and rigorous engagement with material remains—produced fresh, tangible connections that resonated with the Blue Bird's stakeholders. Few of these stakeholders were archaeologists. They were an unconventional group of musicians, grassroots preservationists, residents, journalists, and educators. For them, both the music and the remnants of the club were material things worth commemorating by reactivating the building. Considering their perspectives, the contributions of archaeological investigations in this case are difficult to argue against. Archaeology was a critical intervention that reengaged various groups of people and helped to mobilize a major preservation initiative. According to Carleton Gholz, archaeology "added value" to the historic preservation campaign because people could see themselves, and their histories, in the materials and relationships associated with them that were uncovered during the survey.[107]

In the end, a great deal of what we now know about the Blue Bird Inn's history and functioning in late 1940s Detroit comes from the material remains recovered during the Wayne State University archaeological survey. With Paradise Valley destroyed by the urban renewal efforts in the 1960s, the Blue Bird's records about its Black-owned businesses also preserve traces of that lost historic neighborhood. The behind-the-scenes glimpses that the document cache and artifacts provide into the Blue Bird's management practices provide an unparalleled account of the intricacy and complexity of Black business operations, social networks, and consumer preferences in mid-twentieth-century Detroit. From an archaeological perspective, these remains tell a story of Detroit, within the contexts of the West Side neighborhood and the Blue Bird's music scene, that actively refutes essentialized notions of Black historical experiences.[108] The DSC's inclusive heritage preservation efforts further this contribution through their creative engagements and activations of material remains in ways that call attention to the Blue Bird's legacy and place-based histories. It is perhaps entirely fitting, then, that if the Conservancy succeeds in their efforts to restore the building, they may rename it "The Legendary Blue Bird Inn."

CHAPTER FIVE

Gordon Park

Commemorating Resilience and Activism at the
Flashpoint of the 1967 Uprising

On the northwest corner of Rosa Parks Boulevard and Clairmount Avenue in Detroit's Virginia Park neighborhood sits Gordon Park, a compact, one-acre public space owned by the city. I first encountered Gordon Park in 2014 when I was biking along the boulevard, scanning the landscape for signs of the vibrant commercial thoroughfare that once flanked the street during the first half of the twentieth century. There were no old storefronts or businesses left to see. The ghostly traces of the Jewish and African American communities who once lived along Twelfth Street, as the boulevard was known prior to the 1970s, remained only in the swaths of open lots that stood in between occasional modern housing complexes or corner stores. I almost rode by the park without noticing it. It was easy to overlook because its small *L*-shaped footprint blended in with the surrounding landscape of vacant lots and unoccupied buildings. Then a ten-foot-tall abstract, metal sculpture caught my eye. It drew my gaze to the park space, a sunken plaza delineated by crumbling concrete walls and lines of young-growth trees. Peeling letters on the park's only sign announced that I had arrived at Gordon Park (Figure 5.1).

No one was in the park on that Saturday morning; the absence of trash cans and even litter suggested that it was not a very popular gathering spot. If I had not known the area's history, I would have dismissed the forlorn park as an artifact of one of the city's many failed neighborhood improvement efforts. But this was no ordinary park. The corner of Twelfth Street (now Rosa Parks) and Clairmount was the location where the Economy Printing shop once stood—the flashpoint for Detroit's 1967 uprising, the most violent civic unrest in the United States during the 1960s. It was useful that I came to the park with this knowledge in mind, because there was no hint of the location's significance as a site of activism and conflict among its signage, artwork, or landscape architecture. This absence of information completely disconnected the place's history from the pivotal roles the site and the people associated with it played in Detroit's twentieth-century civil rights struggles and social justice campaigns.

Figure 5.1. Gordon Park from the northwest corner of Rosa Parks (formerly Twelfth Street) and Clairmount, 2017. (Krysta Ryzewski)

Gordon Park was constructed by the city of Detroit on top of the site of the Economy Printing building in 1976 as an effort to quiet and stabilize the devastated Twelfth Street commercial strip and the surrounding Virginia Park neighborhood.[1] For the next fifty-one years, until 2017, Gordon Park stood in its original configuration, altered only by occasional cosmetic changes that local community groups made to its artwork and vegetation. The city of Detroit neglected the park from the outset, performing only cursory maintenance of the space until 1990, when funding shortages required them to discontinue upkeep altogether. As a result, only fragmented memories survive about the history of the park and the purpose, design, and symbolism of the space.

In contrast to the considerable body of scholarship by urban historians and geographers, there has been little attention by historical archaeologists to the physical remains of the 1967 uprising and its aftermath, despite the fact that visible traces of the violence survive in landscape features, structures, and absences throughout the city.[2] As the fiftieth anniversary of the 1967 uprising approached in 2017, I thought it an appropriate moment to position Gordon Park in a longer-term, or diachronic, archaeological perspective by considering its legacy as conveyed by its physical remains and associated personal stories. I began to visit Gordon Park three years earlier in 2014, first on my own and then with colleagues and students. During each visit I photo-documented the space, noting subtle changes to the park's layout, art, and other signs of usage. Eventually, I developed a more formal archaeological survey approach to the park, involving a larger group of people in the collection of spatial information (mapping, measurements, photo-documentation, inventories). In 2015 I led a group of five students in the first of two archaeological surveys of the park. In April 2017, I conducted a second more extensive landscape survey involving ten Wayne State University urban archaeology students. The group included several Detroiters and one woman who was a teenage resident of Virginia Park at the time of the uprising.

Our archaeological surveys of Gordon Park had three objectives. First, we evaluated the extent to which the park's layout and construction materials communicated city officials' anxieties and approaches toward residents in the lower-income African American neighborhood in the years following the uprising. Then, we aimed to connect the park's tangible remnants with archival sources and oral histories in order to demonstrate the extent to which the city neglected the space over the span of decades. Finally, I employed repeated, iterative surveys to document how local residents took active measures to maintain and modify the park in ways that represented their community values and aspirations for the struggling city's future. Owing to the constraints of the coursework during which most of this work was undertaken, the surveys did not incorporate participants from the various community groups who would later contribute to the park's revitalization. Our attention to Gordon Park over the course of four years was an exercise in "slow archaeology."[3] In other words, it was a deliberately gradual accumulation of information that allowed the time to articulate observations in tandem with ongoing issues in the city and the concerns of local communities.

Gordon Park embodies a place-based history that is shaped by competing processes of forgetting, remembering, commemoration, and future-making.[4] With roots in the sociopolitical climate of late-1960s Detroit, especially the violence of 1967, the park is intimately connected with the legacies of mid-twentieth-century activism as well as the traumatic experiences of a major conflict and an aftermath of neglect. Our archaeological surveys took place when the park was a scar on the post-1967 landscape. The information they recorded captured a city and its residents still in the process of coping with the uprising's aftermath and its decades-long intergenerational trauma. Just one month after our last survey in April 2017, the city of Detroit announced plans to rehabilitate the park in time for the 1967 uprising's fiftieth anniversary that July. In the space of three months, the city of Detroit reactivated the ruined park space. Although the park sat in a state of muted animation for the first fifty-one years of its existence, our surveys and the revitalization efforts confirmed that it was and continues to be a place that is significant and evocative for contemporary communities.[5]

This chapter is an archaeological discussion of Gordon Park. It charts the shift of the park first from a forlorn, neglected place into a community-curated space, and then into a revitalized city park and neighborhood center. I consider how the park's remains, and certain absences among them, ultimately empowered conversations about social justice and contested pasts in ways that resulted in civic revitalization and reconciliation efforts. I begin with a brief background of the 1967 uprising to place the park within the context of the citywide upheaval. I then move backward to focus on the deeper history of the neighborhood surrounding the park in order to illustrate some of the underlying tensions that sparked the 1967 violence. Before detailing our archaeological surveys of the park's remains and the city's treatment of the space, I discuss how ruination and blight management has been a consistent, long-term cause of stress for Virginia Park residents over the past six decades. I conclude with a discussion of the park's aftermath of neglect, focusing on the rather sudden heritage-based reactivation of the park in time for the fiftieth anniversary of the 1967 uprising in July 2017.

THE 1967 UPRISING

In the early morning hours of Sunday, July 23, 1967, chaos erupted across Detroit. Simmering tensions, especially between the city's beleaguered African American population and its predominately White police force, had reached a boiling point.[6] The deadly week of unrest began in a speakeasy (or blind pig) on the second floor of the unassuming Economy Printing building at 9125 Twelfth Street. By day, Bill Scott II, a local political activist, operated the United Community League for Civic Action out of the modest, two-story brick building. By night, Scott converted the vacant second floor of the shop into an illegal after-hours bar, where locals came to drink, gamble, and party. Routine police raids on Scott's blind pig and countless others across the city did little to deter their operations. In a typical raid, male patrons would be escorted downtown to the central police station and released after paying a nominal $27.50 fee.[7] The July 23 raid on Bill Scott's speakeasy was anything but typical.

The exact details of what tipped off the unrest that night vary according to the source and the storyteller. All agree that the blind pig was packed with nearly one hundred people on that sweltering summer night. Many were there to celebrate the homecoming of two local servicemen from Vietnam and to send off another neighborhood man to war. Some say the violence erupted when a policeman pushed an African American woman down the stairs during the raid. Others blame patrons who threw bottles at a police vehicle. A third version credits a man nicknamed Mr. Green Sleeves for inciting the crowds gathered on Twelfth Street to take action.[8] As police raided the Economy Printing building, they scuffled with the customers who fled through the front door. Mr. Green Sleeves stood across the street, frantically waving his green-shirted arms and shouting insults at the authorities.[9] In retrospect, it is clear that while the events at the Economy Printing building may have been a flashpoint for the ensuing violence, there was no singular act that started the uprising against the city's oppressive White power structures. On that night, simultaneous acts of aggression on the part of the police and civilians, White and Black, were responsible for igniting the tensions, distrust, and anger that had been simmering for decades among the city's African American and working-class populations (see chapter 3).[10]

Within hours of the blind pig's raid, protesters vandalized many of the two hundred commercial buildings and businesses that lined Twelfth

Street (Figure 5.2). Although looters targeted some shops for their associations with White owners, their acts of destruction did not discriminate along the color line. Many Black-owned businesses, like Joe Von Battle's record shop at 8434 Twelfth Street, which he had relocated there from Paradise Valley just a few years earlier, were also destroyed.

By mid-afternoon on Sunday July 23, arsonists and looters crept westward toward Dexter, Linwood, and Grand River Avenues, gutting the adjacent Petosky-Otsego neighborhood. They burned and ransacked all of the commercial buildings along the Petosky-Otsego stretch of Grand River except the Grande Ballroom (see chapter 6). To the west of Grand River Avenue, the violence spread to the segregated West Side, but spared most of the structures along the neighborhood's thoroughfare, Tireman Avenue, including the Blue Bird Inn (see chapter 4). Over the course of the next five days the civic unrest extended far beyond Virginia Park to neighborhoods on Detroit's east and west sides, especially those adjacent to the main roads that radiated from the city center (Woodward, Gratiot, Grand River, and Jefferson).

With the city in disarray, Michigan governor George Romney appealed to President Lyndon B. Johnson for federal assistance. Two days after the

Figure 5.2. Twelfth Street on the first day of the July 1967 uprising. The Economy Printing building is visible at top left. (Walter P. Reuther Library, Archives of Labor and Urban Affairs, Wayne State University)

unrest began, 8,000 National Guardsmen arrived to occupy Detroit; an additional 4,700 army paratroopers, diverted from their deployment to Vietnam, soon followed. The troops came prepared for war. To restore order, they lined the streets with armored tanks; soldiers drew their weapons at local residents, and snipers took aim at looters. When the troops withdrew on July 29, officials tallied the casualties. Forty-three people were killed and 1,189 injured. The dead and wounded came from all ranks—civilians, innocent bystanders, children, police officers, soldiers, firemen, and a pregnant woman. Police arrested over 7,200 people, the majority of whom were accused of participating in the looting that reduced the city's commercial thoroughfares to ruins.[11] The Kerner Report, the result of investigations by a presidential advisory commission into the nationwide unrests of 1967, estimated that during Detroit's uprising 10,000 angry and opportunistic people from all backgrounds looted 2,509 stores and burned over 1,600 buildings across the city. In the aerial images captured by media helicopters, Detroit looked like a war zone.

The week of July 23 in Detroit ranks among the most deadly and destructive episodes of civic conflict in American history. This is an indisputable fact supported by quantifiable tolls to human lives and properties. There exists no such agreement, however, about how to refer to the events of that week. In mass media especially, but also among suburban White populations, the violence is most commonly referred to as a "race riot." In the Kerner Report, the United States government called it "civil unrest." Scholars tend to use neutral terms like "civil disorder" or "struggles."[12] Among Detroiters, the events are most often discussed as either an "uprising" or a "rebellion." These two terms connect with the language of the city's civil rights movement, which manifested itself publicly in 1963 when Rev. Martin Luther King Jr. debuted his "I Have a Dream" speech in Detroit and then led at least 125,000 people in the Walk to Freedom down Woodward Avenue.[13]

For Black residents, the city's rebellion, other incidents of unrest nationwide, and the assassination of Reverend King in 1968, prompted the amplification and consolidation of Black Power initiatives in Detroit. Preeminent activists Grace Lee and Jimmy Boggs mentored a new generation of radical organizers throughout the 1960s by establishing the Organization for Black Power in 1965 and the Inner City Organizing Committee in 1967, just months before the uprising. The Boggses designed these organizations with the purpose of promoting Black Detroiters to civic leadership positions through political education and practical activities. In the wake of the uprising, Grace Lee and Jimmy coauthored the *Manifesto for a*

Black Revolutionary Party with the intention of leading Black youth beyond rebellion to revolution.[14] The Boggs's work was programmatic, pragmatic, and focused on the long game.[15] It did not operate at the pace of change that some liberation-oriented contingents favored after the uprising. In response, new groups emerged who promoted overturning the system of White supremacy that governed the city. They included the Black Panthers and the League of Revolutionary Black Workers, whose newspaper, the *Inner City Voice*, disseminated the movements' messages.[16]

A wide variety of terminology is still used today to describe the events of 1967. Perhaps there has never been an agreement about how to talk about July 1967 because there has never been a consensus on the root causes or effects of the conflict with regard to issues of inequality, racism, police brutality, and urban resource management. Nevertheless, as Grace Lee Boggs argued, the terminology that people use to describe the July 1967 events matters—especially for the communities who are still living among and coping with the consequences of such profound social inequity and upheaval. People's word choices when describing the violence of July 1967, Boggs said, "reflect how willing we are to accept the challenge to build a Detroit which is safe and sustainable because it is founded on the conviction that human values of justice and community are more important than material and economic growth."[17] Following Boggs, I agree that how one speaks about the unrest indexes one's own orientations to race and conflict in Detroit. These orientations are inevitably based on a number of implicit demographic, generational, and social justice biases. Here, I alternate between the terms "unrest" and "uprising."

VIRGINIA PARK AND URBAN RENEWAL: A NEIGHBORHOOD IN TRANSITION

The longer history of Virginia Park, especially prior to the 1960s, positions the neighborhood, and the businesses that once stood in the footprint of Gordon Park, at the nexus of a cultural interchange between Detroit's Jewish and African American communities, especially during the years of World War II. During the 1930s Virginia Park was a predominately Jewish neighborhood. Its commercial corridor along Twelfth Street was lined with numerous shops, cocktail bars, and restaurants, including the Purple Gang's favorite, Boesky's Delicatessen, on the corner of Hazelwood, just two blocks south of Gordon Park (see chapter 2).[18] A decade later, wartime increases in local industrial manufacturing jobs attracted a second influx of Great Migration–era African Americans to Detroit. Their arrival exacerbated the city's ongoing housing crisis and coincided with its slum clearance efforts in the lower east side Black Bottom neighborhood. New-comers struggled to find housing options even in the low-income, segregated neighborhoods.

Virginia Park was one of the first White neighborhoods into which displaced African American families moved in the mid 1940s. There, they found a welcoming Jewish community, opportunities to establish businesses, and housing to rent or purchase. One such newcomer was Odis Rencher, an enterprising thirty-four-year-old man who opened his own drug store on Twelfth Street in 1951.[19] At the time, over 50% of the businesses along Twelfth Street were Jewish-owned; they included local staples Greenberg's Restaurant and Zorn's Confectionery.[20] Other Black entrepreneurs followed suit and initiated the area's transition from a primarily Jewish to a mixed-race neighborhood.

Detroit's mainstream media and local real estate agents viewed the integration of the Twelfth Street area and Virginia Park as problematic and they spread rumors about the neighborhood's decline at the hands of its new Black residents. In the initial postwar years, both the Jewish and Black communities publicly disputed these "rumor mongers." In January 1948 the city's primary Black newspaper, the *Michigan Chronicle*, reported on the sentiments of the Jewish Community Council. The Council disputed the rumors and reaffirmed their position in favor of the diversifying neighborhood and admonished the "vicious gossip" that decried the changing character of the Twelfth Street area.[21] They then issued a formal statement about the area's transition, proclaiming that regardless of race, color, creed, or national origin, "the Council stands for more of the wholesome and harmonious relationships which already exist between various groups. We believe in American Democracy."[22]

Unfortunately, the intentions of the Jewish community to live in harmony with their new African American neighbors were fleeting. In the early 1950s, Detroit redoubled its slum clearance efforts with the arrival of federal urban renewal funding. Between 1950 and 1956, slum clearance initiatives displaced residents from over 7,000 dwellings; interstate highway construction would soon erase another 9,000 structures. The Detroit Urban League reported that 85% of the families living in urban renewal zones were non-White. Initially, the city intended to relocate displaced African Americans to extant Black neighborhoods. But the new influx of Great Migration arrivals combined with the large numbers of displaced residents exceeded the capacity of segregated neighborhoods. Instead, by the mid-1950s, Black residents from the lower east side began to relocate to previously White-only neighborhoods across the city.[23]

Within the space of a decade, the once comfortably middle-class, multiethnic Virginia Park neighborhood and the Twelfth Street commercial corridor transformed into an overcrowded, distressed community. The Jewish and middle-class Black residents who could afford to leave Detroit relocated by the tens of thousands to the suburbs.[24] Those who remained lived in congested and unpleasant conditions. Twelfth Street transformed into a dangerous, crime-infested strip, where the few remaining grocers and merchants were outnumbered by twenty-two bars, fifteen liquor stores and pawn shops, and a bustling prostitution scene.

On the eve of the 1967 uprising, Virginia Park housed 21,000 people per square mile. This figure, double the city's average population density, translated to a congested community of 145,000 people living within a 6.5 square mile area. Compounding the discomforts of the neighborhood, 43% of the area's occupied housing units were either deficient or so blighted that they required demolition.[25] The disorderly conditions along Twelfth Street and the surrounding neighborhood attracted unwelcome, and at times, undeserved police attention. Three months after the uprising Philip Meyer, the Detroit Urban League, and the *Detroit Free Press* coordinated a survey of local residents. They asked Virginia Park residents to identify the underlying stresses that they felt were contributing factors of the unrest. The top five factors, in their opinion, were (1) police brutality, (2) poor housing, (3) poverty, (4) lack of jobs, and (5) overcrowded living conditions.[26] The raid on the blind pig in the Economy Printing building sparked a rebellion against the city's decades-long unfair treatment of its marginalized residents. The story of Gordon Park is rooted in these urban renewal transformations that turned an interracial neighborhood into an overcrowded, low-income Black community beset by police harassment.

THE RUINS OF TWELFTH STREET

In the aftermath of the uprising few wanted to live or work among the ruins of the burned and vandalized shops along Twelfth Street, physical reminders of the city's injustices. None of the businesses destroyed by arson or looting reopened in the proximity of Twelfth and Clairmount in the uprising's aftermath. With the commercial center gone, local residents gravitated to new areas that offered better resources, services, and safety.

After the unrest, the Economy Printing building remained standing for at least three years. In 1970 reporter David Smothers described the building and its surroundings. The "building where it all began" is "a gray two-story flat jutting like a visible toothache from the expanse of rubble on the corner of 12th Street and Clairmount."[27] City officials were unmotivated to address the issues of blight and decay by demolishing empty buildings in the neighborhood. As far as they were concerned, the gutted area was quiet, less problematic, and therefore a low priority for expending city funds. An epidemic of vacancy and ruination soon took hold of Virginia Park.

The first efforts to improve Virginia Park in the wake of the uprising arrived with the 1974 election of the city's first Black mayor, Coleman Young. Mayor Young arrived in Detroit from Alabama as a child and lived in Black Bottom, where he encountered firsthand the overcrowding and impoverished conditions that disenfranchised the city's African American population. One of his major campaign pledges promised to address the injustices of urban renewal. His platform resonated with local voters. In 1974 he received 92% of the Black vote, and he then remained in office until 1994.[28] In 1976, two years into his administration and seven years after the uprising, city officials finally turned their attention to the disfigured landscape of Virginia Park. There, they initiated cosmetic changes aimed at both forestalling encroaching blight and establishing goodwill among the remaining residents of the then-majority African American city.

With Mayor Young's support, the Detroit City Council's first change to the area in 1976 was to rename Twelfth Street as Rosa Parks Boulevard. Twelfth Street had acquired a negative association in the wake of the unrest as the origin spot of "the troubles," and the city council thought that renaming the street in recognition of a prominent civil rights icon and Detroit resident would be a respectful nod to the city's African American heritage; it might even help to recast the neighborhood in a positive light.[29] In the same year, the city erected Gordon Park on the site of the demolished Economy Printing building. The few extant records about the park's construction from the Detroit Parks and Recreation Department, newspaper accounts from the time, and oral histories from neighborhood residents offer no evidence that the city constructed the park with input from local residents. None of these records provide direct insight into the planners' motivations for the park's organization. Nevertheless, the park's layout and physical features suggests that decisions were made during the design process to mute, enclose, and abstract the distressed landscape.

When it was completed Gordon Park sat among the ruins of the stagnant Twelfth Street corridor and Virginia Park neighborhood. In 1977, one year into the park's existence, journalist Chris Mead visited (former) Twelfth Street to report on the changes to the area a decade after the uprising. He discovered that, despite its new name, Rosa Parks Boulevard was still a "street of ugly scars, gutted buildings and rubble-strewn vacant lots."[30] The Virginia Park neighborhood had been stifled by a prolonged, unrelenting aftermath of open wounds. In the following years, Detroit city officials struggled to repair the economic, psychological, and physical damage the unrest caused to local communities. By 1981, the city had finally demolished most of the ruined businesses along Rosa Parks Boulevard, widening the street in the process in order to completely erase the landscape of conflict along the thoroughfare, except for Gordon Park.[31]

GORDON PARK

Gordon Park occupies an *L*-shaped, one-acre parcel at the northwest corner of Rosa Parks Boulevard and Clairmount Avenue. Until 2017, the park stood in its original configuration, divided into two sections. Its southern half featured a sunken, brick-paved plaza, enclosed on all four sides by knee-high walls and shaded by over two dozen small trees. Gordon Park's northern section was an open lot. Old playground equipment stood in one corner of the lot, a curved walking path connected the street corner to the plaza along the perimeter, and a basketball court in disrepair occupied the central portion of the parcel. The northern recreational area of the park was separated from the sunken plaza by a six-foot-tall dark brown picket fence. This fence continued around the north and west sides of the plaza, enclosing portions of the park and obstructing views of the homes on the bordering streets of Clairmount and Atkinson.

The archaeological surveys I led between 2014 and 2017 recorded Gordon Park when it was still a scar on the landscape for people who were still actively coping with the aftermath of the 1967 unrest. Our approach to documenting the park's layout and material culture included the conventional tools of landscape and survey archaeology; we did not excavate.[32] We relied instead on standard archaeological recording methods (survey, mapping, illustration, photography, 3D imaging) and other sources of information (architectural elements, portable material culture, archival media, oral histories).

Our archaeological surveys documented how pedestrians enjoyed unfettered access from the sidewalks to the northern recreational area of the park. But entry to the sunken plaza, ground zero of the 1967 conflict, was tightly controlled and constrained by landscaped and architectural elements. The entire plaza was surrounded on all four sides by low concrete retaining walls, encased in dark brown tiles. These retaining walls enclosed five- to six-foot-wide raised beds whose trees and low shrubs created both a buffer zone and visual obstruction between the plaza and the street traffic along the park's perimeter. Only two points of entry granted access into the long, rectangular plaza. Each entry point was a walled, angled brick pathway; the wider of the two pathways extended inward from the southeast corner of the park and the other from the southwest. Next to the wider pathway, anchored into the raised grass bed, stood a green and brown painted sign identifying Gordon Park. It was homemade, fashioned from reclaimed wood. Both entryway paths terminated in front of the park's most prominent feature, an abstract, geometric steel sculpture, vaguely resembling a double helix and towering ten feet above the paved brick surface. No signage provided information about the sculpture, but its placement in the only open-air portion of the plaza suggested its importance.

Regardless of the season or hour of our survey visits, the plaza was always a dark space. This was the fault of the architecture and vegetation. The plaza's dark brown fencing and tiled boundary walls blanketed the perimeter of the park in shadows. Its brick-lined ground surface seemed to swallow up the remaining light. Deep gray concrete furniture, rusted bench bases, tree stumps, piles of dried leaves, and dead plants created a drab, depressed atmosphere year-round. In warmer months, when the two dozen trees within and around the plaza were in bloom, they cast shade over everything in the plaza except the monument.

The city's placement of rows of trees within the plaza, ostensibly to create shade for the patrons who might sit on the furniture underneath them, was incongruent with the plaza's presumed function as a communal space. Three-quarters of the plaza's ground surface was occupied by tree coverage. Our research determined that the park's planners originally organized the trees into four parallel rows, spaced about eight feet apart from one another. The placement of the trees in the center of the plaza served another, more ominous purpose; they restricted movement within the plaza and posed natural deterrents to groups of people who might wish to congregate there. To assert the trees' permanency, and to discourage park visitors from clearing the space, the city installed durable wrought iron braces around the trunks. The braces broadcast the city's determination to enforce order over a once-disorderly space and to ward off vandals. Painted white, the braces were among the brightest objects in the park.

For a public space of its size, Gordon Park's plaza offered few seating options. As part of the original construction of the park in 1976, the city installed two concrete tables, each with a painted chess board on top and surrounded by four concrete chairs. The tables and chairs were cemented into stone slabs on the ground, prohibiting any flexibility in seating arrangements (Figure 5.3). In 2015 and 2017, we documented a thick coating of moss covering the chairs and missing chunks from the tables' corners; these details indicated that the furniture was infrequently used for its intended purpose.

The city also installed six wooden park benches, wide enough to seat two adults, along the perimeter of the plaza. Each bench was nestled in between ground-level garden boxes. These boxes previously housed small trees and seasonal plants, which would have created visual obstructions between people sitting and other park visitors. By 2017, all of the benches had been removed, but their rusted metal bases remained in place. In its original configuration, the plaza never offered seating to accommodate more than four people in one area. Instead, the few visitors we observed in the park sat on the retaining walls. But by 2017, these walls were so poorly maintained that many of their covering tiles had fallen off, exposing crumbling concrete bases underneath.

The extent to which the park was designed as an unwelcoming space is evident by the infrequency with which it was used by local residents. Aside from occasional preplanned neighborhood events, during the course of over a dozen visits to the park on various times and days of the week, we never witnessed more than two people using the space in the plaza or playground. Most of the visitors we observed took refuge in the park's shade while waiting for public transport to arrive at the adjacent Clairmount Avenue bus stop.

The physical elements of Gordon Park that we documented during our archaeological surveys convey the city's continued unwillingness, over the preceding fifty-one years, to grant local residents the freedom to maintain it as a place for community gatherings or to install features that connected with the site's historical significance. The walls, fixed furniture, and disruptive vegetation communicated a continued civic distrust for and anxiety about the residents who visited the park. Its decrepit and inhospitable furnishings made material the city's hesitancy to recognize, and commemorate, the park's location as a site associated with histories of activism and the civil rights era. The creation of Gordon Park may have been intended to bandage a wounded neighborhood, but, initially, it did more to materialize the paranoia and mistrust of African American residents and activist groups than to strengthen the local community.

GRASSROOTS MAINTENANCE AND MEMORY

By 1990 the city ran out of funding to maintain the park, and the space fell to local volunteers to clean and improve. During this period of civic

Figure 5.3. Gordon Park plaza included immovable concrete chairs and chess tables, iron braces around the trees, and homemade wooden benches and planter boxes, 2017. (Krysta Ryzewski)

abandonment, the site became home to grassroots activism once again, attracting occasional community cleanups led by some of the city's most prominent social justice advocates, including late activist Grace Lee Boggs. In a 2010 commentary for the *Michigan Citizen*, Boggs reported how one volunteer likened pulling weeds and building a bench at Gordon Park to a metaphor for Detroit. "If we want to see something different," the volunteer said, "we have to do it ourselves."[33] And so, from the 1990s onward,

Detroiters gradually reclaimed the surfaces of Gordon Park through their own initiatives. Local residents volunteered to install new benches with attached planters around the perimeter of the plaza (they survived into 2017). The fences surrounding the plaza became a canvas for hopeful, forward-thinking artwork, still present during our archaeological survey. Volunteers infused the park with color, first by adding plants, then by periodically redecorating the sculpture at the plaza's entry, and later by painting murals on the wooden fence that ran along the northern and western perimeter of the sunken plaza. In 2017, we recorded twenty-one colorful butterflies adorning the side of the fence facing the plaza (Figure 5.4). Each butterfly included an uplifting message, such as "follow your dream" or "smile." In between the butterflies, along the length of the fence, ran a bright-blue-painted cloud. The vibrant colors injected a burst of life into the otherwise dull, forlorn park. On the side of the fence facing the playground, a local artist painted a large peace sign and a mural of Detroit's downtown skyline. The messaging in these interventions was clear—Gordon Park, and the residents of the area, deserved recognition and respect.

The approaching fiftieth anniversary of the 1967 unrest gradually stimulated public interest in and collective memories about the park site's significance. Grassroots and formal neighborhood groups began to take the first steps toward memorializing the park's connections to the uprising. In the years leading up to the anniversary, people started to search for meaning in the park's layout, sculpture, and namesake. As the process of recollection would reveal, if there was ever any special meaning and intentionality behind these material elements, it had long been forgotten, or at least diluted by a combination of civic erasure, intentional discarding, and humiliation.[34] Unlike the Blue Bird Inn or the Grande Ballroom (see chapters 4 and 6), Gordon Park was not a place attached to fond, nostalgic memories. Generations of neglect, the lack of community consultation during the city's design of the park, and the absence of any sort of posted information about the site's historical significance forced twenty-first-century Gordon Park entirely out of context. The site was left open to interpretation.

Many visitors and city officials simply admitted ignorance about the park's history. "There's nobody walking around in that neighborhood who knows why it's named Gordon Park," bemoaned Andrea Gallucci, archivist for the city of Detroit and an expert on local park history. Some residents speculated about the plaza's function, suggesting that it was originally built as a place of reflection, or a memorial square (it was not).[35] Others assumed that the park was named after Gordon Parks, a prominent African American photojournalist. But no such connections to Black history

Figure 5.4. Archaeologists survey the boundary fences and butterfly artwork attached to them in 2017. Note the condition of the retaining walls on which the fence stands, and the blighted landscape along Clairmount in the background. (Krysta Ryzewski)

were intended by the park's creators. Instead, an obscure footnote confirms that the park was named for a different man, Thomas Gordon, a native of Greensburg, Pennsylvania.[36] Gordon was an intelligence officer during World War II and was killed in action near Corsica. His sole connection to Detroit was that he departed from the city for his tour of duty. Nevertheless, among the absence of information, as time passed, elements of the park and its history gained associations with cultural and historical connections that probably should have been but were decidedly not part of its original design.

REIMAGINING A MONUMENT: JACK WARD'S SCULPTURE

Poignant processes of forgetting and reimagining converge at the plaza's monumental sculpture, the most prominent feature of the park. Over the past three decades, the sculpture's significance has become contested as the public monument assumed center stage in community-led discussions about the park's potential as a place of commemoration. Until the 1990s, the black, fabricated steel sculpture stood mute and unaltered at the entrance to the plaza. As one local resident observed, "There's no history to it, it's of no significance, really."[37] A signature at the sculpture's base identifies its creator as Jack A. Ward, but no other signage has ever existed to provide additional information about the installation's name or purpose. This absence was intentional.

Ward's sculpture is an artifact of the city's efforts to construct Gordon Park as a neutralizing space. In 1976 the Detroit Parks and Recreation Department hosted an open competition in which they invited artists to submit designs for a monumental installation in a plaza. At the time Detroit was home to a burgeoning public art scene that emerged in the wake of the uprising. It involved a proliferation of murals and sculptures designed by Black artists, depicting scenes of Black history and leadership. According to journalist Jeff Hoebner, Detroit became a leader in the United States' community mural movement when Chicago-based artists William "Bill" Walker and Eugene "Eda" Wade came to the city to design Black Power murals in collaboration with local churches and community organizations. Their plan was to install the murals in neighborhoods that had been devastated by the uprising.[38] In 1968, in partnership with eight Detroit artists from the Contemporary Studio Group, Walker and Wade led the design of the *Wall of Pride*. The mural was painted on the facade of Grace Episcopal Church on Twelfth Street, a half mile south of Gordon Park. It covered a triangular portion of the church annex's wall beneath its roofline. Each contributing artist created different scenes for the *Wall of Pride*. One segment depicted W. E. B. Du Bois surrounded by contemporary leaders of African countries. Other sections featured luminaries of the creative arts, literature, and sports worlds: Aretha Franklin, Amiri Bakara, James Baldwin, and Muhammad Ali. Political figures Malcolm X, H. Rap Brown, and Martin Luther King Jr. and Black Power symbolism amplified the mural's themes of hope, leadership, and empowerment. The prominent location of the mural along Twelfth Street was a source of both community pride and contention. Some Detroiters, including members of the Grace Episcopal Church, thought that the religious politics and civil rights agendas promoted by certain figures in the mural were incongruent with their positions. A few years after its creation, in the mid-1970s, church leaders decided that the best way to deal with the uncomfortable debates the mural stimulated was to paint over it. By the time the city announced the challenge for the Gordon Park sculpture, the *Wall of Pride* was gone.

City officials selected Jack Ward's sculpture as the winning entry in the Gordon Park monument competition. His abstract, geometric design won because it was bold enough to draw attention to the space but esoteric enough to avert the sort of discord that the Black Power murals had generated in recent years.[39] In other words, the selection of Ward's sculpture symbolized an ironclad commitment by the city to retreat from the park's controversial roots.

When Ward entered the contest, the city did not provide him with information about the park where the artwork would be installed, and so he created the sculpture's design without a setting in mind. He called his abstract, untethered creation *Untitled*. He also created a smaller duplicate that still stands on the campus of Wayne State University.[40] While the sculpture on Wayne State's campus still retains the *Untitled* name, its counterpart at Gordon Park does not. Later in the 1970s and 1980s Ward began to refer to Gordon Park's sculpture as *Energy Column*. With the passage of time, the park's sculpture accrued new layers of significance. In the 1990s, after Ward learned of the park's association with the 1967 unrest, he renamed it *Detroit 1967*.[41] And so, a sculpture that was created without reference to a particular place or historical event gradually became a monument symbolizing the power of the uprising. Its evolving significance was an accumulative process of place-based associations and renaming, facilitated by resurfaced memories and the long-term coping processes of recovery.

The monument's revised status as a symbol of the uprising coincided with a new phase of community maintenance at the park after 1990. In addition to pulling weeds and planting flowers, local residents also began to alter the sculpture, decorating it without the permission of the city or Jack Ward. They repainted the sculpture multiple times. It was purple, red, half purple/half red, white, black, and sometimes also decorated with stick-on mirrors and sequins. Ward's installation became a participatory, public canvas (Figure 5.5).

There exist no formal accounts of who altered the sculpture or why, but during the decades-long process of occasional modifications, it attracted the international attention of artists Aeron Bergman and Alejandra Salinas, who photo-documented the changes to it between 2007 and 2015. As part of their resulting exhibition, *Monument to Rebellion*, displayed at the Bergen Assembly Triennial in Norway and Kunsthalle Exnergasse in Vienna, they included conflicting accounts of the sculpture's meaning and origins. Bergman and Salinas also documented how Ward's attitude toward the monument evolved over time.[42] "People can create their own significance," Ward commented to the artists when asked about changing the sculpture's name.[43]

Indeed, by the time that Bergman and Salinas completed *Monument to Rebellion* in 2015, the sculpture had accumulated such a mythological status as a symbol of local resistance and empowerment that some Detroiters

Figure 5.5. Changes to Jack Ward's monument since 2010. During the time of the archaeological surveys, between 2014 and 2017, the monument was white. It was returned to its original flat black surface during the park's 2017 renovations. (*Left*, courtesy of Kevin Mueller, 2010; *middle and right*, Krysta Ryzewski)

ardently refused any suggestion that it was originally created without connection to the uprising site's history. One well-known local journalist interviewed by Bergman and Salinas insisted, "It is common knowledge here [in Detroit] that Jack Ward's sculpture was commissioned for the 1967 rebellion—if in an indirect way. Because that park was made INTO a park in the first place because that's where the riots started."[44] Her sentiments were certainly grounded in her knowledge of the place-based history of the uprising—and recognition of the events at Twelfth Street and Clairmount—but they also privileged a community's aspirations to commemorate the conflict in ways that disregarded the actual circumstances of the park's original construction. The sculpture, which originated as one of the city's "aesthetic cover-ups" in the wake of the uprising, evolved simultaneously into a hotly contested object of history, or a history-less object, depending on who one asked.[45] In the process of its reinterpretation, discussions about the monument pointed out significant gaps in the memories of Gordon Park's history.[46] These memory gaps and related points of tension inspired our archaeological survey. More importantly, they also initiated separate grassroots and community-based movements that would eventually mobilize Gordon Park as a site whose revitalized components addressed and filled in the memories of the 1967 uprising.

WHY EXCAVATE?

The week after the conclusion of our April 2017 survey, the city suddenly erected a fence around Gordon Park and hung a sign announcing its plans to refurbish the park in time for the fiftieth anniversary of the uprising that July. Mayor Mike Duggan's announcement in the local media about the park's improvements came as a surprise to us and to members of the various historic preservation-based entities in the city. His administration's motivations may have been well-timed with the fiftieth anniversary, but they were not completely unselfish; it was an election year, after all. In his bid for reelection Duggan was eager to draw attention to how his administration contributed to improving neighborhoods outside of the hotspot revitalization areas in Downtown and Midtown. As in 1976 when Gordon Park was built, city officials in 2017 saw the creation and renovation of public parks as a quick-fix strategy to improving neglected landscapes and boosting morale in depressed neighborhoods. The city's improvements to Gordon Park were not designed with the specifics of the site's uprising-related history in mind; the upgrade included the same furnishings as all of the other city parks involved in Duggan's 40 Neighborhood Parks program, an initiative he launched to improve the landscaping, play equipment, walking paths, and seating in parks citywide.[47] Ten weeks after the city erected fences around the old space, Mayor Duggan reopened a completely updated Gordon Park.

After the city announced its plans for the park's renovations, I was in conversation with the Detroit Parks and Recreation staff about the possibility of conducting an archaeological excavation at the site before the new concrete surface was installed in the plaza. The bulldozers were not going to be digging much below the surface, so any archaeological excavations would not have been a rescue or salvage operation. Instead, they would have been an opportunity to recover physical traces of the buildings that stood at the site prior to 1967. Based on the materials and processes used to construct the park in 1976, and the visibility of structural debris in the adjoining vacant lots, I was confident that if we dug beneath the brick surface of the park we would find charred remnants of the buildings that stood at the uprising's flashpoint. I wondered what purposes our excavation of tangible remains related to the uprising might serve, and more so, how they might impact people who were still healing from its aftermath. As archaeologist Gabriel Moshenska's research on sites of recent conflict demonstrates, archaeological work at places associated with contested and violent histories has the potential to generate adverse effects for the people who have been traumatized by such events.[48]

The excavated remains of burned buildings underneath Gordon Park would have certainly elicited considerable public attention and strong reactions, ranging from curiosity to sadness and anger. These sentiments are not uncommon at sites of contested or dark heritage. If we had decided to excavate at Gordon Park, I would have anticipated and welcomed such strong reactions as part of a wider occasion to discuss legacies of racism and conflict in the city. But as archaeologist Sara Gonzalez and colleagues have stressed in their collaborative research on the Grande Ronde Land Tenure Project in Oregon, it is important to ask whether it is appropriate to use archaeology to study a particular place, especially in considering how resulting archaeological finds might strengthen or weaken connections with the needs of communities associated with it.[49] Ultimately, I decided to end conversations about excavating at the Gordon Park. I felt strongly that it was not appropriate to excavate the site at that point in time. In the spring of 2017 Gordon Park was situated within a struggling neighborhood still beset by widespread blight and poverty. The very first signs of home reoccupation and renovation were beginning across the street from Gordon Park; real estate investors identified the area as a target for growth and investment in the coming decade. The community was finally ready to address the events of 1967 in Gordon Park's design with the erection of commemorative signage. There was no immediate need, in my opinion, for us to see or touch the ashes of the uprising to better understand the effects of a decades-long posttraumatic recovery process or to revisit the city's active sidelining of social justice heritage in the name of redevelopment.

A NEW BEGINNING FOR GORDON PARK

On July 23, 2017, the day of the fiftieth anniversary of the uprising's start, Mayor Duggan proclaimed a new beginning for Gordon Park (Figure 5.6).[50] Within three short months the city completely transformed the park into a bright, accommodating public space. In his speech during the park's ribbon-cutting ceremony, Duggan recalled the former park: "It was OK the way it was . . . but it wasn't the kind of quality park, that as far as I was concerned, said to our children, you are valued, you're important, you deserve the best."[51] The findings from our archaeological surveys were more definitive in their assessment of the park's vitality: the park was definitely *not* "OK the way it was." The resulting news media coverage of the reopening event credited the city with revitalizing the space, paying less attention to the underlying community-based contributions to the improvements.

In fact, the park's redesign was partially a response to local grassroots groups who, for years, campaigned the city to recognize the site's history.

Figure 5.6. The renovated Gordon Park plaza, June 2020. The retaining walls were leveled, bench seating installed around the park's perimeter, braces removed from tree trunks, new signage installed, and trash cans placed at the entry paths to prevent vehicular traffic. (Krysta Ryzewski)

During the uprising's fiftieth anniversary year, members of the local community group Brothers Always Together and the Virginia Park Neighborhood Association worked with one another on plans to redesign and reorient the park as a commemorative space.[52] Their efforts were supported by the Detroit Historical Society and amplified by the organization of a major exhibit and oral history project, *Detroit '67: Looking Back to Move Forward*, at the Detroit Historical Museum.[53]

The fast-moving renovation of the park included limited consultations among the city, local community groups, and heritage organizations about the park's physical space. Ultimately, the city led the design of the park's infrastructure. In the playground area in the northern half of the park they installed a new picnic shelter, swing set, and an odd assortment of elliptical machines and other exercise equipment (cemented to the ground). City park designers removed the fencing that divided the plaza from the playground and enclosed the north and west edges of the park. Their efforts to open up the space and integrate it within the surrounding residential landscape erased the personal, community touches that previously adorned Gordon Park—the painted butterflies as well as the murals of Detroit's skyline and a peace sign. In the end, the northern half of the park was reinvigorated, but with the same indistinct, generic furniture and landscaping as the other renovated city parks in the citywide 40 Neighborhood Parks program.

In the southern half of Gordon Park, the city transformed the plaza on the site of the Economy Printing building into a more welcoming, community-centered gathering space. First, the city raised the surface of the plaza to an elevation equal with the sidewalks, eliminating its sunken effect by removing the retaining walls between it and Rosa Parks Boulevard and leveling the grass along the plaza's perimeter. Then they brightened the sidewalks and resurfaced the crumbling retaining walls with light gray concrete. They also installed ample communal seating, adding wooden benches that wrapped, uninterrupted, around two sides of the plaza. New chairs and tables with chess boards, made of a light-colored wood, replaced the immovable, concrete predecessors. At the entryway a new, standardized city sign identified the park's namesake, Thomas Gordon.

In the center of the plaza the city kept the rows of trees, but they removed the iron braces from their trunks. At the urging of local community groups, designers added a raised wooden stage with a roof among the trees in the middle of the plaza to accommodate local events. Finally, they stripped the layers of white, red, and purple paint from Jack Ward's sculpture and restored the steel artwork to its original flat black surface. The new Gordon Park is a bright, welcoming, accessible, and fluid space that conveys a mutual respect for local residents and acknowledges the park's heritage.

The most significant change to Gordon Park during its rehabilitation was the installation of signage connecting the site to the 1967 uprising. As a result of advocacy by local community groups in partnership with the Detroit Historical Society and the Michigan Historical Designation Board, Gordon Park received an official state historical marker.[54] The tall green sign stands at the approximate location of the Economy Printing shop, near the plaza's midpoint. It reads:

Detroit July 1967

In July 1967 the civil unrest that had been spreading across the United States reached Detroit. In the early morning hours of July 23, Detroit police officers raided a blind pig, an illegal after-hours bar, where patrons were celebrating the return of Vietnam War servicemen.

Located at Clairmount Avenue and Twelfth Street (later Rosa Parks Boulevard), the bar was within a mostly African-American business district that had an active nightlife. While the police arrested all eighty-five people inside, a crowd formed outside. Reacting to the arrests, a few people threw rocks and bottles at the police. By eight a.m., the crowd had grown to an estimated 3,000 people, and arson and looting were underway.

Mayor Jerome Cavanagh and Governor George Romney agreed to deploy the Michigan National Guard that afternoon. Federal Army troops joined the guard two days later.

Detroit's civil unrest on Twelfth Street continued for four days until July 27, 1967. More than 1,600 buildings were destroyed after fires spread from the business district to nearby residences.

Property damage was estimated to be $132 million. Around 7,200 people were arrested, hundreds were injured and forty-three people died, including bystanders, looters, a fireman and a National Guardsman.

In response to the conflicts in Detroit and throughout the country, President Lyndon B. Johnson created the Kerner Commission to investigate the causes of the violence.

It concluded that although the specific episodes of violence were spontaneous, they were in response to poverty, segregation, racism, unemployment, "frustrations of powerlessness" and police actions that enforced a double standard for how people of different races were treated.

The historical marker uses the term "civil unrest" to describe the events of 1967. Bob Bury, executive director of the Detroit Historical Society and contributing author of the marker's text, said that the writers carefully crafted the text and intentionally omitted the words "riot," "rebellion," and "uprising" because they remain contested terms used differentially according to age, race, and geography.[55] On the new state historical marker, Gordon Park is positioned as an active site of social justice rather than a place of continued tension, or an ahistorical void on the landscape. The marker's authors chose to articulate the memories of conflict in ways that *Detroit '67* director Marlowe Stoudamire suggested would "not move past what happened, but move the conversation forward."[56] And so, the new Gordon Park not only affords people a welcoming place for reflection and recreation, but it also encourages people to gather and remember the significance of the site's history. As Lamont Causey, president of Brothers Always Together, proclaimed at the park's 2017 reopening ceremony, the new space is more than a park. Like the Blue Bird Inn or Grande Ballroom once were, it is a venue, an anchor for the community, a place designed for experiences, and a site that facilitates connecting and healing.[57] Nowadays Causey and his fellow Virginia Park residents host regular community events at Gordon Park, including a neighborhood oral history project and fundraisers to assist local families.

The inclusion of the marker in the rennovated plaza represents initial steps by the city to recognize Gordon Park's historical significance and to support place-based commemorations of the 1967 uprising. Despite the involvement of local residents in the creation of its text, the marker was part of the formal statewide, government-sanctioned Michigan Historical Marker Program. Its descriptive and impersonal language ultimately exemplifies a commemorative action undertaken within an official, state-led framework.

Beyond the confines of Gordon Park two other prominent and contrasting tributes emerged nearby to commemorate the fiftieth anniversary of the uprising. A week after the renovated park's opening ceremony, renowned Detroit artist Hubert Massey announced his plans to hang a 240-by-360-foot canvas mural on the side of an unoccupied house on the southeast corner of Atkinson and Rosa Parks, directly across the street from Gordon Park (Figure 5.7).

Figure 5.7. *Evolution: Rising Strong*, a mural created by Hubert Massey in 2017, hangs on a canvas banner on the wall of an unoccupied house across from Gordon Park, on the southeast corner of Rosa Parks Boulevard and Atkinson, 2020. (Krysta Ryzewski)

Massey's mural, titled *Evolution: Rising Strong*, forms a vibrant backdrop to the new park. Following in the city's half-century-long tradition of public art and community murals, Massey selected its imagery with, in his words, the intention of stimulating "discussion of important historical benchmarks and memories that enable the community to immerse itself in Detroit pride, while also setting the cultural record straight."[58] In the center of the mural are a cluster of black-and-white signs associated with prominent places involved in the 1967 uprising, including the Economy Printing building and the Algiers Motel. These remnants of a landscape lost to conflict are flanked by unifying scenes of contemporary Detroit whose elements represent a local heritage shaped by mobility, creativity, and industry.

Another memorial stands a half mile south of Gordon Park on Rosa Parks Boulevard at the Joseph Walker Williams Community Center, a popular recreational venue and community space for Virginia Park residents. In 2017 a group of local artists and organizations led a community-based effort to commemorate the uprising on its grounds. Funding from the Community and Public Arts Detroit (CPAD) program at the College for Creative Studies supported the Oakland Avenue Artists Coalition (a grassroots community organization that uses public art to transform and reclaim the North End), and several other partners, in their creation of a monument, pavilion, and mural.[59] When the resulting *12th Street 1967 Memorial* was unveiled in July 2017 it received considerably less media attention than Mayor Duggan's launch of Gordon Park, but it was no less important to the local community (Figure 5.8).

The *12th Street 1967 Memorial* includes a five-by-seven-foot steel marker listing the names of the forty-three people who lost their lives during the uprising. Three flagstones at the base of the marker note the distance between the memorial and particularly significant sites of violence. A small wooden pavilion stands to the left of the marker. Its back wall and roof panels display images that connect the area's legacy of activism with depictions of community and symbols of hope. Although there are some overlapping elements of commemoration between the city-led revitalization at Gordon Park and the artist- and community-led tribute at the Williams Community Center, there are also notable differences in the degrees to which the individuals and suffering associated with the uprising are acknowledged and recognized at each site.

HISTORICAL ARCHAEOLOGY AND SOCIAL JUSTICE LEGACIES

At times over the past fifty years, Gordon Park appeared dormant and lifeless. As a consequence of its inhospitable design and its blighted location people disengaged from the space, forgetting about the origins of the park's namesake, the significance of its sculpture, and even the connections between the site and the 1967 unrest. The archaeological survey results and civic initiatives in the years leading up to the 2017 anniversary of the uprising demonstrated, through attention to its material remains and interactions with its space, how the park was never truly unused or abandoned. Despite the lack of civic upkeep and recognition of the site's significance, Gordon Park remained anchored to its history of grassroots activism. In this case historical archaeology provided a means to reveal the long-standing connections between Gordon Park and its social justice legacies.

Gordon Park took fifty-one years to mature partly because of the city's inaction and its continual repression of memories associated with Detroit's past conflicts and injustices. Jack Ward's abstract sculpture is an artifact of the city's desire to edit certain spaces and the memories associated with them. The slow emergence of Gordon Park as a commemorative space is also partly due to the fact that residents chose to distance

Figure 5.8. The *12th Street 1967 Memorial*, created in 2017 by the Oakland Avenue Artists Coalition and their community partners, stands outside of the Joseph Walker Williams Community Center on Rosa Parks Boulevard, a half mile south of Gordon Park, 2020. (Krysta Ryzewski)

themselves from using and maintaining the park, perhaps as a mechanism for coping with the intergenerational trauma tied to the losses of 1967 and its aftermath. While it is commendable that the city is now working with community stakeholders and heritage professionals to recognize places associated with its painful heritage, it is noteworthy that officials have made no public efforts to reconcile or reflect on the historic roles that their short-sighted land management practices have had on minority and low-income communities over the course of the past century. As the archaeological perspective and survey results in this chapter illustrate, Gordon Park's existence over the past six decades, and the transformations to Virginia Park, were direct consequences of the city's urban renewal practices and civic management decisions.

This case study, focused on one of the city's most noteworthy twentieth-century heritage sites, is the outcome of archaeological analysis and therefore differs in its scope from the perspectives on Gordon Park that a historian or urban studies scholar might offer. It began from the starting point of the park's physical remains, employed a long-term perspective, and wove together strands of material culture, land use, historic, and ethnographic (personal) evidence to tell a story of neglect followed by accounts of community-based interventions, and commemoration. In the archaeological story of Gordon Park processes of commemoration and countermonumentality are in action. They are visible in the physical and intangible acts of remembrance tied to the park—anniversary celebrations, performances, murals, oral history events—and in their increase over time, especially from the 1990s to the present. Current revitalization efforts aim to create a more inclusive park space without muting conversations about the legacy of racism and conflict in the city's past and present. The new physical elements of the park, its signage, furniture, layout, and stage, mediate these aims and install hope that the park's future will occupy the unified vision of Detroit promoted by activist Grace Lee Boggs, who dreamed of a city that provided residents the opportunity to live with and learn from people of many different backgrounds.[60]

CHAPTER SIX

Grande Ballroom
*Counterculture Archaeology and Grassroots
Preservation*

On Sunday night, January 19, 1969, a new British band called Led Zeppelin took the stage at the Grande Ballroom. It was the last night of their three-show gig at Detroit's hippest live music venue. Over the weekend word had spread across the city and suburbs about the band's must-see theatrical performances of blues-infused hard rock. That Sunday the ballroom filled to capacity with an audience of 1,500 teenagers and young adults. Detroit's most famous local rock musicians, the MC5 and the Amboy Dukes, were in the crowd. Everyone came ready to enjoy a thrilling concert.

With the stage hovering just three and a half feet above the wooden dance floor, there was no buffer between the band and the audience. Jaan Uhelszki, a Grande soda pop server, propped her elbows on the band's amplifier; other fans sat along the perimeter of the stage, within an arm's reach of the musicians.[1] Led Zeppelin's lead guitarist, Jimmy Page, formerly of the Yardbirds, arrived onstage in an "exquisite red satin suit," and the band opened with "Train Kept a Rollin'." The hype was short-lived. When the first song ended, an unimpressed crowd barely reacted. The next few songs bombed too. Some fans remained seated cross-legged on the dance floor, others stood motionless, lounging against the surrounding promenade's railings. For the ticket price of $3.50, the band delivered a lackluster, uncoordinated performance; the only notable moment was when Jimmy Page played his guitar with a bow, producing a weird but controlled sound that fans described as "mind-bending." Led Zeppelin failed to meet expectations that night because they underestimated the Detroit crowd's discriminating tastes. The young audience members were electronic music connoisseurs, accustomed to more polished, progressive, and edgy performances at the Grande. In a review of the show, Pat Brent, reporter for the music magazine *Creem*, suggested that if Led Zeppelin would just "get it together" they "might become a major force on the rock scene."[2]

THE COUNTERCULTURE-ERA GRANDE BALLROOM

Between 1966 and 1972 the Grande Ballroom was the epicenter of

Detroit's counterculture scene, a hub for innovative performances and radical activism. The baby boomer generation revered the Grande (pronounced "grand-/ē/") as a haven for promoting up-and-coming musicians, creative expression, and social justice agendas. Young people from all walks of life mingled there—urban and suburban, Black and White. On weekend nights they enjoyed psychedelic light shows choreographed to a variety of music: rock, blues, folk, and proto-punk. They also interacted with local activist groups who were, at the time, as essential to the Grande's success as the music.[3]

The Grande Ballroom is most fondly remembered today for the reputation it garnered during this short six-year period of its history. In the late 1960s the Grande rose to prominence as a venue that supported local musical talents, like the MC5 or Iggy and the Psychedelic Stooges, alongside (soon-to-be) legendary, world-famous bands, including The Who, Jethro Tull, Pink Floyd, Cream, Jefferson Airplane, Fleetwood Mac, Van Morrison, Sun Ra, Creedence Clearwater Revival, The Byrds, Howlin' Wolf, the Jeff Beck Group, and the Grateful Dead, among many others (Figure 6.1).

The Grande's manager, "Uncle" Russ Gibb, reopened the ballroom as a rock music venue in October 1966 and quickly established its reputation as a center for social justice advocacy and antiauthoritarian activism. Nine months later the July 1967 uprising ravaged the surrounding Petosky-Otsego neighborhood (see chapter 5). Proof that the Grande was already a well-respected champion of change was evident in the fact that it was left completely unscathed by those who ransacked and burned adjacent businesses.[4] Detroiters viewed the Grande as a welcoming place for people who rejected the status quo and "who were frustrated and angry with social, racial, and political events occurring at that time."[5] After the uprising these sentiments inspired the organization of Trans-Love Energies (TLE), the White Panther Party, and the *Fifth Estate* (a local anarchist, anticapitalist newspaper). All of these outlets used the Grande Ballroom to disseminate their messages and recruit supporters.[6]

The atmosphere of the counterculture-era Grande—distinguished by long-haired hippies, loud electric guitars, antiestablishment protestors, Hare Krishnas, and clouds of marijuana smoke—was a far cry from the elegant Moorish art deco ballroom that speakeasy owner and Purple Gang affiliate Harry Weitzman envisioned when he commissioned the building's construction in 1927 (see chapter 2). Weitzman designed the Grande Ballroom as a live music venue for well-heeled, clean-cut Detroiters. In its initial years of operation, the Grande often hosted special events for society groups and religious organizations. Swing musicians Hank

Figure 6.1. British rock band the Jeff Beck Group performs at the Grande Ballroom in 1968. The aluminum foil covering the proscenium arch and the circular light fixture overhanging it were installed to augment the Grande's multisensory psychedelic experience. (Courtesy of Michael Bolan)

Fomish and His Orchestra (1931) and singers Grace Baruth and Margaret Maischein (1933) entertained dances for groups like the Guardian Junior Bankers' Club, the Detroit Chiropractic Society, and Kroger Grocery, as well as local Catholic parishes, Jewish community groups, and universities.[7] It is impossible to predict how Weitzman, who died in 1942, might have reacted to "Uncle" Russ Gibb's conversion of his big band–era, high-society ballroom into an emporium of electrified music, light shows, and rebellious youths. Although Weitzman and the baby boomers identified with radically different manifestations of the Grande Ballroom, they may have shared similar nostalgic sentiments of shock and dismay about the Grande's eventual fate.

Today the Grande Ballroom is unoccupied (Figure 6.2). It sits in a state of decay and disrepair, much as it has since the venue's last show in 1972. Gaping holes puncture the building's roof. All of the windows are missing. The once-elegant maple dance floor is buckled and rotten from exposure to the weather. Vandals have removed the ballroom's distinctive ornamental architectural fixtures. As of 2020 the Grande has existed in this state of decay for forty-eight years; that is four years longer than its run as an entertainment venue between 1928 and 1972.

As a place tied to a still-living population's firsthand memories, the Grande Ballroom receives considerably more attention in the media and in preservation conversations than any of the other heritage sites discussed in this book. A vocal contingency of grassroots preservationists, including nostalgic patrons of the 1960s and 1970s, mourn the state of dereliction into which the Grande has fallen over the past five decades. Under the leadership of the nonprofit Friends of the Grande Ballroom, a dedicated group of former concertgoers and music history buffs have been working over the past two decades to restore and reinvigorate the ballroom. Their efforts, which include various place-based and regional commemorative activities, are firmly tied to the Grande that they experienced. The productive preservation campaigns they spearhead celebrate both the creative and political accomplishments of counterculture-era performers and patrons. As the following discussion reveals, although these efforts are well-intentioned, they are not immune to resistance.

One consequence of the prevailing contemporary focus on the Grande Ballroom's period of living memory is that the building's long-term history is underrecognized. This chapter presents the outcomes of the Grande Ballroom Archaeological Survey, a collaborative project that involved applying historical archaeological methods to understanding the ballroom's multifaceted history through its material remains. Our approach treated the Grande Ballroom as an archaeological site. We conceived of the ballroom as both a formerly active commercial and performance space *and* as an unoccupied, neglected building. These periods of activity before and after 1972 represent two distinct phases in the Grande's archaeological record, but they are part of the same story.

In this chapter I combine archaeological, historical, and oral history sources to portray the Grande Ballroom as a space of evolving twentieth-century popular music, a venue of social inclusion and exclusion, and a site of willful neglect and ruination over the span of its nearly century-long existence. The majority of the discussion relates to the counterculture era and the building's decay post-1972; this bias is a reflection of

Figure 6.2. Grande Ballroom occupied the second floor of this building on the corner of Grand River Avenue and Beverly Court from 1928 to 1972. Photo taken from Grand River Avenue, 2014. (Krysta Ryzewski)

the available historical sources and the extant physical remnants of the Grande. My account differs from other popular histories of the ballroom because it foregrounds material remains and then considers them in relation to their historical and contemporary contexts. By approaching the building in its totality, I illustrate why the Grande of the counterculture era was so meaningful and why its legacy continues to be relevant and celebrated today.

AN ENTERTAINMENT VENUE EVOLVES

The Grande Ballroom occupies the second floor of a two-story building at 8952 Grand River Avenue. Grand River is one of Detroit's main arterial roadways; it extends from the city center to the northwest, forming a boundary between west side neighborhoods. When the ballroom opened in 1928 it joined the Petosky-Otsego neighborhood's thriving commercial strip of retail shops, grocers, butchers, and movie theaters. By automobile (Detroiters' preferred mode of transport), the Grande Ballroom was just a three minute drive (1.2 miles) from the Blue Bird Inn jazz club and five minutes (1.8 miles) from the blind pig above the Economy Printing building, the flashpoint for the 1967 unrest at Twelfth and Clairmount (see chapters 4 and 5). But for the first forty years of its existence the Grande was, culturally, a world away from these contemporaneous entertainment venues. Until the 1960s the neighborhood surrounding the Grande Ballroom was predominately White, middle class, and home to a sizeable Jewish community. Between 1928 and 1962 the Grande showcased the standard big band–era swing music and orchestral jazz that was in line with the mainstream popular radio hits of the time, and the conventional tastes of its White clientele (Figure 6.3).

In 1927, at the same time as he operated the Little Harry speakeasy downtown (chapter 2), Harry Weitzman commissioned distinguished Detroit architect Charles N. Agree to design the Grande Ballroom. Builders from the W. E. Wood Company completed the Grande's construction a year later.[8] The square-shaped, two-story building on the corner of Grand River Avenue and Beverly Court housed retail spaces on the ground floor and the largest dance floor in the Midwest (at the time) upstairs. Its exterior design shared similar aesthetics with the other Spanish Revival–style theaters, ballrooms, and residences Agree designed across the fast-growing city during the 1920s—red terra-cotta roof tiles, tall, arched windows, limestone carvings, yellow buff brick, stucco, and ornamental wrought iron.[9] As he did with the Hollywood Theatre, Vanity Ballroom, Belcrest Apartments, and Whittier Hotel in Detroit, Agree executed a plan

Figure 6.3. Grande Ballroom in the 1940s, during its swing dancing years. (Courtesy of the Burton Historical Collection, Detroit Public Library)

for the Grande Ballroom that, as he stated, prioritized aesthetics, durability, strength, adaptability, and lowest possible cost.[10]

The Grande was intended to be one of the city's premiere entertainment venues. Agree promoted this status by incorporating commanding architectural elements into its exterior design. The most notable features were the grandiose towers that protruded from the building's four corners. Each tower was topped by a triangular, red-tiled roof and flagpole. In-between them, placed at equal intervals around three sides of the building, were five arched window bays; each tower face also had a bay. Augmenting the Spanish Revival roof and tower elements, Agree added carved stone hoods above the windows and wrought iron balconettes below them.[11] Originally, some of the window arches also boasted a limestone tympanum of winged griffins between a crowned shield as well as urn and scroll motifs.[12] Along the south facade of the tower at the corner of Grand River and Beverly Court, the builders mounted a one-story-tall vertical sign. Over the course of the ballroom's occupational history it was illuminated with different titles, including "Ballroom," "Grande," and "Grande Dancing." The sign was removed after 1972, and today only its metal brackets survive, protruding from the second story facade along Grand River. Harry Weitzman added a personal touch to the building's ornamentation by commissioning the architectural firm to insert limestone plaques underneath the corner towers' windows. The plaques bear the letters "CDSW"—the names of his children: Clement, Dorothy, and Seymour (see Figure 6.16). The fact that Weitzman chose to memorialize his family in the building's architecture signals his expectation that the Grande would enjoy a long, distinguished life.[13]

Agree's practice of selecting building materials for their durability and strength is perhaps the major factor contributing to the Grande's physical resilience and survival, especially during the period of its neglect and unoccupancy over the past fifty years. In 1930 Agree authored an informative article in the journal *Theatre Engineering* detailing his process of brick use in construction projects. He reported how in the architecture of the 3,400-seat Hollywood Theatre on West Fort Street, which he designed the same year as the Grande, he carefully selected common brick for its walls. He praised common brick for its strength and bonding capabilities, attractive appearance from weathering over time, long life span, low cost, and—perhaps most importantly—resistance to fire.[14] As detailed later, Agree also selected locally produced common bricks for the Grande's walls.

Patrons accessed the second floor ballroom from an entrance on Beverly Court. After ascending two flights of stairs they arrived in the southeast corner of a wide promenade that encircled three sides of a 5,000-square-foot sunken dance floor (Figure 6.4).[15] To access the main attraction, the "sprung" maple dance floor, guests took two steps down from the *u*-shaped promenade at designated entry points. The ballroom's promoters praised the floor's accommodating bounce in advertisements, leading dancers and some building historians to believe that there were actually metal springs placed underneath the maple planks to add extra buoyancy to dancers' steps (archaeological investigations proved otherwise).

In between a series of archways onlookers lounged in seating along the promenade. Each arch was supported by rectangular pilasters and bordered with cabled columns of molded plaster.[16] Hybrid ram and griffin head corbels topped each column. Waist-high wrought iron gates stood between most of the archways, limiting direct access to the dance floor below (Figure 6.5). On the north side of the dance floor still stands a wooden stage. Almost two-thirds of the stage is enclosed by a proscenium arch, originally painted and stenciled with ornate red, blue, and gold floral designs. The portion of the stage underneath the proscenium arch is twenty-four feet wide; a three-foot section that extends beyond the arch out toward the dance floor is four feet wider. Flanking the sides of the stage were small lounge rooms, restrooms, and utility closets.

Figure 6.4. Archways separated the dance floor (*foreground*) from the promenade. (Krysta Ryzewski)

In the aftermath of the 1967 uprising, most of the Grande's neighboring businesses never recovered. For a few short years, the Grande was an exception; in its counterculture heyday the ballroom thrived in an environment of otherwise increasing blight and out-migration. After a few years though, it too became part of a new ghost town along Grand River Avenue. In the Grande's case, it was not the violent social upheaval that ended its operation but rather the changing commercialization of the music industry and demands from the next generation of 1970s concertgoers. With the exception of a few short-lived attempts by community groups to use the building for storage and charity organizations, the Grande Ballroom has now been unoccupied and unmaintained for the majority of its existence. Since the building's abandonment in the 1970s, all of the ground floor retail spaces and the second floor ballroom have incurred heavy damage from scrapping, decay, and weathering. To an untrained eye, the Grande is an irretrievable, epic, and untimely ruin. To structural engineers, architects, preservationists, and archaeologists, the Grande still has integrity. Vandalism has not caused irreparable damage to the main structural supports and architectural materials of the building, most of which remain intact and viable, but in its current state of dilapidation, the Grande's physical survival is a race against time.

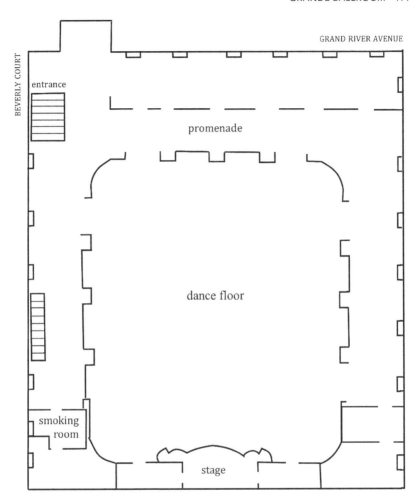

Figure 6.5. Plan map of the Grande Ballroom based on the original 1928 building blueprints by architect Charles N. Agree. (Katharine Blatchford and Krysta Ryzewski)

GRASSROOTS PRESERVATION AND ARCHAEOLOGY

It was not until nature started to reclaim the Grande Ballroom that its potential loss began to resonate with those who shared attachments to the building and its history. By the early 2000s trees sprouted out of the building's windows, rain and snow poured onto the wooden dance floor, plaster walls caved in, and segments of the ceiling dangled from open holes in the roof. Rubble choked the main stairway, blocking access to the ballroom for all but the most intrepid trespassers. Images portraying the Grande as an "incredible ruin" soon started to fill pages of urban explorers' blogs and photographers' coffee table books.[17] These indicators of demolition by neglect alarmed historic preservationists and the diffuse but widespread community of baby boomers who frequented the Grande as young adults.

The first formal attempt to mobilize protections for the Grande coincided with the fortieth anniversary of the Grande's opening as a rock music venue in 1966. Local musician, historian, and preservationist Leo Early, who was already maintaining a website about the Grande's history, formed the Friends of the Grande in 2006 as a grassroots preservation group in response to a groundswell of anniversary-based nostalgia. The Friends of the Grande's objectives are to "preserve the history of the Grande Ballroom and its physical edifice while promoting the culture fostered by its patrons, performers and promoters."[18] Initially, the group's ambitions to organize preservation protections for the Grande were met with ambivalence by the building's current owner, the Chapel Hill Missionary Baptist Church. The significance of the musical and architectural heritage that preservationists celebrated was not enough to persuade the current owners to undertake what they worried would be a cost prohibitive and logistically complicated renovation project.

Over the course of the next decade, Early persisted. He kept the Grande Ballroom at the forefront of local advocacy conversations and worked tirelessly to sway the building owner's support for historic preservation protections. Early mobilized the Friends of the Grande through various events, oral history recordings, and web-based engagements. The group developed a blog, website, and Facebook group. With over 2,600 members, the Facebook group continues to provide a forum for people to share memories about the so-called Grande Experience and to discuss its future. These discussions, in turn, have spurred major commemorative events, including a sold-out fiftieth anniversary concert in 2016 featuring the Yardbirds, the publication of Early's definitive book *The Grande Ballroom: Detroit's Rock 'n' Roll Palace*, a documentary film, *Louder Than Love*, and successful fundraising campaigns. In 2016, as the Grande approached the fiftieth anniversary of its counterculture era, mounting pressure and advocacy on behalf of these nostalgic fans, musicians, and local preservationists finally persuaded the current owners to endorse actions that might forestall further decay.

The critical first step in the preservation initiative was to assess the current state of the building and determine whether it was even feasible to safeguard the Grande Ballroom from advancing decay. The Chapel Hill church agreed to allow the Friends of the Grande to proceed with

preservation initiatives if an inspection deemed the building to be structurally viable, and if enough of the ballroom's historic architectural features remained present and intact. Based on his familiarity with our work
at the Little Harry speakeasy and the Blue Bird Inn jazz club, Early recognized that archaeological techniques were appropriate for systematically
documenting and interpreting the extant remains of the Grande Ballroom.
In October 2016, at the invitation of Early and with the permission of the
building owners, I led a team of seven archaeologists from Wayne State
University on an archaeological survey of the ballroom. Our group was
part of a larger inspection team, which included two architects, a historian, and historic preservationists from the Detroit Sound Conservancy
and Preservation Detroit.

It took Early three years to coordinate the 2016 inspection with the
building owners.[19] During the prior decade numerous trespassers had entered the building illegally, scrapping piping and fixtures from the ballroom, tagging walls and floors with graffiti, dumping trash, and looting
ornamental architectural elements. Out of concern for people's safety and
the building's condition, the owners had, by 2012, installed wooden boards
over the ground-floor windows and doors, barring entry to the building.
Access to the ballroom's interior required dismantling the church's bar-
ricades. When we finally entered the Grande, we were the first group of
sanctioned visitors inside the space in years.

Up until the moment when the first member of the inspection team
ascended the rubble-filled staircase to the second floor, we were unsure
whether we would be able to access the ballroom. We also knew that the
remains might not be intact or stable enough to document once we arrived on the second floor. The building's precarious future loomed over
the inspection team; all of us approached the survey as if it might be the
last time anyone would set foot in the Grande Ballroom.

Given the situation surrounding the Grande Ballroom's structural integrity, preservation, and future prospects, I designed the archaeological
survey to gather as much information as possible about the building's
extant architectural remains and ballroom-era material culture. My approach to the Grande was based on a similar survey I codirected of a late
twentieth-century popular music recording complex at AIR Studios on
the Caribbean island of Montserrat.[20] AIR Studios met an untimely end
in 1989 when it was damaged by Hurricane Hugo and eruptions of the
Soufriere Hills volcano, beginning in 1995. Beatles' producer and studio
owner Sir George Martin eventually abandoned plans to rebuild the studios after decades worth of ongoing eruptions from the volcano deposited

feet of ash on the property and contributed to the eventual collapse of the main house's roof. In 2010 I led an archaeological team in conducting a building survey of AIR Studios, a survey of its interior spaces, and an excavation of its courtyard sidewalk. We then subsequently visited the property in 2012, 2016, and 2019 to document the aggressive decay of its buildings in the inhospitable tropical environment.

As at AIR Studios, our objectives with the Grande Ballroom survey were twofold: to document the archaeological record of the building and to inform future strategies for the Grande Ballroom's stabilization and rehabilitation.[21] Like most of our archaeological interventions in Detroit, the Grande Ballroom survey involved elements of "punk archaeology" in moments when we had to improvise ways of accessing or collecting information from certain spaces.[22] For the most part though, the survey employed conventional archaeological recording methods.

The inspection team entered the Grande's ground floor through a doorway into one of the former retail shops. Inside we were met by a dark, open room filled with rubble and trash; the dividing walls between the shops were long since demolished. A stairway to the ballroom led upstairs from the back of one shop. Its steps were totally covered by fallen portions of the roof and walls, and debris, making our ascent slow and perilous. Fortunately, we reached the second floor to discover that the ballroom was still intact and its floors were sturdy enough for us to conduct a full pedestrian survey and documentation (Figure 6.6).

Our time inside of the building was limited to a few daytime hours, and so we had to work quickly and efficiently. These constraints required an archaeological team whose members had previous survey experience. Before entering the building, I divided the archaeologists into three two-person work groups. One group, composed of Samantha Ellens and Bridget Bennane, was in charge of documenting the layout of the ballroom and how its configurations changed over time. They photo-documented modifications to the interior space and mapped them onto a copy of Charles Agree's original 1928 architectural blueprint for the ballroom. During their portion of the survey, Ellens and Bennane investigated all accessible sections of the ballroom, including the dance floor, stage, office space, lounge areas, and smaller rooms. Within these areas they examined structural elements for signs of age and modifications (e.g., doors, walls, windows, access points, paint, ornamentation).

Archaeologists Athena Zissis and Jeri Pajor led the second group in a systematic pedestrian survey of the ballroom floor, promenade, and side rooms. Their task was to identify and photo-document portable objects

Figure 6.6. Grande Ballroom archaeological survey team receives a briefing from Leo Early and structural engineers. In the foreground the maple dance floor is succumbing to moisture from holes in the roof. In the background the well-preserved stage is covered by an intact proscenium arch, above which two banks of lights installed by Russ Gibb still hang. (Krysta Ryzewski)

and furnishings related to the Grande's ballroom-era occupancy. They also recorded damage to the ballroom's architectural elements as a result of the building's neglect. Some of these in situ features, like ceiling-mounted stage lights and mural fragments, helped us identify past activity areas and conveyed sensory information about the Grande Experience. Other objects, like disarticulated plaster ornamentation, which had fallen from the ceiling and columns, provided information about the building's construction techniques and modifications. Once the systematic recording was finished, we collected samples of the most diagnostic objects and architectural elements for further analysis in our laboratory and display in local museum exhibits.

Brendan Doucet and Beau Kromberg led the third archaeological survey group. They collected a comprehensive set of digital photographs for the ballroom's dance floor, stage, and promenade. From these, they later created prototype 3D visualizations of the space so that those interested in the ballroom's history, state of preservation, and potential future uses might visit the site virtually without trespassing into hazardous conditions. My role during the survey was to direct and assist the three work groups. I also inspected the stage using a camera scope, collected wood, plaster, and brick samples, probed the more hazardous areas of the building, documented the building's exterior, and consulted with the other half of the nonarchaeological inspection team.

Before and after our visit to the ballroom, we gathered additional sources about the Grande from archival records, material culture collections, and oral histories. We integrated these sources into our analysis of the ballroom's interior space, the objects we recovered, and the memories former patrons shared with us in order to position the Grande within a longer-term framework of reference as an archaeological site with many different layers of occupancy, history, and public conceptions.[23] Two months after the survey, each member of the archaeological team authored a chapter in the narrative report, which I then submitted to the Friends of the Grande, the Chapel Hill Missionary Baptist Church, and the State Historic Preservation Office.[24] I turn now to situate the physical and archival findings from our survey within their historical and contemporary contexts. I will then discuss how what began as a standard archaeological survey eventually turned into a platform for advocacy.

ORNAMENTAL DESIGN AND ACOUSTIC ARCHAEOLOGY

Our archaeological documentation of the ballroom's spatial layout determined that during its forty-four years as an entertainment venue the Grande's interior retained most of its original configuration. It was still easy in 2016 to identify particular rooms and architectural features that were labeled on Agree's 1928 blueprint and that are also remembered by patrons of the 1960s-era Grande. The major structural elements of the ballroom—the stage, proscenium arch, promenade, columns, plasterwork, dance floor and side rooms—were never moved or demolished. When concertgoers in 1966 entered into the foyer at the top of the carpeted staircase, they would have encountered the same view and layout of the ballroom as patrons did nearly forty years earlier.

When the Grande opened in 1928 it offered a new outlet for Detroit's thriving, Prohibition-era entertainment scene. At the time the city's most popular live music and dancing venue was the Graystone Ballroom, opened in 1922. Centrally located on Woodward Avenue, it accommodated over 3,000 dancers underneath its sixty-foot-tall domed ceiling and boasted the region's most popular performers, including Jean Goldkette's Orchestra and McKinney's Cotton Pickers.[25] The Grande, and its sister venue, the Vanity Ballroom (1929), expanded the city's ballroom-centered nightlife beyond the city center to the west and east side neighborhoods. Agree designed both venues as large, second-story ballrooms suitable for over 1,000 dancers, using layouts and design elements that were typical of Detroit's 1920s dance hall architecture. In the Grande Ballroom the ceiling was embellished with ornate, multicolor stenciled designs and ornamental plaster grills, including fleur-de-lis and pineapple motifs. The plaster column and pilaster bases surrounding the promenade were finished with braided designs. All were topped with detailed geometric shapes, scrolls, and hybrid ram/griffin animal head reliefs. Some historians attribute the Grande's plasterwork to the sculptor Corrado Parducci, although no documentation has yet been located to confirm the potential link.[26] Nevertheless, the quality craftmanship of the Grande's decorative elements, at least on their exterior surface, was so detailed that some patrons of the 1960s-era Grande mistook the plaster columns for marble.[27]

Eventually, the plaster decor of the pilasters, columns, and ceiling reliefs was no match for the rain and snow that fell through the roof over the years. About one-third of the plasterwork inside the ballroom has broken off from the surfaces of underlying supports. From an archaeological perspective, the decay of the decorative surfaces proved to be useful for our assessment of the building's architectural process since the crumbling plaster revealed the base supporting the column's plasterwork—chicken wire (Figure 6.7). We confirmed that the Grande's builders used wire mesh to fashion the pilaster and column bases; this choice of expedient building material reflects Agree's low-cost priorities and the quick time frame in which Weitzman required the ballroom to be completed.

The ballroom's fragments also revealed information about how the space was purpose-built to maximize sound quality. Performers from all periods of the Grande's music history praised the ballroom's acoustics, especially the clarity with which sound projected outward from the stage and across the expansive dance floor. During our survey, we collected fragments of plasterwork that had fallen from the walls and columns. The plaster's lime and sand matrix was tightly packed with bundles of animal hair and other fibers (Figure 6.8). In addition to binding the plaster constituents together, hair was considered an acoustic innovation in 1920s dance hall architecture and was purposefully included in the design of the Grande and other music venues, including Orchestra Hall. "Uncle" Russ Gibb encountered the Grande's fiber-packed plaster when performing minor upgrades to the ballroom after he acquired it in 1966. Gibb attributed the ballroom's quality sound to the materials and reportedly insisted on using horsehair in the alterations he made.[28] Invisible to the Grande's

Figure 6.7. Promenade pilaster with eroding plasterwork reveals chicken wire mesh underneath. Voids are visible at the top of the cabled columns, where salvagers removed the hybrid
ram/griffin heads that were attached to them. (Krysta Ryzewski)

patrons, these fibers reduced echo by absorbing sound. They were critical
for creating the ballroom's renowned acoustics.[29]

Although there were no portable remains to collect from the Grande's
earliest iterations as a swing music venue, there survived enough architectural elements and decorative features to visualize the space at various periods in time and to consider the history of the ballroom before its
counterculture era. Surviving plaster decorations, especially the columns
and cross sections of wall surfaces, revealed different layers of paint. As
the Grande's taste in music changed, so too did its aesthetics. At various

Figure 6.8. Plaster on the columns, walls, and ceiling was mixed with animal hair and fiber to serve dual purposes as a binding agent and an acoustic innovation. This broken column revealed a tuft of horsehair. (Krysta Ryzewski)

points in its history, the walls and columns were painted blue, red, yellow, or gold.

THE GRANDE BEFORE GIBB: A BALLROOM FOR SOME

While our archaeological survey produced information about the Grande's physical appearance from the late 1920s onward, it did not provide direct insight into the social experiences within the ballroom in the decades prior to the 1960s. For this earlier information I turned to various archival repositories and primary source materials.

Some popular historical accounts suggest that the Grande thrived during the big band era of the 1930s, fell dormant during World War II, and then was repurposed for other ventures until it was resurrected by "Uncle" Russ Gibb in 1966. Newspaper archives, especially from the *Detroit Free Press*, prove otherwise; they confirm that the Grande operated as a ballroom—a space for music and dancing—consistently between 1928 and 1962. During that time frame the ballroom was usually open between three and four nights per week, except during the summer months (it was not air conditioned). Even during the difficult economic climate of the Great Depression, the ballroom remained active one night per week.

Although it is beyond the scope of this chapter to provide a comprehensive musical history of the Grande, it is important to highlight how an anthropological reading of archival sources located race and gender-based disparities within the ballroom's operation prior to the 1960s.[30] Owing to labor shortages during World War II, the Grande's managers regularly placed classified advertisements in local newspapers to recruit workers for the ballroom's coat check, soda fountain, personnel, and maintenance staff. The most frequently appearing advertisements sought young men in their late teens and twenties to serve as coat checkers. To be hired, they had to be able-bodied, at least eighteen years old, five feet nine inches tall, and White. If they fit the bill, they would be hired to work at least one weekend night for a salary of three dollars.[31] Young White women were also recruited to work the ballroom's soda fountain; one ad mentioned that the counter was staffed by five women in 1947. While White employees were hired for roles in which they interacted directly with patrons, Black employees were relegated to supplementary and behind-the-scenes positions.

In September 1943, just three months after racially motivated rioting erupted across the city (see chapter 3), the Grande's management sought to hire a "colored couple"; the woman would serve as a matron and the man a porter. Both would also serve as janitors during the course of their forty- to fifty-hour work week.[32] Two months later, managers placed an advertisement for another "colored porter" who would also work four nights per week as a washroom attendant and a shoe shiner. The ad boasted that "the right man should make easily thirty dollars weekly."[33] Unlike his White counterparts at the Grande, his pay would depend on tips rather than a set wage. The differential treatment of Black and White employees by Grande managers demonstrates how segregated labor structures existed in the city's White-owned commercial entertainment venues through the 1950s. These findings stand in contrast to those that detail the operations at the nearby Blue Bird Inn jazz club (see chapter 4). Unlike the Blue Bird, the Grande Ballroom employed a diverse but unequal workforce who catered to maintaining the space for a predominately White clientele.

The Grande Ballroom's owners never publicly excluded non-White patrons from the venue, but prior to 1966 it was certainly not an inviting place for diverse audiences. Nor was it a haven for innovative jazz music and experimentation, like the nightclubs of Paradise Valley or the Blue Bird Inn. Until the early 1960s the Grande was a mainstream swing dancing venue. It hosted weekly dances, usually on Friday and Saturday evenings between 9:30 and 12:30 p.m. Catering to the conservative ideals of the time, managers Don and Helen Hill served as chaperones and hosted jazz ensembles, dance classes, and themed events. Performers included well-known orchestras led by Lowry Clark, Elliot Lawrence, Ralph Bowen, and Bobby Rodriguez. In the years before its counterculture transformation, the Grande began to offer trendier Latin-inspired music, but the updated programming failed to connect with the fast-changing tastes and values emerging among the ballroom's target young adult demographic.

REFORMING THE GRANDE

In October 1966 "Uncle" Russ Gibb, a local disc jockey, concert promoter, and high school teacher, purchased the Grande and refashioned it into the midwestern equivalent of San Francisco's Fillmore Auditorium. The Grande fast became an incubator for some of the most influential musicians of the counterculture era. Two or three bands played on the ballroom's lineup each weekend night. Gibb had a talent for attracting national acts, such as Traffic and the Jeff Beck Group, to Detroit, but he also ardently supported the local music scene (Figure 6.9). In the weekend shows he routinely included Michigan-based bands like MC5, Iggy and the Psychedelic Stooges, and the Amboy Dukes, each of whom would debut or experiment with music at the Grande that would be foundational for the later development of punk, progressive, and heavy metal genres.[34] Within a few hours on a Saturday night, fans could witness a wildly eccentric performance by Iggy Pop—with theatrics inspired by his browsing of anthropology books in the University of Michigan library—and then stay on for a blues set by the British-American band Fleetwood Mac.[35]

The Grande Ballroom of the Woodstock era stood in stark contrast to the commercially manufactured and generally apolitical Motown productions that dominated Detroit's music industry and garnered worldwide fame during the 1960s. In contrast to Berry Gordon Jr.'s tightly

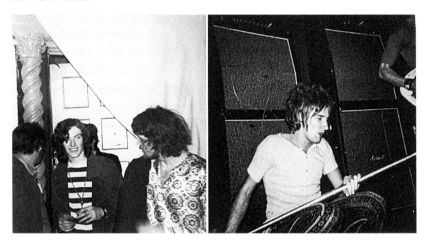

Figure 6.9. Scenes from the Grande captured by concertgoer Michael Bolan in 1968 include a backstage encounter with Steve Winwood and Jim Capaldi of the English band Traffic (*left*), and Rod Stewart performing with the Jeff Beck Group (*right*). (Courtesy of Michael Bolan)

choreographed Motown sound, Gibb designed the Grande to be an unbounded, unfettered space of musical acceptance. He presented the widest range of popular and emergent electronic music to his young audiences. By design, the Grande was an experiment in music archaeology; the venue's musicians routinely incorporated elements of older genres and artists into their new electronic rock music experiments. Performers typically aligned with one or two particular genres by virtue of their own tastes and experience. But even the heaviest proto-punk rockers consciously drew influences from earlier jazz, folk, and blues artists into their performances.[36] Such was the case with the Grande's house band, the MC5. Short for the "Motor City Five," the band of five suburban teenagers from Lincoln Park, Michigan, was credited by music critic Thomas Erlewine as "crystallizing the counterculture movement at its most volatile and threatening."[37] John Sinclair, the band's manager from 1966 until 1969, described the MC5 as pioneers who combined "jazz and rock to make a new musical form infused with unbridled energy and improvisational freedom"; think a visceral mix of high-energy rock paired with John Coltrane and Sun Ra.[38]

As the Grande's house band and most frequent performer, the MC5 set the tone for the counterculture-era ballroom as a place where music was inextricably linked with social issues. In Sinclair's words, they created "the template for socially conscious popular musicians" by tying their music and their performances to special radical causes, including fundraising campaigns for activist organizations, community groups, political prisoners, and various antiestablishment causes.[39] Echoing the sentiments of pragmatists like Detroit activist Grace Lee Boggs, Sinclair described the MC5's proto-punk music as "a real thing . . . not just a theory. [To them], it's a way of life and a way to play music."[40] Among the band's most popular songs were "Kick Out the Jams" and "Motor City Is Burning," the latter of which was their adaptation of the song John Lee Hooker wrote in response to Detroit's 1967 uprising. MC5 would have heard Hooker perform "Motor City Is Burning" at the Grande when he headlined shows there on December 29 and 30, 1967.[41] Soon thereafter, they transformed Hooker's mournful song into a loud, forcefully delivered diatribe that expressed their own frustrations about pervasive class and race-based injustices in and around Detroit. They played their rendition of Hooker's song so often that it became the hallmark song of the counterculture-era Grande and their band—memorized by the generation of young adult music fans and activists who spent their weekends at the ballroom.[42]

Today the Grande is remembered as a "rock 'n' roll palace," where the most acclaimed bands tend to be the radical performers, like MC5, and those who eventually rose to chart-topping status, especially The Who.[43] These performers are foregrounded in the ballroom's narratives in a way that might suggest that the Grande was a scene of White, rock-centric performers. But this impression is simply a reflection of contemporary storytellers' tastes and memories. During Gibb's management the Grande was never defined by one particular musical genre or type of performer.[44]

The Grande's counterculture music and activism scene was intimately connected to the blues and jazz music pioneered by musicians who played in Paradise Valley's nightclubs and the Blue Bird Inn jazz club a generation earlier. During the 1960s and 1970s, these connections were established and expanded on by the MC5 and Iggy Pop (as is often reported), but also frequently showcased by acclaimed African American musicians or racially integrated combinations of performers. From its earliest days under Gibb's management, the Grande featured legendary blues, funk, and jazz performers like B. B. King (the "King of the Blues"), Howlin' Wolf, John Mayall, and Taj Mahal. A review of B. B. King's performance on September 13, 1968, reported that he "blew minds" at the Grande during his performances on the previous Friday and Saturday.[45]

The appearance of blues music at the Grande reflected the popular music trends of the day, where rock music emulated blues chord progressions and other stylistic elements.[46] The marriage between the genres of rock and blues music resulted in collaborations between Grande performers, including the 1971 double album *Hooker n' Heat*, by John Lee Hooker and blues-rock band Canned Heat. Similarly, the connection between jazz and rock music was highlighted by one of the Grande's first major benefit concerts in September 1967, an "Homage to John Coltrane." Billed as the first musical memorial for Coltrane, who died on July 17, 1967, Gibb organized the concert to coincide with the saxophonist's birthday.[47] The Coltrane tribute featured diverse musical genres and performers, with individual and collaborative performances by the MC5 as well as the UP and the Charles Moore Ensemble—the Charles Moore Ensemble was promoted as Detroit's "first and most forward avant-garde jazz unit."[48] Coltrane was a notable presence in Detroit during the 1950s and 1960s, including at the nearby Blue Bird Inn. Gibb designed the tribute concert's lineup to recognize Coltrane's contributions to modern music in general and to the city's musical heritage in particular. His advertisement for the event emphasized how all of the performers "have translated Coltrane's huge energy force into the electronic rock medium and are putting it to work in a popular context."[49]

AN ACTIVIST SPACE

At any other venue, it would have been perfectly acceptable for the Coltrane tribute to be a stand-alone celebration of bebop jazz's legacy in contemporary rock music. But when the Grande hosted major events, creative expression and political causes always went hand-in-hand. The "Homage to John Coltrane" was also an important fundraising benefit for the radical, antiestablishment Trans-Love Energies group (TLE). John Sinclair, the MC5's manager and prominent poet, writer, and activist, cofounded Trans-Love with his wife Leni and local artist Gary Grimshaw in 1967. The group incorporated the remainder of an earlier cooperative of artists and jazz musicians, the Detroit Artists Workshop (1964–1967), whose cofounder, trumpeter Charles Moore, also headlined the Coltrane tribute.[50] Members of the far-left TLE, including several regularly performing Grande musicians, saw rock music as a vehicle for radical social and cultural change.[51] By 1967 the group of self-described "hippie entrepreneurs" incorporated as a nonprofit organization.[52] The Grande's operation was interwoven with the Trans-Love organization. Its founders and members managed the ballroom's bands, ran its light shows, and sold handcrafted jewelry and clothing. In return for their logistical support, Gibb set up a "store" for the TLE to distribute media, fundraise, and sell merchandise from the concession area along the promenade's back wall.[53] From Gary Grimshaw's promotional posters to Leni Sinclair's handmade beaded necklaces, Trans-Love

Energies effectively created and marketed the psychedelic material culture that was emblematic of the Grande Experience (Figure 6.10).[54]

Most of the Grande Ballroom's patrons were committed to the anti–Vietnam War and civil rights movements of the late 1960s and early 1970s. In the aftermath of Detroit's 1967 uprising and in the wake of similar conflicts across the country, the efforts of Trans-Love Energies to promote progressive cultural changes through mind-expanding hallucinogenic trips, literature, and light shows were grounded by the formation in 1968 of the White Panther Party by John Sinclair, Leni Sinclair, Pun Plamondon, and members of the MC5. The White Panthers were an antiracist, militant, socialist political collective established on the recommendation of Black Panther leader Huey P. Newton.[55] Like their Black Panther counterparts, the White Panther Party sought radical cultural revolution. Sinclair described the White Panther Party as "an organization of fiercely resistant white youths committed to the principles and practice of the Black Panther Party for Self-Defense."[56] The MC5 and their music became the organization's propaganda machine.[57]

The Grande's reputation as a hotbed of activism and antiauthoritarianism did not go unnoticed by the authorities. Its events attracted unwelcome attention from the FBI, local police, and mainstream media. Among the many controversial law enforcement actions of the era, the Detroit police arrested Sinclair in 1969 for the possession of two marijuana cigarettes. His subsequent sentencing to a ten-year jail term ignited international protests and inspired several special events held at the Grande and elsewhere.[58]

Figure 6.10. Promotional postcards advertising upcoming shows and designed by Gary Grimshaw were distributed weekly at the Grande, at local shops, and by other venues in Metro Detroit. (Courtesy of Michael Bolan)

The most vivid tangible remains of the Grande's activist-oriented, psychedelic music experience survive in the traces of the smoking room, a small vestibule separating the promenade from the men's bathroom (Figure 6.11). The room's name dates back to the original 1928 blueprints of the building, but by the late 1960s the space also functioned as a metaphorical cosmic gateway for patrons who sought a more intimate experience during performances. Russ Gibb enlisted local artists Carl Lundgren, Gary Grimshaw, and Judy Janis from the Detroit Artists Collective to paint a vibrant mural over the room's light blue walls.[59] In line with the design aesthetic of the time, Gibb also covered the floor with a fluffy red and orange shag carpet, affording patrons a comfortable surface for lounging. By the time of our archaeological survey in 2016 the smoking room had been subjected to extensive damage from moisture due to a missing window along its east wall. Only fragments of the mural and the room's carpeting survived. From these traces it was impossible to discern what the mural or smoking room looked like in its 1960s iteration. Yet we could still see the artists' brushstrokes in the swirls of fluorescent blue, pink, orange, and green paints that adorned the remaining mural fragments. When illuminated by overhanging ultraviolet black lights, the colors would have created a portal whose energy elevated the smoking room experience to the next level (Figure 6.11).

In the aftermath of our survey, counterculture-era music and art enthusiasts remarked on how the fragmented mural was an important, if not obscure, artifact of collaborative psychedelic artwork. One of the mural's painters was Gary Grimshaw, the graphic designer for the Grande's promotional materials. His illusionist posters and postcards comprise a body of psychedelic concert art that defined an entire genre of counterculture imagery.[60] The recovery of the smoking room mural fragments recorded an example of this genre's artwork that was a few rainstorms away from being lost.

THE GRANDE EXPERIENCE

The many trends and audiences to pass through the Grande between the 1920s and 1970s evidently inspired no major alterations to the ballroom's layout or its prominent architectural features. Instead, our archaeological surveys documented more subtle spatial changes, including artifacts of period-specific design aesthetics and remnants of performance-enhancing technologies. Since the counterculture-era Grande was the most recent iteration of the ballroom's musical occupancy, most of the spatial modifications we documented related to electronic music performance and

Figure 6.11. Remains of the smoking room include fragments of the counterculture-era fluorescent mural and red-orange shag carpet. (Krysta Ryzewski)

the manufacturing of the multisensory experiences that accompanied it. These remnants and the so-called Grande Experience that they represent feature most prominently in the surviving memories of the ballroom's former patrons and performers.

The Grande Experience was an aesthetic that Gibb carefully choreographed with a combination of brightly painted walls, colorful light shows, and abstract liquid light projections. His pairing of music with multisensory effects created an immersive and mind-altering environment. At the time, light shows were new additions to electronic music performances. Gibb relied on a combination of cutting-edge lighting technology and

homespun experimental techniques to stage them. Traces of these technologies survive in the Grande and were documented during the archaeological survey. Two well-preserved light fixtures remain suspended from
the ceiling in front of the stage's proscenium arch—one houses a set of
colored bulbs, and another encloses a secondary row of white bulbs. These
lights are artifacts of Russ Gibb's proudest technological innovation, the
Grande's psychedelic light shows.

The light shows were coproduced by Leni Sinclair, Gary Grimshaw, and
Robin Sommers—members of Trans-Love Energies, and often involved
artists from collectives with names like the Leprechaun Marmalade Company or the High Society. In a 2013 interview, Leni Sinclair recalled how
Gibb paid the crew $25 per night to perform liquid light shows (although
they gave their earnings to TLE).[61] From the top of a twelve-foot-high scaffold tower in the back of the ballroom the artists projected "throbbing
amoeba-like" figures onto the stage behind and above the performers.[62]
The job was demanding and required creative adaptations of everyday
materials to produce otherworldly effects. With temperatures in the light
tower often exceeding 100 degrees Fahrenheit, artists created imagery using four 1500 watt overhead projectors and four carousel slide projectors.
Into the projectors Sommers inserted thin glass slides with colorful designs, and he coated the platform of an overhead projector with dyed water
and oils to create swirling imagery on the stage backdrop.[63] The operators
combined the effects of the liquid light show with film clips, black ultraviolet lights along the promenade, and the overhanging colored and flashing
strobe lights. The objective of this sensory overload, as Gary Grimshaw reported in 1966, was to "create the feeling of being inside something alive
. . . to break down one's symbolizing capacity and expand awareness."[64]

Musicians also enlisted their own special effects to enhance their performances. Their props included lightweight, portable materials like plastic confetti, aluminum foil, glitter, and smoke bombs. Our archaeological
survey recovered traces of these materials, including pieces of circular,
red confetti lodged in the cracks of the stage floorboards. Between the
stage floorboards and wall, we also recovered three used turquoise smoke
bombs. With the Grande being a popular place for unsanctioned urban
exploration and vandalism, and in the absence of any markings to indicate
their date of manufacture, we initially suspected that the smoke bombs
were of more recent vintage. Upon further examination, in consideration
of their in situ location in between the front framing boards of the stage
apron, coupled with stories from former Grande patrons, we confirmed
that they dated to the 1960s or 1970s. Smoke bombs, it turns out, were

integral parts of the Grande performers' special effects repertoires during the ballroom's counterculture era (Figure 6.12). Former Grande patrons recall how some bands, including The Who, often used smoke bombs in their performance, especially to exit the stage from behind a smokescreen. To enhance their performances, the Grande's musicians depended on smoke, lights, and mirrors. Pyrotechnic displays and more elaborate special effects were later embellishments for the arena-rock concerts of the 1980s.

In their memories of the counterculture-era Grande, former patrons and performers foreground these multisensory effects as an essential, if not emblematic, facet of the ballroom's allure. Guitarist Herman Daldin played seven shows at the Grande Ballroom, beginning in 1968 as a fifteen-year-old, with his band Train and Kingdom Come. His most lucid memories recall "a huge ballroom with a light show, strobe lights and fog machines all running simultaneously."[65] Daldin noted how the sensory effects created an echo off of the back wall, which made it difficult to focus on his sound and keep the music's beat. Nevertheless, with his band's performance augmented by the special effects, he "felt strong and totally immersed in [his] music." Performing at the Grande was, he recalls, "a dynamic feeling."[66]

Jaan Uhelszki, who worked as a writer for *Creem* and a soda pop vendor at the Grande, shared mixed recollections of the Grande Experience. She recalled the ballroom as a "very hip spot" with "moments of pure luminosity."[67] In the same breath, however, she noted that the audiences tended to be made up of "a horde of drug-sloppy concertgoers." Indeed, to maximize the sensory effects of the Grande performances, many patrons openly consumed marijuana and acid (LSD).[68] John Sinclair recounted how, at about ten o'clock on Friday nights, a man by the name of Neal routinely appeared on a staircase leading from the ballroom to an attic utility closet. There he would "just hang out with a big smile. Everybody would go to Neal, and he'd give them samples of this week's acid, and all the acidheads would drop. The first band played at nine. The second band at 10:15. And at 11 o'clock it was time for the MC5, when everybody was peaking on acid—the audience and, often, the band."[69]

As a consequence of the ballroom's mind-altering substances, memories about the Grande Experience tend to be a bit fuzzy. Regular concertgoer Tom Skinner recalled that "the Third Power were one of the best power trios I ever saw at the Grande Ballroom."[70] But, he added, "I just wish I could remember the Grande Ballroom!"[71] For the most part, the individual accounts that survive about the Grande Ballroom are fragmented

Figure 6.12. Artifacts recovered during the Grande Ballroom archaeological survey included fragments of the smoking room mural and shag carpet as well as used smoke bombs and confetti (*not pictured*). (Krysta Ryzewski)

and selective memories. Many are altered by hallucinogens, smoothed into collective experiences, and focused on the venue's most noteworthy performances, events, and personalities. Nevertheless, one of the constant features of patrons' recollections are the Grande's special effects. The smoking room mural, light shows, and other creative interventions formed lasting impressions that are now cherished by former patrons, some of whom are actively involved in attempts to restore the ballroom. As anthropologist Joy Sather-Wagstaff argues, such complexities of affect and sensory elements, and their impacts on memory-making, are critical for understanding the current social construction of the Grande Ballroom as a place of experience, nostalgia, and potential revitalization.[72]

THE END OF AN ERA

The MC5 headlined the final performance at the Grande on New Year's Eve 1972. Electronic music, and the political messages tied to it, may have saved the Grande from damage during the 1967 uprising, but it could not spare the ballroom from the emergent mass-marketed, profit-oriented concert industry. Even though the Grande's performers, patrons, and staff espoused the antiestablishment sentiments of the counterculture movement, the Grande, it turned out, was never immune to capitalist forces.[73] In fact, the ballroom's operations, its staff, and its musicians (several of whom would go on to produce commercially successful albums), relied on the revenues the Grande generated through ticket sales, concessions, sponsors, and fundraising events. By 1972 larger venues increasingly lured the Grande's artists to their stages, and the next generation of young concertgoers gravitated to the arenas that hosted nationwide touring acts and accommodated several thousand spectators. Popular music performances became less intimate events, and their ties to political and social justice causes diminished as the importance of entertainment value and choreographed spectacles took priority. After a six-year run, the Grande's distinct experience became obsolete and the ballroom joined the ranks of the ephemeral popular music acts who once played its stage.

MOURNING LOSS

As the Grande fell into a state of decay after 1972, its physical remains became the basis for inspiring and mobilizing preservation efforts in the decades to come. The sense of loss that former patrons felt for the Grande building, and the memories of the events that took place there, have been the underlying forces motivating these efforts. One member of our archaeological survey team, Jeri Pajor, a graduate student in anthropology in her sixties, frequented the ballroom as a teenager. Her visit to the Grande in 2016 was the first time she entered the building since the 1970s. Before our survey Jeri regularly shared stories about the ballroom with me and others. Like many former concertgoers, her accounts were filled with descriptions of the building's layout, details about eccentric performers (especially Iggy and the Psychedelic Stooges), and reminiscences about the smells, sounds, and special effects that accompanied her favorite bands.[74] Still a fan of the Grande's counterculture-era rock music, Jeri became an active follower of the Friends of the Grande group in the years leading up to our survey. As an area resident, she was well aware of the Grande's considerable state of decay; she certainly did not expect to find a space that looked identical to the ballroom of her youth when our team entered the building. Yet she was unprepared for the side effects of encountering such utter dereliction. In her contribution to the Grande Ballroom narrative survey report, she reflected on her first impressions of the space: "Once I reached the top of the stairs and moved away from the stairs and around the promenade to look at the ballroom, I was shocked to see the level of devastation of the Grande Ballroom, where I used to attend concerts in the 1960s and '70s. I stood there paralyzed at the sight before me. It took me several minutes to get my bearings. . . . It was heartbreaking for me to see the old girl in such poor overall shape."[75]

Jeri's return to the Grande was fraught with unanticipated emotions of loss. In the aftermath of the visit, her nostalgia turned mournful as she grieved the destruction of the Grande and her passing youth. Her experience with the Grande's remains is a reminder about the lasting psychological effects that ruins of any sort might have on the people who once experienced them as active places (Figure 6.13).

For Jeri, the breathtaking decay of the ballroom's infrastructure was a poignant, emotional reminder of the passage of time. In her opinion, this temporal gap made the small, mundane objects, architectural fragments, and movable fixtures from the Grande even more worth saving; the smoke bombs, mural fragments, light boxes, and dance floor boards afforded powerful and lasting connections to the Grande. She saw her own story through the material remains. The materials were therapeutic, tangible lifelines to the ballroom, a place whose experiences shaped her lifelong appreciation for music, social justice causes, and Detroit history.

NOSTALGIA AND THE POWER OF OBJECTS

Jeri was one of many former patrons and music history fans who embrace the power of unassuming objects from the building as a way to maintain their connections to the Grande Experience. Three months after our survey was completed, a heated debate erupted on the Friends of the Grande Facebook page when Leo Early, the group's facilitator, publicly decried an act of vandalism against the building. In a post from February 28, 2017, Early described how a Grande fan posted a photo in which he held a brick that he had pried from the building's exterior wall with a crowbar.[76] The brick was especially meaningful for the fan because it was stamped with the letters J.A.M.

At that point we realized that our public dissemination of our survey findings (via the Friends of the Grande blog and our own social media outlets) may have, unintentionally, drawn collectors' attention to the building's materials. We recovered J.A.M. bricks from the crumbling ballroom walls during our archaeological survey (Figure 6.14). The bricks are not especially remarkable on their own. The initials refer to James A. Mercier, a Detroit-based brick manufacturer who, during the city's architectural boom of the 1920s, provided the building materials for many of the skyscrapers and other major buildings constructed during that decade.[77] For fans of the counterculture-era Grande though, the building's bricks have a significant, ascribed value because of their association with house band MC5's most popular song, "Kick Out the Jams."

Leo Early was outraged by the fan's illegal act of destruction. He insisted that the issue was much more serious than the removal of one brick. "The building is in the condition it is today largely thanks to these two groups [souvenir hunters and scrappers]," he protested. Early ended

Figure 6.13. Archaeologist and former Grande patron Jeri Pajor stands at the spot along the promenade where she and her friends used to sit during performances in the late 1960s and early 1970s. (Krysta Ryzewski)

Figure 6.14. The Grande was constructed with bricks produced by the John A. Mercier Brick Company using clay extracted from deposits in southwest Detroit. Collectors seek these bricks for their attributed connection to the MC5's song "Kick Out the Jams," which was recorded live at the Grande Ballroom in 1969. (Krysta Ryzewski)

his post by asking the 2,600 Facebook group members for advice about how to handle the incident.[78] The thirty responses to his question were uniformly passionate but widely divergent in their views of how the ruined building and its portable remains should be treated. It was a contentious debate. For some, the Grande Experience had nothing to do with the building's infrastructure. One commenter asked, "What are you going to do? Cream gonna play there again? The people who went to the Grande are starting to be fewer and fewer. They were the Grande not the bricks. Let it go." This comment garnered nine "likes." Another replied, "Concert's over, folks."

These commenters identified the Grande's significance with the music performed there, not the building itself. Such sentiments echo archaeologist Paul Graves-Brown's words of caution. He warns archaeologists, heritage professionals, and other scholars with interests in the places associated with popular music production to be careful about monumentalizing music as if it were a static, physical entity.[79] In the case of the Grande, however, an archaeological focus positioned the ballroom within the context of the building's design elements, sociopolitical settings, and longer term history as an entertainment venue. This approach recognized the building as part of a broader cultural landscape of music-making and activism in Detroit.[80]

In the course of the J.A.M. brick Facebook debate, several preservation-oriented commenters countered the anti-place-based perspectives by emphasizing the integral role the building's design and materials played in creating the memorable performance space. They also stressed the illegality of vandalism, the ongoing efforts of the building owners to maintain the space, and the potential to restore the building—citing examples of recently rehabilitated buildings that were once in worse states of decay. Other commenters asserted that by removing pieces of the building, vandals were stealing collective memories. Our archaeological findings supported their arguments. Despite crumbling walls and open holes in the ceiling, the ballroom's stage and proscenium arch remained remarkably well-preserved. Investigations underneath the stage floor revealed that its underlying supports were also in excellent condition. It was entirely possible, based on our observations, to sustain the heart of the ballroom.

Despite these facts, preservationists held the minority voice in the J.A.M. brick debate. Most of the commenters entered into the conversation from the position that the Grande was in a state of irreversible decay; the building, in their eyes, was already lost. People like the man who pried the brick from the Grande's wall, or those who removed the plaster ram/griffin head corbels from the pilasters around the ballroom promenade, deserved credit for saving elements of the building, they argued—these were acts of conservation by destruction. In the end, there was no consensus; the Grande's significance as a physical remain is still contested.

The materials, archives, and oral histories we recovered as part of our survey-based research activated different memories and inspired debates about whether to preserve the Grande Ballroom building. In the process, these conversations demonstrated that there was never one, singular Grande Experience, but rather many different encounters with the space, the music, and its associated activist agendas. In our case, archaeological approaches provided a baseline for understanding the complexity of the Grande Experience, before, during, and after its counterculture heyday. Thanks in part to the J.A.M. brick debate and other comments on social media, what began as an archaeological inspection of the building's integrity and remains had its own, public-facing and activist outcomes. Our archaeological findings were ultimately referenced in social media debates, they featured in exhibitions in the Grosscup Museum of Anthropology and the Detroit Historical Museum, and they were used to openly advocate for the building's maintenance. In 2017 Leo Early enlisted them in his efforts to secure federal recognition for the Grande on behalf of the building's owner.[81]

PRESERVATION AND COMMEMORATION

It took over a decade for Early and the Friends of the Grande group to mobilize formal historic preservation protections for the ballroom. Motivated by the outpouring of attention during the fiftieth anniversary events of the Grande's 1966 debut as a rock music venue, and also by the accelerating decay of the building due to structural issues and looting, the Chapel Hill church finally approved Leo Early's request to nominate the Grande to the National Register of Historic Places.[82] Grassroots preservation efforts officially paid off in September 2018, when Michigan's State Historic Preservation Review Board enthusiastically approved the ballroom for nomination to the National Register at the local level under Criterion A, as a building whose associated activities made a major contribution to events in American history.[83] The nomination, which included details of our survey's archaeological findings, then progressed to the federal level, and the US Department of the Interior officially certified it in December 2018.[84]

The Grande's addition to the National Register yielded no direct financial gains or immediate protections against the advancing decay. It did, however, inspire the building owners to pursue steps toward its stabilization. In January 2019 they permitted the Friends of the Grande to raise funds for engineers to conduct a structural evaluation; the subsequent survey deemed the building stable.[85] In October 2019, the group ran another fundraising campaign to install a temporary cover over the roof.

According to engineers, the Grande Ballroom is now officially salvageable. While enthusiasm will not stop the constant damage that the ballroom incurs from being open to the elements, the Grande's new National Register status qualifies the owners to apply for historic property tax credits and grants to offset the costs of renovating the building. Whether its rehabilitation among a strip of otherwise empty, decaying commercial buildings along Grand River Avenue will anchor the neighborhood's revitalization is another matter.

With new hope for the Grande's future, some of the people who retrieved objects or architectural elements from the Grande for "safekeeping" have begun to repatriate them to the Friends of the Grande and the building owners.[86] Such was the case with one of the hybrid ram/griffin corbel heads, which Early brought to the Wayne State archaeology laboratory in 2018 for 3D imaging, and eventually placed on display in the Detroit Historical Museum and Detroit Sound Conservancy's *Salvaging Sound* exhibit (Figure 6.15).

Recognizing that it will be some time before the building can be

Figure 6.15. Following the archaeological survey and the Grande's nomination to the National Register for Historic Places, a collector returned this hybrid ram/griffin corbel to Leo Early. Archaeologists created a 3D model of it, and it was exhibited in the Detroit Historical Museum's *Salvaging Sound* exhibit in 2018. (Krysta Ryzewski)

transformed into a venue again, Grande fans recently turned their attention to the building's exterior. A month after the State Historic Preservation Review Board voted on the Grande's National Register nomination, a brightly painted red, white, and blue mural appeared on the boards covering the first story of the building. The 2,000-square-foot painting, wrapped around the two street-facing sides of the building, is intended to reactivate the ballroom's musical and activist legacies within the context of the surrounding sparsely occupied area (Figure 6.16).

Margaret Saadi Kramer, music producer and wife of MC5 guitarist Wayne Kramer, designed the mural and commissioned Los Angeles–based artist Gabe Gault to paint it in commemoration of the fiftieth anniversary of the band's song "Kick Out the Jams," which they recorded live at the Grande in 1969. On the Grand River Avenue side of the building, Wayne Kamer is the mural's central (and only) figure. He is depicted playing his famous stars-and-stripes Fender Stratocaster guitar. Four red roses and a burst of white stars cascade from the guitar's head. Around the corner on Beverly Court the mural celebrates the White Panther Party with its logo and a montage of black-and-white photos depicting members and messages from the political group. As *Detroit Free Press* journalist Ryan

Figure 6.16. Margaret Saadi Kramer deigned this mural commemorating the MC5 and White Panther Party. She commissioned artist Gabe Gault to paint it on the corner of the building in 2018 in celebration of the band's fiftieth anniversary of its "Kick Out the Jams" recording there. The initials below the windows over the mural belong to the three children of Harry Weitzman, the financier of the Grande and likely operator of Little Harry speakeasy (see chapter 2). (Krysta Ryzewski)

Patrick Hooper commented, the mural has "just as many layers of meaning as there are coats of paint."[87] This may be the case with respect to its counterculture-era connections, but in actuality the mural's complexity centers on one band and one political movement; it barely scratches the surface of the building's longer-term social and creative legacies and their remains.

POPULAR MUSIC ARCHAEOLOGY

As our survey of the Grande Ballroom demonstrated, the relationships between popular music, memory, and archaeological remains are evident in physical, human, and sensory traces. A small but growing number of archaeologists, urban geographers, and music historians have also illustrated in their respective research projects how these relationships might be studied through music's material culture (e.g., recording devices, promotional posters, records), by examining music as a facet of cultural heritage, or by recognizing music as a communicative medium.[88] Popular music, as performed by counterculture-era Grande performers, cultivated memories among concertgoers that relate particular experiences in their youth with the space and experiences of the Grande Ballroom.[89] These lasting connections between ephemeral sounds, personal and collective memories, and physical remains are powerful catalysts for heritage management and revitalization strategies in Detroit.

Over the course of its history, the Grande Ballroom's music and patrons embodied the conditions, transitions, and tensions of twentieth-century Detroit.[90] This was especially the case during the counterculture era, when music and activism were inextricable in Grande events and performances. In Detroit countless places associated with 1960s activism and music heritage have been erased from the city's landscape as a result of neglect and aggressive urban renewal activities over the past fifty years. Such erasure has had adverse effects on the commemoration of the city's counterculture, social justice, and civil rights histories.[91] Thanks to grassroots preservation efforts, the Grande Ballroom may soon become a notable exception. Its remains, as well as its creative and its activist legacies, continue to inspire place-based community action decades after the building began to succumb to neglect. In this case, where an empowered place connects archaeological approaches with social justice legacies, the same spirit of activism that characterized a considerable part of the Grande Experience may wind up saving it for the enjoyment of future generations.

CHAPTER SEVEN

The Halleck Street Log Cabin
An Inconvenient Past

One of Detroit's most distressed residential areas is an enclave of about 135 acres on the city's east side. It is a marginal place in every sense of the word. On city maps the area has no name. Residents disagree about whether it is either an extension of Detroit's North End district, part of the Banglatown neighborhood, or more akin to the adjacent city of Hamtramck (*ham-TRAM-ick*). The area's physical isolation magnifies its uncertain identity.[1] Four major thoroughfares enclose it, two freeways to the north and west, and the municipal boundaries between Detroit and Hamtramck to the south and east.[2] These roads effectively sever the area from other neighborhoods and discourage outside vehicular traffic from traversing its narrow one-way streets.

Thirty-five blocks are nestled within this compact, rectangular enclave. Along the gridded streets named after Civil War generals, clusters of small, run-down houses are interspersed with tracts of vacant lots. In its mid-twentieth-century heyday, nearly seven hundred houses stood along these streets; today, there remain just a few dozen. Some of Detroit's most underserved and impoverished citizens live in the surviving homes. Most neighborhood residents are African American, but there is also a visible minority of Arab Americans who affiliate with the large community of Muslim immigrants living in the adjacent city of Hamtramck.

Over the past twenty years this diffuse, nameless neighborhood bore the brunt of crippling economic downturns. It was first ravaged by the national foreclosure and mortgage crises of the early 2000s, and then it was left to decay by the reduction of city services in the years before and during Detroit's 2013 municipal bankruptcy. By 2014, the city of Detroit owned 70% of the area's buildings and parcels.[3] Today the surviving homes, and the sweeping voids where houses used to stand, create the impression of a vast postapocalyptic landscape whose derelict physical remains are a testimony to the failures of industrial capitalism (Figure 7.1). To local residents, these remains are the festering wounds of pervasive inequality, government mismanagement, and civic disregard.

Figure 7.1. Eastward view of Halleck Street from the log cabin house at no. 2038. Only one of the houses pictured was occupied at the time this photograph was taken in 2019. (Krysta Ryzewski)

A century ago, city officials would have designated a blighted, liminal place like this a slum worthy of aggressive clearance, much as they did with the poor, dilapidated areas of Tin-Can Alley downtown and the Corktown neighborhood that once stood at the site of Roosevelt Park.[4] Yet in the 1920s, and in the decades to come, this was no slum. It was a fast-growing, vibrant working-class neighborhood whose tightly spaced homes were built to accommodate the massive influx of African American and eastern European migrants who relocated to Detroit. The unsegregated neighborhood was especially attractive to newcomers because it was located within convenient walking distance of several manufacturing plants: Gray Motor Company; Maxwell Motors; the Borg-Warner Corporation's clutch manufacturing plant; Chrysler's Highland Park assembly; and a number of smaller factories and machine shops along Dequindre, the neighborhood's western boundary road. For the remainder of the twentieth century the area was home to a close-knit, low-income, and predominately African American community.

Between 1920 and 1921 the modern house at 2038 Halleck Street was constructed as a one-and-a-half-story detached frame dwelling (Figure 7.2). Detroit city directory records list Anthony Ament, an oiler, and Elliott Gelyard, a laborer, as the home's first residents in 1922. The home's construction was an unremarkable episode in a building spree that brought rows of dwellings to Halleck and its parallel streets. Resembling the mill towns of New England, the houses were spaced just three to four feet apart. The majority had rectangular footprints and were set back from the street along an even sight line. The house at 2038 Halleck was a notable exception; according to the Sanborn Fire Insurance

Figure 7.2. Modern house at 2038 Halleck at the time of the archaeological survey in December 2018. The log cabin occupied the front one-and-a-half stories of the structure. (Krysta Ryzewski)

map of 1921, it was purposefully built to be narrower and shorter than its neighbors.

Throughout the 1920s the house at 2038 Halleck accommodated short-term residents who worked for nearby automotive manufacturers, including Adam Binder, a Hungarian immigrant, and John Heskinen, a northern Michigander of Finnish descent. In 1929 the first African American residents moved in. They included Wylie C. Wells, an interior decorator and painter who was born around 1880 in Alabama; his wife Carrie, a hotel cook; James, a barber; Viola Sharp, a housekeeper; Georgia-born Walter Blunt, an automotive factory laborer; his wife Essie, and their two children Carrie (age 8) and Tommy (age 5). The fact that this unnamed, marginal neighborhood of Detroit was welcoming to Black renters and homeowners from the 1930s onward is largely unrecognized in historical discussions about city housing. Yet, for the next seventy-seven years, as the area transitioned from an integrated to a predominately Black neighborhood, the house would continue to be occupied by a mixture of African American families and their renters.

In 2018, nearly one hundred years after its construction, our archaeological survey revealed that the front half of the house at 2038 Halleck was built around the remains of an earlier log cabin. The modern house's builders apparently appreciated the cabin's sturdy architecture and decided to keep its walls in place. For decades thereafter the cabin's durable timbers and original features survived relatively unscathed, hidden underneath a facade of wall plaster, modern siding, and roof shingles.

This nameless, derelict neighborhood is among the last places in Detroit that any of us, scholars, historic preservationists, and local residents alike, expected to find the remains of a remarkably well-preserved nineteenth-century log cabin. During the unsteady course of the Halleck Street Log Cabin Recovery Project, conducted jointly between my team of Wayne State University archaeologists and colleagues from the Hamtramck Historical Museum, we would come to appreciate how the neighborhood's twentieth-century history was vital for both understanding the cabin's inadvertent preservation and for envisioning its future potential as a cultural heritage resource in not one, but two multiethnic, working-class cities: Detroit and Hamtramck.

This chapter tells the story of a collaborative, community-based archaeology and historic preservation project that did not succeed as planned. It does not have a happy ending. The story recounts how our collaborative attempts to study and preserve the Halleck Street log cabin—a quintessential historic midwestern dwelling—became embroiled in a highly visible blight management controversy that pitted the two cities of Detroit and Hamtramck and various groups of stakeholders against each other. On one side of the struggle were interest groups concerned with the cabin's future: archaeologists, historic preservationists, local Hamtramck politicians, and residents. The other side was composed of stakeholders propelled by stringent economic and political agendas: developers, contractors, city agencies in Detroit, and federal authorities. The bitter outcome, the cabin's careless destruction by city-backed contractors, immersed an archaeology and preservation-oriented project within a fraught political milieu, one that deemed unanticipated archaeological finds, and the people invested in their preservation, inconvenient and disruptive to civic improvement initiatives.

As circumstances evolved unfavorably for archaeology and preservation interests during the course of the Log Cabin Recovery Project, our group faced two choices: retreat quietly or step up and take public action. We chose the latter course. Part of our response involved launching an investigation into the patterns and circumstances of federally funded blight removal demolitions in Detroit. Our research revealed an exemption to federally mandated historic preservation and archaeological resource protections. By design, the preservation exemption accelerated the removal of the most impoverished and blighted neighborhoods in Detroit and other struggling postindustrial cities nationwide. Even though we failed to achieve our initial objectives, the Log Cabin Recovery Project team ultimately succeeded by increasing public awareness about policy and development issues affecting historic and archaeological resources.

Here I recount the contentious Log Cabin Recovery Project in its four chronological phases: (1) the start of a conventional collaborative, community-based archaeology project; (2) an innovative community-led preservation initiative; (3) a controversial demolition; and (4) a process of recalibration and reconciliation.

HAMTRAMCK ARCHAEOLOGY

The story of the Log Cabin Recovery Project begins with another archaeological excavation project, 1.5 miles to the southeast, at the former location of Old Hamtramck Center. During the fall of 2018 I directed excavations of Old Hamtramck Center as part of my biannual Archaeological Field Methods class. Our twenty-person team included Wayne State University students who were enrolled in the class as well as alumni, local volunteers, a retired police officer, and members of the Hamtramck Historical Commission. The excavations took place with permission of the landowner and in partnership with the Hamtramck Historical Museum on a privately owned vacant lot along the west side of Joseph Campau Avenue. A century ago a bustling strip of retail shops and offices stood on the lot alongside Hamtramck's main road. Within our excavation area there used to stand two shops, a bar called the Nut House, two single family homes, various outbuildings, and Hamtramck's first municipal building, Village Hall, constructed between 1914 and 1915. Village Hall housed local government offices, the fire department, police station, and jail. Old Hamtramck Center and its archaeological remains were a microcosm of life in fast-growing Hamtramck during the years of its rapid transition from a village outpost to a small but mighty 2.1-square-mile industrial city.

The city of Hamtramck has a history and cultural identity that is distinct from, but complementary to, its neighbor, Detroit. Hamtramck is an independent municipality located within the boundaries of Detroit. Like Highland Park to the northwest, Hamtramck's origins as an incorporated city date to the automobile manufacturing boom of the 1910s. In 1910 the Dodge Brothers opened their automotive plant in the township of Hamtramck. Immigrants from eastern Europe arrived to Hamtramck in droves, boosting the town's population from 3,500 in 1910 to 48,000 in 1920.[5] By 1921, Hamtramck was one of the most densely populated cities in the United States, with an estimated 24,000 residents per square mile, 80% of whom were born in Poland. To protect its assets from being subsumed by Detroit, Hamtramck incorporated as its own city in 1922. It quickly developed a reputation as a prosperous industrial city, whose residents took pride in their work ethic, Polish American culture, and independence from Detroit.

Hamtramck's immigrant population began to diversify in the 1970s. With the arrival of newcomers from Bangladesh, Pakistan, Yemen, and Serbia, it gradually transitioned into the first Muslim-majority city in the United States. Today, with a population of nearly 22,000, Hamtramck is among the most culturally diverse cities in the country. Although Hamtramck suffered from out-migration and economic downturns as a result of late twentieth-century deindustrialization and government mismanagement, the city's built environment is generally well maintained. It has not suffered from epidemics of blight comparable to those in Detroit prior to its 2013 bankruptcy.

At the Old Hamtramck Center site my archaeology team excavated the remains of six buildings over the course of eleven weeks (Figure 7.3). With just a chain-link fence separating the lot from busy Joseph Campau Avenue, our presence piqued the attention of neighborhood businesspeople,

Figure 7.3. Wayne State University excavations at Old Hamtramck Center with Neal Rubin and other media personnel in the background, October 2018. (Krysta Ryzewski)

children walking home from school, firefighters, journalists, and city politicians. We always took the time to speak with curious onlookers, and we also organized a public open house on a Saturday in October during which over one hundred visitors braved torrential rains to meet the team and learn about our finds.

One of the site visitors was Neal Rubin, a reporter for the *Detroit News* whose coverage of local history and archaeology is noteworthy for its careful attention to detail. Rubin wrote a feature story about the excavations, and as soon as it appeared in the newspaper on October 28, 2018, I began to receive emails from strangers who wanted to share bits of local history, archaeological hunches, and urban legends with me.[6] Few of these stories related directly to the Old Hamtramck Center site's history, but they were valuable nonetheless because they contributed to a more vibrant picture of the city's social history. One such message came from an inspector who worked for Michigan's state environmental agency.[7] His job was to examine condemned buildings for asbestos before their demolition. Acting as a concerned citizen, he reached out to me to report how he had come across what appeared to be the remains of an old log cabin during a local house inspection. The alleged cabin's squared, hand-hewn logs had been exposed after construction workers removed the interior plaster walls of a modern house. He provided me with the street address, attached pictures of the timber-built walls, and suggested that I might be interested in visiting the house to determine whether it was of historical and archaeological significance. I was.

I shared the news about the potential log cabin with the local Historical Commission and the Hamtramck Historical Museum, both of which are directed by my colleague Greg Kowalski, a historian, journalist, and lifelong Hamtramckan. Kowalski and I planned an initial reconnaissance visit to the Halleck Street home in late November 2018. During our preparations for the visit we entered the property's address into Google Maps. The results produced two listings for the same address; one placed the house in Hamtramck and the other put it in Detroit. There is, in fact, a historical basis for the home's confusing geographic association. Between 1798 and 1917 Halleck Street and its environs were part of Hamtramck Township (a much larger twenty-square-mile tract of land that extended from present-day 8 Mile southward to the Detroit River).[8] By 1915, as its economic and population base expanded, Detroit annexed all of Hamtramck Township except for the village center, which would later become the city of Hamtramck. Since 1922 uncontroversial municipal boundaries have existed between the two cities. Yet somehow Google and other geospatial databases, including the Detroit Land Bank Authority's parcel maps, still seem uncertain, or perhaps ambivalent, about where the homes in the borderland neighborhood belong.[9]

The modern Halleck Street home was, in fact, located within present-day Detroit, just a few blocks north of the Hamtramck-Detroit border. While the modern iteration of the house may have belonged to Detroit, as far as Kowalski and the Historical Commission were concerned, if the log cabin structure encased within it predated 1917, then it—the cabin—was "Hamtramck's own."[10]

A FORGOTTEN LOG CABIN

My first visit to 2038 Halleck took place on a cold Friday afternoon in November with Greg Kowalski and three Hamtramck Historical Museum board members. In our approach to the property, we turned onto Halleck Street from Dequindre, the subdivision's western boundary, and drove slowly down a desolate block interspersed with poorly maintained single-family houses. Along that one block of Halleck between Dequindre and Goddard, about half—thirty-six of the sixty-seven parcels—still had houses standing on them. Twenty of these thirty-six homes were owned by the city of Detroit; they were vacant and had been formally condemned as "blight" by the Detroit Land Bank Authority. Only a handful of the other sixteen privately owned houses appeared to be occupied. It was easy to discern most of the Land Bank–owned properties along Halleck because the agency had installed wooden boards over the houses' doors and windows and affixed yellow condemnation signs to them.

We arrived at 2038 Halleck to discover the front entrance wide open. Proceeding with caution, our reconnaissance group walked into a dark, open living room that comprised the front half of the modern house. The entire home's interior had been stripped to a skeleton of wooden framing and flooring, and so we were immediately able to discern clear architectural differences between the front and back sections of the first story. The back, southern half of the house was constructed of modern vertical framing, while the front half was supported by horizontally aligned timbers (Figure 7.4). At a later date, builders had installed drywall supports over the log timbers. The modern, back section of the house had a basement and amenities (bathroom, kitchen area). By contrast, the front portion of the house was raised eighteen inches above the ground surface, presumably during construction of the newer house, at which point builders added concrete blocks underneath to elevate the older portion of the house.

We carefully examined the architectural details in the older, front portion of the house. Robust horizontal timbers held together all four of its walls. Based on our inspections of the timbers and the architectural techniques and materials used to connect them to one another, we concluded that the front portion of the house was clearly part of a different, earlier building episode than the modern structure. On the first floor the timbers enclosed a rectangular footprint of sixteen-and-three-quarters by twenty-one feet and extended halfway up into the second story of the modern house. The horizontal logs were intact, well preserved, and stable, as well as relatively unaffected by generations of occupancy, the decay of the modern house, and exposure to weather. Traces of hand-hewn ax marks, remnants of the construction techniques used to cut and square the timbers, were visible along the beams' edges (Figure 7.5). The presence of hand-wrought square nails in some of the timbers suggested that the log structure was built prior to the widespread introduction of round-headed, machine-cut nails in the late 1880s.[11] Our reconnaissance team agreed

Figure 7.4. Horizontal timbers of the log cabin's east wall are visible behind the framing for the modern house's interior drywall. (Krysta Ryzewski)

that there was indeed an authentic log cabin encased within the modern house, and that it appeared to have been constructed prior to 1890.

We were all thrilled by this rare find, a long-forgotten log cabin in the middle of the city. Its rediscovery boosted the number of surviving historic log cabins known in Detroit to three. The best-known log cabin was built as an upscale retreat in 1885 by architects Mason and Reed for Senator Thomas Palmer and his wife, Lizzie.[12] It still stands in Palmer Park and is a popular space for public events and programming. The second cabin, located at 2015 Clements Street on the city's west side, is more ordinary and comparable with the Halleck Street home. The James Smith Farmhouse was originally built as a one-and-a-half story log cabin between 1830 and 1850.[13] At a later date, its owners constructed an aluminum-sided house around it. Like the Halleck Street cabin, the Detroit Land Bank Authority (DLBA) assumed ownership of the Smith Farmhouse after it fell into foreclosure. But unlike the Halleck Street property, the log cabin inside the Smith Farmhouse was not a chance discovery; occupants and local historians knew about its existence underneath the modern building facade and advocated for its protection. As a result, the DLBA was willing to protect the Smith Farmhouse by including it on their "Do Not Demolish" list, where it remained until its return to private ownership on February 18, 2019.[14]

Given the dilapidated state of the modern Halleck Street home and the impending winter weather, we agreed that a more thorough documentation of the log cabin was a time-sensitive priority. We also planned to start exploring ways to protect the structure from further decay. As we exited the home, one member of our group spotted a plywood board buried under debris on the porch. When he picked it up to reposition it over the front door, we noticed the Detroit Land Bank's telltale yellow condemnation notice affixed to it, announcing that the building was earmarked for demolition. At that point, we realized that time was not on our side. We needed to take immediate action if there was to be a future for the cabin.

PRELUDE TO PRESERVATION

Greg Kowalski and I divided up advocacy and research tasks according to our own professional expertise. With decades worth of experience in local politics, communications, and reporting, Kowalski took the lead on notifying local politicians and government offices in Hamtramck and Detroit about the log cabin. I notified local and state preservation authorities, including the state archaeologist, the Michigan Historic Preservation Network, and my archaeology colleagues. I informed them of our plans to conduct an immediate archaeological survey of the log cabin and sought their advice about comparative examples and suitable analytical techniques. All of us agreed that this was not an appropriate moment for media exposure because the property was easily accessible, and we wanted to prevent it from vandalism. The property's precarious situation, poor preservation, and our need for privacy also meant that it was not a suitable locale for developing an open, community-involved and participatory recovery project from the outset. That opportunity would feature prominently later on in our emergent plan for the cabin.

To proceed with a full-scale archaeological documentation of the log cabin and any sort of recovery or restoration plans, we required cooperation from the property's manager, the DLBA. The DLBA is a legal entity and corporation (a body public) charged with managing the city's blighted and vacant properties through sales and demolitions, for the purpose of returning them to "productive use."[15] The agency's origins and its journey to amassing a level of unquestioned power and authority over Detroit's built environment coincide with the city's reintroduction of aggressive

Figure 7.5. Sections of two adjoining logs removed for dendrochronology analysis. Hand-carved wooden pegs held the timbers together, and their ends were tapered to accommodate the adjacent door frame. (Krysta Ryzewski)

blight removal practices over the past decade. This process is important to understand in order to appreciate the circumstances behind the modern Halleck Street home's dereliction and the log cabin's eventual fate.

BLIGHT MANAGEMENT AND THE DETROIT LAND BANK AUTHORITY

Five years after the passage of Michigan's Land Bank Fast Tract Act in 2003, the city of Detroit and the state of Michigan's Land Bank Fast Track Authority established the first iteration of the Detroit Land Bank Authority in September 2008.[16] The purpose of the DLBA, as stated in the intergovernmental agreement that initiated the authority, was to strengthen the city's economy and revitalization efforts by assembling and disposing public property in "a manner that fosters development and promotes economic growth."[17] The DLBA quickly stalled because of the dual effects of the 2008 mortgage crisis and the mismanagement of resources by Mayor

Kwame Kilpatrick's administration. Lacking the municipal funds to manage the city's blight issues, by early 2013 the city of Detroit pursued alternative land management strategies, including a partnership with the Detroit Blight Authority, a nonprofit organization established by CEO Bill Pulte (of Pulte Capital Partners).[18] Supported by a combination of private and public funds, the Detroit Blight Authority began to manage demolition and land vacancy in Eastern Market and other target neighborhoods by applying "high-tech and mass-production techniques to housing demolition."[19] Later that fall, six months after Michigan governor Rick Snyder placed Detroit under the control of an Emergency Manager (Kevyn Orr), the Obama administration established another initiative, the Blight Removal Task Force. The Task Force granted Detroit $300 million of federal funds to focus on blight, public safety, and public works.[20] The Detroit Blight Removal Task Force originated as an outgrowth of this funding arrangement. Its organizers structured the entity as a public-private partnership, made up of nonprofit leaders, real estate developers, and representatives from various federal, state, and local government agencies. As their first task the Detroit Blight Removal Task Force commissioned a comprehensive citywide land parcel survey to determine the state of the city's housing stock, lot conditions, and land use. Their data collection process, and the results, would inform future land management strategies and development initiatives.[21]

The Detroit Blight Removal Task Force's citywide survey of property conditions began in November 2013. The survey took ten weeks to complete and involved 150 local residents as "surveyors" during the parcel-by-parcel property assessment. The avocational surveyors collected data about land use within designated quarter-mile "microhood" areas.[22] At each property, they used tablet computers to take photographs and answer a list of predesigned, closed questions about the property's apparent function and condition. Evaluations of property conditions fell within the subjective constraints of what the task force determined to be indicators of blight, vacancy, fire damage, dumping, and structural stability.[23] After completing the questions for each property, surveyors uploaded their assessments to a master database. In partnership with Data Driven Detroit and Loveland Technologies, the task force developed a digital open source citywide map, the Motor City Mapping Project, to visualize the data compiled for 377,602 surveyed properties.[24] The scale of blight recorded in the citywide property survey was staggering. Surveyors designated 30% of the city's housing stock—78,506 of 263,569 structures—as subpar and in need of "intervention."[25] Of these buildings, over half, 40,077, met the task force's definition of blight and therefore merited immediate demolition. The remaining 38,429 subpar properties showed indications of encroaching blight and, the report concluded, would eventually require similar intervention.[26]

When Mayor Mike Duggan assumed office in January 2014, Detroit lacked a plan to manage the nearly 80,000 structures that existed across the city in a state of seemingly irreversible decay. At the beginning of his term, Duggan issued a ten-point plan called "Every Neighborhood Has a Future." Five of the ten points concerned blight removal issues—boarding up vacant homes, increasing rates of demolition, and addressing maintenance issues.[27] The plan reinvigorated the DLBA and asserted it as the city's authoritative blight removal agent.[28] As described in the 2014 Detroit Blight Removal Task Force Report, the DLBA was reestablished as "a strong agent for *preservation, revitalization, and transformation of blighted properties* in Detroit through a range of interventions, from stabilization of structures and returning them to private ownership to removal of hazardous conditions and dangerous buildings."[29]

In its efforts to combat the city's property vacancies and to justify the clearance of tens of thousands of decaying buildings, the Blight Removal Task Force and the Detroit Land Bank Authority reintroduced the concept of "blight" to Detroit's city planning vocabulary.[30] For longtime Detroiters, this rhetoric was nothing new. Blight removal proposals have been perennial fixtures of Detroit's city planning efforts for the best part of a century, especially in the wake of economic downturns and population changes.[31] As with earlier generations' blight removal campaigns, in 2014 the scale and speed of demolitions under the DLBA's management depended on the availability of funds. Unfortunately, for the Halleck Street log cabin, federal funding was readily available. I will return to the particulars of this funding and how the DLBA executed it later.

Immediately after our November 2018 reconnaissance visit, Kowalski began petitioning the DLBA to remove 2038 Halleck from their demolition list, even if just temporarily, so that my colleagues and I could survey and document the cabin. He first spoke with a colleague at the Land Bank in early December. The staff member assured him that they would support removing the property from the demolition list. We trusted that with over 91,976 properties to manage, and over 40,000 buildings slated for demolition, pausing the plans for 2038 Halleck would not cause undue interruptions to the DLBA's scheduled blight elimination operations.[32] With reassurance from the Land Bank office staff, we shifted gears and proceeded with our documentation and recovery plans.

ARCHAEOLOGICAL SURVEY

Three days after our initial visit to 2038 Halleck, on a snowy Monday morning in December, I returned with a team of five archaeologists (all of whom were part of the Old Hamtramck Center excavations). Our objectives that day were to conduct a thorough survey and documentation of the visible elements of the log cabin's interior and exterior faces. Our work was noninvasive. We planned to photograph, measure, and map only what we saw on the surface in order to gather more information about the cabin's construction, age, and state of preservation. These data, which I compiled into a twenty-seven-page report, were necessary for crafting subsequent research and recovery plans.[33] Part of those plans would include more extensive archaeological investigations inside and outside of the cabin in the spring or summer of 2019, after the ground thawed.

The archaeology team carefully inspected each architectural element within the interior area of the log cabin—flooring, doors, windows, interior walls, a chimney, and hardware—to determine which elements were associated with it and which belonged to the modern house. The interior walls of the log cabin were fully exposed and visible in the front half of the modern house. Our systematic documentation detailed how the cabin was carefully constructed with hardwood logs, later determined to be black ash (*Fraxinus nigra*).[34] Each of the walls of the cabin's first story were built with a series of eleven or twelve single logs placed on top of one another and held together by interlocking double-pegged joinery. The only places where the long logs were cut was at the terminal ends of walls or along the edges of the cabin's two doors and one surviving window (Figures 7.6 and 7.7).

The wooden pegs joining the timbers together were so strong, and the logs were cut to such a precise fit with one another, that no mortar was used to secure the walls. To insulate the walls, the cabin's occupants stuffed moss and newspapers in between the timbers. Four rectangular voids in the east and west walls marked the former location of beams that once supported a ceiling between the ground floor and a half-story loft above (the cabin's ceiling was six inches lower than the modern home's ceiling).

Based on its extant architectural features, we concluded that the log cabin was a one-and-a-half story (twelve and three-quarters feet tall), 350 square-foot home. The rectangular structure's north and south walls spanned sixteen and three-quarters feet, and its east and west walls were twenty-one feet long. It had two entryways, one along the south wall and another along the east. Remarkably, it was still possible to see these entryways in the remains of the cabin walls. We determined the difference between modern and historic doorways by the ways in which the log timbers were cut. For example, two doorways stood along the southern wall, one modern and one historic (see Figures 7.6 and 7.7). The logs bordering the historic doorframe were carved to a taper so that the door (to

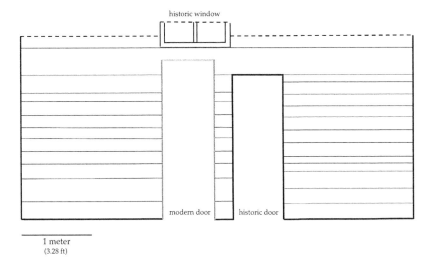

Figure 7.6. Plan drawing of the south interior wall of the log cabin based on measurements taken during the archaeological survey. (Krysta Ryzewski)

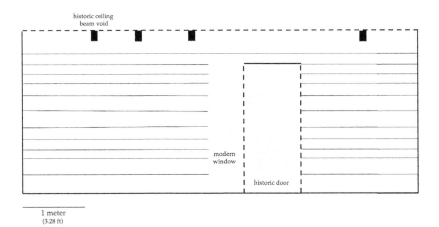

Figure 7.7. Plan drawing of the east interior wall of the log cabin based on measurements taken during the archaeological survey. (Krysta Ryzewski)

the outside) would fit into the frame; the logs on either side of the door frame were of different widths, indicating that the cabin's builders placed the timbers to accommodate the shape of the door rather than building the wall first and then cutting out a space for the door. The modern door, by contrast, was cut out of the preexisting log wall. The same was true of the historic two-pane window in the second-story loft; the logs surrounding it were tapered to accommodate a snug fit for the window frame (Figure 7.8).

In addition to the cabin's extant window and doors, there were traces of a brick chimney set toward the northern edge of the structure. The position of the doors and window suggested that if the cabin still stood in its original orientation, its frontage was oriented to the south, in the opposite direction of the modern house's northern entrance. The cabin's doorway orientation was another indication that it was constructed before Halleck and the other streets named after Civil War generals were laid out in the area around 1890.

Along the east wall of the cabin we documented fragments of hand-stenciled wallpaper adhered directly to the surface of the log timbers (Figure 7.9). The elaborate stenciled and painted designs included white flower and scrolls, green latticework, and a tan background.

We concluded that the wallpaper dated to one of the earliest phases of the cabin's occupancy based on the remnants of other wall treatments

Figure 7.8. Interior south wall of the log cabin and the cabin's historic doorway and window above it. The back half of the modern house is visible through the doorway. (Krysta Ryzewski)

Figure 7.9. Remnants of stenciled and painted wallpaper adhered to the surface of the log cabin's walls. (Krysta Ryzewski)

placed on top of it. Some pieces of it were covered over by a more recent gray paint or plaster. The wallpaper was remarkable for its survival despite numerous alterations to the wall surfaces, but also because it hinted that the earlier structure was, to its occupants, much more than an expediently built shelter.

According to a 1991 National Park Service Preservation Brief on historic log buildings, there exists an important distinction to make between log cabins and log houses.[35] A log cabin is typically a "simple one, or one-and-a-half story structure, somewhat impermanent . . . usually constructed with round rather than hewn, or hand-worked, logs, and it was the first generation homestead erected quickly for frontier shelter." A log house

"denotes a more permanent, hewn-log dwelling, either one or two stories
. . . often built as a second generation replacement." Many log houses were
"traditionally clad, sooner or later, with wood siding or stucco." Given the
permanency of the structure's architecture and its decorative elements,
the Halleck Street dwelling seems to fit well within the definition of a log
house. Nevertheless, until we had the opportunity to conduct further research, we continued to refer to the structure as a log cabin—mainly because the term conjured a more familiar reference among stakeholders
than the "log house" designation.

Although we did not plan to probe beneath the surface of the cabin
during our initial survey, we made two exceptions. First, we cut small sections of two log timbers from the southern wall of the cabin. We submitted these samples to our colleague at Michigan Technological University
for dendrochronology analysis. If enough information was present in the
logs' annual growth rings, then it would be possible for Zachary Merrill
to narrow down the year when the tree was cut and approximately when
the cabin was constructed. Second, we collected subsurface soil data by
inserting a six-foot-long soil probe through a hole in the cabin's floor into
the ground beneath the structure. We made six soil borings with the two-
inch-wide probe to get a better indication of the stratigraphic deposits
underneath the cabin and whether they might suggest that the cabin was
standing at its original location or if it had been relocated there during
the construction of the modern house. The soil we collected was relatively
undisturbed, suggesting that it was not affected by the construction of the
modern house. This finding supported the likelihood that the log cabin
stood at or very near its original location. Our last soil probe produced our
first nineteenth-century artifact, a shell button, perhaps dropped through
the floorboards of the cabin over a century ago. This was an encouraging
discovery. If we could locate a historic button with a few soil probes, then
future archaeological excavations were likely to yield more material culture related to the log cabin's occupants.

DATING THE CABIN FROM HISTORIC MAPS

During our archaeological survey a neighbor who lived across the street
walked into the house, curious about why we had descended on the building with an arsenal of lights, cameras, and tools. He was a retired union
electrician and took great interest in the remnants of the well-built cabin.
Until then, he had no idea that there was such a rare historic structure
within sight of his own home. Later, another neighbor came by. She told
us that she knew the last owners of the house and that she used to style

their daughter's hair in a front room on the second floor (the loft of the log cabin). Neither she nor her former clients knew that they were working and living within the remains of a historic home. Among current residents, there appeared to be no surviving recollections of the Halleck Street log cabin.

With few clues available from living memories, Kowalski and I turned to archival sources to gather information about the property and the historical development of the land on which the cabin once stood. Unfortunately, we did not locate any records that depict the cabin on historic maps or any other conclusive evidence of its date of construction or occupants. We did, however, amass considerable corroborating evidence from historic maps, which became the basis of our timeline for the area's urbanization. When we paired this land-use information with the archaeological materials—the wall timbers, wallpaper, button, and square-cut nails—we arrived at an estimation of the log cabin's construction date.

The earliest depiction of the area around present-day Halleck Street appears on the 1855 Map of Wayne County, published in the Farmer Atlas.[36] This map portrays the surrounding area as a sparsely populated agricultural hinterland on the outskirts of Detroit. Along Detroit's northern border there existed a portion of land straddling Greenfield Township to the west and Hamtramck Township to the east called "Ten Thousand Acre Tract." Within this tract were sixty square parcels, ranging in size from 91 to 160 acres; forty-four of the sixty parcels belonged to a Thomas Palmer, including Parcel 19, which spanned the entire modern-day Grace & Roos subdivision through which Halleck Street runs. Ten Thousand Acre Tract remained in place five years later, but by the time the 1860 Map of Wayne County was published Thomas Palmer no longer owned any properties within it. Instead, new landowners had recently carved smaller, narrow tracts, many as small as 20 acres, from preexisting parcels.[37] In Parcel 19 half of the 160-acre lot was divided into four 20-acre holdings, and the remaining lot was an 80-acre parcel owned by the McLeod family. Based on the changing settlement configurations within Ten Thousand Acre Tract, it may be inferred that the cabin's construction postdates 1855. Modern-day Halleck Street and the log cabin, if it existed in 1860, would have stood on the McLeod's property (Figure 7.10).

Sixteen years later, a map of Hamtramck Township published in the 1876 Wayne County Atlas shows a similar configuration of parcel size and ownership. The 76-acre parcel where the cabin stood then belonged to a James Wallace.[38] On all three of these early Hamtramck Township maps no buildings appear in the vicinity of the log cabin's location. It is worth

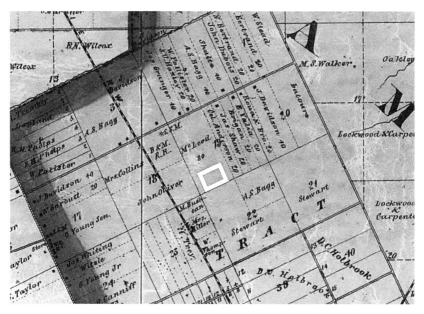

Figure 7.10. General location of the Halleck Street log cabin on the 1860 map of Wayne County published by Geil, Harley, and Siverd. (Library of Congress)

noting, however, that the only buildings included on the 1855, 1860, and 1876 maps are those located along main thoroughfares. It is quite possible that smaller buildings situated in the interior of larger tracts were omitted by surveyors and mapmakers.

Sometime between 1876 and 1891 Wallace sold the parcel on which the log cabin stood to the developers of the Grace & Roos subdivision. The subdivision, and Halleck Street, first appear on the 1891 Hamtramck Township map in the Wayne County Atlas.[39] The subdivision's design was well ahead of its time in anticipating Detroit and Hamtramck's rapid urbanization in the decades to come. When surveyors plotted the nine narrow rectangular blocks named after Civil War generals, they introduced a new configuration of urban dwelling to the otherwise open, pastoral landscape. Each parcel within the subdivision was arranged into thirty-eight uniform thirty-foot-wide lots, and each lot assigned an address. The property where the log cabin once stood appears on the map with the address of 601 Halleck (it was changed in 1922 when all addresses in the Metro Detroit area were reconfigured). By 1915 the Sanborn Fire Insurance map of the area depicts a scatter of houses interspersed among the subdivision's streets.[40] At first there were only three or four homes built on each block, but over the course of the next six years the neighborhood was utterly transformed by the housing boom that accommodated the influx of newcomers from the American South and eastern Europe. By 1921 new houses stood on every one of the over 680 parcels along the streets of the Grace & Roos subdivision, including at 2038 Halleck Street (Figure 7.11).[41]

Our archival research confirmed that the modern house at 2038 Halleck was constructed around the preexisting log cabin between 1920 and 1921. The historic maps convey how the land in the vicinity of the cabin was increasingly occupied by Euro-American settlers by 1860. Based on the available clues from the cabin's architecture, material culture, and archival information, we concluded that the log cabin was built to be a permanent dwelling, and that it was most likely constructed between 1855 and 1880. The orientation of the cabin's two doors to the south and east strongly suggests that it was in place before 1891. After that date the Grace & Roos subdivision's developers reoriented the area's domestic landscape by introducing northward-facing homes along that side of Halleck Street. While our archival and archaeological investigations were helpful in confirming a mid to late nineteenth-century date for the log cabin's occupancy, there remain many unanswered questions about specific dates and, of course, the people who lived there.

PRESERVATION MEETS POLITICAL ACTION

There was no question that the modern house at 2038 Halleck needed to be demolished. In the back of the house, crumbling walls were destabilizing the structure; in the front, dangling siding and collapsing ceilings posed serious safety hazards. The log cabin that survived inside of the front half of the house was a different story though. Armed with information about its age and construction, Greg Kowalski and the Hamtramck Historical Commission envisioned a scenario where it could be saved, relocated, and reinvented as an educational resource and heritage site for the benefit of Hamtramck residents. This vision was not unprecedented. Kowlaski based his plan on examples of another log cabin relocation in the Detroit suburb of Bloomfield Township.

With suggestion from the Detroit Land Bank Authority that the property would be temporarily spared from demolition, in early January 2019 our group shifted gears toward planning for the cabin's future. The planning process involved consulting with various politicians, developers, contractors, and community members in Hamtramck and Detroit about the logistics of the cabin's relocation and its potential public uses in the future.

Kowalski quickly gained the support of local politicians for the project, including Hamtramck mayor Karen Majewski. He then identified a

Figure 7.11. Sanborn Fire Insurance map of 1921 of a portion of the neighborhood between Dequindre to the west and Arlington Avenue to the east illustrates the area's rapid transformation since 1915 when the previous Sanborn map of the area was published. The log cabin house at 2038 Halleck (denoted by the black rectangle) is irregularly shaped among the rows of homes with identical dimensions.

potential location for the cabin—Zussman Park, a public green space in front of Hamtramck City Hall. He also consulted with local heavy equipment operators, builders, and carpenters about the feasibility of the relocation idea. All agreed that it was possible, and some even offered to donate their equipment and labor to the project. Members of the Historical Commission took to the streets of Hamtramck, where they carefully measured the width of roads and overhanging obstacles along the route between Halleck Street and Zussman Park to ensure that the cabin might be relocated without complications. After laying the groundwork for the cabin's relocation, Kowalski drafted a six-page proposal outlining plans to carefully dismantle, rebuild, and reinterpret the cabin.[42] Based on comparable projects, he estimated the cost of the recovery at $60,000. With the city's official approval, the Hamtramck Historical Museum planned to launch a fundraiser to finance the cabin's move. According to the community-led plan, our group of archaeologists and preservationists, along with qualified contractors, would work closely with the DLBA during their demolition process of the modern house. Together, we would dismantle the cabin, reconstruct it, and design interpretive and educational programming around it. Kowalski circulated the proposal to the DLBA, city officials in Hamtramck and Detroit, local politicians, preservationists, and other decision-makers.

There was no response from the DLBA. We figured they were disinterested in the proposal because the Halleck Street property was no longer a priority on their demolition schedule. By contrast, there was an enthusiastic response from local politicians in Hamtramck. Encouraged by their support, we decided to formalize the process for moving forward by proposing a resolution to the Hamtramck City Council. The resolution, if passed, would approve negotiations with the city of Detroit to transfer the cabin's ownership to Hamtramck and would permit the museum to initiate fundraising efforts to relocate the cabin to Zussman Park.

On January 22, 2019, our group squeezed into the Hamtramck City Council chambers and listened to Kowalski as he petitioned the city council to support the Halleck Street log cabin resolution. We were unsure how the proposal would be received. Hamtramck's mayor Karen Majewski, who holds a PhD in American culture, was an unwavering supporter of the plan, but flanking her at the meeting was the first majority-Muslim city council in the United States and a contentious public audience rearing to fight over the city's proposed ordinance prohibiting marijuana sales.

One of the challenges we addressed in the cabin's preservation plan was how to connect its distant history and associations with Euro-American settlers with Hamtramck's diverse community of recent immigrants. By relocating the cabin and placing it in a public space, we hoped that it would become what archaeologist Christopher Matthews describes as an assemblage around which various interest groups would cohere, rather than an object or site designed to conjure a specific experience for a limited or predefined group of stakeholders.[43] This resolution was a test of whether the log cabin might succeed as part of the city's present and future heritage or languish as a relic of a distant, disconnected past.

The city council meeting began with a public comment session. A dozen local residents took turns standing at the podium in front of the council members and mayor to advocate for various issues and air grievances. Nobody aside from our group came there prepared to speak about the log cabin, but somehow word had spread about it, and to our surprise, several commenters paused their remarks on other issues to champion its preservation. As one middle-aged woman ended her heated tirade about city mismanagement, her voice calmed and she declared, "I'm also pro-cabin. I hope it's open to the public." The audience laughed approvingly. Another local resident, a young man of about thirty who was employed at the local automotive assembly plant, took to the podium to plea for poverty exemptions to local property taxes. He bemoaned the economic struggles Hamtramck faced but ended his commentary by upholding the log cabin as a symbol of hope. "I get the sense that this is going to be a tough year for Hamtramckans," he started, "Please approve the resolution to rescue the historic log cabin. I can't even rationalize my support of it. It's purely emotional. In the words of a neighbor, 'This resonates within me.' I just get a feeling like we're going to need it. Some stupid, little, wonderous thing that we can celebrate. Have a parade. Be excited, and happy, and proud together for no reason we can even figure."[44] His sentiments about the log cabin seemed to resonate with the audience and with the city council, who unanimously passed the resolution later in the meeting.

The resolution asserts clear language about the city's support for the cabin's future and its ties to Hamtramck's past:

> WHEREAS, The Hamtramck Historical Commission, along with Wayne State University is currently evaluating the historic significance of the site, and has produced a plan to possibly restore and move the structure; and
>
> WHEREAS, The City of Hamtramck wishes to preserve this piece of Hamtramck Township history.
>
> NOW THEREFORE BE IT RESOLVED by the City Council of the City of Hamtramck, Wayne County, Michigan that the

Hamtramck Historical Commission shall pursue the necessary avenues to present a comprehensive plan for the funding
and rescue of the historic Halleck St. Hamtramck Township
Log Cabin.

During his comments to the city council, Kowalski described how,
when the cabin was relocated to Zussman Park, it would not need modern
utilities, but it would require basic maintenance from staff of the Historical Museum, a roof, concrete slab foundation, and insurance. It was an
expensive though not unattainable goal. On our way out of the chambers,
one resident handed him a check for $3,000 to support the log cabin's relo-
cation costs. After we posted about the resolution's passage on social media, colleagues as far away as England inquired about how to make dona-
tions. Our fundraising campaign had not yet begun but there was already
an international community invested in the future of the log cabin.

RESISTANCE AND DEMOLITION

Sadly, the situation in Hamtramck was too good to be true. Kowalski
reached out to the DLBA after the Hamtramck City Council meeting to
update them about the resolution's passage. For the first time the DLBA
replied promptly, but with their own update: it would not be possible for
us to pursue the log cabin recovery plan. The house at 2038 Halleck was
still on the DLBA's demolition list. Despite assurances to the contrary, it
had never actually been removed from the list. In mid-January, just days
before the Hamtramck City Council voted in favor of the cabin's preservation, the DLBA had quietly issued a demolition contract for the Halleck
Street property. It was no coincidence that the DLBA directorial staff's first
conversation with Kowalski (or any collaborator on our project) came after they issued this contract. The DLBA spokeswoman explained to Kowalski that once the organization issued a demolition contract to a private
company, it was simply impossible for them to halt the process. From that
point onward, as far as the DLBA was concerned, the fate of the Halleck
Street log cabin was out of their hands.

With the news that the 2038 Halleck property was to be demolished,
our group launched into a frenzy of activity. We placed numerous calls
to officials in Detroit and Hamtramck. We notified state historic preservation authorities. We consulted with reporters in the local media. Kowalski
reached out to managerial authorities at the Detroit Land Bank, requesting meetings so that we could petition to have the property spared from
imminent demolition. We were even prepared to compromise, if it was

truly impossible to halt demolition, by requesting time to recover more archaeological information from the cabin. At the very least, we wanted to collect more samples for dendrochronology analysis and excavate a few areas underneath the cabin to locate temporally diagnostic artifacts.

The messages Kowalski left for the DLBA over the course of a month went unanswered. In the absence of direct communication, we were left in the dark about the timeline for the impending demolition plans. We were hopeful that the snowy, frigid winter weather would bide us a bit more time to negotiate and leverage support from our allies. Meanwhile, a group of colleagues affiliated with the statewide preservation nonprofit the Michigan Historic Preservation Network (MHPN) had the financial means to pursue a more drastic and immediate intervention. On Monday, February 18, 2019, one MHPN member called the DLBA with an offer to purchase 2038 Halleck Street in order to forestall the log cabin's demolition. Nobody at the DLBA responded to her offer. Three days later, in the early Thursday morning hours of February 21, when we least expected it, bulldozers from the Smalley Construction company in Scottville, Michigan, appeared on site. Within a few hours the modern house and log cabin at 2038 Halleck were demolished and their remains carted away to a landfill in suburban Northville. Our colleague from the MHPN, who had taken to driving by the property on a daily basis, discovered the demolition (Figure 7.12).

The news about the log cabin's demolition felt like a punch to the gut. We worried whether our public and vocal advocacy for the cabin's preservation accelerated the demolition process. Had we made the DLBA eager to remove the structure before it attracted more attention and disrupted their demolition timeline?

RATIONALIZING REMOVAL

When pressed by reporters, the DLBA defended the log cabin's demolition as a cost-saving measure executed in the best interest of both Detroit residents and federal taxpayers. Land Bank spokeswoman Alyssa Strickland explained that even before the bulldozer arrived on site, the DLBA had already spent at least $10,000 to remediate and prepare the home for demolition.[45] She argued, "Without a way to recoup that significant cost of time spent . . . it would be a waste of taxpayer dollars" to halt the property's demolition.[46] "Pulling it from the list and losing the $10,000 already spent," she insisted, "wasn't a viable option."[47] Never mind the MHPN member's offer to buy the property from the Land Bank or our plan to fundraise for the cabin's recovery. Our plans were "purely theoretical,"

Figure 7.12. Only the porch and the basement foundation remained after the Detroit Land Bank demolished the home at 2038 Halleck in February 2019. (Krysta Ryzewski)

she alleged; she claimed she had never seen or heard of them prior to the demolition.[48]

The DLBA intended for the removal of 2038 Halleck to be a routine demolition, executed quickly and quietly, in the same capacity as their contractors had erased 11,000 buildings from other city-owned properties between 2014 and 2019. Like those homes, 2038 Halleck's demolition was financed by the Hardest Hit Fund. These federal funds were due to expire in 2020, but there still remained several DLBA-owned homes on Halleck Street (and dozens within the neighborhood) designated to be cleared with the monies before then. For the DLBA, time was of the essence. Demolition delays, like those caused by chance discoveries of previously unknown historic structures or archaeological remains, added to the DLBA's maintenance costs, impeded the city's blight removal agenda, and burdened taxpayers. The log cabin's rediscovery posed an inconvenience, and rather than take the time to discuss how the historic remains might be addressed, the DLBA grew impatient and instead removed the structure from the neighborhood landscape, hoping to silence the issue once and for all. Their decisions generated the opposite effect: vocal opposition and widespread national media coverage.

In speeding through the demolition process, the DLBA made several critical oversights that, at least circumstantially, revealed their disregard for the concerns of local residents living in distressed neighborhoods and for preservation and cultural resource management professionals. The DLBA's first misstep was assuming that contemporary neighborhood residents would not care about the discovery and demolition of a historic log cabin. The unassuming homes belonging to low-income residents on Halleck Street, and along the neighboring streets, offered little economic or aesthetic incentives to developers or historic preservationists, and so the DLBA chose not to initiate consultations with heritage management specialists to consider the neighborhood's historic or archaeological resource potential in advance of their demolition plans. But to the working-class African American and Euro-American families whose ancestors relocated to the subdivision during the Great Migration era, the homes were a source of pride, hope, and new beginnings. In fact, our research revealed that such stories of resilient local Halleck Street residents and their fondness for the area span a century.

Take Douglas Ford Sr. and his wife, Mabel. Within a month of their arrival in Detroit from Tennessee in 1922, Ford Sr. was able to purchase a home, as a thirty-four-year-old Black man, at 1950 Halleck Street (the corner lot on the same block as 2038 Halleck). From their home, the Fords established the D. Ford Company, a business that supplied wood and coal for residential stoves and space heaters. From the back of his truck, Douglas Ford delivered fuel to residents in all areas of Detroit and neighboring suburbs, crossing into segregated neighborhoods and securing loyal customers of all backgrounds in the process. Douglas cleverly navigated the prejudices of Great Migration–era Detroit by leveraging his surname's connection to the Ford family of auto-manufacturing fame. Instead of identifying himself as the company's namesake, he posed as a fictitious man called "Jim Hines," a driver for the D. Ford

Company. As a result many of his regular customers simply assumed he worked for a White-owned business. The D. Ford Company thrived as a result of his strategy and continued to operate as a prosperous business out of his Halleck Street home through the Great Depression and into the 1950s.[49]

When disguised as delivery driver "Jim Hines," Douglas Ford Sr. would have had to dodge the dozens of children who transformed Halleck Street's sidewalks, yards, and roadway into their playground space outside of school hours during the 1940s and 1950s. Like the Fords, most of their parents had also recently migrated from the South. While they labored in local manufacturing and service industries, the children entertained themselves by working local newspaper routes and playing games in the street outside of their homes. Through countless rounds of jacks, hopscotch, and tag, the "Halleck Street Kids," as they called themselves, formed a community of their own, one that would remain intact for over fifty years, even after most of them moved away from the area. In 1993 the "Halleck Street Kids" planned a reunion. Many of them were turning fifty that year, and they decided that the birthday anniversary was an opportune moment to gather and share their "very fond memories of their close-knit neighborhood." On August 13, 1993, dozens of former residents convened at Detroit's American Serbian Memorial Hall for the celebration.[50]

One of these "Halleck Street Kids" was Carolyn Shepherd, a life-long resident of the neighborhood. Like Douglas Ford Sr., she is an entrepreneur, a hairdresser who has over the years visited many of the homes in the neighborhood to cut and style residents' hair. One of her clients in the early 2000s was Laschella Johnson, then a resident of 2038 Halleck (the log cabin/house). Johnson's father Willie first purchased 2038 Halleck in 1954 when he was working as a laborer at the nearby Ford automotive plant. The Johnsons then kept the house in the family into the 2000s. Shepherd initially reported that the Johnsons never mentioned that a log cabin was part of their home, so she figured they were probably unaware of it.[51] Over the course of our recovery efforts, Shepherd became fascinated by the cabin and its history. She visited with us during our surveys and began to keep watch over, and report to us, the movements of DLBA contractors around the property. On February 21, 2019, she watched the demolition from her home across the street. Later, she told me that as she watched the bulldozer level the house she felt sad. She was upset by how an artifact that spoke to the industriousness of local residents was erased without any sort of community consultation. Her interest in the site encouraged her to reconnect with Laschella's mother, Mary Johnson, also a former resident of the house. Mary, it turns out, always suspected that there was something different, and older, about the architecture of the house with the log cabin inside of it. She, too, regretted that she never got the chance to learn more about the log cabin before it was demolished.

To the local residents of Halleck Street, and also to those of Hamtramck and nearby neighborhoods in Detroit, the log cabin represented a spirit of ingenuity, resilience, and sweat equity with which they identified. As an archaeological remain and historic resource, its heritage was much more relatable to them than the Gilded Age mansions of Brush Park (see chapter 3). Local residents instead connected with stories of migration and having to generate income in creative ways, often through informal means. In the case of the log cabin, the DLBA neglected to consider how the connections between communities, memories, and Halleck Street's built environment still ran deep. Given the scope of the histories and personal connections that emerged during the resolution and demolition processes, it stung to imagine what a community-involved archaeology project centered on the log cabin's recovery and relocation might have been like, if we just had the time.

OUTRAGED AND OUTSPOKEN

Things got messy after the demolition. The local coverage of the log cabin's discovery and demolition spread on social media and soon reached a national audience. The Associated Press recirculated the stories about the DLBA's careless demolition of the log cabin to news outlets nationwide. People from as far afield as California, North Carolina, and Florida reached out to us to share their regrets about the cabin controversy.

Locally, the demolition triggered outrage among Hamtramck officials, tearing a rift between two cities that could have been productive partners on the cabin recovery project. Hamtramck mayor Karen Majewski put her feelings about the DLBA bluntly, "Heads should roll," she told *The Review*, Hamtramck's newspaper.[52] In another newspaper story on March 22, Greg Kowalski reported how, in Hamtramck, "Everybody is furious." He continued, "Detroit has a long history of allowing historic buildings to be demolished for supposed redevelopment—redevelopment that rarely occurs or ends up being worth it."[53] Kowalski concluded his piece with a scathing critique of the DLBA: "Detroit officials have long had no appreciation of their own past. It's no surprise they have no interest in saving Hamtramck's past either."[54]

Officials with the Michigan Historic Preservation Network issued their own censure about the process and outcome of the demolition. Detroit preservation specialist Melissa Arrowsmith stressed that once historic structures are gone, "they're gone for good." In the case of the Halleck Street log cabin, she emphasized that privately funded preservation efforts by the MHPN members would have recouped and saved the cost of demolition for the DLBA. She lamented, "when we have a place that the community has raised their voice in support of preserving rather than demolishing, [it is important] that we work together."[55]

The log cabin incident was not the first time the DLBA's questionable tactics attracted negative media attention, public scrutiny, federal investigations, or even prison sentences. In recent years the DLBA's reputation had become tarnished in the wake of various scandals involving accusations, investigations, and convictions of: bid-rigging, dubious inflation of demolition costs, safety violations, environmental contamination, and mismanagement of federal funds.[56] In the context of these controversies, one would think that the DLBA might have seized on the excitement generated by the log cabin's discovery as a positive public relations opportunity. Instead, in the wake of the public outcry, a thin-skinned DLBA assumed an offensive posture and doubled down on their attack. We were in their crosshairs. In various newspaper accounts, television reports, and a segment on Detroit's National Public Radio affiliate, the DLBA spokeswoman alternately accused our group of collaborators of illegally trespassing onto the property, delaying communications, providing undeveloped plans, and failing to pursue proper procedures for removing 2038 Halleck from their demolition list.[57]

By waging this attack, the DLBA once again hoped to silence a group of stakeholders. But they underestimated the strength and professionalism of preservation-oriented advocates—our group and our allies—historic preservationists, archaeologists, planners, activists, community leaders, and local politicians. Judging by their initial response to our efforts, they considered us to be little more than annoying local obstacles. They were not interested in our professional roles and did not appreciate that we had certain knowledge, expertise, and influence that might have facilitated a slower-paced outcome that would have been satisfactory to all parties. Unlike the local residents, those of us who led the project team occupied certain positions of authority in local government, heritage institutions, and academia. Our proposal to recover the log cabin failed, and the cabin was demolished, but as far as we were concerned, our project was far from over. We recalibrated our approach to the cabin's recovery, and in doing so we knowingly assumed more vocal public leadership roles.

DIGGING INTO BLIGHT REMOVAL STRATEGIES

Before we could begin to advocate for more attention to cultural resources during Detroit's blight removal process, we agreed that it was important to understand the circumstances, timeline, and decisions surrounding the removal of the log cabin. We reached out to Neal Rubin of the *Detroit News*, the same reporter who published the story about our excavations at Old Hamtramck Center that led to the state inspector's tip about the cabin. Rubin agreed to investigate the cabin's demolition and the Land Bank's policy toward historical and archaeological remains. In the course of his research he tracked down and interviewed the contractors from the Smalley Company who demolished the house, DLBA staff, and employees at the Northville dump where the cabin remains were deposited. He also spoke with local Halleck Street residents and former occupants of 2038 Halleck. His resulting exposé, published in the *Detroit News* on March 11, 2019, revealed how, despite widespread public interest, the DLBA demolished the cabin under problematic and suspicious circumstances.[58]

In the wake of Rubin's investigations and our conversations with local officials, two critically important questions remained unresolved: Why was the 2038 Halleck Street house a priority for demolition when so many other homes in the neighborhood were also on the list? And why could it not be removed from the list when a significant historical archaeological feature was identified within it? We decided to put our forensic archival skills to work and launch our own investigation. Our decision would lead us into a dark tangle of politics involving blight removal policies, historic preservation exemptions, and federal mandates.

THE HARDEST HIT FUND

The DLBA contractors who demolished the Halleck Street log cabin were financed with federal money from the Hardest Hit Fund. In 2010 the Hardest Hit Fund was established as a federal loan program "to assist states with their foreclosure prevention and neighborhood stabilization efforts."[59] Its origin was the Emergency Economic Stabilization Act of 2008 (EESA), or Troubled Asset Relief Program (TARP), which allocated funding for states like Michigan that had been devastated by the foreclosure and mortgage crises in the years leading up to the Great Recession. Initially, Hardest Hit Funds were intended to help residents whose properties were at risk of foreclosure by assisting them with mortgage modifications. Had the funds been put to such use, Laschella Johnson, the owner of 2038 Halleck in 2007, would have been able to keep living in the home (and log cabin) that her family owned since 1954 and that her parents Willie and Mary sold to her for $54,773 in 2001.[60] Instead, unable to pay an outstanding mortgage bill, the Federal National Mortgage Association foreclosed on her home in 2007. The mortgage company then sold the home to Ali Said for $2,400 before it fell into the hands of the Michigan Land Bank, which later transferred it to the Detroit Land Bank in 2014.[61] In the case of 2038 Halleck, the very funds that could have spared the property were redirected to demolish it.

In 2013 the US Treasury revised the remit of the Hardest Hit Funds and reallocated them for blight removal rather than mortgage assistance. The Michigan State Housing Development Authority (MSHDA) then created the Michigan Homeowner Assistance Nonprofit Housing Corporation (MHA) to oversee the distribution of Hardest Hit Funds statewide. The MHA, in turn, created the Hardest Hit Fund Blight Elimination Program, whose stated goals were to work with local leaders to "identify and demolish dilapidated abandoned homes . . . [and] stabilize property values by establishing more green space and making way for future development."[62] These state-level efforts dovetailed with concurrent blight elimination and right-sizing initiatives in Detroit and other Michigan cities, including the Detroit Blight Removal Task Force.[63]

In June 2013, the US Treasury granted Michigan $100 million to pilot a blight elimination program in five cities: Detroit, Flint, Grand Rapids, Pontiac, and Saginaw. With the exception of Grand Rapids, the pilot cities were all notable for their high rates of poverty and crime as well as their association with working-class and non-White populations. Of the eighteen states to receive Hardest Hit Funds, Michigan's allocation was among the largest, at $761 million.[64] With ample funding available, the state set a national precedent for its approach to blight elimination.

The house at 2038 Halleck was one of more than 11,000 buildings removed in Detroit with Hardest Hit Funds. The scale and speed of Detroit's federally funded demolition efforts, mobilized primarily by the Detroit Land Bank Authority, has earned the city a dubious distinction: operator of the largest blight removal initiative of its kind in the United States.[65] In the end, it cost $15,913.33 to demolish the log cabin and modern home at 2038 Halleck Street, a small fraction of the $259 million in federal money that Detroit had thus far received from the fund.[66]

The Hardest Hit–funded Blight Elimination Program poses a double-edged sword for historic preservationists, as Amy Arnold noted in Michigan's 2014 State Historic Preservation Plan.[67] She and other heritage practitioners agree that blight removal and right-sizing strategies might be effective in increasing property values and addressing changes in areas that experienced drastic reductions in their population and tax base. Neither historic preservationists nor historical archaeologists are opposed to the concept of removing dilapidated structures per se, but they are critical of the process of removal decision-making. With city managers eager to spend federal Hardest Hit Funds before their expiration in 2020, plans for blight removal proceeded at a swift pace with minimal attention to planning and selection criteria for historic or archaeological resources. Blight elimination plans have focused on the removal and erasure of eyesores from the landscape, bypassing options to create sustainable communities over a longer term by mothballing, reusing, or rehabbing properties with the concerns in mind of local residents and preservationists.[68] Arnold warns that such a hasty approach to blight management has the potential to destroy a community's historic fabric and usher in long-term and unintended consequences, as was the case with past urban renewal programs.[69] Her predictions would come to fruition twice over at 2038 Halleck—first with Johnson's eviction from her family home and then with the log cabin's demolition.

DEMOLISHING HALLECK STREET'S HOMES

To appreciate the influence the DLBA and the Hardest Hit Funds had on reshaping Halleck Street, and to determine why the home at 2038 Halleck was demolished with such urgency, it is useful to consult some land-use and housing data. Following the recommendations of the Detroit Blight Removal Task Force and the DLBA, the city of Detroit began to maintain an open, online information portal with parcel-level data on city-owned properties.[70] I consulted this database to understand the DLBA's presence on Halleck Street and to assess whether the speed with which 2038 Halleck was demolished fit within the pattern of their demolitions and property management practices in the neighborhood since 2013.

According to the database, there are eighty-six empty parcels and forty-one parcels with standing structures on them spread across the two blocks of Halleck Street, between Dequindre to the west and Arlington to the east (Figure 7.13). As of September 2019, Detroit owned 61% of these parcels (fifty-two of eighty-six) and 49% (twenty of forty-one) of the buildings.[71] In 2014, when the DLBA first began demolitions on Halleck Street, the city owned twenty-eight homes. Since then their contractors have demolished eight of these houses and scheduled another ten for removal at an unspecified future date (Figure 7.14).

Interestingly, only four of the eight homes demolished on Halleck

Figure 7.13. Parcel map of Halleck Street and the wider neighborhood depicting the large number of properties owned by the Detroit Land Bank, slated for demolition, and recently demolished as of October 2019. (Detroit Street View, open access GIS)

Figure 7.14. House two doors to the east of 2038 Halleck (*left*) and the house directly across the street (*right*) were both owned by the Detroit Land Bank and were on their demolition list at the time that the log cabin house was demolished. They were demolished four months after the cabin. (Krysta Ryzewski)

since 2014 have been funded by Hardest Hit Funds. The house at 1955 Halleck was the first property to be removed with the funds; that demolition occurred on May 9, 2016. Three years passed before the next round of Hardest Hit–funded demolition commenced with the removal of the log cabin at 2038 Halleck in February 2019. The infrequency with which Hardest Hit–funded demolitions occurred on Halleck Street does not correspond with comments made to us by DLBA authorities in the aftermath of the log cabin's demolitions, which stressed their urgent need to proceed with demolition because of predetermined timelines.

DLBA records reveal that of the three Halleck Street homes demolished with Hardest Hit Funds in 2019, the log cabin property at 2038 Halleck was the first to go. The DLBA spokeswoman explained to me that the agency typically issues demolition contracts for bundles of properties rather than individual structures. Contractors bid on these bundles, and then, once they win the contract, it is up to them to determine the order in which structures are dismantled. The DLBA, she insisted, had no authority to influence contractors' demolition priorities or to remove properties from the demolition list once the contracts are issued.

In January 2019 Scottville-based Smalley Construction Inc. won the DLBA contract to demolish three homes on Halleck Street using Hardest Hit Funds: 2051, 2146, and the log cabin house at 2038. When reporter Neal Rubin contacted a representative from Smalley in the wake of the cabin's demolition, he asked whether they had been notified by the DLBA about the presence of a historic log cabin inside of the modern house. They had not. Their representative expressed regret about its loss and suggested that if they had known about it, they could have at least scheduled the demolition of the other two properties first to allow our project team more time. There was no identifiable reason why 2038 Halleck had to be demolished before the other two homes. Those homes—at 2051 and 2146 Halleck—were torn down on June 20, 2019, four months after the cabin.

The statistics about city property ownership and demolitions on Halleck Street revealed more issues than answers. There was nothing in the data to support the DLBA's claims about the demolition's urgency, or to justify the removal of 2038 Halleck before any of the other city-owned properties on Halleck Street that also appeared on their demolition list. Although they had known about the log cabin, the DLBA chose not to notify the contractors (or anyone else) about its presence. Whenever pressed on the matter by us or the media, the DLBA spokesperson mechanically repeated the claim that once a property is on their demolition list and has been contracted for demolition, it is impossible for the DLBA to remove it. It would be far too costly to do so, they argued. Our suspicions that this was a scripted talking point were verified when, later in the spring, we learned of two properties that were recently removed from their demolition list, one of which was the Blue Bird Inn jazz club on the west side (see chapter 4).

CULTURAL RESOURCE MANAGEMENT
VERSUS FAST CAPITALISM

We hit a dead end in our attempts to understand the DLBA's blight removal strategies, and so we turned inward to our own professional community to explore how we might prevent a situation like the log cabin demolition from happening again. By now, any professional North

American archaeologist reading this will be wondering why no historic re-source or archaeological assessments were undertaken on Halleck Street prior to the expenditure of the Hardest Hit Funds. Since the log cabin's demolition was financed by federal funds, and since it had potential to meet National Register criteria for "significance" and "integrity," it would have qualified for consideration in the Section 106 review and compliance process, as mandated by the National Historic Preservation Act of 1966 (NHPA).[72] The NHPA and the implementation regulations outlined in Section 106 require all federal agencies to "take into account" the effects of their undertakings on properties that are either listed or eligible for listing on the National Register of Historic Places.[73] These undertakings include projects conducted on federal lands and also situations like the log cabin demolition—where federal funding is allocated to construction, land mod-ification, and resource planning projects on nonfederal lands, including state and municipal properties. As part of the consultation process, federal agencies are required to provide the Advisory Council on Historic Preser-vation an opportunity to comment on their assessments before alterations to buildings or landscapes occur. The impact of the NHPA on shaping his-toric preservation, heritage management, and archaeological professions in the United States cannot be overstated; the Advisory Council on His-toric Preservation estimates that more than 90% of all archaeological exca-vations in the United States are conducted as part of Section 106 reviews.[74]

Under a routine Section 106 assessment for historic resources and ar-chaeological remains, federal agencies and contractors are not required to identify and research all sites within an area of potential effect (APE). In-stead, agencies are expected to make a "reasonable and good faith effort" to account for the presence and potential significance of historic proper-ties within affected areas as well as the extent to which their undertakings may impact historic properties.[75] During the Section 106 review process, historic properties or archaeological sites are determined to be eligible for inclusion on the National Register of Historic Places if they meet one of four criteria for significance and demonstrate integrity, that is, "the ability to convey significance through intact physical features and context."[76]

Section 106 not only requires federal agencies to consider evaluating properties or sites and their historic values during planning processes but also public interest.[77] Participation by both State Historic Preservation Officers (SHPOs) and public stakeholders is integral to the Section 106 compliance process. As stated in the National Park Service Cultural Re-source Management Guidelines, under the Section 106 review process, federal agencies "must recognize properties *important to communities* as well as to the nation as a whole, so they need to be aware of the *interest of local groups* and individuals. The goal of the process is to make sure that preservation is *fully considered* in federal actions, thereby protecting our shared heritage from thoughtless or ill-considered damage" (emphasis added). At 2038 Halleck, such an evaluation process may have verified the log cabin's significance as a historic and archaeological resource and effectively connected the DLBA with Halleck Street communities and other stakeholders.

Today, the majority of the United States' cultural resource management industry hinges on federal agencies' willingness to undertake Section 106 compliance in "good faith." The procedures outlined in the NHPA have become so enshrined in historic preservation and archaeological practice that heritage professionals tend to be unfamiliar with places in the legislation where language affords federal agencies the wiggle room to bypass the Section 106 process under certain circumstances. In fact, the process of considering the "effects of their undertakings" on potentially significant historic or archaeological resources only requires federal agencies to *consider* historic preservation; there is no absolute requirement to undertake it. Instead, Section 106 requires agencies to reconcile preservation of historic and archaeological resources with other considerations, including financial costs and public benefits. The process does not always ensure a positive outcome for preservation-oriented interests.

In the case of the log cabin's demolition with Hardest Hit Funds, the US Treasury's position was clear. Blight elimination in Detroit and other poor, postindustrial cities was a matter of public benefit; land management and its profitability was the city's pathway to future economic development. These priority benefits outweighed historic preservation concerns. The Treasury publicized its position in a memo to the MSHDA, the state agency that managed Michigan's Hardest Hit Funds. It announced, "The US Treasury does not consider Hardest Hit Funds to be an undertaking for purposes of Section 106 of the NHPA of 1966. The Michigan Homeowner Assistance Nonprofit Housing Corporation (MHA) is not obligated to take into account adverse effects on historic resources targeted for demolition under the Hardest Hit Funds."[78] The US Treasury identified space for exceptions in the language of Section 106 and, technically, were not acting in violation of the NHPA mandate.

When this memo was first circulated in 2013, historic preservationists nationwide were alarmed by the Treasury's disqualification of what amounted to hundreds of thousands of properties from potential Section 106 review in the eighteen states that received Hardest Hit Funds. In a letter dated October 2, 2013, Erik M. Hein, executive director of the National Council of State Historic Preservation Officers, admonished US Treasury officials for "directly facilitating demolition actions without the evaluation of impacts, the consideration of alternatives, or the opportunity for public impact and consultation provided by the Section 106 process."[79] He added that the NCSHPO "strongly disagrees with the interpretation of the [NHPA] law and believes it is entirely feasible to both accommodate Treasury's goals while at the same time satisfying Section 106 of the Act."[80] In Michigan officials within the State Historic Preservation Office joined the protests. They asserted that the US Treasury's position set a dangerous precedent for how historic properties and sites were to be managed in the face of large-scale demolitions and developments. This precedent, they argued, also threatened the stability of historic preservation and cultural resource management professions.

The national and state-level protests made no difference to the US Treasury's position. Back in Michigan, preservation officials scored a minor victory when the MHA agreed to insert a carrot into the Historic Preservation Parameters section of their 2016 Hardest Hit Fund Handbook. The language requested that blight removal partners in Michigan cities take into account "the potential effects of the Hardest Hit Funds on historic resources if it can reasonably do so without delaying the intent and purpose of the Hardest Hit Funds."[81] Although the memo reiterated that the state was "not obligated" to consider the funds' effects on historic resources, MHA officials advised that in the event that blight removal targets fell within a National Register historic district, the blight partner should consult with the State Historic Preservation Office. In the case of locally designated resources, blight removers were encouraged to consult with the relevant municipal historic designation advisory board to obtain a Notice to Proceed in accordance with state law 1970 PA 169 and local ordinances.

The Hardest Hit Funds memo, the MHA Handbook, and the situation surrounding large-scale blight removal represent an impossible logistical challenge for the Michigan State Historic Preservation Office (SHPO) to manage. The Detroit Land Bank applied federal funds to the demolition of over 11,000 properties between 2014 and 2019; there was no way that the small staff of preservationists and archaeologists in the Michigan SHPO could handle even a fraction of the routine Section 106 paperwork from Detroit let alone the other Michigan cities to receive federal demolition funding. Ultimately, preservation interests in Michigan's cities were completely overwhelmed and defeated by the sheer volume and speed of demolition activities across the state.

The inducement added to the 2016 MHA notice transferred decisions about whether to undertake preservation considerations to local agencies. In Detroit, these decisions rested with the DLBA, an organization that did not employ professionally trained cultural resource management or historical preservation specialists. On Halleck Street, and in the majority of other cases, the DLBA chose not to engage Section 106, perhaps out of ignorance for the Section 106 process or perhaps because they chose to prioritize their demolition agenda at all costs. The added language to the MHA notice made no difference for the DLBA's treatment of 2038 Halleck. Even if they had established a Section 106 process to review properties in Detroit, Halleck Street would not have been a focus since it was not part of a local or federally designated historic district. As far as both historic preservation officials and the DLBA were concerned, the Halleck Street site, and by extension, the stakeholders' place-based histories, were outliers.

DEVALUING ARCHAEOLOGY AND HISTORIES OF MARGINALIZED COMMUNITIES

Our digging into the operations of the Hardest Hit Fund revealed how preservation and archaeological interests were being quietly pushed aside by federal and state-level policies. In the process of shifting the oversight and responsibilities of Section 106 reviews to local blight removal agencies, the US Treasury Department devalued the cultural resource management industry, the opinions of local stakeholders, and the historic value of resources in urban, low-income communities. In Michigan and elsewhere, state historic preservation officials were only given the opportunity to react to the Treasury's parameters; they were not involved in the design or implementation of the federal Blight Elimination Task Force's agenda. Their recourse was to include language in the state-level Hardest Hit Fund manual that urged local demolition agencies to recognize potentially significant and already-protected historic resources. There were no contingency plans at any level, federal, state, or local, for when blight contractors encountered historic properties or archaeological finds during a Hardest Hit–funded demolition project.

It was not until April 2019, two months after the log cabin's demolition, that I obtained the MHA memo describing the Hardest Hit Fund's historic preservation parameters. The first colleague I contacted was Misty Jackson, director of Arbre Croche Cultural Resources, a historic preservation and archaeological consulting company that is active in Michigan and Indiana. She was unaware of the US Treasury's exemption of Hardest

Hit–funded properties from Section 106 review and equally alarmed at the prospects of the potential impact of the policy on the cultural resource management industry. At the time, Jackson and I held the two seats designated for archaeologists on Michigan's governor-appointed State Historic Preservation Review Board. As public officials, we held positions of authority and responsibility. We wondered whether we might use our positions to call attention to the need for contingency plans when blight removers encounter historic and archaeological resources in the future. In May 2019, we brought the matter to the attention of the State Historic Preservation Review Board at our triannual meeting.

During the meeting, the board members unanimously passed a motion requesting that the State Historic Preservation Office expand the section about historic resources in the MHA's Hardest Hit Fund manual with language that advised demolition agencies to contact the SHPO in the event of unanticipated archaeological or historic discoveries during the process of preparing a property for demolition. The review board also requested that the director of the SHPO draft a letter (to be cosigned by the board) to federal congresswomen Rashida Tlaib and Brenda Lawrence, state representative LaTonya Garrett, and Detroit City Council president Brenda Jones that elaborated on the Hardest Hit Fund's treatment of historic preservation and the adverse effects it posed for the protection of resources in blighted urban communities. When the SHPO director, who was present at the meeting, agreed to fulfill the board's request, we were optimistic that we had used our role as a historic preservation board to initiate change. But then nine months passed before the SHPO took action. Rather than follow the recommendation of the board, the SHPO director ultimately pursued an entirely different course of action. He invited lawyers from the Michigan Attorney General's office to our January 2020 meeting to inform us that, in their opinion, the motions we passed in May 2019 posed apparent and potential conflicts of interest between our professional roles and our appointed positions on a governmental body. We were instructed to retract the motions and pursue any further advocacy as private citizens.

COPING AS A COMMUNITY

Back in Detroit and Hamtramck, our group of collaborators thought long and hard about how we wanted to pursue our research about the cabin after its demolition. Local residents and preservationists were still fuming a month after the demolition, but it was important to us that any initiatives we organized were not inflammatory but rather productive toward a larger agenda that promoted more inclusive and community-involved preservation efforts. The first step of the Log Cabin Recovery Project 2.0 was a public event designed to increase transparency and visibility about the handling of the 2038 Halleck Street demolition. On March 28, 2019, five weeks after the demolition, Kowalski hosted "The Lost Log Cabin" event at the Hamtramck Historical Museum. The evening's program focused on bringing stakeholders into conversation about the demolition. It featured talks by Kowalski and Wayne State University archaeology graduate student Luke Pickrahn (who participated in the survey), a question and answer session, and a display of the few finds recovered during the December survey. About fifty people attended, including Halleck Street residents.

Kowlaski and I agreed that it was in nobody's best interest, even the DLBA's, to become embittered in fights over the management of historic resources in Detroit or Hamtramck. With over 90,000 parcels under city ownership and the DLBA's management, we were all but certain that more archaeological sites and significant historic structures were to be located in future demolitions or land alterations. Nobody wanted another log cabin debacle. We thought we might use this occasion to connect the DLBA with preservationists and archaeologists with whom they might consult in the future.

I found an unlikely arbitrator in a popular local television news anchor, Roop Raj. In the wake of Neal Rubin's newspaper story of the log cabin's demolition, and in true small-town Detroit fashion, Raj offered to put me in phone contact with the DLBA spokeswoman, Alyssa Strickland. We had a productive conversation that day and agreed that our two factions were better off as collaborative partners than adversaries. She expressed interest in working together in the future. As the initial step toward establishing this working relationship, I proposed conducting an archaeological excavation at the demolition site to recover any architectural and artifact remains that might help us refine a date for the log cabin and better understand the people who once resided in it. After the excavations, Kowalski and I would organize a follow-up public event in which we would invite the public to the Hamtramck Historical Museum to assist with artifact processing; both activities would be advertised as cosponsored by Wayne State University, the Hamtramck Historical Museum, and the DLBA. She and the DLBA were amenable to the proposal, not least, one suspects, because it offered the DLBA a measure of damage control over their handling of the situation. In the following days, Strickland and I worked together to arrange the logistics for the excavations.

ARCHAEOLOGY IN THE AFTERMATH

Although the DLBA readily granted my team permission to excavate at 2038 Halleck Street, they restricted our time on the site to one day. Our work had to accommodate their contractor's scheduled plans to finish clearing debris from the site and backfill the modern home's exposed cellar hole. On March 11, 2019, I assembled a team of fifteen archaeologists and local volunteers to assist with excavations within the footprint of the demolished log cabin (Figure 7.15). The team included Wayne State graduate students and alumni, Megan McCullen (director of the Wayne State Grosscup Museum of Anthropology), archaeologist Misty Jackson, board members of the Hamtramck Historical Museum, and two local community volunteers. It was a freezing cold day; the barely thawed ground turned what might have been an accommodating soil into thick, soupy mud.

Digging conditions were less than ideal, but given the time constraints, we employed a strategy to maximize our coverage of the site over the course of a day's worth of work. The footprint where the log cabin once stood was still visible, as were the concrete supports that the modern house's builders installed to raise the cabin above the ground surface. We divided the internal space of the log cabin into four quadrants, and each

Figure 7.15. Archaeological excavations of the log cabin's footprint after demolition, March 2019. (Krysta Ryzewski)

small group focused on the interior and immediate exterior areas of the cabin within their work area. The muddy conditions disrupted the visibility of stratigraphic deposits, but our team was able to recover 354 artifacts nonetheless. The vast majority of the artifacts related to the modern house's occupants; they included seventeen toys (fifteen of which were glass marbles) as well as eight fully intact and eleven partial bottles whose contents once included milk, soda pop, medicine, and alcohol. Within the excavated assemblage we recovered over a dozen household artifacts of nineteenth-century manufacture, including whiteware pottery with transfer-print and flow blue decorations, mold-blown glass bottles, and a shell button. We also recovered sixty-five square-cut nails whose manufacture predated 1890. The presence of these nineteenth-century materials at the location of the demolished cabin suggested that it was positioned on, or at least very close to, its original location when the modern house was constructed around it.

During the excavation day, a steady stream of visitors appeared on site, as if they were paying their last respects to it (Figure 7.16).[82] First to arrive was one of the members of the Michigan Historic Preservation Network (MHPN), who offered to purchase the house from the DLBA and spare it from demolition. Then came other preservation officials from the MHPN and the Detroit Planning and Development Department. Two television news trucks arrived to cover the excavations for their headline evening news stories. Hamtramck's city council president and cabinet members watched the excavations from the modern house's front porch, which demolition crews left intact. As the day went on neighborhood residents, Wayne State administrators, and Alyssa Strickland from the DLBA also came by. We brought back to the site the timbers, wallpaper, and artifacts that we recovered during the initial December survey of the cabin. Everyone who visited was impressed by these remains and fascinated by the cabin's discovery. Most left downtrodden, weighed down by thoughts of what more could have been done.

Six weeks after the excavations, on a Saturday in early June, the Hamtramck Historical Museum invited the public to work alongside our Wayne State archaeology team to wash and process the artifacts recovered during the excavations (Figure 7.17). Eight volunteers came to assist our group. Two men from Hamtramck with Polish American backgrounds were drawn to the event because of their interest in local history. A teenage boy and his parents came in from the suburbs to help; he was hoping to study archaeology in a university program. Two additional residents from Detroit assisted with artifact washing; they

Figure 7.16. Greg Kowalski and Joe Kochut (Hamtramck historical commissioners) and Kathy Angerer (acting Hamtramck city manager) observe the log cabin site excavations from the former porch of the modern house. (Krysta Ryzewski)

had heard about the log cabin incident on the news and were curious to learn more about it.

The public events and archaeological excavations should have been the start rather than the end of the log cabin recovery process, but we made the most of what remained of the cabin nonetheless. After we cleaned the artifacts from the cabin survey and excavations, the Hamtramck Historical Museum added them to their collections and created a special exhibit showcasing the finds and the circumstances of their discovery. They used the proceeds of an outreach award that we received from the Conference on Michigan Archaeology to install a permanent exhibit about the log cabin.

Figure 7.17. Wayne State University archaeologists and volunteers clean artifacts from the log cabin excavations at an open day hosted at the Hamtramck Historical Museum, June 2019. (Krysta Ryzewski)

AN UNTIMELY DISCOVERY

Initially, following the log cabin's rediscovery in 2018, my colleagues and I questioned whether residents in the distressed, nameless neighborhood along the Detroit-Hamtramck border would care about protecting the remains of what seemed like a distant, unfamiliar heritage. Likewise, the Detroit Land Bank Authority assumed communities who live in such blighted neighborhoods are disinterested and detached from neglected buildings. We were both wrong. During the process of the Log Cabin Recovery Project we gradually witnessed how a simple, unassuming nineteenth-century structure connected deeply with local residents' own bootstrapping work ethic and migrant/immigrant experiences. To local residents in Detroit and Hamtramck, the log cabin and the people who built it were not artifacts of a distant, detached past. The structure was a symbol of continuity and a physical manifestation of the qualities of ingenuity and perseverance that are so ingrained in the spirit of local civic and community identity.

There are unlikely to be any further collaborations between preservationists and the DLBA. Just days after I received permission to conduct limited excavations at 2038 Halleck, Detroit mayor Mike Duggan announced that by the end of 2019 the "beleaguered" DLBA will no longer oversee the city's demolition program.[83] Several months later, on September 15, 2019, as part of the process to phase out the DLBA from blight removal efforts, Duggan submitted a $250 million, thirty-year bond proposal to the Detroit City Council. Duggan's proposal outlined the city's ambitious plans to remove all residential blight from Detroit by mid-2025 without raising residents' taxes.[84] Duggan estimated total blight removal costs at $420 million, inclusive of the bond. His new demolition program proposed to reduce the timeline for blight eradication from thirteen to five years, during which time the city would demolish 19,000 properties and renovate 8,000 vacant homes. City Council members were wary of the proposal's motivations and consequences. In particular, they expressed concerns over the long-lasting socioeconomic and financial implications of the bond and its treatment of neighborhoods. In her response to the plan, city council president pro tempore Marry Sheffield reminded Mayor Duggan that tearing down homes did not equate to "building up neighborhoods."[85] In November 2019, the Detroit City Council rejected the bond proposal with a 6–3 vote. The majority of council members agreed that the city's proposal hinged on a short-term vision. It presumed that blight is an acute problem that, if extinguished now, will not return. No new blight management schemes emerged from city planners subsequently (during the first six months of 2020). The arrival of the COVID-19 pandemic strained the city's finances and resulted in severe budget cuts and layoffs at the DLBA.[86] It may be the case that postpandemic Detroit will be back to where it began in 2014 in terms of its blight removal strategies.

The log cabin at 2038 Halleck Street was an untimely, burdensome discovery. Nobody quite knew what to do about it. The cabin elicited surprise because it was a rare find. It also generated curiosity because, for many, it seemed out of place among the history and communities of a working-class Great Migration–era neighborhood. Its structural integrity and durability was incongruent with a landscape defined by vacant lots and crumbling, derelict houses. The area surrounding Halleck Street was a no-man's-land slated for erasure; blight elimination strategies treated it as if it did not deserve to have historic resources or residents who cared about them.

While our project did not yield the collaborative outcomes or the changes to preservation policies that we tried to achieve, it did raise historical consciousness about the significance of place-based local heritage and the risks that careless blight removal practices pose to it. It also exposed the fact that historic preservation, in Detroit, has been a luxury extended to only a handful of communities and certain notions of heritage (e.g., prominent downtown and Midtown sites associated with wealthy, elite White residents). Nevertheless, the fact that the log cabin controversy elicited such a strong backlash among various stakeholder groups, and more so, that the reaction caught both the DLBA and historic preservation officials off guard, should underscore the theme that prevails in each of this book's case studies: the need for planners, preservationists, and politicians to reexamine the processes and lasting effects of urban erasures on American cities' most vulnerable populations and their historic and archaeological remains.

CHAPTER EIGHT

Rethinking Detroit
Reflections from the Trenches

Historical archaeology in Detroit lends itself to a collaborative and inclusive practice in its efforts to interpret the material remains of past communities in the present. With respect to the city's recent past, especially the time frame that includes living, first-person memories, it is impossible to separate historical archaeology projects or other heritage-based initiatives from the pervasive issues of race, inequality, politics, and access that have shaped modern Detroit.

Archaeological research that engages these issues elicits strong responses; it triggers debate, generates backlash, attracts media attention, and motivates people to share their stories and participate in the research or preservation advocacy process. Such passion demonstrates the investment local communities have in their heritage and affirms that historical archaeology has relevant contributions to make in strengthening connections with place-based histories.

In Detroit historical archaeologists have not had direct effects on altering government policies, changing laws, preventing the careless management of blighted neighborhoods, or diversifying the profession of historic preservation. Nor have such objectives been the primary aims of their project designs. Despite professional commitments to advocacy, antiracism, and equity across the subdiscipline, the reality is that the vast majority of community-based archaeological interventions simply do not have the capacity and expertise to lead or execute such systemic changes single-handedly. This is not to say that archaeological work and archaeologists cannot initiate or participate in larger-scale, systemic, and bureaucratic transformations in coordination with local leaders, lawmakers, and other community stakeholders. They can and should. But archaeologists can rarely initiate such changes on their own, or by only promoting radical ideas for transformations in practice and policy among like-minded colleagues within the discipline.

As the preceding case studies have illustrated, the processes and outcomes of community-involved archaeological investigations in contemporary Detroit extended far beyond the confines of academic archaeology. They have inspired action locally by raising historical consciousness among communities and stimulating grassroots participation in heritage advocacy. Historical archaeology has heightened awareness about various local heritage management issues, and over the long term this increased visibility will hopefully persuade civic leaders to include contributions from archaeological research, and historical archaeologists, into main-stream conversations about city planning, educational curricula, land management policies, and preservation law.

AFTERTHOUGHTS

I chose to end this book with the story of the Halleck Street log cabin, a case study that lays bare the challenges of practicing local and community-based, collaborative archaeology, for two reasons. There exist very few dis-cussions in scholarly literature and popular media about how archaeolo-gists respond to unanticipated situations and shortcomings, from denied permits and stakeholder disagreements, to public media scrutiny and full-blown political controversies. I also wanted to debunk the myth that the pursuit of collaborative projects, or projects conducted in the public eye, promises an enjoyable, productive, and agreeable process and outcome. As archaeologist Laurie Wilkie notes, engaged heritage work is hard and often uncomfortable.[1] Furthermore, community-based archaeology is an uneven, unpredictable practice where the idea of collaboration is often un-derstood differently by the parties involved in a project; it can be received with variable levels of interest, skepticism, and investment by the various stakeholder groups who practitioners seek to involve.[2] There are many dirty little secrets to practicing public and community-based, collaborative archaeology that my colleagues and I seem reluctant to discuss, perhaps out of the fear that people might interpret a project's failures as a sign of fallibility or incompetency.

In retrospect, the case studies in *Detroit Remains* demonstrated three things that publications about collaborative, public, and community-involved projects tend not to acknowledge. First, archaeological proj-ects often incur failures and setbacks. When they do, archaeologists face challenges in locating alternate possibilities and being nimble and mindful about readjusting priorities so that they respond appropriately to logistical, stakeholder, and broader political issues. Second, when ar-chaeologists conduct their work in public, especially in high-traffic, ur-ban areas, the work is likely to generate considerable attention, not all of which will be positive. Some of my colleagues have been caught off guard when their projects triggered widespread social media attention or when their research created its own political dialogue.[3] The majority of these unanticipated situations are avoidable, I argue, if archaeologists are prepared to navigate conversations with the media, negotiate with politicians and contractors, and identify policies or issues that might trigger opposition. Third, if historical archaeologists witness injustices when cultural resources are handled carelessly in the communities where they work, they have the option of leveraging their professional expertise and assuming positions of vocal leadership in protest. This sort of action may require operating beyond the idealized level playing field of collaborative relationships and entering into a sphere of responsibility, exposure, and influence that may seem antithetical to the fundamental aims of collaborative archaeology. It is not. Sometimes it is necessary to assume a position of expertise in order to draw attention to policy, legal, and social issues that affect the respect for shared heritage as well as the profession. If archaeologists are unwilling to act as leaders and public advocates then they risk undermining the very purpose of community archaeology.[4]

SLOW ARCHAEOLOGY VERSUS DETROIT

In recent years the notion of "slow archaeology" has gained traction in professional discourse as a practice that follows the principles of the slow science movement, especially in its call for more engaged, collaborative, and critical work.[5] Although I would argue that there are considerable overlaps between emergent conceptions of slow archaeology and the decades-old practices of public archaeology, an explicit and perhaps more refined aim of slow archaeology is that it encourages archaeologists to pursue more ethical and activist stances as they approach projects with a measured pace and deliberate sense of care. Given that slow archaeology is relatively new to the discipline's vocabulary, there are certainly more questions than clarity to provide when it comes to understanding its identity, utility, and feasibility in urban settings.

I offer the preceding case studies for readers to use in reflecting critically on the extent to which slow, community-involved archaeology might be possible and equitable in fast-changing Detroit (and in other comparable settings). In urban, postindustrial cities historic preservationists and archaeologists are forced to adjust to real-time, fast-moving agendas in ways that bring them into different types of relationships and conversations than one might expect to encounter based on the prevailing scholarship about collaborative archaeological practice.[6] This scholarship tends to promote collaborative fieldwork as a process that unfolds gradually between stakeholders and is oriented toward decolonizing archaeological research processes and outcomes. While I have no objection to the scope or purpose of such aims, these academic conversations do not consider the complicated dynamics of urban archaeological projects, which are often messier, more unpredictable, involve more stakeholders, and are higher visibility than those that take place in more remote and accommodating locales.

In many of the *Detroit Remains* cases, the Ransom Gillis house, Gordon Park, and the Halleck Street log cabin especially, slow-paced intentionality, care, and collaboration at the local level were no match for developers' interests and government policies. In contrast with these experiences, the success of slow, community-involved archaeological practices appears to hinge on a set of optimal circumstances that are kept under control by a project's principal archaeologist and her collaborating partners. These circumstances involve projects that are almost always led by people in positions of academic privilege, are not in the crosshairs of fast capitalist interests (e.g., development and blight removal), and have the luxury of time and funding on their side. The *Detroit Remains* case studies illustrate how some aspects of slow archaeological practice may wind up unintentionally excluding some of the less visible communities, histories, and practitioners (including those who are CRM-based) who archaeologists aim to involve in their collaborative and public-facing projects. Where the slow archaeology factors into the *Detroit Remains* cases is an important matter for further discussion.

CONTOURS OF CAPITALISM

Detroit Remains set out to trace the contours of the city's underrepresented communities and their place-based histories through a combination of historical archaeological research and storytelling.[7] In the process of writing each chapter I began to recognize how the heterogeneity of capitalism has been expressed in Detroit in relation to local circumstances, communities, and particular time periods. On the surface, and to outsiders, Detroit appears to be a city both gripped and leveled by hurricane-force effects of industrial capitalism. Detroit has all of the hallmarks of one of the "core" capitalist cities in the United States. It is a bastion of manufacturing, the birthplace of the American middle class, a city with a history of explosive violence and rampant inequality, and a landscape scarred by economic failures. Beneath the surface though, historical archaeologists have paid little attention to how capitalism and the cracks in its system manifest themselves within the contexts of local situations, relationships, and practices. In other words, aside from the examples presented in the *Detroit Remains* case studies, it is difficult to identify what capitalist exploitation and local responses to it look(ed) like on the ground in Detroit, and how these relationships have changed over time.

As anthropologist Shannon Lee Dawdy suggests, recognizing the specific processes and practices of accumulation and dispossession in localized contexts may demystify capitalism and facilitate comparisons with other archaeological settings.[8] One of the outcomes of *Detroit Remains* is a historical archaeological account of the local currents of twentieth-century capitalism. None of the case studies touch directly on automobile production, the juggernaut of industrial Detroit. Instead, they focus on the communities, landscape transformations, creative expressions, and wealth that emerged during the cycles of economic boom and bust that transformed and continue to shape the city.

As illustrated by archaeological findings, people's responses to the processes of dispossession, violence, and inequality that accompanied Detroit's economic growth ran the gamut from criminal and covert, to creative and entrepreneurial. One might be inclined to identify many of the examples of bootstrapping ingenuity presented in *Detroit Remains* as examples of anticapitalist or informal economic strategies designed to operate under the radar, outside of the prevailing system—cashing weekly paychecks at the Blue Bird Inn, styling hair for neighbors in the attic of the Halleck Street house, operating a speakeasy in a restaurant basement, repurposing a horse stable as a pottery studio, changing one's name to operate a truck-driving business in segregated neighborhoods, the invention of bebop jazz, counterculture musicians and "hippie entrepreneurs," or the grassroots volunteer cleanup crews at Gordon Park. In some of these cases, such as the Grande Ballroom's antiauthoritarian White Panther Party or the Purple Gang's bootlegging operations, people openly flaunted the city's established system of capitalist exchange.

Indeed, it was certainly the case that the communities whose histories are represented in this book expected more than financial profit from their undertakings. Symbolic, political, and experiential values coincided with their ambitions. In large part, these latter motivations are the associations people still highlight when they recount their attachments to individual sites today. Nevertheless, the archaeological stories of *Detroit Remains* detail how capitalism, in its various guises of accumulation, was always an undercurrent. No matter how hard people tried to evade or resist its restrictive structures, the system always caught up. Large concert arenas eliminated the Grande Experience. The Purple Gang's illicit alcohol smuggling, production, and distribution network required established banking infrastructure to manage its lucrative enterprise. Progressive jazz music became commercialized and outgrew the city's small jazz rooms. Private developers restored the Ransom Gillis house into expensive apartments whose design elements harken back to a particular moment in time. Tour bus operators profited from the Little Harry Speakeasy's rediscovery. Construction companies reaped gains from blight elimination contracts as they demolished tens of thousands of homes with little regard for their histories or prior inhabitants. These historical and localized manifestations of Detroit's complicated and variable capitalist structures expose the relations, including anticapitalist and anarchist agendas, that have propelled the ebb and flow of the city's economic engine for more than a century.

Detroit Remains responds to historical archaeologist Guido Pezzarossi's call for debunking notions of an abstract, monolithic approach to defining capitalist systems.[9] Its case studies offer opportunities to rethink capitalism from more diverse theoretical orientations, including pragmatism and feminism, and from the perspectives of more inclusive histories of underrepresented people in urban communities. Ultimately, the *Detroit Remains* sites suggest that perhaps there is a fertile space in between the extremes of corporate manufacturing and antiauthoritarianism where historical archaeology might make a contribution to understanding the evolution of industrial capitalism and its lasting effects on urban settings and their residents.

A SEAT AT THE TABLE

In their seminal 1995 textbook *Historical Archaeology*, archaeologists Charles Orser and Brian Fagan begin with a claim that historical archaeology "is important not only because it is a means of studying the past, but because it has the potential to teach us about ourselves."[10] There are historical circumstances that archaeologists and others will never be able to relate to directly, but, they add, historical archaeology can aid in gaining a better understanding of them.

From my perspective the processes of community-involved and collaborative archaeology that I detailed in *Detroit Remains* have taught me a considerable amount about myself as a professional archaeologist and about how others perceive my role and purpose. I have also learned many lessons about how to conduct collaborative research. If I could begin these projects all over again, knowing half of what I do now, I would change something about every single one of them. By organizing the case studies chronologically, in the order that I undertook the projects, I hope readers will be able to detect some of the ways in which I adjusted my own approaches as I learned from previous successes and failures.

If there is to be a take-home message from *Detroit Remains*, I would like it to be that historical archaeology has relevant contributions to make in present-day urban situations, from historic preservation and educational programming to community organizing and policy revision. Historical archaeologists deserve a seat at decision-making and policy tables in conversations about urban heritage, revitalization, and preservation. In the end, the real "slow" work for historical archaeologists working in Detroit and elsewhere is to figure out how to establish and maintain a foothold as stewards and advocates, especially in the eroding historical landscapes of our poorest cities.

NOTES

INTRODUCTION

1. For a discussion of multiscalar historical archaeological methods and documentary records as material culture, see Hicks and Beaudry, introduction to *The Cambridge Companion to Historical Archaeology*; and Wilkie, "Documentary Archaeology."

2. Hamlin, *Legends of Le Détroit*.

3. Ryzewski, "Ruin Photography as Archaeological Method."

4. Detroit Blight Removal Task Force, *Every Neighborhood Has a Future*, 15.

5. Prior to the 1863 emancipation of slavery in the United States, the Underground Railroad was a network of clandestine safe houses that enslaved laborers traveled between as they fled from conditions of bondage in the South to free northern states and Canada.

6. Kiddey and Graves-Brown, "Reclaiming the Streets."

7. Apel, *Beautiful Terrible Ruins*, 3.

8. Herron, *After Culture*, 9.

9. The historical origins of Detroit's urban crisis and blight epidemic are beyond the scope of this book. There exists a substantial body of literature on the topic that readers may wish to consult for more in-depth historical discussions, including Sugrue, *Origins of the Urban Crisis*; and Dewar and Thomas, *The City after Abandonment*.

10. Gallagher, *Reimagining Detroit*, 30.

11. Duggan, "Annual State of the City Address."

12. Detroit's population in 2004 was 924,000 and 680,000 in 2014. New Orleans, which experienced Hurricane Katrina in 2005, had a population of 462,000 in 2004 and 384,000 in 2014. Duggan, "Annual State of the City Address."

13. According to the 2010 US census, the suburban region of Metro Detroit, with over 3.7 million residents, ranks as the eleventh largest metropolitan population in the United States.

14. DeSilvey and Edensor, "Reckoning with Ruins"; Edensor, *Industrial Ruins*.

15. Austin, "Post-Post-Apocalyptic Detroit"; Austin and Doerr, *Lost Detroit*.

16. Detroit Future City, *139 Square Miles*, 69.

17. Ryzewski, "Detroit 139."

18. As of the time of this book's completion, the media reported on the possibility that Kilpatrick might be released twenty-one years early due to an outbreak of COVID-19 among inmates in the Louisiana prison where he is housed. Elrick and Baldas, "COVID-19 Outbreak"; Elrick and Baldas, "Kilpatrick Denied Early Release." Kilpatrick has also sought clemency from President Donald Trump.

19. Wilkinson, "Detroit Police Improve Response Times"; Kurth, "Detroit Pays High Price for Arson Onslaught."

20. Apel, *Beautiful Terrible Ruins*, 5.

21. Detroit's unemployment rate, based on 2010 census figures, was 23%, the highest among the United States' fifty largest cities. In 2015 nearly half (40%) of the city's streetlights did not work, leaving dark side streets unsafe for motorists and pedestrians. Apel, *Beautiful Terrible Ruins*, 4. In 2014 Detroit had the country's highest poverty and murder rate. Duggan, "Annual State of the City."

22. On December 10, 2014, Detroit had emerged from bankruptcy and Orr resigned as emergency manager. Apel, *Beautiful Terrible Ruins*, 29; Davey and Walsh, "Billions in Debt, Detroit Tumbles into Insolvency"; Dolan, "Record Bankruptcy for Detroit."

23. Arnold, *Michigan's State Historic Preservation Plan*; Williams, "Historic Tax Credit."

24. The Detroit Institute of Arts is the fifth largest encyclopedic museum in the United States.

25. Finley, "Face It, DIA Artwork Will Be 'Monetized'"; Apel, *Beautiful Terrible Ruins*.

26. Kennedy, "Fate of City's Art Hangs in the Balance"; Stryker, "Detroit Rising."

27. Kennedy, "Fate of City's Art Hangs in the Balance."

28. Eisinger, "Is Detroit Dead?," 1; Tabb, "If Detroit is Dead," 1; Morton, "Something, Something, Something, Detroit."

29. Hitchens, "From Motown to Ghost Town."

30. "Derelict Detroit" *Daily Mail*, October 1, 2012; Finnis, "Left to Rot."

31. Finelli, *Last Days of Detroit*; Locke et al., "Urban Heritage as a Generator of Landscapes."

32. Kinney, "America's Great Comeback Story," 779; Ryzewski, "Ruin Photography as Archaeological Method."

33. Pétursdóttir and Olsen, "Imaging Modern Decay"; Marchand and Meffre, *Ruins of Detroit*.

34. Apel, *Beautiful Terrible Ruins*, 23.

35. Detroit Future City, *139 Square Miles*; Detroit Future City, *Detroit Strategic Framework Plan*; Ryzewski, "Detroit 139."

36. City Form Detroit, *7.2 SQ MI*.

37. Safransky, "Rethinking Land Struggle in the Postindustrial City," 1086.

38. United States Census Bureau, "Detroit, Michigan. State and County Quick Facts." On the Great Migration experience, see Wilkerson, *The Warmth of Other Suns*.

39. United States Census Bureau, "Detroit, Michigan. State and County Quick Facts." In 1940 the US census recorded 149,119 African American residents in Detroit. The number may have been closer to 200,000 by 1943.

40. Of the thirty-four people who were killed, twenty-five were Black. Seven-

teen of the twenty-five Black Detroiters were reportedly shot by the police. Detroit Historical Society, "Race Riot of 1943."

41. Sugrue, *Origins of the Urban Crisis*.

42. Thomas, *Redevelopment and Race*, 130.

43. On the statewide inventory of archaeological sites, the Little Harry speakeasy is site 20WN1200.

44. On the statewide inventory of archaeological sites, the Ransom Gillis House is site 20WN1199.

45. On the statewide inventory of archaeological sites, the Blue Bird Inn is site 20WN1201.

46. Högberg, Holtorf, and Wollentz, "No Future in Archaeological Heritage Management?," 645; Perry, "Enchantment of the Archaeological Record"; Schlanger, Nespoulous, and Demoule, "Year 5 at Fukushima."

CHAPTER ONE

1. In US academia, archaeology is considered to be one of the four subfields of anthropology.

2. The timeframe that archaeologists of the contemporary past consider spans the period of living memory and extends into the present. For a discussion of contemporary archaeology in urban settings, see McAtackney and Ryzewski, *Contemporary Archaeology in the City*.

3. The first European to explore Michigan, Étienne Brûlé, arrived in about 1620. Dunbar and May, *Michigan*, 19.

4. Beaudry, *Documentary Archaeology in the New World*; Beaudry, Cook, and Mrozowski, "Artifacts and Active Voices"; Leone and Knauf, *Historical Archaeologies of Capitalism*; Wilkie, "Documentary Archaeology."

5. Wurst, "Toward a Collective Historical Archaeology."

6. On dark heritage, see McAtackney, *An Archaeology of the Troubles*; Uzzell and Ballantyne, "Heritage That Hurts."

7. Surface-Evans "Landscape of Assimilation and Resistance"; Clark and Amati, "Powerful Objects, Difficult Dialogues"; Camp, "Landscapes of Japanese American Internment"; McAtackney, "Repercussions of Differential Deindustrialization in the City"; Mullins, "Politics, Inequality, and Engaged Archaeology."

8. Hicks and Mallet, *Lande*. On civic and political action, see McGuire, "Won with Blood"; Kiddey, *Homeless Heritage*; Zimmerman, Singleton, and Welch, "Translational Archaeology of Homelessness."

9. Little, "Archaeology as a Shared Vision." See also Gonzalez-Tennant, "Anarchism, Decolonization, and Collaborative Archaeology."

10. Moshenska, "Working with Memory," 41.

11. Dawdy, *Patina*; La Roche and Blakey, "Seizing Intellectual Power"; Tilley, "Archaeology as Socio-Political Action in the Present"; Moshenska, "Working with Memory," 44.

12. Kiddey, *Homeless Heritage*, 2; Jones, "Wrestling with the Social Value of

Heritage." For a review of approaches to heritage from different disciplines, see Harrison, "On Heritage Ontologies."

13. Perry, "Enchantment of the Archaeological Record."

14. Cherry and Ryzewski, *Archaeological History of Montserrat.*

15. The Michigan Consolidated Gas Company building was designed by Minoru Yamasaki, architect of the World Trade Center in New York City. Prior to Pilling's excavations there had been several salvage projects undertaken in Detroit by relic hunters during the nineteenth and early twentieth centuries. Pilling, "Detroit"; Pilling, "Skyscraper Archaeologist."

16. The French were the first European settlers in Detroit. They arrived in 1701.

17. In a controversial move, which Pilling vehemently protested against, the Michigan Consolidated Gas Company banned women from working on the site, alleging that they would distract workers and compromise site safety. Pilling, "Memo"; McElvenny, "RE: Official Sidewalk Superintendent Membership Card."

18. Pilling kept detailed records of the project's procedures and correspondence between himself and Michigan Consolidated Gas Company's officials. These records are now artifacts in their own right because they provide such valuable insights into the managerial dynamics of Detroit's early archaeological recovery projects.

19. McElvenny, "RE: Official Sidewalk Superintendent Membership Card."

20. Bunge was blacklisted as a communist sympathizer and subsequently fired from Wayne State University shortly after publishing the project's resulting book. Bunge, *Fitzgerald.*

21. Pilling, "Bunge Site Files, 20WN348, 1971"; also see Pilling in Bunge, *Fitzgerald*, xx; Pilling, "Skyscraper Archaeologist"; Pilling, "Detroit."

22. It was also distinct from earlier examples because it focused on the archaeology within the city rather than the story of urbanization, or the archaeology of the city, distinctions that were hotly debated within historical archaeology in the 1960s and 1970s.

23. The Gordon L. Grosscup Museum of Anthropology at Wayne State University houses a collection of over 500,000 artifacts, the majority of which were recovered from over three dozen archaeological sites in Detroit.

24. The 1805 fire destroyed the buildings of eighteenth-century Detroit. There exist very few archaeological remains from the first century of European settlement in Detroit as a result.

25. Unearthing Detroit Project, Wayne State University, principal investigator, Krysta Ryzewski, https://unearthdetroit.wordpress.com/.

26. Detroit Urban League, *Detroit Urban League (1950–1953)*; Detroit Housing Commission, *Urban Renewal and Public Housing in Detroit, 1954.*

27. Branstner, "Historical Archaeology in Detroit."

28. Cutoff dates are implemented in archaeological practice in other midwestern states, including Indiana.

29. Ryzewski, "'No Home for the Ordinary Gamut.'"

30. Roby and Starzmann "Techniques of Power," cited in Wurst, "Toward a Collective Historical Archaeology."

31. Wurst, "Toward a Collective Historical Archaeology"; Bernbeck and Pollock, "'Grabe, wo du stehst!'"

32. Kinney, "America's Great Comeback Story."

33. These approaches have proven to be unproductive. Instead, as Paul Mullins argues, notions of ethnicity—understood to be indexes of shared historical experiences and collectively articulated identity—are most effectively employed by efforts that seek to understand how its construction relates to structural power relations, expectations, and social tensions. Mullins, "Excavating America's Metaphor," 111. See also Orser, *Race and Practice*; Orser, "Twenty-First-Century Historical Archaeology."

34. Examples of such work in Chicago and New Orleans include Graff, *Disposing of Modernity*, and Gray, *Uprooted*.

35. Franklin, "A Black Feminist-Inspired Archaeology?," 109; Mullins, "Race and the Genteel Consumer"; Singleton, "Facing the Challenges"; Wilkie, *Creating Freedom*.

36. Battle-Baptiste, *Black Feminist Archaeology*, 19.

37. Mullins, "African-American Heritage," 68.

38. See figure 1 in Moshenska and Bonacchi, "Critical Reflections on Digital Public Archaeology"; Moshenska, *Key Concepts in Public Archaeology*, 6; Shackel, introduction to *Places in Mind*.

39. McGimsey, *Public Archaeology*.

40. Moshenska, *Key Concepts in Public Archaeology*, 5; Atalay, *Community-Based Archaeology*; Merriman, *Public Archaeology*.

41. Lamphere, "Applied, Practicing, and Public Anthropology," 431.

42. McDavid, "Archaeologies That Hurt; Descendants That Matter," 311–312.

43. Little, "Public Benefits of Public Archaeology."

44. Agbe-Davies, "Concepts of Community," 377.

45. Agbe-Davies, "Concepts of Community"; Little and Shackel, *Archaeology, Heritage, and Civic Engagement*, 83; Smith and Waterton, *Heritage, Communities, and Archaeology*.

46. Agbe-Davies, "Concepts of Community," 374.

47. Atalay, *Community-Based Archaeology*; Atalay, "Indigenous Archaeology as Decolonizing Practice."

48. Agbe-Davies, "Inside/Outside, Upside Down"; Wilkie, "Heritage Inheritances," 150.

49. Mullins, "African-American Heritage."

50. Gadsby and Chidester, "Heritage in Hampden"; Gadsby, "Urban Heritage in Troubled Times."

51. Gadsby, "Urban Heritage in Troubled Times," 20; also see successful examples in other cities and/or involving collaborations with communities as part of cultural resource management projects by Agbe-Davies, "Inside/Outside, Upside

Down"; Franklin and Lee, "African American Descendants"; Mullins, "Politics, Inequality, and Engaged Archaeology"; Díaz-Andreu and Ruiz, "Interacting with Heritage."

52. Singleton, "Facing the Challenges," 150–151.

53. Atalay, *Community-Based Archaeology*; Gonzalez, Kretzler, and Edwards, "Imagining Indigenous and Archaeological Futures"; Surface-Evans, "Landscape of Assimilation"; Mrozowski, "Imagining an Archaeology of the Future."

54. Gonzalez, Kretzler, and Edwards, "Imagining Indigenous and Archaeological Futures," 88.

55. Agbe-Davies, "Concepts of Community," 374; on service learning in western Michigan, see also Nassaney, "Implementing Community Service Learning," 97.

56. For example, see the Society of Black Archeologists' collaborations with professional organizations and SHPOs across the United States to ascertain the frequency with which African diaspora sites are considered eligible for the National Register of Historic Places and to increase statewide best practices for education and outreach efforts within Black communities; Franklin et al., "The Future Is Now," 760.

57. The emphasis on public archaeology as a form of civic engagement aligns with various other calls by scholars for activist archaeology, applied heritage, and action-oriented practice. See Stottman, *Archaeologists as Activists*; Kiddey, *Homeless Heritage*; Zimmerman, Singleton, and Welch, "Translational Archaeology of Homelessness."

58. Wurst, "Toward a Collective Historical Archaeology," 123.

59. Wurst, "Toward a Collective Historical Archaeology," 129.

60. Caraher, Kourelis, and Reinhard, *Punk Archaeology*.

61. DeLeón, *Land of Open Graves*; Gokee and DeLeón, "Sites of Contention"; Matthews, "Archaeology of Race and African American Resistance"; Leone, LaRoche, and Babiarz, "Archaeology of Black Americans in Recent Times."

62. Little and Shackel, *Archaeology, Heritage, and Civic Engagement*; Little and Shackel, *Archaeology as a Tool*.

63. University of Maryland's Coalition for Civic Engagement and Leadership (2005), cited in Little and Shackel, *Archaeology as a Tool*, 47.

64. Little and Shackel, *Archaeology as a Tool*, 47.

65. Little and Shackel, *Archaeology as a Tool*, 13.

66. Matthews, "Assemblages, Routines, and Social Justice Research."

67. Little and Zimmerman, "In the Public Interest," 158.

68. Pyburn, "Engaged Archaeology."

69. Agbe-Davies, "Inside/Outside, Upside Down," 574; Carman, "Stories We Tell," 495.

70. Kiddey, *Homeless Heritage*.

71. Kiddey, *Homeless Heritage*, 2; Graves-Brown and Kiddey, "Reclaiming the Streets"; Zimmerman, Vitelli, and Hollowell-Zimmer, *Ethical Issues in Archaeology*.

72. Little and Zimmerman, "In the Public Interest," 158; Wurst, "Toward a Collective Historical Archaeology," 124.

73. Agbe-Davies, "Where Tradition and Pragmatism Meet," 10; Agbe-Davies, "How to Do Things with Things"; Harris and Cipolla, *Archaeological Theory in the New Millennium*; Horning, "Politics, Publics, and Professional Pragmatics"; Larkin and McGuire, *Archaeology of Class War*; Mrozowski, "Pragmatism and the Relevancy of Archaeology"; Preucel and Mrozowski, "New Pragmatism"; Saitta, *Archaeology of Collective Action*; Wurst, "Toward a Collective Historical Archaeology."

74. Pyburn, "A Response to 'Herding Cats,'" 55.

75. Pyburn, "A Response to 'Herding Cats,'" 56.

76. Preucel and Mrozowski, "New Pragmatism," 3.

77. Klein et al., "Future of American Archaeology."

78. Boggs, with Kurashige, *Next American Revolution*; Boggs, *Living for Change*; Boggs and Boggs, *Revolution and Evolution in the 20th Century*; Ward, *In Love and Struggle*.

79. Boggs, "Metaphor for Detroit."

CHAPTER TWO

1. By 1920, twenty-nine different automobile companies operated within the city or in the immediate suburbs of Detroit. Waltzer, "East European Jewish Detroit," 291.

2. *Detroit News*, January 1, 1924, cited in Okrent, *Last Call*, 260.

3. Occasional high-profile raids led by federal officials did make headlines. "Business Men Arrested in Liquor Raid," *Detroit Free Press*, May 28, 1927, 1; "Seize $80,000 Holiday Liquor in Three Raids," *Detroit Free Press*, November 20, 1927, 1; "Hamtramck, City of Contrasts," *Detroit Free Press*, March 2, 1924, 66; "U.S. Dry Agents Stage Raids," *Detroit Free Press*, September 26, 1926.

4. "Detroit Is Wettest City He Worked In, Dry Administrator Says in Resigning," *New York Times*, November 4, 1925.

5. "Thirsty Americans Drink 250,000,000 Gallons of Rum," *Detroit Free Press*, May 28, 1927.

6. On the statewide inventory of archaeological sites, the Little Harry speakeasy is site 20WN1200.

7. Lyons, "Dry Times."

8. Carrie Nation made several visits to Detroit, but accounts of her destroying saloon property are difficult to verify. On August 24, 1908, she reportedly stormed Considine's Crescent Bar at 20 Monroe Avenue in Detroit, caused a commotion and lectured the customers, but did not destroy the bar with her signature hatchet. Lyons, "Hatchetations in Holly and Detroit."

9. Business leaders and manufacturers, including Henry Ford, were proponents of Prohibition because they figured that sober employees would be more productive and less truant in the workplace. On state legislation, see "Dry Laws Provide Sure Prohibition," *Detroit Free Press*, April 26, 1917, 10.

10. United States Constitution, Amendment XVIII (repealed 1933).

11. The Damon Act, passed in 1917, amended Michigan's state constitution to prohibit alcohol manufacturing, distribution, and consumption. It went into effect on May 1, 1918. The federal Volstead Act was passed in October 1919 and was enacted nationwide on midnight of January 17, 1920.

12. Rockaway, "Notorious Purple Gang," 118.

13. In addition to the Purple Gang there were also secondary Hamtramck, Irish, Downriver gangs. According to Wilson and Cohassey, each gang supplied whiskey outlets, clubs, and after-hours spots, in different territories. Historians estimate that the Purple Gang controlled at least 50% of the alcohol trafficked into Detroit during the twelve years of federal Prohibition (1919–1933). Wilson and Cohassey, *Toast of the Town*, 50; Rockaway, "Notorious Purple Gang," 113; Vachon, *Legendary Locals*, 124–25.

14. "Thirsty Americans Drink 250,000,000 Gallons of Rum," *Detroit Free Press*, May 28, 1927.

15. Vachon, *Legendary Locals*, 125.

16. Engelmann, *Intemperance*, 125; Rockaway, "Notorious Purple Gang," 120.

17. Kavieff, *The Purple Gang*, 77; Kavieff, *Detroit's Infamous Purple Gang*; Kavieff, *The Violent Years*.

18. Rockaway, "Notorious Purple Gang," 120–21. The Purple Gang is credited with over five hundred killings in the space of a decade, more than Al Capone's mob at the time.

19. African Americans comprised 4% of the population. See Bolkosky, *Harmony and Dissonance*, 19; United States Census Bureau, Detroit, Wayne, Michigan, Population, III, 1910, 953; United States Census Bureau, Detroit, Wayne, Michigan, Population, III, 1920, 496–497; Waltzer, "East European Jewish Detroit."

20. Ford automobile dealers often included subscriptions to the *Dearborn Independent* into the purchase price of Model T cars.

21. "Police Get Orders o Close Detroit's 7,500 Blind Pigs," *Detroit Free Press*, May 12, 1933, 2; Englemann, *Intemperance*, 126; Rockaway, "Notorious Purple Gang," 116.

22. Moon, *Untold Tales, Unsung Heroes*, 46; Vachon, *Legendary Locals*, 125; advertisement, Blossom Heath Inn, *Detroit Free Press*, May 16, 1920, 16; "Blossom Heath Inn Again Raided," *Detroit Free Press*, May 1, 1921, 6.

23. Wayne County Register of Deeds, Parcel 04003331, Sale History, 624 Third, Detroit, 48226.

24. The tasks into which I divided team members aligned with people's interests, expertise, abilities, and schedule availability.

25. Moloney and Ryzewski, *Report on the 2013 Speakeasy Project Excavations*.

26. There is disagreement about when the brick incarnation of the Tommy's bar building was first constructed. City land deed records on file at the Wayne County Records Office list an incorrect construction date of 1920. Present-day bar

staff suggest that the brick building dates to around 1850. This very early date is not, however, supported by archival records. It is most likely that the brick building's earliest iteration was constructed sometime during the 1860s or even early 1870s. Two sources of evidence support this. The property appears listed for the first time in the 1869 city directory under the ownership of Dr. Davis Henderson, and it was subdivided as a separate property lot in 1871. A photograph taken of the Fort Street Presbyterian Church in the 1860s, shortly after it opened in 1855, clearly shows earlier wooden buildings standing where the brick structure would eventually be constructed.

27. "Sayings and Doings," *Detroit Free Press*, June 10, 1898, A5; "Various Thefts Reported," *Detroit Free Press*, September 26, 1898, 5.

28. Andrew Healey, 1892/93–1918; Joseph Teman, 1906–1910; Louis Gianotti, 1921–1926; Harry Weitzman, 1927–1930; Harry Bianchini, 1933; Louis Gianotti, 1931, 1934–1937.

29. Advertisement, barber chair for sale, *Detroit Free Press*, June 22, 1900, 8.

30. Healey was born around 1860 in Virginia, see United States Census Bureau, Detroit, Ward 8, Wayne, Michigan, Roll T624_683, 1910, 10A.

31. *Sanborn Fire Insurance Map from Detroit, Wayne County, Michigan*, vol. 1, sheet 6, 1884.

32. The Michigan Central Railroad Depot was closed after a catastrophic fire in 1913 and demolished in 1966. In the years between 1913 and 1966 the back of the station continued to be used for railroad traffic and storage. This station is not to be confused with Fort St. Union Depot or the second incarnation of Michigan Central in Corktown.

33. "Third Street Matters," *Detroit Free Press*, May 27, 1892, 5.

34. It operated until 1971.

35. "Passing of Fort Street West: Once a Social Center," *Detroit Free Press*, November 9, 1913, H3.

36. *Sanborn Fire Insurance Map from Detroit, Wayne County, Michigan*, vol. 1, sheet 8, 1897; Baist, *Baist's Property Atlas of the City of Detroit, Michigan* (1896).

37. Baist, *Baist's Property Atlas of the City of Detroit, Michigan* (1915).

38. "Healey's Saloon," in *Polk's Detroit City Directory* (1917).

39. Gianotti's surname has multiple spellings in archival records.

40. United States Census Bureau, Detroit, Ward 18, Wayne, Michigan, Roll T625_817, 1920, 45B.

41. Weitzman was remembered by friends and family as a "tough guy"; McCormick, "Al Wertheimer Dies."

42. Nelson, "Weitzman Family Oral History."

43. "Ticket Seller under Arrest," *Detroit Free Press*, October 11, 1907, 1; "Weitzman Loans," *Detroit Free Press*, September 18, 1916, 12; "Money Loaned on Diamonds—Weitzman's," *Detroit Free Press*, May 17, 1919, 1; "Harry Weitzman Bond Sales," *Detroit Free Press*, June 21, 1925, 95.

44. "Business Corner Resold," *Detroit Free Press*, January 24, 1915, D3; "Centrally Located Business Block Valued at $175,000 Figures in Sale," *Detroit Free Press*, April 18, 1915, C2.

45. The Purple Gang began to unravel by 1930; "Detroit Purple Gang Smashed by Own Greed," *Washington Post*, February 25, 1934.

46. "Restaurant for Sale," *Detroit Free Press*, July 19, 1930, 20; "Cuneo Restaurant," *Detroit Free Press*, November 26, 1931, 19.

47. "Café Operator Fined," *Detroit Free Press*, August 24, 1934, 7.

48. Mason, *Rumrunning and the Roaring Twenties*.

49. The city's homeless population slept in culverts underneath Third Avenue; see Nelson, "Police Explore Detroit's Jungles."

50. "Royal Glass," *Electrical World T&D* 93, no. 6 (1929): 324.

51. Hartnett and Dawdy, "Archaeology of Illegal and Illicit Economies"; Nyman, Fogle, and Beaudry, *Historical Archaeology of Shadow and Intimate Economies*.

52. Delle, "Tale of Two Tunnels"; Graff, "Ardent Anti-Slavery Tale"; Fruehling and Smith, "Subterranean Hideaways"; LaRoche, "On the Edge of Freedom"; Vlach, "Above Ground on the Underground Railroad."

53. "Police Get Orders to Close Detroit's 7,500 Blind Pigs." *Detroit Free Press*, May 12, 1933, 2.

54. "Little Harry's Restaurant," *Detroit Free Press*, November 28, 1934, 21; Steinmetz, "Bianchini Family Oral History."

55. "Little Harry's Restaurant," *Detroit Free Press*, November 28, 1934, 21; "Café Operator Fined," *Detroit Free Press*, August 24, 1934, 7.

56. "Detroit Purple Gang Smashed by Own Greed," *Washington Post*, February 25, 1934. During the 1930s the FBI tracked the Purple Gang's movement across the country, from Michigan to Florida, San Francisco, Tulsa, Oklahoma, New York, and New Jersey; see Federal Bureau of Investigation (1933–1948), Purple Gang, File 62-HQ-29632.

57. "3 Killed by Gang: 5 Jailed," *Detroit Free Press*, September 17, 1931, 1; Rockaway, "Detroit's Purple Gang," 23–25.

58. "Deutches Haus Faces Padlock," *Detroit Free Press*, October, 25, 1928.

59. Nelson, "Weitzman Family Oral History"; Hill, "Weitzman Family Oral History"; Finsilver, "Weitzman Family Oral History"; Whiteman, "Weitzman Family Oral History."

60. Hill, "Weitzman Family Oral History."

61. Rubin, "Clues at Downtown Bar"; Headapohl, "Digging for Purple"; Reed, "Digging Detroit."

62. Caraher, "Slow Archaeology, Punk Archaeology"; Caraher, "Slow Archaeology"; Cunningham and MacEachern, "Ethnoarchaeology as Slow Science."

63. Lennon, "Conclusion," 242.

64. Graff, "Ardent Anti-Slavery Tale," 85.

65. Beisaw, "Ghost Hunting as Archaeology," 192. On the intersection of archaeology and ghosts as a mechanism for negotiating difficult aspects of his-

torical legacies, see Surface-Evans, Garrison, and Supernant, *Blurring Timescapes, Subverting Erasure*.

CHAPTER THREE

1. *Sanborn Fire Insurance Map from Detroit, Wayne County, Michigan*, vol. 3, sheet 4, 1897; Detroit Free Press Club, *Detroit Blue Book*.

2. Ninety percent of the historic homes in Brush Park had been demolished by 2012; Barrionuevo, "Detroit's Billionaires."

3. McLauchlin, *Alfred Street*.

4. McLauchlin, *Alfred Street*, 1.

5. Marchand and Meffre, *Ruins of Detroit*.

6. On the statewide inventory of archaeological sites, the Ransom Gillis House is site 20WN1199.

7. Ryzewski, "Detroit 139."

8. Advertisement for Edson Moore & Co Wholesale Dealers in Dry Goods, *Detroit Free Press*, April 6, 1875, 2.

9. Between 1920 and 1922 the city of Detroit renumbered all addresses in the city to accommodate rapid urbanization. Prior to 1921 the Ransom Gillis House's address was 63 Alfred; it was then changed to 215 Alfred.

10. Ryzewski, "Historical Archaeology."

11. Kossik, *63 Alfred Street*, 8–9; State Historic Preservation Office of Michigan, *Ransom Gillis House, Brush Park, Detroit, Michigan*.

12. John R. Street is named for John R. Williams (1782–1854), the first mayor of Detroit after the city's reincorporation.

13. Kossik, *63 Alfred Street*, 29.

14. Maynard, "Detroit Polishes, and Demolishes, for the Super Bowl."

15. Kossik, *63 Alfred Street*, 105.

16. United States Department of the Interior, *Mothballing Historic Buildings*.

17. For a photographic sequence of the Ransom Gillis House's decay and rehabilitation from the late 1990s to 2015, see Vergara, *Tracking Time*.

18. Barrionuevo, "Detroit's Billionaires"; Brush Park Development Company, "City Modern Design Process."

19. Quicken Loans Press Room, "HGTV and Quicken Loans Collaborate."

20. May, "Heritage, Endangerment and Participation."

21. *Sanborn Fire Insurance Map from Detroit, Wayne County, Michigan*, vol. 3, sheet 16, 1950; *Sanborn Fire Insurance Map from Detroit, Wayne County, Michigan*, vol. 3, sheet 16, 1921; *Sanborn Fire Insurance Map from Detroit, Wayne County, Michigan*, vol. 3, sheet 4, 1897.

22. Mary Chase Perry (b. March 15, 1867) married William Buck Stratton in 1918. During the time she worked in the Stable Studio at 63 Alfred Street she was unmarried. Therefore, I refer to her throughout the text by her maiden name, as it was at the time.

23. Branstner, *Cultural Resource Overview*.

24. Pear, *Pewabic Pottery*, 12.

25. Green, "Mary Chase Perry Stratton"; Ars Ceramica, *Highlights of Pewabic Pottery*; Pear, *Pewabic Pottery*; Callen, *Women Artists of the Arts and Crafts Movement*; Detroit Historical Society, "Stratton, Mary Chase Perry."

26. Kossik, *63 Alfred Street*, 54.

27. Green, "Mary Chase Perry Stratton," 6.

28. Pear, *Pewabic Pottery*, 23, 28.

29. Green, "Mary Chase Perry Stratton," 6.

30. Kossik, *63 Alfred Street*, 59.

31. We excavated all four units to a depth of about 1 meter (3.3 ft). The maximum depths for the excavation units were Unit 1, 90 centimeters below the unit datum point (cmbd); Unit 2, 103 cmbd; Unit 3, 90 cmbd; Unit 4, 84 cmbd.

32. Level 4 of Unit 4.

33. Demeter, *Expanded Phase I/II Archaeological Evaluation*.

34. McLauchlin, *Alfred Street*.

35. Kossik, *63 Alfred Street*, 29, 31–32, 59.

36. "Local Musical Notes," *Detroit Free Press*, October 16, 1898, A5.

37. "Alanson J. Fox Is Dead," *Detroit Free Press*, October 30, 1903, 1.

38. Kossik, *63 Alfred Street*, 54.

39. Personals, *Detroit Free Press*, June 6, 1909, B4.

40. Kossik, *63 Alfred Street*, 55.

41. Reverend Fike owned the Ransom Gillis House until 1919 but moved out by 1916 and allowed Noeske to run it as a rooming house.

42. Kossik, *63 Alfred Street*, 55; United States Census Bureau, Detroit, Ward 1, Wayne, Michigan, Roll T624_679, 1910, 130.

43. "City Sightings," *Detroit Free Press*, May 18, 1916, 5; "Harry Vrooman," *Detroit City Directory*, 1915.

44. Kossik, *63 Alfred Street*, 58; United States Census Bureau, Detroit, Ward 1, Wayne, Michigan, Roll T625_803, 1920, 9A.

45. United States Census Bureau, Detroit, Wayne, Michigan, 1930, 16A.

46. Kossik, *63 Alfred Street*, 60.

47. Kossik reports that they were immigrants from the towns of Adana and Tel Kaif in Syria. Kossik, *63 Alfred Street*, 72.

48. Kossik, *63 Alfred Street*, 72; *Sanborn Fire Insurance Map from Detroit, Wayne County, Michigan*, vol. 3, sheet 16, 1950.

49. Kossik, *63 Alfred Street*, 74.

50. Black Bottom and Paradise Valley were the neighborhoods with the largest concentrations of African American residents in Detroit. Paradise Valley was the entertainment center of the city. Both were displaced by urban renewal. The Brewster Douglass Projects were the first federally funded housing projects built to accommodate African Americans in the United States. The Essas did not live at the Ransom Gillis House; they lived off-site at 161 Atkinson. See Lauterbach, *Chitlin' Circuit*; United States Census Bureau, Detroit, Wayne, Michigan, 1940, 10A.

51. "View of Riotous Scene," Acme News Service, Getty Images, June 22, 1943.

52. McLauchlin, *Alfred Street*.

53. Zunz, *Changing Face of Inequality*.

54. "2 Landlords in Slum Area Draw Big Fines," *Detroit Free Press*, January 8, 1955, 1.

55. Kossik, *63 Alfred Street*, 89.

56. Kossik, *63 Alfred Street*; see also chapter 5.

57. McMahon, "Woodward East Seeks Designation."

58. Lenhausen, "Abandoned Victorian Homes Periled."

59. Lenhausen, "Abandoned Victorian Homes Periled."

60. Branstner, *Cultural Resource Overview*, 18.

61. Branstner, *Cultural Resource Overview*, 18; McMahon, "Woodward East Seeks Designation."

62. Fox, "Neighborhood's Dream of Revival Going Sour," 1A + 4A.

63. Fox, "Neighborhood's Dream," 1A.

64. Rick Ratliff, "Buy for a Song—Renovations Extra."

65. Gram and Barton, *Literature Cultural Resource Survey*.

66. Gram and Barton, *Literature Cultural Resource Survey*, 23–25.

67. Ratliff, "Buy for a Song—Renovations Extra."

68. Kossik, *63 Alfred Street*, 102.

69. Ratliff, "City's Brush Park Houses Unsold after a Year."

70. King, "Archer, Developers Want Mansions Moved."

71. Branstner, *Cultural Resource Overview*, 30.

72. Demeter, *Expanded Phase I/II Archaeological Evaluation*.

73. On the relationship between gentrification, heritage, and history, see Herzfeld, "Engagement, Gentrification, and the Neoliberal Hijacking of History"; DeCesari, Chiara, and Rozita Dimova, "Heritage, Gentrification, Participation"; DeCesari and Herzfeld, "Urban Heritage and Social Movements."

74. Ramirez, "Hundreds Get Sneak Peek."

75. Pinho, "City Modern Construction."

76. Afana, "16 Condos Sold"; Candice Williams, "Officials Celebrate."

77. Stoler, introduction to *Imperial Debris*.

78. González-Ruibal, "Ruins of the South," 159; Apel, *Beautiful Terrible Ruins*.

79. Stoler, introduction to *Imperial Debris*; Thomas, *Redevelopment and Race*, 10–11.

80. Meskell, *A Future in Ruins*, 1. See also Kinney, "Longing for Detroit," 7.

CHAPTER FOUR

1. Bjorn and Gallert, "Bebop in Detroit," 8.

2. For a discussion of how bebop emerged as a reflection of mid-twentieth-century urban Blackness, see Neal, *What the Music Said*, 26; Malcolm, "'Myriad Subtleties.'"

3. The musicians initially earned about $41.40 per night; Dulzo, "Remembering the Bebop at the Blue Bird."

4. Beatty, "Hitting the Hot Spots."

5. McCallum, "Jazz Lives."

6. Various grassroots heritage efforts are currently underway, led by the site's owner and our collaborator, the nonprofit Detroit Sound Conservancy.

7. Ryzewski, "Making Music in Detroit," 69–90.

8. Making Music in Detroit videos, Wayne Archaeology, March 2014, www. youtube.com.

9. Detroit Sound Conservancy, "Vision, Mission, and Goals."

10. Cherry, Ryzewski, and Pecoraro "'A Kind of Sacred Place'"; see also Arjona, "Homesick Blues."

11. I arranged the survey, supervised its methodology, and coordinated with the survey team. In the survey's aftermath, I continued collaborations with the DSC and conducted artifact analysis and historical background research on the survey findings. I was, however, unable to enter the Blue Bird during the April 2015 archaeological survey due to my late stage pregnancy and the potential risks that the building posed. My work on the survey portion of the project was conducted remotely and I designated my graduate students Lorin Brace and Samantha Ellens to act as the on-site survey supervisors; see Brace and Ellens, "Archaeology at the Blue Bird."

12. Brace, "'Nothing Phony about It in Any Way.'"

13. Molin's building measured thirty feet wide and sixty feet long and was twelve feet high. City of Detroit, Historic Designation Advisory Board, *Proposed Blue Bird Inn Historic District*, 3–4; *Sanborn Fire Insurance Map from Detroit, Wayne County, Michigan*, vol. 6, sheet 3, 1917.

14. Thomas, *Redevelopment and Race*.

15. See summary 1910–1970 census data in Sugrue, *Origins of the Urban Crisis*.

16. Stryker, *Jazz from Detroit*, 4; Sugrue, *Origins of the Urban Crisis*.

17. City of Detroit, Historic Designation Advisory Board, *Proposed Blue Bird Inn Historic District*, 3–4; "Son Shoots Father Who Beat Mother," *Chicago Defender*, November 20, 1937, 2; "Son Gets Life Sentence in Slaying of His Father," *Detroit Free Press*, March 8, 1938, 4.

18. LaJean Dubois Black, Death Certificate, State of Michigan, May 28, 1998, #1335957.

19. Advertisement for Blue Bird Inn jam sessions, *Detroit Tribune* April 30, 1938, n.p.

20. Seven years later Buddy was killed when he was shot at close range a few blocks from the Blue Bird, allegedly in a dispute over a woman with whom he was romantically involved. "Link Woman to Dubois Slaying: Manager Shot in Face by Assailant," *Michigan Chronicle*, September 29, 1955, 1.

21. Borden, *Detroit's Paradise Valley*.

22. Stryker, *Jazz from Detroit*, x.

23. Williams, *Detroit: The Black Bottom Community*.

24. Moon, *Untold Tales, Unsung Heroes*, 176.

25. The Chitlin' Circuit was a network of performance venues that welcomed African American musicians and entertainers during the period of twentieth-century racial segregation. The network spread across the southern, eastern, and midwestern United States and included Detroit. Lauterbach, *Chitlin' Circuit*; "Lionel Hampton at the Paradise Theatre," *Michigan Chronicle*, March 27, 1948, 17.

26. In Detroit during the 1930s and through the 1950s, entertainment venues that welcomed mixed crowds were referred to in the media and by residents as "black-and-tans."

27. Wilson and Cohassey, *Toast of the Town*, 44–45.

28. Neal, *What the Music Said*, 27.

29. "Detroit Music Scene," *Michigan Chronicle*, September 10, 1949, n.p.

30. "Interracial Goodwill Hour," *Michigan Chronicle*, January 10, 1948, 47; "Column on Michigan Radio Shows," *Michigan Chronicle*, March 28, 1948, 18.

31. Lane, "Swinging Down the Lane, Rockin' with LeRoy."

32. O'Neal and van Singel, *Voice of the Blues*.

33. "Joe's Record Shop," *Michigan Chronicle*, September 4, 1948, 11.

34. "Staff Record Company and Dessa Label," *Michigan Chronicle*, May 7, 1949, 21; "Dessa Malone," *Michigan Chronicle*, February 5, 1949, 18.

35. "Staff Record Company and Dessa Label," *Michigan Chronicle*, May 7, 1949, 21; O'Neal and van Singel, *Voice of the Blues*, 214.

36. "Dessa Malone," *Michigan Chronicle*, February 5, 1949, 18; Malone left the record business in the following years and became a reputable gospel music deejay in Lonoke, Arkansas; O'Neal and van Singel, *Voice of the Blues*, 214.

37. "Jimmy Caldwell at the Royal Blue," *Michigan Chronicle*, January 17, 1948, 16.

38. Advertisement for the Royal Blue featuring Bebop, *Michigan Chronicle*, June 18, 1948, 19.

39. United States Department of Labor, *Wage Chronology*, 14.

40. We know from newspaper advertisements that Hill continued to play as the Blue Bird's house band through much of 1949, but no records of the band's wages survive from that period.

41. Advertisement, *Michigan Chronicle*, October 20, 1948, 10.

42. By March 1949 the combo included Phil Hill, Eddie Jackson on the alto saxophone, Jimmy Richardson on bass, and Art Mardigan on the drums. They played Thursdays through Sundays. "Blue Bird Inn Features Hill and Orchestra," *Michigan Chronicle*, March 19, 1949, 20.

43. "Jazz Wars," *Michigan Chronicle*, March 19, 1949, 21.

44. Stephens, Stemmin' with Steve, *Michigan Chronicle*, October 30, 1948, 11.

45. Stephens, "Jazz in Detroit Is Terrific and 'Crazy'"; Stephens, Stemmin' with Steve, *Michigan Chronicle*, October 10, 1948, 10.

46. "Blue Bird Inn Features Hill and Orchestra," *Michigan Chronicle*, March 19, 1949, 20.

47. "Dessa Malone," *Michigan Chronicle*, February 5, 1949, 18; Hays, "The Focal Scrip."

48. "Blue Bird Inn Features Hill and Orchestra," *Michigan Chronicle*, March 19, 1949, 20.

49. Stryker, *Jazz from Detroit*, 7. For earlier detailed accounts of Detroit's musical heritage, see reports by Walter Kim Heron, including "Detroit Music: The Ultimate Sightseer's Guide," *Metro Times*, December 14, 2011.

50. Metzger and Booza, *African Americans in the United States, Michigan, and Metropolitan Detroit*.

51. *Polk's Detroit City Directory* (1927, 1929, and 1935).

52. United States Census Bureau, Detroit, Wayne, Michigan, 1930, 8A; United States Census Bureau, Detroit, Wayne, Michigan, 1940, 7A.

53. Thomas, *Redevelopment and Race*, 17, cites US Home and Housing Finance Agency, *Housing Commission Report*, January 21, 1948, Burton Mayors, 1948, box 4, "Housing Commission (1)," folder 5, Burton Historical Collection, Detroit Public Library.

54. Advertisement, *Michigan Chronicle*, January 20, 1945, 1.

55. Sugrue, *Origins of the Urban Crisis*, 133.

56. Freund, *Colored Property*, 42.

57. Sojourner Truth Housing Project, Walter Reuther Library, Wayne State University.

58. Twenty-five of the victims were Black, nine were White.

59. White and Marshall, *What Caused the Detroit Riot?*

60. Harris, "Whiteness as Property."

61. "20 Fined for Liquor Violations," *Detroit Free Press*, July 23, 1950, 6.

62. "Two Bars Cited after Dope Raids," *Detroit Free Press*, May 17, 1951, 13; Lane, "Padlocking for Serving Underworld."

63. Dulzo, "Remembering the Bebop at the Blue Bird."

64. Dulzo, "Remembering the Bebop at the Blue Bird."

65. They routinely advertised positions seeking "colored" applicants in local Black and White newspapers. See, for example, classified ad for staff, *Detroit Free Press*, May 19, 1944, 20.

66. This figure is based on the average amount of cash received for the bar in one month, May 1–June 30, 1948—$11,485.64 as recorded in the Blue Bird Inn cash ledger found during the archaeological survey.

67. "Jumpin' Jive," *Detroit Tribune*, June 6, 1942, 13.

68. Advertisement for Blue Bird Inn Thanksgiving dinners, *Detroit Tribune*, November 23, 1940, 6.

69. Brace, "'Nothing Phony about It in Any Way,'" 37.

70. Blue Bird Inn receipts, May 4, 1949 (documents recovered from archaeological survey).

71. Blue Bird Inn receipts, May 4, 1949.

72. Blue Bird Inn cash ledger, 1948–1949 (recovered from archaeological survey).

73. Blue Bird Inn receipts, May 10, 1949, and May 4, 1949.

74. Brace, "'Nothing Phony about It in Any Way,'" 57.

75. Brace, "'Nothing Phony about It in Any Way,'" 37.

76. Blue Bird Inn receipts, May 4, 1949.

77. Blue Bird Inn receipts, November 10, 1948, and May 6, 1949.

78. Brace, "'Nothing Phony about It in Any Way,'" 17.

79. *Wikipedia*, "1948 in Television."

80. Bjorn and Gallert, "Bebop in Detroit," 116.

81. Sugrue, *Origins of the Urban Crisis*, 47.

82. Kingsdale, "The 'Poor Man's Club.'"

83. Sugrue, *Origins of the Urban Crisis*, 92.

84. Blue Bird Inn cash ledger, 1948–1949; Blue Bird Inn checks, 1948–1949.

85. Blue Bird Inn cash ledger, 1948–1949.

86. Blue Bird Inn cash ledger, 1948–1949; Blue Bird Inn checks, 1948–1949.

87. Advertisement, Paradise Valley Distributing Company, *Detroit Tribune*, September 6, 1941, 6; advertisement, Paradise Valley Distributing Company, *Detroit Tribune*, November 7, 1942.

88. Williams, *Detroit: The Black Bottom Community*, 17.

89. Blue Bird Inn receipts, May 6, 1949.

90. Wilson and Cohassey, *Toast of the Town*, 46–47.

91. Associates Advertisers Service, *Directory of Negro Businesses, Professions, and Churches for Detroit and Environs*. The Blue Bird Inn and the West Side businesses that the management frequented are not mentioned in the directory.

92. Borden, *Detroit's Paradise Valley*.

93. Mullins, "Race and the Genteel Consumer," 34.

94. Bjorn and Gallert, "Bebop in Detroit," 10. According to Gholz, there may be a connection between the stage's design motif and local midcentury Freemason symbolism (personal communication, March 2020).

95. Bjorn and Gallert, "Bebop in Detroit," 11.

96. Dulzo, "Remembering the Bebop at the Blue Bird."

97. Heron, "They Went to Europe to Find a Jazz Festival."

98. The National Register nomination process was never completed; Stryker, "ReBop," 1G + 7G.

99. Bjorn and Gallert, "Bebop in Detroit," 8.

100. Stryker, "ReBop," 1G + 7G.

101. Wayne County Register of Deeds, Parcel 16001965, Sale History, 5021 Tireman, Detroit, 48204, 2018.

102. Detroit Sound Conservancy, "Restaging the Stage."

103. Detroit Sound Conservancy, "A Site of Sonic Resistance Is Reborn"; Henderson, "Legendary Blue Bird Inn Stage Restored."

104. Basso, *Wisdom Sits in Places*, 5.

105. Frank, "Detroit Sound Conservancy Plots Future for Historic Jazz Club.'"
106. Gholz, "Magic, Liberation, and Architecture."
107. Carleton S. Gholz to Krysta Ryzewski, personal communication, February 5, 2020.
108. Mullins, "Excavating America's Metaphor," 104.

CHAPTER FIVE

1. Today Twelfth Street is known as Rosa Parks Boulevard. It was renamed in 1976, nine years after the 1967 uprising.
2. References to the extensive body of scholarship by historians, geographers, urban studies, and other scholars can be found in Stone, *Detroit 1967*.
3. Caraher, "Slow Archaeology, Punk Archaeology"; Caraher, "Slow Archaeology"; Cunningham and MacEachern, "Ethnoarchaeology as Slow Science."
4. Ashplant, "War Commemoration in Western Europe"; Basso, *Wisdom Sits in Places*; Dawson, *Commemorating War*. On memory in Detroit, see Chenoweth, "Natural Graffiti and Cultural Plants."
5. McAtackney and Ryzewski, *Contemporary Archaeology in the City*.
6. Black Detroiters' history of activism and resilience in the face of police brutality and oppressive restrictions is chronicled in Boyd, *Black Detroit*.
7. Calvert, "Oral History Interview."
8. Detroit Historical Museum, Oral History Collection, 2017.
9. McGraw, "He Helped Start 1967 Detroit Riot."
10. Sugrue, *Origins of the Urban Crisis*.
11. United States National Advisory Commission on Civil Disorders and Kerner, *Report*.
12. Thomas, *Redevelopment and Race*, 127.
13. Boggs, "Detroit 1967."
14. Boggs, *Manifesto for a Black Revolutionary Party*, 158.
15. Boggs, *Detroit, Birth of a Nation*.
16. Boggs, with Kurashige, *Next American Revolution*, 140.
17. Boggs, "Detroit 1967."
18. Rockaway, "Notorious Purple Gang," 126.
19. Moon, *Untold Tales, Unsung Heroes*, 345.
20. Moon, *Untold Tales, Unsung Heroes*, 345.
21. "Jewish Council Blasts 12th St. Area 'Rumor-Mongers,'" *Michigan Chronicle*, January 3, 1948, 2.
22. "Jewish Council Blasts 12th St. Area 'Rumor-Mongers,'" 2.
23. Thomas, *Redevelopment and Race*, 60; Detroit Urban League, *Brief of Urban Renewal Activity in the City of Detroit, November 29, 1956*.
24. On White flight: 22,000 White residents left the city on average each year from 1964 to 1966. In 1967, 47,000 White residents left; 80,000 left in 1968 and 46,000 in 1969. Detroit's non-White population increased from 12.5% of the city's total population in 1950 to over 30% in 1960 (304,000 to 487,000). In 1950, 35%

of the city's African American population were homeowners, in 1960 the number rose to 41%. White home ownership rose from 65% in 1950 to 76% in 1960. See Thomas, *Redevelopment and Race*, 130.

25. Thomas, *Redevelopment and Race*, 130; United States National Advisory Commission on Civil Disorders and Kerner, *Report*, 86–87; John Lowell, "Violence on 12th—Street of Nightmares."

26. Thomas, *Redevelopment and Race*, 130–131; Meyer, "Return to 12th Street."

27. Smothers, "Visit to 12th Street."

28. Thomas, *Redevelopment and Race*, 150; city police chief Nichols received 91% of the vote from White residents.

29. Mead, "Scars Linger in Detroit."

30. Mead, "Scars Linger in Detroit," 85.

31. Peterson, "Street Awakening from '67 Detroit Riot."

32. Cherry, "Still Not Digging, Much."

33. Boggs, "Metaphor for Detroit." The *Michigan Citizen* was a weekly newspaper founded in 1978 oriented toward the state's African American and progressive-minded communities. It should not be confused with the *Michigan Chronicle*.

34. On types of forgetting see Connerton, "Seven Types of Forgetting," 67–68.

35. "Jack Ward's Detroit Riot Monument," *Discuss Detroit* (electronic forum), postings from 2009.

36. "Jack Ward's Detroit Riot Monument."

37. "Jack Ward's Detroit Riot Monument."

38. Huebner, *Walls of Prophecy and Protest*; Huebner, "In Search of Detroit's Lost Walls." The *Wall of Pride* mural on Twelfth Street was one of three major installations in areas affected by the uprising whose design was led by Walker and Wade in 1968–1969. The other two were the *Wall of Dignity* on the Fairview Gardens building at 11000 Mack Avenue and the *Harriet Tubman Memorial Wall (Let My People Go)* at St. Bernard Catholic Church. All three murals were either erased or dismantled (in the case of the *Harriet Tubman Memorial* Wall) by the 1980s. No traces of them survive today.

39. Ward, "Detroit 1967 Sculpture."

40. Ward, "Detroit 1967 Sculpture."

41. Ward, "Detroit 1967 Sculpture."

42. Bergman and Salinas, *Monument to Rebellion*, 2015. "Exhibit of the origin site of the 1967 Great Rebellion or 12th Street Riots, at Clairmount Ave. and 12th Street, Detroit," shown at the 1st Bergen Assembly Triennial and Kunsthalle Exnergasse, Vienna, exhibit description accessed February 12, 2019, www.alejandra-aeron.com.

43. Ward, "Detroit 1967 Sculpture."

44. Emphasis in original; Mazzei, "Monument Email."

45. Bergman and Salinas, *Monument to Rebellion*.

46. Meskell, "Negative Heritage and Past Mastering," 558.

47. Lee, "Detroit Plans to Renovate 40 Neighborhood Parks."

48. Moshenska, "Working with Memory in the Archaeology of Modern Conflict," 33–48, 45; Moshenska, "Charred Churches or Iron Harvests?"

49. Gonzalez, Kretzler, and Edwards, "Imagining Indigenous and Archaeological Futures," 95.

50. Aguilar, "Site Where 1967 Uprising Began."

51. American Black Journal, "Gordon Park: Reborn."

52. American Black Journal, "Gordon Park: Reborn."

53. Detroit Historical Museum, *Detroit 1967*; Stone, *Detroit 1967*.

54. John Wisely, "Historic Marker Unveiled."

55. Bill Kubota, "Detroit's 1967 Uprising Gets Historical Marker."

56. American Black Journal, "Gordon Park: Reborn."

57. American Black Journal, "Gordon Park: Reborn."

58. Allen, "Muralist Says."

59. In the creation of the Twelfth Street memorial, the Oakland Avenue Artists' Coalition partnered with the Virginia Park Community District Citizen's Council, the Greening of Detroit, NEWCO, MDDDinc, and the Detroit Department of Parks and Recreation. Solis, "Childhood Memories from Detroit 1967"; Galbraith, "New Parks in Downtown and Morningside."

60. Boggs, with Kurashige, *Next American Revolution*, 223.

CHAPTER SIX

1. Uhelszki, "Twenty-Five Years of *Creem*," 290.

2. Brent, "Press Review, Led Zeppelin."

3. For a comprehensive history of the rock 'n' roll era at the Grande Ballroom, see Early, *Grande Ballroom*.

4. Thurston, "City's Nightlife Landmarks Escape Serious Damage"; Gibb believed the Grande was spared because of its music and reputation; see Early, *Grande Ballroom*, 136.

5. Walsh and Early, "Grande Ballroom," National Register of Historic Places Inventory/Nomination Form, 10, 31.

6. Edsall, "Capturing Detroit through an Underground Lens"; Walker, "Voice of the Budding Underground."

7. "Henry 'Hank' Fomish and His Orchestra," *Lansing State Journal*, May 30, 1931, 19; "Entertain at Dance—Singers Grace Baruth and Margaret Maischein of Detroit," *Detroit Free* Press, February 12, 1933, 23.

8. "Jewett Plant Built by Wood," *Detroit Free Press*, January 20, 1924, 7.

9. Walsh and Early, "Grande Ballroom."

10. Agree, "Use of Brick Construction for Modern Playhouse," 15–16.

11. Walsh and Early, "Grande Ballroom," 7–8.

12. Walsh and Early, "Grande Ballroom," 8–9.

13. Walsh and Early, "Grande Ballroom," 7–8; Moloney and Ryzewski, *Report on the 2013 Speakeasy Project Excavations at Tommy's Bar, Detroit, MI.*

14. Agree, "Use of Brick Construction for Modern Playhouse"; Agree, "Record of Projects Undertaken During the Last Ten Years or More."

15. Walsh and Early, "Grande Ballroom," 10.

16. Walsh and Early, "Grande Ballroom," 9–10.

17. Atlas Obscura, "Incredible Ruins in Detroit—Grande Ballroom"; see critique of ruin photography in Ryzewski, "Ruin Photography as Archaeological Method."

18. Early, "Friends of the Grande Ballroom Mission Statement."

19. Early, "Grande Ballroom Inspection."

20. Cherry, Ryzewski, and Pecoraro, "'A Kind of Sacred Place'"; Ryzewski and Cherry, "On AIR." In 1969 the late Beatles producer Sir George Martin established AIR Studios' headquarters in London; a decade later he opened the satellite studio on Montserrat as a recording retreat for the company's artists. Between 1979 and 1989, performers like the Rolling Stones, Elton John, and The Police recorded chart-topping albums on the remote island using AIR Studios Montserrat state-of-the-art recording technology. When working at AIR Montserrat, artists operated out of the studio's modest complex, which included a lodging house, a patio and pool area for entertaining, a business office, and a two-room recording studio. In between the house and recording studio was a courtyard and a bordering sidewalk, into which artists and production staff impressed their handprints and autographs.

21. Ryzewski, *Grande Ballroom Archaeological Survey Report.*

22. Klein et al., "Future of American Archaeology"; Caraher, Kourelis, and Reinhard, *Punk Archaeology*; Morgan, "Punk, DIY, and Anarchy."

23. Moshenska, "Working with Memory," 37.

24. Ryzewski, *Grande Ballroom Archaeological Survey Report.*

25. Milan, *Detroit*, 17.

26. Early, "Grande Column Corbels Repatriated."

27. Alterman, "Teen Club That's Absolutely Wow."

28. Vachon, *Legendary Locals*, 14.

29. Ryzewski, *Grande Ballroom Archaeological Survey Report*, 50.

30. See overview in Early, *Grande Ballroom.*

31. Classified ad for coat checkers, *Detroit Free Press*, March 2, 1945, 21.

32. Classified ad for matron, porter, and janitors, *Detroit Free Press*, September 5, 1943, 12.

33. Classified ad for shoe shiner and washroom attendant, *Detroit Free Press*, November 10, 1943, 19.

34. Bartkowiak, *MC5 and Social Change*; Carson, *Grit, Noise, and Revolution.*

35. Callwood, *The Stooges*; Sheehan, "Iggy's Blues"; Concert Database—Grande Ballroom, "Fleetwood Mac, December 27, 1968."

36. Daldin, "Grande Daze, Bubble Puppies, and Suburban Hippies," 420.

37. MC5 included Rob Tyner (vocals), Wayne Kramer (guitar), Fred "Sonic" Smith (guitar), Michael Davis (bass), and Dennis Thompson (drums); Erlewine quoted in Ankeny, "MC5."

38. Sinclair, "DKT/MC5."

39. Sinclair, "DKT/MC5," 225.

40. Sinclair, "DKT/MC5," 223.

41. Concert Database—Grande Ballroom, "John Lee Hooker, December 29, 1967"; Concert Database—Grande Ballroom, "John Lee Hooker, December 30, 1967."

42. Bartkowiak, *MC5 and Social Change.*

43. Early, *Grande Ballroom.*

44. Ryzewski, "Making Music in Detroit."

45. "Review of B. B. King," *Detroit Free Press*, September 13, 1968.

46. Sheehan, "Iggy's Blues."

47. Fifth Estate Collective, "Coltrane Memorial."

48. Fifth Estate Collective, "Coltrane Memorial."

49. Fifth Estate Collective, "Coltrane Memorial."

50. Chadbourne, "Charles Moore." The Detroit Artists Workshop formed in November 1964. It was originally a group of sixteen young writers, musicians, and artists living near Wayne State University. Its founding members included twenty-three-year-old John Sinclair, trumpeter Charles Moore, drummer Danny Spencer, painter Ellen Phelan, photographer Leni Sinclair (neé Magdalene Arndt), poets George Tysh and Jim Semark, and poet-filmmaker Robin Eichele. Other influential members included drummer Ronnie Johnson, pianist Stanley Cowell, drummer Doug Hammond, and pianist Harold McKinney; Stryker, *Jazz from Detroit*, 181.

51. "Trans-Love Evolves," *Detroit Fifth Estate*, August 15, 1967.

52. Early, *Grande Ballroom*, 141.

53. Early, *Grande Ballroom*, 142.

54. "Trans-Love Evolves," *Detroit Fifth Estate*, August 15, 1967.

55. Bartkowiak, "Motor City Burning."

56. Sinclair, "DKT/MC5," 224.

57. Bartkowiak, "Motor City Burning."

58. Sinclair was released from prison in 1971 after a protracted legal battle; Buchanan, "John Sinclair Freed from 10 Year Sentence"; "Benefit Held for Sinclair," *Detroit Free Press*, January 25, 1970, 31.

59. Early, *Grande Ballroom*, 144–145.

60. Carson, *Grit, Noise, and Revolution*, 100.

61. Vachon, *Legendary Locals*, 13.

62. Vachon, *Legendary Locals*, 13.

63. Vachon, *Legendary Locals*, 14.

64. Gary Grimshaw, "Detroit Freaks Out."

65. Daldin, "Grande Daze," 481.

66. Daldin, "Grande Daze," 481.

67. Uhelszki, "Twenty-Five Years of *Creem*," 290.

68. Sinclair quoted in Vachon, *Legendary Locals*, 11.

69. Vachon, *Legendary Locals*, 11.

70. Skinner quoted in Sinclair, "DKT/MC5," 222.

71. Skinner quoted in Sinclair, "DKT/MC5," 222–223.

72. Sather-Wagstaff, "Making Polysense of the World."

73. Mullins, "Optimism of Absence."

74. Pajor, "Oral History Interview."

75. Pajor, "State of Preservation," 68–69.

76. Early, Friends of the Grande Ballroom Facebook Page.

77. Ryzewski, *Grande Ballroom Archaeological Survey Report*, 64.

78. Early, Friends of the Grande Facebook Page.

79. Graves-Brown, "Nowhere Man"; see also Ceraso, "(Re) Educating the Senses," 102; Ryzewski, "Making Music in Detroit," 75.

80. Ryzewski, "Making Music in Detroit," 75; Penrose, "Recording Transition in Post-Industrial England"; Ryzewski, "Multiply Situated Strategies?"

81. Early, "Grande Ballroom Green Lit."

82. Early, "Grande Ballroom Green Lit."

83. At the time of the Grande's National Register nomination I was serving as a gubernatorial appointee to Michigan's State Historic Preservation Review Board. Since the authors of the Grande's National Register nomination cited substantial information from the archaeological survey report that I authored, the board's legal advisors identified a potential conflict of interest between my role as an archaeological investigator at the Grande and as a review board member. I therefore abstained from voting on or discussing the nomination during the board meeting.

84. Kelliher and McCollum, "Grande Ballroom Added to National Historic Registry."

85. Jerilyn Jordan, "Detroit's Historic Grande Ballroom Holds Promise for Restoration."

86. Early, "Grande Column Corbels Repatriated."

87. Hooper, "Impressive New Mural Commemorating MC5."

88. See Darvill, "Rock and Soul"; O'Keeffe, "Performance, Materiality, and Heritage"; O'Keeffe, "Street Ballets in Magic Cities"; Cherry, Ryzewski, and Pecoraro, "'A Kind of Sacred Place'"; Graves-Brown, "Where the Streets Have No Name"; Graves-Brown and Schofield, "The Filth and the Fury"; Ouzounian, "Recomposing the City"; Parkman, "A Hippie Discography"; Roberts, "Marketing Musicscapes"; Schofield, *Who Needs Experts?*

89. Ryzewski, "Making Music in Detroit," 74; Keeling, "Iconic Landscapes," 113; Long, "Popular Music, Psychogeography, Place Identity and Tourism."

90. After O'Keeffe, "Street Ballets," for the value of music as indicator of urban conditions.

91. Moshenska, "Charred Churches or Iron Harvests?," 5–27, at 6.

CHAPTER SEVEN

1. The enclave is adjacent to but not officially part of the Banglatown neigh-

borhood. The city of Detroit treats it as part of the Campau/Banglatown area in its landholding records.

2. The area's four bounding thoroughfares are the Davison freeway (north), Dequindre Street and Chrysler freeway (west), Carpenter Avenue (south), and Joseph Campau Avenue (east).

3. City of Detroit, "Detroit Property Parcels"; Detroit Blight Removal Task Force, *Every Neighborhood Has A Future.*

4. Ryzewski, "Historical Archaeology."

5. Kowalski, *Wicked Hamtramck*, 23.

6. Rubin, "Dig It."

7. I have chosen to not to provide his name in this text.

8. WDET News, "Why Do Hamtramck and Highland Park Exist Inside the City of Detroit?"

9. When one searches the Detroit Land Bank's database on the city of Detroit's open data portal, the property at 2038 Halleck is listed in Hamtramck; see City of Detroit, "Detroit Street View."

10. Kowalski, "Detroit's Disregard."

11. Ryzewski and Gordon, "Historical Nail-Making Techniques Revealed."

12. Carlisle, "Detroit's Oldest Cabin"; see also Detroit 1701, "James Smith Farm House."

13. Detroit 1701, "James Smith Farm House."

14. It was then purchased along with the adjoining multifamily dwelling by a private developer; see listing on Estately.com.

15. Detroit Land Bank Authority, "Who We Are."

16. Land Bank Fast Track Act of 2003, PA 258, MCL 124.751 to 124.774, 2003.

17. Homan and Orr, "Second Amended and Restated Intergovernmental Agreement," 1.

18. The Blight Authority, "Who We Are."

19. Runk, "In Detroit, A Nonprofit Fights Urban Blight"; Detroit Land Bank Authority, "Who We Are."

20. Detroit Blight Removal Task Force, *Every Neighborhood Has a Future*, 1.

21. Klinefelter, "Battling Blight"; Ryzewski, "Detroit 139."

22. Detroit Blight Removal Task Force, *Every Neighborhood Has a Future*, 10–11.

23. Detroit Blight Removal Task Force, *Every Neighborhood Has a Future*, 13. According to the task force, blight is defined as a public or attractive nuisance, fire hazard, or a tax-reverted property. A property may also be considered blighted if it has been vacant and under control of the Land Bank for five consecutive years; has code violations posing a severe and immediate health or safety threats; has utilities disconnected, removed, or rendered ineffective; is not structurally sound; and/or has been turned into a dumping ground.

24. Initially publicized by the Motor City Mapping Project, the data for 263,569 structures and 114,033 lots is now available in the City of Detroit's Open Data Portal; see City of Detroit, "Detroit Street View."

25. Detroit Blight Removal Task Force, *Every Neighborhood Has a Future*, 15.

26. Detroit Blight Removal Task Force, *Every Neighborhood Has a Future*, 15–16.

27. Duggan, *Every Neighborhood has a Future*.

28. Homan and Orr, "Second Amended and Restated Intergovernmental Agreement."

29. Detroit Blight Removal Task Force, *Every Neighborhood Has a Future*, 4; emphasis added.

30. Herstad, "'Reclaiming' Detroit."

31. See, for example, Detroit Housing Commission, *The Detroit Plan: A Program for Blight Elimination*, and Blessing, *An Evaluation of the Urban Renewal Program in Detroit*. Also see discussion in Thomas, *Redevelopment and Race*, 48. As Thomas discusses, although slum clearance efforts began in earnest in the early twentieth century, the Detroit Housing Commission issued one of the first formal policy documents in 1947 with *The Detroit Plan: A Program for Blight Elimination*. The sixteen-page document laid out the city's plans to clear blighted neighborhoods, or slums, as they were then called, using public funds in the name of economic redevelopment and aesthetic improvement. The plan detailed how the city planned to acquire, clear, and sell to developers 100 acres of blighted properties per year. Their first target for "blight elimination" was part of Black Bottom, the city's most densely populated African American neighborhood, to be replaced by the Gratiot redevelopment site. Like most of the city's blight removal efforts, the initial Detroit Plan was short-sighted and rendered obsolete by the arrival of new city governments. Fifteen years later, in 1962 blight continued to be a pressing issue for city officials. City planner Charles Blessing reported widespread blight covering 10,000 acres—or 15% of the city's total net area—with 18% of all structures in a state of deterioration (Blessing, *An Evaluation of the Urban Renewal*, 13).

32. This is the figure as of May 1, 2019. See City of Detroit, "Detroit Property Parcels."

33. Ryzewski, *Log Cabin Historic Building and Archaeological Survey*.

34. The results of dendrochronological analysis were inconclusive because of the limited sample size of two timbers and the absence of a black ash tree sequence for the region. Merrill, *Dendrochronology Report*.

35. Bomberger, *Preservation and Repair of Historic Log Buildings*.

36. Farmer, *Map of Wayne County, Michigan* (1855).

37. *Map of Wayne County, Michigan* (1860).

38. Belden, "Map of Hamtramck Township" (1876).

39. Sauer, "Map of the City of Detroit, Details of Hamtramck" (1893), plate 1, plate 15, and plate 62.

40. Sauer, *Map of Wayne County, Michigan* (1915); *Sanborn Fire Insurance Map from Detroit, Wayne County, Michigan*, vol. 10, sheet 96, 1915.

41. *Sanborn Fire Insurance Map from Detroit, Wayne County, Michigan*, vol. 10, sheet 101, 1921.

42. Kowalski, *Proposal to Rescue and Restore Historical Log Cabin*.

43. Matthews, "Assemblages, Routines, and Social Justice Research."

44. Perotta, "Hamtramck City Council Meeting, January 22, 2019."

45. The final amount spent on remediation and demolition was $15,913.33 according City of Detroit, "Detroit Property Parcels."

46. Rubin, "Historic Log Cabin Found in Detroit—and Then Demolished."

47. Rubin, "Historic Log Cabin."

48. Rubin, "Historic Log Cabin"; Fox 2 Staff, "Demolished Wooden Cabin."

49. Fuqua, "Family Overcame Prejudice to Build Business in Detroit."

50. Denise White Matthews, "Halleck St. Kids, Now Turning 50, Plan Reunion."

51. Rubin, "Historic Log Cabin."

52. Sercombe, "And Then There Were Just Two . . ."

53. According to the 2010 US census, African Americans make up 5.1% of Hamtramck's population vs. 83% in Detroit. The crisis of abandonment did not have as widespread an effect in Detroit as it did in Hamtramck. Kowalski, "Detroit's Disregard"; Kowalski, "Hamtramck's Log Cabin."

54. Kowalski, "Detroit's Disregard."

55. Rubin, "Historic Log Cabin."

56. Bach, "DLBA Reach Settlement"; Neavling, "Councilwoman Calls for Federal Probe"; Snell, "Feds Issue First Charges"; Stafford, "Bribes, Bid-Rigging Alleged."

57. Rubin, "Historic Log Cabin"; Fox 2 Staff, "Demolished Wooden Cabin"; Henderson, "Why Did Detroit Land Bank Demolish Historic Log Cabin?"

58. Rubin, "Historic Log Cabin."

59. Michigan was one of the first recipients of Hardest Hit Funds in 2013 and has since benefited from $761 million of funding. See Michigan State Housing Development Authority (MSHDA), "Step Forward."

60. Wayne County Register of Deeds, Sale of 2038 Halleck St from Willie and Mary Johnson to Laschella Johnson (for $54,773), 2001.

61. Wayne County Register of Deeds, Foreclosure Notice (Federal National Mortgage Association forecloses on property owned by Laschella C. Johnson), 2007; Wayne County Register of Deeds, Sale of 2038 Halleck (sold from Federal National Mortgage Association to Ali Said for $2,400), August 21, 2007.

62. Townley, "Memo."

63. On right-sizing, see Advisory Council on Historic Preservation, *Managing Change*, 4, 11.

64. MSHDA, "Step Forward"; Bach, "DLBA Reach Settlement."

65. Detroit has the largest demolition program of its kind in the United States. See Snell, "Feds Issue First Charges"; Stafford, "Bribes, Bid-Rigging Alleged."

66. City of Detroit, "Detroit Property Parcels."

67. Arnold, *Michigan's State Historic Preservation Plan*, 15.

68. Advisory Council on Historic Preservation, *Managing Change*, 51.

69. Arnold, *Michigan's State Historic Preservation Plan*, 15.

70. City of Detroit, "Detroit Property Parcels"; City of Detroit, "Detroit Street View."

71. City of Detroit, "Detroit Property Parcels."

72. National Historic Preservation Act of 1966, 16 U.S.C. 470h-2(a)(2)(E)(ii), 1966.

73. Little et al., *Guidelines for Evaluating and Registering Archaeological Properties.*

74. Advisory Council on Historic Preservation, "National Historic Preservation Act."

75. Emphasis added; Advisory Council on Historic Preservation, "Section 106 Archaeology Guidance."

76. National Register of Historic Places, *How to Apply the National Register Criteria for Evaluation.*

77. National Park Service, *NPS-28 Cultural Resource Management Guideline.*

78. Townley, "Memo."

79. Hein, "Letter."

80. Hein, "Letter."

81. Townley, "Memo."

82. Fox 2 Detroit, "Archaeologists Excavate Site."

83. Stafford, "Beleaguered Detroit Demo Program."

84. Stafford, "Duggan Seeking Residential Blight Removal."

85. Stafford, "Duggan Seeking Residential Blight Removal."

86. Johncox, "Detroit Land Bank Authority to Terminate, Lay Off Employees."

CHAPTER EIGHT

1. Wilkie, "Heritage Inheritances," 149.

2. Hart, "Gender, Masculinity, and Professional-Avocational Heritage Collaborations," 58.

3. Moshenska, "Working with Memory"; Beck, Schofield, and Drollinger, "Archaeologists, Activists, and a Contemporary Peace Camp."

4. Matthews, "Assemblages, Routines, and Social Justice Research"; González-Ruibal, González, and Criado-Boado, "Against Reactionary Populism."

5. Slow Archaeology was the theme of the TAG 2019 conference in Syracuse; Caraher, "Slow Archaeology"; Cunningham, and MacEachern, "Ethnoarchaeology as Slow Science."

6. Silliman, *Engaging Archaeology*; Harris and Cipolla, *Archaeological Theory in the New Millennium.*

7. On contours of communities, see Agbe-Davies, "Inside/Outside, Upside Down."

8. Dawdy, "Clockpunk Anthropology."

9. Pezzarossi, "Rethinking the Archaeology of Capitalism," 453.

10. Orser and Fagan, *Historical Archaeology.*

BIBLIOGRAPHY

Advertisement. *Michigan Chronicle*, January 20, 1945, 1.

Advertisement. *Michigan Chronicle*, October 20, 1948, 10.

Advertisement, barber chair for sale. *Detroit Free Press*, June 22, 1900, 8.

Advertisement, Blossom Heath Inn. *Detroit Free Press*, May 16, 1920, 16.

Advertisement, Paradise Valley Distributing Company. *Detroit Tribune*, September 6, 1941, 6.

Advertisement, Paradise Valley Distributing Company. *Detroit Tribune*, November 7, 1942.

Advertisement for Blue Bird Inn jam sessions. *Detroit Tribune* April 30, 1938, n.p.

Advertisement for Blue Bird Inn Thanksgiving dinners. *Detroit Tribune*, November 23, 1940, 6.

Advertisement for Edson Moore & Co Wholesale Dealers in Dry Goods. *Detroit Free Press*, April 6, 1875, 2.

Advertisement for the Royal Blue featuring Bebop. *Michigan Chronicle*, June 18, 1948, 19.

Advisory Council on Historic Preservation. *Managing Change: Preservation and Rightsizing in America*. Washington, DC: ACHP, 2014.

———. "National Historic Preservation Act." www.achp.gov.

———. "Section 106 Archaeology Guidance." January 1, 2009. www.achp.gov.

Afana, Dana. "16 Condos Sold before They're Built in Detroit Brush Park Development." *MLive*, March 18, 2017.

Agbe-Davies, Anna S. "Concepts of Community in the Pursuit of an Inclusive Archaeology." *International Journal of Heritage Studies* 16, no. 6 (2010): 373–389.

———. "How to Do Things with Things; or, Are Blue Beads Good to Think?" *Semiotic Review* 4, December 16, 2016. www.semioticreview.com.

———. "Inside/Outside, Upside Down: Including Archaeologists in Communities." *Archaeologies* 7, no. 3 (2011): 574–595.

———. "Where Tradition and Pragmatism Meet: African Diaspora Archaeology at the Crossroads." *Historical Archaeology* 51, no. 1 (2017): 9–27.

Agree, Charles N. "A Record of Projects Undertaken during the Last Ten Years or More, Arranged in Yearly Group." Charles N. Agree Inc., Architects Manuscript Collection, Burton Historical Collection, Detroit Public Library, undated document.

———. "Use of Brick Construction for Modern Playhouse." *Theatre Engineering* (June 1930): 5–16.

Aguilar, Louis. "Site Where 1967 Uprising Began Sees New Signs of Life." *Detroit News*, July 20, 2017.

"Alanson J. Fox Is Dead." *Detroit Free Press*, October 30, 1903, 1.

Allen, E. B. "Muralist Says Artwork Will Symbolize Former 12th Street's Ongoing Recovery." *The Hub Detroit*, July 31, 2017.

Alterman, Loraine. "Teen Club That's Absolutely Wow." *Detroit Free Press*, October 21, 1966.

American Black Journal. "Gordon Park: Reborn." *Detroit Public TV*, July 23, 2017. www.youtube.com.

Ankeny, Jason. "MC5—Artist Biography." AllMusic.com.

Apel, Dora. *Beautiful Terrible Ruins: Detroit and the Anxiety of Decline*. New Brunswick, NJ: Rutgers University Press, 2015.

Arjona, Jamie M. "Homesick Blues: Excavating Crooked Intimacies in Late Nineteenth- and Early Twentieth-Century Jook Joints." *Historical Archaeology* 51, no. 1 (2017): 43–59.

Arnold, Amy L. *Michigan's State Historic Preservation Plan, 2014–2019*. Lansing: Michigan State Housing Development Authority, 2014.

Ars Ceramica. *Highlights of Pewabic Pottery*. Lansing, MI: Ars Ceramica Ltd., 1977.

Ashplant, Timothy G. "War Commemoration in Western Europe: Changing Meaning, Divisive Loyalties, Unheard Voices." In *The Politics of Memory: Commemorating War*, edited by Timothy G. Ashplant, Graham Dawson, and Michael Roper, 263–270. London: Routledge, 2004.

Associates Advertisers Service. *Directory of Negro Businesses, Professions, and Churches for Detroit and Environs*. Detroit: Associates Advertisers Service, 1952.

Atalay, Sonya. *Community-Based Archaeology: Research with, by, and for Indigenous and Local Communities*. Berkeley: University of California Press, 2012.

———. "Indigenous Archaeology as Decolonizing Practice." *American Indian Quarterly* (2006): 280–310.

Atlas Obscura. "Incredible Ruins in Detroit—Grande Ballroom." www.atlasobscura.com.

Austin, Ben. "The Post-Post-Apocalyptic Detroit." *New York Times*, July 11, 2014.

Austin, Dan, and Sean Doerr. *Lost Detroit: Stories behind the Motor City's Majestic Ruins*. Charleston, SC: History Press, 2010.

Bach, Katie. "DLBA Reach Settlement Regarding Improper Invoicing for Hardest Hit Fund Demolition Work." Michigan State Housing Development Authority. June 22, 2017. www.michigan.gov/mshda.

Baist, George W. *Baist's Property Atlas of the City of Detroit, Michigan*. Philadelphia: Baist, 1896.

———. *Baist's Property Atlas of the City of Detroit, Michigan*. Philadelphia: Baist, 1915.

Barrionuevo, Alexei. "Detroit's Billionaires Hope to Change Downtown with Development Spree." *Detroit Curbed*, March 30, 2016.

Bartkowiak, Mathew J. *The MC5 and Social Change: A Study in Rock and Revolution*. Jefferson, NC: McFarland, 2015.

———. "Motor City Burning: Rock and Rebellion in the WPP and the MC5." *Journal for the Study of Radicalism* 1, no. 2 (2008): 55–76.

Basso, Keith H. *Wisdom Sits in Places: Landscape and Language among the Western Apache.* Albuquerque: University of New Mexico Press, 1996.

Battle-Baptiste, Whitney. *Black Feminist Archaeology.* Walnut Creek, CA: Left Coast Press, 2011.

Beatty, Robert Allen. "Hitting the Hot Spots." *Detroit Tribune,* October 2, 1948, 13.

Beaudry, Mary C., ed. *Documentary Archaeology in the New World.* Cambridge: Cambridge University Press, 1993.

Beaudry, Mary C., Lauren J. Cook, and Stephen A. Mrozowski. "Artifacts and Active Voices: Material Culture as Social Discourse." In *Images of the Recent Past: Readings in Historical Archaeology,* edited by Charles E. Orser Jr., 272–310. Walnut Creek, CA: AltaMira Press, 1996.

Beck, Colleen M., John Schofield, and Harold Drollinger. "Archaeologists, Activists, and a Contemporary Peace Camp." In *Contemporary Archaeologies: Excavating Now,* edited by Cornelius Holtorf and Angela Piccini, 95–111. Berlin: Peter Lang, 2009.

Beisaw, April M. "Ghost Hunting as Archaeology: Archaeology as Ghost Hunting." In *Lost City, Found Pyramid: Understanding Alternative Archaeologies and Pseudoscientific Practices,* edited by Jeb J. Card and David S. Anderson, 185–198. Tuscaloosa: University of Alabama Press, 2016.

Belden, H. "Map of Hamtramck Township." In *Illustrated Atlas of the County of Wayne, Michigan.* Chicago: H. Belden, 1876.

"Benefit Held for Sinclair." *Detroit Free Press,* January 25, 1970, 31.

Bergman, Aeron, and Alejandra Salinas. *Monument to Rebellion.* Exhibit shown at the First Bergen Assembly Triennial and Kunsthalle Exnergasse, Vienna, Austria, 2015.

Bernbeck, Reinhard, and Susan Pollock. "'Grabe, wo du stehst!' An Archaeology of Perpetrators." In *Archaeology and Capitalism: From Ethics to Politics,* edited by Yannis Hamilakis and Philip Duke, 217–234. Walnut Creek, CA: Left Coast Press, 2007.

Bjorn, Lars, and Jim Gallert. "Bebop in Detroit: Nights at the Blue Bird Inn." In *Heaven Was Detroit: From Jazz to Hip-Hop and Beyond,* edited by M. L. Leibler, 8–11. Detroit: Wayne State University Press, 2016.

Black, LaJean Dubois. Death Certificate. State of Michigan, May 28, 1998, #1335957.

Blessing, Charles A. *An Evaluation of the Urban Renewal Program in Detroit. Renewal and Revenue: A Demonstration Grant Study.* Detroit: City Plan Commission, 1962.

The Blight Authority. "Who We Are." www.theblightauthority.com.

"Blossom Heath Inn Again Raided." *Detroit Free Press,* May 1, 1921, 6.

"Blue Bird Inn Features Hill and Orchestra." *Michigan Chronicle,* March 19, 1949, 20.

Boggs, Grace Lee. *Detroit, Birth of a Nation.* Detroit: Weekly Guardian Associates, 1967.

———. "Detroit 1967: Riot or Rebellion?" *Michigan Citizen,* April 8–14, 2007.

———. *Living for Change*. Minneapolis: University of Minnesota Press, 1998.

———. "Living for Change: Metaphor for Detroit." *Michigan Citizen* 32, no. 40 (August 15, 2010): A10.

Boggs, Grace Lee, with Scott Kurashige. *The Next American Revolution: Sustainable Activism for the 21st Century*. Berkeley: University of California Press, 2012.

Boggs, James. *Manifesto for a Black Revolutionary Party*. Philadelphia: Pacesetters Publishing, 1969.

Boggs, James, and Grace Lee Boggs. *Revolution and Evolution in the 20th Century*. New York: Monthly Review Press, 1974.

Bolkosky, Sidney. *Harmony and Dissonance: Voices of Jewish Identity in Detroit, 1914–1967*. Detroit: Wayne State University Press, 1991.

Bomberger, Bruce D. *The Preservation and Repair of Historic Log Buildings*. National Park Service Preservation Brief 26. Washington, DC: US Department of the Interior, 1991.

Borden, Ernest H. *Detroit's Paradise Valley*. Charleston, SC: Arcadia, 2003.

Boyd, Herb. *Black Detroit: A People's History of Self-Determination*. New York: HarperCollins, 2017.

Brace, C. Lorin, VI. "'Nothing Phony about It in Any Way': Archaeological Analysis of the Blue Bird Inn Jazz Club in Post-War Detroit." Master's thesis, Department of Anthropology, Wayne State University, 2016.

Brace, C. Lorin, VI, and Samantha Ellens. "Archaeology at the Blue Bird." *Detroit Sound Conservancy* (blog), November 7, 2015. https://detroitsound.org/archaeology-at-the-blue-bird/.

Branstner, Mark C. *Cultural Resource Overview and Sensitivity Model: Brush Park Project Area, Detroit, Michigan*. Report prepared for Zachary and Associates, Detroit, MI, by Great Lakes Research Associates Inc., 1996. On file with the State Historic Preservation Office, Lansing, Michigan, ER-890283.

———. "Historical Archaeology in Detroit: The Evolution of an Urban Management Strategy." Paper presented to the Symposium on Ohio Valley Urban and Historic Archaeology, Cincinnati, Ohio, March 17, 1989. On file at the Grosscup Museum of Anthropology, Wayne State University, Detroit, Michigan.

Brent, Pat. "Press Review, Led Zeppelin—Jan. 19, 1969." *Creem*, March 1969. Text available at https://www.ledzeppelin.com/show/january-19-1969.

Brush Park Development Company. "City Modern Design Process." Accessed October 24, 2019. www.citymoderndetroit.com/story.html.

Buchanan, Michael. "December 13, 1971: John Sinclair Freed from 10 Year Sentence for Possessing Two Joints." *Today in Crime History*, December 12, 2011. Accessed February 12, 2019. http://reasonabledoubt.org/index.php/criminallawblog.

Bunge, William. *Fitzgerald: Geography of a Revolution*. Cambridge, MA: Schenkman, 1971.

"Business Corner Resold." *Detroit Free Press*, January 24, 1915, D.

"Business Men Arrested in Liquor Raid." *Detroit Free Press*, May 28, 1927, 1.

"Café Operator Fined." *Detroit Free Press*, August 24, 1934, 7.

Callen, Anthea. *Women Artists of the Arts and Crafts Movement, 1870–1914*. New York: Pantheon Books, 1979.

Callwood, Brett. *The Stooges: Head On*. Detroit: Wayne State University Press, 2011.

Calvert, Al. "Oral History Interview." *Detroit '67 Project*. Detroit: Detroit Historical Museum, July 18, 2017. https://detroit1967.detroithistorical.org.

Camp, Stacey Lynn. "Landscapes of Japanese American Internment." *Historical Archaeology* 50, no. 1 (2016): 169–186.

Caraher, William. "Slow Archaeology, Punk Archaeology, and the 'Archaeology of Care.'" *European Journal of Archaeology* 22, no. 3 (2019): 372–385.

———. "Slow Archaeology: Technology, Efficiency, and Archaeological Work." In *Mobilizing the Past for a Digital Future: The Potential of Digital Archaeology*, edited by Erin Walcek Averett, Jody M. Gordon, and Derek B. Counts, 421–442. Grand Forks, ND: Digital Press, 2016.

Caraher, William, Kostis Kourelis, and Andrew Reinhard. *Punk Archaeology*. Grand Forks, ND: Digital Press, 2014.

Carlisle, John. "Detroit's Oldest Cabin Lies Hidden in a Neighborhood." *Detroit Free Press*, February 27, 2016.

Carman, John. "Stories We Tell: Myths at the Heart of 'Community Archaeology.'" *Archaeologies* 7, no. 3 (2011): 490–501.

Carson, David A. *Grit, Noise, and Revolution: The Birth of Detroit Rock 'N' Roll*. Ann Arbor: University of Michigan Press, 2005.

"Centrally Located Business Block Valued at $175,000 Figures in Sale." *Detroit Free Press*, April 18, 1915, C2.

Ceraso, Steph. "(Re) Educating the Senses: Multimodal Listening, Bodily Learning, and the Composition of Sonic Experiences." *College English* 77, no. 2 (2014): 102.

Chadbourne, Eugene. "Charles Moore." Detroit Artists Workshop. www.detroitartistsworkshop.com/moore-charles.

Chenoweth, John. "Natural Graffiti and Cultural Plants: Memory, Race, and Contemporary Archaeology in Yosemite and Detroit." *American Anthropologist* 119, no. 3 (2017): 464–477.

Cherry, John F. "Still Not Digging, Much." *Archaeological Dialogues* 18, no. 1 (2011): 10–17.

Cherry, John F., and Krysta Ryzewski. *An Archaeological History of Montserrat in the West Indies*. Oxford: Oxbow, 2020.

Cherry, John F., Krysta Ryzewski, and Luke J. Pecoraro. "'A Kind of Sacred Place': The Rock-and-Roll Ruins of AIR Studios, Montserrat." In *Archaeologies of Mobility and Movement*, edited by Mary C. Beaudry and Travis Parno, 181–198. New York: Springer, 2013.

City Form Detroit. *7.2 SQ MI: A Report on Greater Downtown Detroit*. 2nd ed. Detroit: City Form Detroit, 2015.

City of Detroit. "Detroit Property Parcels, City of Detroit—Open Data DET." Demolition Tracker App, 2019. Accessed October 24, 2019. https://data.detroitmi. gov/app/demolition-tracker-map.

———. "Detroit Street View—Open Data DET." 2019. Accessed October 24, 2019. https://gis.detroitmi.gov/dsv.

City of Detroit, Historic Designation Advisory Board. *Proposed Blue Bird Inn Historic District, 5021 Tireman Avenue.* Draft Preliminary Report prepared by the Historic Designation Advisory Board, Detroit, 2020.

"City Sightings." *Detroit Free Press,* May 18, 1916, 5.

Clark, Bonnie J., and Anne Amati. "Powerful Objects, Difficult Dialogues: Mobilizing Archaeological Exhibits for Civic Engagement." *International Journal of Heritage Studies* 25, no. 7 (2019): 708–721.

Classified ad for coat checkers. *Detroit Free Press,* March 2, 1945, 21.

Classified ad for matron, porter, and janitors. *Detroit Free Press,* September 5, 1943, 12.

Classified ad for shoe shiner and washroom attendant. *Detroit Free Press,* November 10, 1943, 19.

Classified ad for staff. *Detroit Free Press,* May 19, 1944, 20.

"Column on Michigan Radio Shows." *Michigan Chronicle,* March 28, 1948, 18.

Concert Database—Grande Ballroom. "Fleetwood Mac, December 27, 1968." The Concert Database. https://theconcertdatabase.com.

———. "John Lee Hooker, December 29, 1967." The Concert Database. https://theconcertdatabase.com.

———. "John Lee Hooker, December 30, 1967." The Concert Database. https://theconcertdatabase.com.

Connerton, Paul. "Seven Types of Forgetting." *Memory Studies* 1, no. 1 (2008): 59–71.

"Cuneo Restaurant." *Detroit Free Press,* November 26, 1931, 19.

Cunningham, Jerimy J., and Scott MacEachern. "Ethnoarchaeology as Slow Science." *World Archaeology* 48, no. 5 (2016): 628–641.

Daldin, Herman. "Grande Daze, Bubble Puppies, and Suburban Hippies." In *Heaven Was Detroit: From Jazz to Hip-Hop and Beyond,* edited by M. L. Leibler, 417–421. Detroit: Wayne State University Press, 2016.

Darvill, Timothy. "Rock and Soul: Humanizing Heritage, Memorializing Music, and Producing Places." *World Archaeology* 46, no. 3 (2014): 462–476.

Davey, Monica, and Mary Williams Walsh. "Billions in Debt, Detroit Tumbles into Insolvency." *New York Times,* July 18, 2013.

Dawdy, Shannon Lee. "Clockpunk Anthropology and the Ruins of Modernity." *Current Anthropology* 51, no. 6 (2010): 761–793.

———. *Patina: A Profane Archaeology.* Chicago: University of Chicago Press, 2016.

Dawson, Graham, ed. *Commemorating War: The Politics of Memory.* London: Routledge, 2017.

DeCesari, Chiara, and Rozita Dimova. "Heritage, Gentrification, Participation:

Remaking Urban Landscapes in the Name of Culture and Historic Preservation." *International Journal of Heritage* Studies 25, no. 9 (2019): 863–869.

DeCesari, Chiara, and Michael Herzfeld. "Urban Heritage and Social Movements." In *Global Heritage: A Reader,* edited by Lynn Meskell, 171–195. London: Wiley-Blackwell, 2015.

DeLeón, Jason. *The Land of Open Graves: Living and Dying on the Migrant Trail.* Oakland: University of California Press, 2015.

Delle, James A. "A Tale of Two Tunnels: Memory, Archaeology, and the Underground Railroad." *Journal of Social Archaeology* 8, no. 1 (2008): 63–93.

Demeter, C. Stephan. *Expanded Phase I/II Archaeological Evaluation of the Brush Park Project Site, Detroit, Michigan.* R-0278. Prepared for Detroit Economic Growth Corporation by Commonwealth Cultural Resources Group Inc., 1998.

"Derelict Detroit: Gloomy Pictures Chart the 25-Year Decline of America's Motor City." *Daily Mail,* October 1, 2012.

DeSilvey, Caitlin, and Tim Edensor. "Reckoning with Ruins." *Progress in Human Geography* 33, no. 5 (2013): 646–666.

"Dessa Malone." *Michigan Chronicle,* February 5, 1949, 18.

Detroit 1701. "James Smith Farm House, 2015 Clements in Detroit." Detroit1701. org. http://detroit1701.org/SmithFarm.htm.

Detroit Blight Removal Task Force. *Every Neighborhood Has A Future . . . And It Doesn't Include Blight.* Detroit Blight Removal Task Force Plan. Detroit: Inland Press, 2014. https://datadrivendetroit.org.

Detroit Free Press Club. *Detroit Blue Book: A Society Directory for the City of Detroit, Containing the Names of Several Thousand Householders and Prominent Citizens.* Detroit: Detroit Free Press Club, 1885.

Detroit Future City. *Detroit Strategic Framework.* Detroit: Inland Press, 2012.

———. *139 Square Miles.* Detroit: Inland Press, 2017.

Detroit Historical Museum. *Detroit 1967: Looking Back to Move Forward.* Exhibit shown at Detroit Historical Museum, 2017. https://detroit1967.org.

———. Oral History Collection, 2017. https://detroit1967.detroithistorical.org.

Detroit Historical Society. "Race Riot of 1943." In *Encyclopedia of Detroit.* Detroit: Detroit Historical Society, 2019. https://detroithistorical.org/learn/encyclopedia-of-detroit.

———. "Stratton, Mary Chase Perry." *Encyclopedia of Detroit.* Detroit: Detroit Historical Society, 2019.

Detroit Housing Commission. *The Detroit Plan: A Program for Blight Elimination.* Detroit: Detroit Housing Commission, 1947.

———. *Urban Renewal and Public Housing in Detroit, 1954.* Booklet, Bentley Historical Library, University of Michigan, Urban League Records, 1916–1992, Folder A6-1.

"Detroit Is Wettest City He Worked In, Dry Administrator Says in Resigning." *New York Times,* November 4, 1925.

Detroit Land Bank Authority. "Who We Are." https://buildingdetroit.org.

"Detroit Music Scene." *Michigan Chronicle*, September 10, 1949, n.p.

"Detroit Purple Gang Smashed by Own Greed." *Washington Post*, February 25, 1934.

Detroit Sound Conservancy. "Restaging the Stage." *Detroit Sound Conservancy* (blog), November 22, 2016. https://detroitsound.org/restaging-the-stage/.

———. "A Site of Sonic Resistance Is Reborn as the World's Only Historic Mobile Stage." *Detroit Sound Conservancy* (blog), April 25, 2019. http://detroitsound.org/blue-bird.

———. "Vision, Mission, and Goals." Updated June 14, 2019. http://detroitsound.org/mission.

Detroit Urban League. *Detroit Urban League (1950–1953)*. Bentley Historical Library, University of Michigan, Detroit Urban League Records, 1916–1992, Folder A4-18.

———. *The Detroit Urban League's Brief of Urban Renewal Activity in the City of Detroit, November 29, 1956.* Document in Detroit Urban League Collections, Bentley Historical Library, University of Michigan, File A8-28.

"Deutches Haus Faces Padlock." *Detroit Free Press*, October, 25, 1928.

Dewar, Margaret, and June Manning Thomas, eds. *The City after Abandonment.* Philadelphia: University of Pennsylvania Press, 2012.

Díaz-Andreu, Margarita, and Apen Ruiz. "Interacting with Heritage: Social Inclusion and Archaeology in Barcelona." *Journal of Community Archaeology and Heritage* 4, no. 1 (2017): 53–68.

Dolan, Matthew. "Record Bankruptcy for Detroit." *Wall Street Journal*, July 19, 2013.

"Dry Laws Provide Sure Prohibition." *Detroit Free Press*, April 26, 1917, 10.

Duggan, Mike. "Annual State of the City Address." Detroit, March 6, 2018. https://detroitmi.gov.

———. *Every Neighborhood Has a Future—10-Point Plan for the Next Four Years.* Detroit: City of Detroit, 2014. https://detroitmi.gov.

Dulzo, Jim. "Remembering the Bebop at the Blue Bird." *Detroit News*, September 26, 1992, C1 + 6C.

Dunbar, Willis F., and George F. May. *Michigan: A History of the Wolverine State.* 3rd ed. Grand Rapids: William B. Eerdmans, 1995.

Early, Leo. Friends of the Grande Ballroom Facebook Page. Post by Leo Early, February 2, 2017.

———. "Friends of the Grande Ballroom Mission Statement." The Grande Ballroom. http://thegrandeballroom.com/friends-of-the-grande.

———. *The Grande Ballroom: Detroit's Rock 'n' Roll Palace.* Charleston, SC: History Press, 2016.

———. "Grande Ballroom Green Lit for National Register of Historic Places Process/Restoration." The Grande Ballroom. March 1, 2017. http://thegrandeballroom.com/grande-ballroom-register-of-historic-places.

———. "The Grande Ballroom Inspection." The Grande Ballroom. October 5, 2016. http://thegrandeballroom.com/october-5-2016-grande-ballroom-inspection.

———. "Grande Column Corbels Repatriated." The Grande Ballroom. January 19, 2019. http://thegrandeballroom.com/grande-column-corbels-repatriated.

Edensor, Tim. *Industrial Ruins: Space, Aesthetics, and Materiality*. New York: Berg, 2005.

Edsall, Harold Bressmer, III. "Capturing Detroit through an Underground Lens: Issues of the Sixties Inside Pages of the Detroit Fifth Estate, 1965–1970." Master's thesis, Department of American Culture, University of Michigan, Flint, 2010.

Eisinger, Peter. "Is Detroit Dead?" *Journal of Urban Affairs* 36, no. 1 (2014): 1–12.

Engelmann, Larry. *Intemperance: The Lost War against Liquor*. New York: Free Press, 1979.

Elrick, M. L., and Tresa Baldas. "COVID-19 Outbreak That Killed His Fellow Inmates Will Help Set Kwame Kilpatrick Free." *Detroit Free Press*, May 22, 2020.

———. "Kwame Kilpatrick Denied Early Release from Federal Prison." *Detroit Free Press*, May 26, 2020.

"Entertain at Dance—Singers Grace Baruth and Margaret Maischein of Detroit." *Detroit Free* Press, February 12, 1933, 23.

Estately. Listing for Ransom Gillis House, 2019. Accessed October 24, 2019. www.estately.com/listings/info/2009-clements-street.

Farmer, John. *Map of Wayne County, Michigan*. Detroit: John Farmer, 1855. Retrieved from the Library of Congress. www.loc.gov.

Federal Bureau of Investigation. Purple Gang, File 62-HQ-29632, 1933–1948.

Fifth Estate Collective. "Coltrane Memorial." *Fifth Estate*, no. 38, September 15–30, 1967.

Finelli, Mark. *The Last Days of Detroit: Motor Cars, Motown, and the Collapse of an Industrial Giant*. London: Bodley Head, 2013.

Finley, Nolan. "Face It, DIA Artwork Will Be 'Monetized.'" *Detroit News*, September 29, 2013.

Finnis, Alex. "Left to Rot: Detroit's 40,000 Abandoned and Empty Buildings Awaiting Demolition as Decaying City Nears Bankruptcy." *Daily Mail*, August 13, 2014.

Finsilver, Bruce. "Weitzman Family Oral History." Recorded by Krysta Ryzewski, October 1, 2013.

Fox, Thomas. "Neighborhood's Dream of Revival Going Sour." *Detroit Free Press*, October 6, 1977, 1A + 4A.

Fox 2 Detroit. "Archaeologists Excavate Site of Demolished Civil War–Era Log Cabin in Detroit." *Fox 2 Detroit*. March 18, 2019.

Fox 2 Staff. "Demolished Wooden Cabin from 1800s Causes Tension between Detroit Land Bank, Historians." *Fox 2 Detroit*, March 11, 2019.

Frank, Annalise. "Detroit Sound Conservancy Plots Future for Historic Jazz Club,

Designated 'Dangerous.'" *Crain's Detroit Business*, March 14, 2019.

Franklin, Maria. "A Black Feminist-Inspired Archaeology?" *Journal of Social Archaeology* 1, no. 1 (2001): 108–125.

Franklin, Maria, Justin P. Dunnavant, Ayana Omilade Flewellen, and Alicia Odewale. "The Future is Now: Archaeology and the Eradication of Anti-Blackness." *International Journal of Historical Archaeology* 24 (2020): 753–766.

Franklin, Maria, and Nedra Lee. "African American Descendants, Community Outreach, and the Ransom and Sarah Williams Farmstead Project." *Journal of Community Archaeology & Heritage* 7, no. 2 (2020): 135–148.

Freund, David M. P. *Colored Property: State Policy and White Racial Politics in Suburban America*. Chicago: University of Chicago Press, 2010.

Fruehling, Byron D., and Robert H. Smith. "Subterranean Hideaways of the Underground Railroad in Ohio: An Architectural, Archaeological, Historical Critique of Local Traditions." *Ohio History* 102 (1998): 97–117.

Fuqua, Jean Ford. "Family Overcame Prejudice to Build Business in Detroit." *Detroit Free Press*, April 30, 1992, 19A.

Gadsby, David. "Urban Heritage in Troubled Times." *Practicing Anthropology* 31, no. 3 (2009): 20–23.

Gadsby, David A., and Robert C. Chidester. "Heritage in Hampden: A Participatory Research Design for Public Archaeology in a Working-Class Neighborhood, Baltimore, Maryland." In *Archaeology as a Tool of Civic Engagement*, edited by Barbara J. Little and Paul A. Shackel, 223–342. Lanham, MD: AltaMira, 2007.

Galbraith, M. J. "New Parks in Downtown and Morningside among City's Latest Outdoor Developments." *Model D*, July 18, 2017.

Gallagher, John. *Reimagining Detroit: Opportunities for Redefining an American City*. Detroit: Wayne State University Press, 2010.

Gholz, Carleton S. "Magic, Liberation, and Architecture: Placekeeping Musical Space in Detroit." *Paprika! Journal of the School of Architecture*, Yale University, September 12, 2019. https://yalepaprika.com.

Gokee, Cameron, and Jason De León. "Sites of Contention." *Journal of Contemporary Archaeology* 1, no. 1 (2014): 133–163.

Gonzalez, Sara L., Ian Kretzler, and Briece Edwards. "Imagining Indigenous and Archaeological Futures: Building Capacity with the Confederated Tribes of Grand Ronde." *Archaeologies* 14, no. 1 (2018): 85–114.

González-Ruibal, Alfredo. "Ruins of the South." In *Contemporary Archaeology and the City*, edited by Laura McAtackney and Krysta Ryzewski, 149–170. Oxford: Oxford University Press, 2017.

González-Ruibal, Alfredo, Pablo Alonso González, and Felipe Criado-Boado. "Against Reactionary Populism: Towards a New Public Archaeology." *Antiquity* 92, no. 362 (2018): 507–515.

Gonzalez-Tennant, Edward. "Anarchism, Decolonization, and Collaborative Archaeology." *Journal of Contemporary Archaeology* 5, no. 2 (2018): 238–244.

Graff, Rebecca S. "An Ardent Anti-Slavery Tale: Narrating Resistance through

Chicago's Underground Railroad, 1856–Present." *Journal of Community Archaeology and Heritage* 6, no. 2 (2019): 85–97.

———. *Disposing of Modernity: The Archaeology of Garbage and Chicago's 1893 World's Fair*. Gainesville: University Press of Florida, 2020.

Gram John M., and David F. Barton. *A Literature Cultural Resource Survey and Field Inspection of the Brush Park Project Area, Detroit, Michigan*. Report submitted to the Community and Economic Development Department, City of Detroit, by Resource Analysts Inc., Bloomington, Indiana, 1981. Report on File at the State Historic Preservation Office, Lansing, Michigan.

Graves-Brown, Paul. "Nowhere Man: Urban Life and the Virtualization of Popular Music." *Popular Music History* 4, no. 2 (2009): 220–241.

———. "Where the Streets Have No Name: A Guided Tour of Pop Heritage Sites in London's West End." In *The Good, the Bad, and the Unbuilt: Handling the Heritage of the Recent Past*, edited by Sarah May, Hilary Orange, and Sefryn Penrose, 63–76. London: Archaeopress, 2012.

Graves-Brown, Paul, and Rachael Kiddey. "Reclaiming the Streets: The Role of Archaeology in Deconstructing the Myths of Contemporary Society." *Archaeological Review from Cambridge: Myths Within and Without* 30, no. 2 (2015): 135–147.

Graves-Brown, Paul, and John Schofield. "The Filth and the Fury: 6 Denmark Street (London) and the Sex Pistols." *Antiquity* 85, no. 330 (2011): 1385–1401.

Gray, Ryan D. *Uprooted: Race, Public Housing, and the Archaeology of Four Lost New Orleans Neighborhoods*. Tuscaloosa: University of Alabama Press, 2020.

Green, J. L. "Mary Chase Perry Stratton and the Pewabic Pottery." Pewabic Pottery Archives, Detroit, undated manuscript. www.arts-crafts.com/archive/pewabic.pdf.

Grimshaw, Gary. "Detroit Freaks Out with First Participatory Zoo Dance." *Detroit Fifth Estate*, October 16, 1966.

Hamlin, Marie Caroline Watson. *Legends of Le Détroit*. Detroit: Thorndike Nourse, 1884.

"Hamtramck, City of Contrasts." *Detroit Free Press*, March 2, 1924, 66.

Harris, Cheryl I. "Whiteness as Property." *Harvard Law Review* (1993): 1707–1791.

Harris, Oliver J. T., and Craig N. Cipolla. *Archaeological Theory in the New Millennium: Introducing Current Perspectives*. New York: Routledge, 2017.

Harrison, Rodney. "On Heritage Ontologies: Rethinking the Material Worlds of Heritage." *Anthropological Quarterly* 91, no. 4 (2018): 1365–1383.

"Harry Vrooman." *Detroit City Directory*, 1915.

"Harry Weitzman Bond Sales." *Detroit Free Press*, June 21, 1925, 95.

Hart, Siobhan M. "Gender, Masculinity, and Professional-Avocational Heritage Collaborations." *Archaeological Papers of the American Anthropological Association* 31, no. 1 (2020): 54–65.

Hartnett, Alexandra, and Shannon Lee Dawdy. "The Archaeology of Illegal and Illicit Economies." *Annual Review of Anthropology* 42 (2013): 37–51.

Hays, Mary Patterson. "The Focal Scrip." *Detroit Tribune*, January 18, 1947, 5.

Headapohl, Jackie. "Digging for Purple." *Jewish News*, September 26, 2013.

Hein, Erik M. "Letter from Erik M. Hein, Executive Director National Council of State Historic Preservation Officers (NCSHPO), RE: Hardest Hit Fund to Maureen Quinn, Mark McArdle, Eric Rosenfeld, US Department of the Treasury." October 2, 2013. Accessed October 24, 2019. http://ncshpo.org/hardesthitfundletter.pdf.

Henderson, Stephen. "Legendary Blue Bird Inn Stage Restored, Goes to France for Exhibition." *Detroit Today*, WDET/NPR, April 6, 2017.

———. "Why Did Detroit Land Bank Demolish Historic Log Cabin?" *Detroit Today*, WDET/NPR, April 24, 2019.

"Henry 'Hank' Fomish and His Orchestra." *Lansing State Journal*, May 30, 1931, 19.

Heron, Walter Kim. "Detroit Music: The Ultimate Sightseer's Guide." *Metro Times*, December 14, 2011.

———. "They Went to Europe to Find a Jazz Festival; The Music Started Here." *Detroit Free Press*, August 24, 1980, 117.

Herron, Jerry. *After Culture: Detroit and the Humiliation of History*. Detroit: Wayne State University Press, 1993.

Herstad, Kaeleigh. "'Reclaiming' Detroit: Demolition and Deconstruction in the Motor City." *Public Historian* 39, no. 4 (2017): 85–113.

Herzfeld, Michael. "Engagement, Gentrification, and the Neoliberal Hijacking of History." *Current Anthropology* 51, S2 (2010): S259–S267.

Hicks, Dan, and Mary C. Beaudry. Introduction to *The Cambridge Companion to Historical Archaeology*, edited by Dan Hicks and Mary C. Beaudry, 1–12. Cambridge: Cambridge University Press, 2006.

Hicks, Dan, and Sarah Mallet. *Lande: The Calais' Jungle and Beyond*. Bristol: Bristol University Press, 2019.

Hill, Jaqueline Ogus (neé Jacqueline Weitzman). "Weitzman Family Oral History." Recorded by Brenna Moloney, November 8, 2013.

Hitchens, Peter. "From Motown to Ghost Town: How the Once Mighty Detroit Is Heading Down a Long, Slow Road to Ruin." *Daily Mail*, July 9, 2011.

Högberg, Anders, Cornelius Holtorf, Sarah May, and Gustav Wollentz. "No Future in Archaeological Heritage Management?" *World Archaeology* 49, no. 5 (2017): 639–647.

Homan, Kim, and Kevyn D. Orr. "Second Amended and Restated Intergovernmental Agreement between the Michigan Land Bank Fast Track Authority and the City of Detroit Creating the Detroit Land Bank Authority." December 19, 2013. Accessed October 24, 2019. https://s3.us-east-2.amazonaws.com/dlba-production-bucket/cms/IGA+-+2nd+Amended+EXECUTED+121913.pdf.

Hooper, Ryan Patrick. "Detroit's Grande Ballroom Gets Impressive New Mural Commemorating MC5." *Detroit Free Press*, October 31, 2018.

Horning, Audrey. "Politics, Publics, and Professional Pragmatics: Re-envisioning

Archaeological Practice in Northern Ireland." In *The Public and the Recent Past*, edited by Chris Dalglish, 95–110. Woodbridge: Society for Post-Medieval Archaeology, 2013.

Huebner, Jeff. "In Search of Detroit's Lost Walls of Dignity, Freedom, and Pride." *Metro Times*, February 26, 2020.

———. *Walls of Prophecy and Protest: William Walker and the Roots of a Revolutionary Public Art Movement*. Evanston, IL: Northwestern University Press, 2019.

"Interracial Goodwill Hour." *Michigan Chronicle*, January 10, 1948, 47.

"Jack Ward's Detroit Riot Monument." *Discuss Detroit* (electronic forum). Postings from 2009. Accessed February 12, 2019. www.atdetroit.net/forum/messages/5/177235.html?1235000258.

"Jazz Wars." *Michigan Chronicle*, March 19, 1949, 21.

"Jewett Plant Built by Wood." *Detroit Free Press*, January 20, 1924, 7.

"Jewish Council Blasts 12th St. Area 'Rumor-Mongers.'" *Michigan Chronicle*, January 3, 1948, 2.

"Jimmy Caldwell at the Royal Blue." *Michigan Chronicle*, January 17, 1948, 16.

"Joe's Record Shop." *Michigan Chronicle*, September 4, 1948, 11.

Johncox, Cassidy. "Detroit Land Bank Authority to Terminate, Lay Off Employees Due to $5.8M in 'Budget Shortfall.'" *Local 4 NBC News Detroit*, April 22, 2020.

Jones, Siân. "Wrestling with the Social Value of Heritage: Problems, Dilemmas, and Opportunities." *Journal of Community Archaeology and Heritage* 4, no. 1 (2016): 21–37.

Jordan, Jerilyn. "Structural Inspection Reveals Detroit's Historic Grande Ballroom Holds Promise for Restoration." *Detroit Metro Times*, February 4, 2019.

"Jumpin' Jive." *Detroit Tribune*, June 6, 1942, 13.

Kavieff, Paul R. *Detroit's Infamous Purple Gang*. Charleston, SC: Arcadia, 2008.

———. *The Purple Gang: Organized Crime in Detroit, 1910–1945*. New York: Barricade Books, 2000.

———. *The Violent Years: Prohibition and the Detroit Mobs*. Fort Lee, NJ: Barricade Books, 2013.

Keeling, David J. "Iconic Landscapes: The Lyrical Links of Songs and Cities." *FOCUS on Geography* 54, no. 4 (2011): 113–125.

Kelliher, Fiona, and Brian McCollum. "Grande Ballroom Added to National Historic Registry." *Detroit Free Press*, December 17, 2018.

Kennedy, Randy. "Fate of City's Art Hangs in the Balance." *New York Times*, December 4, 2013.

Kiddey, Rachael. *Homeless Heritage: Collaborative Social Archaeology as Therapeutic Practice*. Oxford: Oxford University Press, 2017.

Kiddey, Rachael, and Paul Graves-Brown. "Reclaiming the Streets: The Role of Archaeology in Deconstructing the Myths of Contemporary Society." *Archaeological Review from Cambridge* 30, no. 2 (2015): 135–147.

King, R. J. "Archer, Developers Want Mansions Moved to Allow Condos in Brush Park Neighborhood." *Detroit News*, February 5, 1994, 1A + 8A.

Kingsdale, Jon M. "The 'Poor Man's Club': Social Functions of the Urban Working-Class Saloon." *American Quarterly* 25, no. 4 (1973): 472–489.

Kinney, Rebecca J. "'America's Great Comeback Story': The White Possessive in Detroit Tourism." *American Quarterly* 70, no. 4 (2018): 777–806.

———. "Longing for Detroit: The Naturalization of Racism through Ruin Porn and Digital Memories." *Media Fields Journal* 5 (2012): 1–14.

Klein, Terry H., Lynne Goldstein, Deborah Gangloff, William B. Lees, Krysta Ryzewski, Bonnie W. Styles, and Alice P. Wright. "The Future of American Archaeology: Engage the Voting Public or Kiss Your Research Goodbye!" *Advances in Archaeological Practice* (2018): 1–18.

Klinefelter, Quinn. "Battling Blight: Detroit Maps Entire City to Find Bad Buildings." *National Public Radio, Morning Edition*, February 18, 2014.

Kossik, John. *63 Alfred Street: Where Capitalism Failed; The Life and Times of a Venetian Gothic Mansion in Downtown Detroit*. Detroit: John Kossik, 2010.

Kowalski, Greg. "Detroit's Disregard for Its Past Has Encroached on Hamtramck." *Review Hamtramck*, March 22, 2019.

———. "Hamtramck's Log Cabin: The Treasure Was Lost, Found . . . and Lost Again." *Review Hamtramck*, March 15, 2019.

———. *Proposal to Rescue and Restore Historical Log Cabin*. Prepared by the Hamtramck Historical Commission/Hamtramck Historical Museum in cooperation with Wayne State University, January 2019. On file with the Hamtramck Historical Commission and City of Hamtramck.

———. *Wicked Hamtramck: Lust, Liquor and Lead*. Charleston, SC: History Press, 2010.

Kubota, Bill. "Detroit's 1967 Uprising Gets Historical Marker at Gordon Park." *Daily Detroit*, July 21, 2017.

Kurth, Joel. "Detroit Pays High Price for Arson Onslaught." *Detroit News*, February 18, 2005.

Lamphere, Louise. "The Convergence of Applied, Practicing, and Public Anthropology in the 21st Century." *Human Organization* (December 1, 2004): 431–443.

Land Bank Fast Track Act of 2003, PA 258, MCL 124.751 to 124.774, 2003.

Lane, Bill. "Padlocking for Serving Underworld." *New Tribune*, June 2, 1951, 10.

———. "Swinging Down the Lane, Rockin' with LeRoy." *Michigan Chronicle*, November 26, 1949, 21.

Larkin, Karin, and Randall H. McGuire. *Archaeology of Class War: The Colorado Coalfield Strike of 1913–1914*. Boulder: University Press of Colorado, 2009.

LaRoche, Cheryl J. "On the Edge of Freedom: Free Black Communities, Archaeology, and the Underground Railroad." PhD diss., Department of American Studies, University of Maryland, 2004.

LaRoche, Cheryl J., and Michael L. Blakey. "Seizing Intellectual Power: The Dialogue at the New York African Burial Ground." *Historical Archaeology* 31, no. 3 (1997): 84–106.

Lauterbach, Preston. *The Chitlin' Circuit: And the Road to Rock 'n' Roll*. New York: W. W. Norton, 2011.

Lee, Ardelia. "Detroit Plans to Renovate 40 Neighborhood Parks across City over Next Two Years." *Daily Detroit*, March 18, 2016.

Lenhausen, Don. "Abandoned Victorian Homes Periled." *Detroit Free Press*, May 7, 1973, 8C.

Lennon, John J. "Conclusion: Dark Tourism in a Digital Post-Truth Society." *Worldwide Hospitality and Tourism Themes* 9, no. 2 (2017): 240–244.

Leone, Mark P., and Jocelyn E. Knauf, eds. *Historical Archaeologies of Capitalism*. New York: Springer, 2015.

Leone, Mark P., Cheryl J. LaRoche, and Jennifer J. Babiarz. "The Archaeology of Black Americans in Recent Times." *Annual Review of Anthropology* 34 (2005): 575–598.

"Link Woman to Dubois Slaying: Manager Shot in Face by Assailant." *Michigan Chronicle*, September 29, 1955, 1.

"Lionel Hampton at the Paradise Theatre." *Michigan Chronicle*, March 27, 1948, 17.

Little, Barbara J. "Archaeology as a Shared Vision." In *Public Benefits of Archaeology*, edited by Barbara J. Little, 1–19. Gainesville: University Press of Florida, 2002.

———. "Public Benefits of Public Archaeology." In *The Oxford Handbook of Public Archaeology*, edited by Robin Skeates, Carol McDavid, and John Carman, 395–413. Oxford: Oxford University Press, 2012.

Little, Barbara, Erika M. Seibert, Jan Townsend, John H. Sprinkle Jr., and John Knoerl. *Guidelines for Evaluating and Registering Archaeological Properties*. National Register Bulletin No. 36. Washington, DC: US Department of the Interior, National Park Service, 2000.

Little, Barbara J., and Paul A. Shackel, eds. *Archaeology as a Tool of Civic Engagement*. Lanham, MD: AltaMira Press, 2007.

———. *Archaeology, Heritage, and Civic Engagement: Working toward the Public Good*. Walnut Creek, CA: Left Coast Press, 2014.

Little, Barbara J., and Larry J. Zimmerman. "In the Public Interest: Creating a More Activist, Civically Engaged Archaeology." In *Voices in American Archaeology*, edited by Wendy Ashmore, Dorothy Lippert, and Barbara Mills, 131–159. Washington, DC: Society for American Archaeology Press, 2010.

"Little Harry's Restaurant." *Detroit Free Press*, November 28, 1934, 21.

"Local Musical Notes." *Detroit Free Press*, October 16, 1898, A5.

Locke, Ryan, Michael Mehaffy, Tigran Haas, and Krister Olsson. "Urban Heritage as a Generator of Landscapes: Building New Geographies from Post-Urban Decline in Detroit." *Urban Science* 2, no. 92 (2018): 1–16.

Long, Philip. "Popular Music, Psychogeography, Place Identity, and Tourism: The Case of Sheffield." *Tourist Studies* 14, no. 1 (2014): 48–65.

Lowell, John. "Violence on 12th—Street of Nightmares." *Detroit News*, July 24. 1967.

Lyons, Mickey. "Dry Times: Looking Back 100 Years after Prohibition." *Hour Detroit*, April 20, 2018.

———. "Hatchetations in Holly and Detroit: Carrie Nation Comes to Town." *Prohibition Detroit* (blog), August 26, 2017. http://prohibitiondetroit.com.

Malcolm, Douglas. "'Myriad Subtleties': Subverting Racism through Irony in the Music of Duke Ellington and Dizzy Gillespie." *Black Music Research Journal* 35, no. 2 (2015): 185–227.

Map of Wayne County, Michigan. Philadelphia: Geil, Harley, and Siverd, 1860. Retrieved from the Library of Congress. www.loc.gov.

Marchand, Yves, and Romaine Meffre. *The Ruins of Detroit.* Göttingen: Steidl Publishers, 2010.

Mason, Philip P. *Rumrunning and the Roaring Twenties: Prohibition on the Michigan-Ontario Waterway.* Detroit: Wayne State University Press, 1995.

Matthews, Christopher N. "The Archaeology of Race and African American Resistance." In *The Archaeology of American Capitalism*, edited by Christopher N. Matthews, 177–195. Gainesville: University Press of Florida, 2010.

———. "Assemblages, Routines, and Social Justice Research in Community Archaeology." *Journal of Community Archaeology and Heritage* 6, no. 3 (2019): 220–226.

Matthews, Denise White. "Halleck St. Kids, Now Turning 50, Plan Reunion." *Detroit Free Press*, July 1, 1993, 11C.

May, Sarah. "Heritage, Endangerment, and Participation: Alternative Futures in the Lake District." *International Journal of Heritage Studies* (2019): 1–16. https://doi.org/10.1080/13527258.2019.1620827.

Maynard, Micheline. "Detroit Polishes, and Demolishes, for the Super Bowl." *New York Times*, January 22, 2006.

Mazzei, Rebecca. "Monument Email. Email to Alejandra Salinas, 2008." Displayed as part of the *Monument to Rebellion* exhibit, by Aeron Bergman and Alejandra Salinas, 2015.

McAtackney, Laura. *An Archaeology of the Troubles: The Dark Heritage of Long Kesh/Maze Prison.* Oxford: Oxford University Press, 2014.

———. "Repercussions of Differential Deindustrialization in the City: Memory and Identity in Contemporary East Belfast." In *Contemporary Archaeology and the City*, edited by Laura McAtackney and Krysta Ryzewski, 190–210. Oxford: Oxford University Press, 2017.

McAtackney, Laura, and Krysta Ryzewski, eds. *Contemporary Archaeology in the City: Creativity, Ruin, and Political Action.* Oxford: Oxford University Press, 2017.

McCallum, Robert. "Jazz Lives: The Blue Bird Spreads Its Wings Again." *Metro Times*, June 7–13, 1995, 20–21.

McCormick, Ken. "Al Wertheimer Dies." *Detroit Free Press*, June 9, 1953, 28.

McDavid, Carol. "Archaeologies That Hurt; Descendants That Matter: A Pragmatic Approach to Collaboration in the Public Interpretation of African-American Archaeology." *World Archaeology* 34, no. 2 (2002): 303–314.

McElvenny, Ralph T. "Ralph T. McElvenny, President of Michigan Consolidated

Gas Company to Arnold Arnoldy, RE: Official Sidewalk Superintendent Membership Card." February 7, 1961. Grosscup Museum of Anthropology Archives, Wayne State University, Accession 104/249.

McGimsey, Charles Robert, III. *Public Archaeology.* New York: Seminar Press, 1972.

McGraw, Bill. "He Helped Start 1967 Detroit Riot, Now His Son Struggles with the Legacy." *Detroit Free Press,* July 20, 2017.

McGuire, Randall H. "Won with Blood: Archaeology and Labor's Struggle." *International Journal of Historical Archaeology* 1, no. 2 (2014): 259–271.

McLauchlin, Russell. *Alfred Street.* Detroit: Conjure House, 1946.

McMahon, Bryan T. "Woodward East Seeks Designation." *Detroit Free Press,* November 22, 1973, 31.

Mead, Chris. "Scars Linger in Detroit Despite Changes." *Lubbock Avalanche-Journal,* July 17, 1977.

Merrill, Zachary. *Dendrochronology Report for 2038 Halleck Street Log Cabin, Detroit.* Prepared for the Hamtramck Historical Museum, August 27, 2019. On file with the Hamtramck Historical Museum.

Merriman, Nick, ed. *Public Archaeology.* London: Routledge, 2004.

Meskell, Lynn. *A Future in Ruins: UNESCO, World Heritage, and the Dream of Peace.* Oxford: Oxford University Press, 2018.

———. "Negative Heritage and Past Mastering in Archaeology." *Anthropological Quarterly* 75, no. 3 (2002): 557–574.

Metzger, Kurt, and Jason Booza. *African Americans in the United States, Michigan, and Metropolitan Detroit.* Detroit: Center for Urban Studies Archives, Wayne State University, 2002.

Meyer, Philip. "Return to 12th Street: A Follow-up Survey of Attitudes of Detroit Negroes." *Detroit Free Press,* 1968, 7.

Michigan State Housing Development Authority. "Step Forward Mortgage Assistance and Hardest Hit Blight Program." www.michigan.gov/mshda.

Milan, Jon. *Detroit: Ragtime and the Jazz Age.* Charleston, SC: Arcadia, 2009.

Moloney, Brenna, and Krysta Ryzewski. *Report on the 2013 Speakeasy Project Excavations at Tommy's Bar, Detroit, Michigan.* Report on file in the Grosscup Museum of Anthropology, Wayne State University, Detroit, 2013.

"Money Loaned on Diamonds—Weitzman's." *Detroit Free Press,* May 17, 1919, 1.

Moon, Elaine Latzman. *Untold Tales, Unsung Heroes: An Oral History of Detroit's African American Community, 1918–1967.* Detroit: Wayne State University Press, 1994.

Morgan, Colleen. "Punk, DIY, and Anarchy in Archaeological Thought and Practice." *Online Journal in Public Archaeology* 5 (2015): 123–146.

Morton, Thomas. "Something, Something, Something, Detroit." *Vice Magazine,* July 31, 2009.

Moshenska, Gabriel. "Charred Churches or Iron Harvests? Counter-Monumentality and the Commemoration of the London Blitz." *Journal of Social Archaeology* 10, no. 1 (2010): 5–27.

———. *Key Concepts in Public Archaeology.* London: University College London Press, 2017.

———. "Working with Memory in the Archaeology of Modern Conflict." *Cambridge Archaeological Journal* 20, no. 1 (2010): 33–48.

Moshenska, Gabriel, and Chiara Bonacchi. "Critical Reflections on Digital Public Archaeology." *Internet Archaeology*, no. 40 (2015). https://doi.org/10.11141/ia.40.7.1.

Mrozowski, Stephen A. "Imagining an Archaeology of the Future: Capitalism and Colonialism Past and Present." *International Journal of Historical Archaeology* 18, no. 2 (2014): 340–360.

———. "Pragmatism and the Relevancy of Archaeology for Contemporary Society." In *Archaeology in Society: Its Relevance in the Modern World,* edited by Marcy Rockman and Joe Flatman, 239–243. New York: Springer, 2012.

Mullins, Paul R. "African-American Heritage in a Multicultural Community: An Archaeology of Race, Culture, and Consumption." In *Places in Mind: Public Archaeology as Applied Anthropology,* edited by Paul A. Shackel and Erve Chambers, 57–70. New York: Routledge, 2004.

———. "Excavating America's Metaphor: Race, Diaspora, and Vindicationist Archaeologies." *Historical Archaeology* 42, no. 2 (2008): 104–122.

———. "The Optimism of Absence: An Archaeology of Displacement, Effacement, and Modernity." In *Contemporary Archaeology in the City,* edited by Laura McAtackney and Krysta Ryzewski, 262–274. Oxford: Oxford University Press, 2017.

———. "Politics, Inequality, and Engaged Archaeology: Community Archaeology along the Color Line." In *Archaeology as a Tool of Civic Engagement,* edited by Barbara J. Little and Paul A. Shackel, 89–108. Lanham, MD: AltaMira Press, 2007.

———. "Race and the Genteel Consumer: Class and African-American Consumption, 1850–1930." *Historical Archaeology* 33, no. 1 (1999): 22–38.

Nassaney, Michael S. "Implementing Community Service Learning through Archaeological Practice." *Michigan Journal of Community Service Learning* Summer (2004): 89–99.

National Historic Preservation Act of 1966. 16 U.S.C. 470h-2(a)(2)(E)(ii)(1966).

National Park Service. *NPS-28 Cultural Resource Management Guideline.* Washington, DC: US Department of the Interior, 1998.

National Register of Historic Places. *National Register Bulletin: How to Apply the National Register Criteria for Evaluation.* Washington, DC: US Department of the Interior, National Park Service, 2002.

Neal, Mark Anthony. *What the Music Said: Black Popular Music and Black Public Culture.* New York: Routledge, 2013.

Neavling, Steve. "Councilwoman Calls for Federal Probe of Detroit Demolition Program." *Metro Times,* February 13, 2019.

Nelson, Marina. "Weitzman Family Oral History." Recorded by Krysta Ryzewski, January 17, 2019.

Nelson, Ralph. "Police Explore Detroit's Jungles to Curb City's Forgotten Men." *Detroit Free Press*, August 16, 1942, 44.

Nyman, James A., Kevin R. Fogle, and Mary C. Beaudry, eds. *The Historical Archaeology of Shadow and Intimate Economies*. Gainesville: University Press of Florida, 2019.

O'Keeffe, Tadhg. "Performance, Materiality, and Heritage: What Does an Archaeology of Popular Music Look Like?" *Journal of Popular Music Studies* 25, no. 1 (2013): 91–113.

———. "Street Ballets in Magic Cities: Cultural Imaginings of the Modern American Metropolis." *Popular Music History* 4, no. 2 (2009): 111–125.

Okrent, Daniel. *Last Call: The Rise and Fall of Prohibition*. New York: Scribner, 2010.

O'Neal, Jim, and Amy van Singel. *The Voice of the Blues: Classic Interviews from Living Blues Magazine*. New York: Routledge, 2002.

Orser, Charles E., Jr. *Race and Practice in Archaeological Interpretation*. Philadelphia: University of Pennsylvania Press, 2004.

———. "Twenty-First-Century Historical Archaeology." *Journal of Archaeological Research* 18, no. 2 (2010): 111–150.

Orser, Charles E., and Brian M. Fagan. *Historical Archaeology*. New York: HarperCollins, 1995.

Ouzounian, Gascia. "Recomposing the City: A Survey of Recent Sound Art in Belfast." *Leonardo Music Journal* 23 (2013): 47–54.

Pajor, Jeri. "Oral History Interview with Jeri Pajor, 2016." Friends of the Grande, January 21, 2018. www.youtube.com.

———. "State of Preservation." In *Grande Ballroom Archaeological Survey Report, Detroit, Michigan, October 5, 2016*, edited by Krysta Ryzewski, 45–69. Report on file with the Grosscup Museum of Anthropology, Wayne State University, Detroit, 2016.

Parkman, E. Breck. "A Hippie Discography: Vinyl Records from a Sixties Commune." *World Archaeology* 46, no. 3 (2014): 431–447.

"Passing of Fort Street West: Once a Social Center." *Detroit Free Press*, November 9, 1913, H3.

Pear, Lillian Myers. *The Pewabic Pottery*. Des Moines, IA: Wallace-Homestead Book, 1976.

Penrose, Sefryn. "Recording Transition in Post-Industrial England: A Future Perfect View of Oxford's Motopolis." *Archaeologies* 6, no. 1 (2010): 167–180.

Perotta, Ian. "Hamtramck City Council Meeting, January 22, 2019." Video retrieved from www.facebook.com/ianperrotta/videos/10106465845470783.

Perry, Sara. "The Enchantment of the Archaeological Record." *European Journal of Archaeology* 22, no. 3 (2019): 354–371.

Personals. *Detroit Free Press*, June 6, 1909, B4.

Peterson, Iver. "Street Awakening from '67 Detroit Riot." *New York Times*, May 21, 1981, A20.

Pétursdóttir, Þóra, and Bjørnar Olsen. "Imaging Modern Decay: The Aesthetics of Ruin Photography." *Journal of Contemporary Archaeology* 1, no. 1 (2014): 7–23.

Pezzarossi, Guido. "Introduction: Rethinking the Archaeology of Capitalism: Coercion, Violence, and the Politics of Accumulation." *Historical Archaeology* 53 (2019): 453–467. https://doi.org/10.1007/s41636-019-00203-w.

Pilling Arnold R. "Bunge Site Files, 20WN348, 1971." Gordon L. Grosscup Museum of Anthropology Archives, Detroit, Michigan.

———. "Detroit: Urbanism Moves West. Palisaded Fur-Trade Center to Diversified Manufacturing City." *North American Archaeologist* 3, no. 3 (1983): 225–242.

———. "Memo Describing the Barring of Women and Non-Wayne County Residents from Participating in Excavations." April 24, 1960. *Michigan Consolidated Gas Company Records*, 11W20-1. Grosscup Museum of Anthropology Archives, Wayne State University, Detroit, Michigan, Accession 104/249.

———. "Skyscraper Archaeologist: The Urban Archaeology in Detroit." *Detroit Historical Society Bulletin* 23, no. 8 (1967): 4–9.

Pinho, Kirk. "City Modern Construction in Brush Park Likely to Begin Next Week." *Crain's Detroit Business*, November 29, 2016.

"Police Get Orders to Close Detroit's 7,500 Blind Pigs." *Detroit Free Press*, May 12, 1933, 2.

Polk's Detroit City Directory. Detroit: R. L. Polk, 1917.

———. Detroit: R. L. Polk, 1927.

———. Detroit: R. L. Polk, 1920.

———. Detroit: R. L. Polk, 1935.

Preucel, Robert W., and Stephen A. Mrozowski. "The New Pragmatism." In *Contemporary Archaeology in Theory: The New Pragmatism*, edited by Robert W. Preucel and Stephen A. Mrozowski, 3–49. Chichester: Wiley-Blackwell, 2010.

Pyburn, K. Anne. "Engaged Archaeology: Whose Community? Which Public?" In *New Perspectives in Global Public Archaeology*, edited by Katsuyuki Okamura and Akira Matsuda, 29–41. New York: Springer, 2011.

———. "A Response to 'Herding Cats': Building Archaeological Communities' by John Carman." *Journal of Community Archaeology and Heritage* 5, no. 1 (2018): 55–57.

Quicken Loans Press Room. "HGTV and Quicken Loans Collaborate to Restore Historic Ransom-Gillis Mansion alongside Brush Park Development Company." *Quicken Loans Press Room*, July 23, 2015.

Ramirez, Charles E. "Hundreds Get Sneak Peek at Rehabbed Ransom Gillis House." *Detroit News*, November 1, 2015.

Ratliff, Rick. "Buy for a Song—Renovations Extra." *Detroit Free Press*, January 16, 1984, 1A + 7A.

———. "City's Brush Park Houses Unsold after a Year." *Detroit Free Press*, February 22, 1985, 3A.

Ray, Reuben, II. *Paradise Valley: Detroit*. Detroit: Xlibris, 2017.

Reed, Tom. "Digging Detroit—Episode 1: Tommy's—Inside a Detroit Speakeasy." 2014. www.youtube.com.

"Restaurant for Sale." *Detroit Free Press*, July 19, 1930, 20.

"Review of B. B. King." *Detroit Free Press*, September 13, 1968.

Roberts, Les. "Marketing Musicscapes, or the Political Economy of Contagious Music." *Tourist Studies* 14, no. 1 (2014): 431–437.

Roby, John R., and Maria Theresia Starzmann. "Techniques of Power and Archaeologies of the Contemporary Past." Paper presented at the Annual Society for Historical Archaeology Conference, Quebec City, Canada, January 8–12, 2014.

Rockaway, Robert A. "Detroit's Purple Gang: Not So Nice Jewish Boys." *Detroit Jewish News*, June 29, 1990, 23–25.

———. "The Notorious Purple Gang: Detroit's All-Jewish Prohibition Era Mob." *Shofar: An Interdisciplinary Journal of Jewish Studies* 20, no. 1 (2001):113–130.

"Royal Glass." *Electrical World T&D* 93, no. 6 (1929): 324.

Rubin, Neal. "Clues at Downtown Bar Point toward the Purple Gang and a Colorful Past." *Detroit News*, August 29, 2013.

———. "Dig It: WSU Archaeology Team Unearths Hamtramck History." *Detroit News*, October 25, 2018.

———. "Historic Log Cabin Found in Detroit—and Then Demolished." *Detroit News*, March 11, 2019.

Runk, David. "In Detroit, A Nonprofit Fights Urban Blight." *Christian Science Monitor*, February 19, 2013.

Ryzewski, Krysta. "Detroit 139: Archaeology and the Future-Making of a Post-Industrial City." *Journal of Contemporary Archaeology* 6, no. 1 (2019): 85–100.

———. ed. *Grande Ballroom Archaeological Survey Report, Detroit, Michigan, October 5, 2016*. Report on file with the Grosscup Museum of Anthropology, Wayne State University, Detroit, 2016.

———. "Historical Archaeology and the Evolution of 20th-Century Slums in Detroit." In *The Oxford Handbook on the History of Slums*, edited by Alan Mayne. Oxford: Oxford University Press, in press.

———. *Log Cabin Historic Building and Archaeological Survey, 2038 Halleck, Detroit, Michigan*. Revised Report prepared for the Hamtramck Historical Museum, City of Detroit, City of Hamtramck, and the State Historic Preservation Office, Lansing, 2018.

———. "Making Music in Detroit: Archaeology, Popular Music, and Post-industrial Heritage." In *Contemporary Archaeology and the City: Creativity, Ruination, and Political Action*, edited by Laura McAtackney and Krysta Ryzewski, 69–90. Oxford: Oxford University Press, 2017.

———. "Multiply Situated Strategies? Multi-sited Ethnography and Archeology." *Journal of Archaeological Method and Theory* 19, no. 2 (2012): 241–268.

———. "'No Home for the Ordinary Gamut': A Historical Archaeology of Community Displacement and the Creation of Detroit, City Beautiful." *Journal of Social Archaeology* 15, no. 3 (2015): 408–431.

———. "Ruin Photography as Archaeological Method: A Snapshot from Detroit." *Journal of Contemporary Archaeology* 1, no. 1 (2014): 36–41.

Ryzewski, Krysta, and John F. Cherry. "On AIR: An Archaeological Riff on Montserrat's World-Famous 1980s Recording Studio." In *Archaeology Out of the Box*, edited by Hans Barnard. Los Angeles: Cotsen Institute Press, forthcoming.

Ryzewski, Krysta, and Robert Gordon. "Historical Nail-Making Techniques Revealed." *Historical Metallurgy* 42, no. 1 (2008): 50–64.

Safransky, Sara. "Rethinking Land Struggle in the Postindustrial City." *Antipode* 49, no. 4 (2017): 1079–1100.

Saitta, Dean J. *The Archaeology of Collective Action.* Gainesville: University Press of Florida, 2007.

Sanborn Fire Insurance Map from Detroit, Wayne County, Michigan. Volume 1, sheet 6, 1884. Retrieved from the Library of Congress. www.loc.gov.

———. Volume 1, sheet 8, 1897. Retrieved from the Library of Congress. www.loc.gov.

———. Volume 3, sheet 4, 1897. Retrieved from the Library of Congress. www.loc.gov.

———. Volume 10, sheet 96, 1915. Retrieved from the Library of Congress. www.loc.gov.

———. Volume 6, sheet 3, 1917. Retrieved from the Library of Congress. www.loc.gov.

———. Volume 3, sheet 16, 1921. Retrieved from the Library of Congress. www.loc.gov.

———. Volume 10, sheet 101, 1921. Retrieved from the Library of Congress. www.loc.gov.

———. Volume 3, sheet 16, 1950. Retrieved from the Library of Congress. www.loc.gov.

Sather-Wagstaff, Joy. "Making Polysense of the World: Affect, Memory, Heritage." In *Heritage, Affect, and Emotion: Politics, Practices, and Infrastructures*, edited by Divya P. Tolia-Kelly, Emma Waterton, and Steve Watson, 30–48. London: Routledge, 2016.

Sauer, William C. "Map of the City of Detroit. Details of Hamtramck." In *General Official Atlas of Wayne County, Michigan: Containing General Maps of Wayne County and City of Detroit, General Township Maps.* Detroit: Wm. C. Sauer, 1893. Retrieved from the Library of Congress. www.loc.gov.

———. *Map of Wayne County, Michigan.* New York: Sauer Bros., 1915. Retrieved from the Library of Congress. www.loc.gov.

"Sayings and Doings." *Detroit Free Press* June 10, 1898, A5.

Schlanger, Nathan, Laurent Nespoulous, and Jean-Paul Demoule. "Year 5 at Fukushima: A 'Disaster-Led' Archaeology of the Contemporary Future." *Antiquity* 90, no. 350 (2016): 409–424.

Schofield, John, ed. *Who Needs Experts? Counter-Mapping Cultural Heritage.* Burlington, VT: Ashgate, 2014.

"Seize $80,000 Holiday Liquor in Three Raids." *Detroit Free Press*, November 20, 1927, 1.

Sercombe, Charles. "And Then There Were Just Two . . ." *Review Hamtramck*, March 15, 2019.

Shackel, Paul A. Introduction to *Places in Mind: Public Archaeology as Applied Archaeology*, edited by Paul A. Shackel and Erve J. Chambers, 1–16. New York: Routledge, 2004.

Sheehan, Thomas W. "Iggy's Blues." *Journal of Popular Music Studies* 19, no. 2 (2007): 133–156.

Silliman, Stephen W. *Engaging Archaeology: 25 Case Studies in Research Practice.* Hoboken, NJ: Wiley-Blackwell, 2018.

Sinclair, John. "DKT/MC5: The Truest Possible Testimonial." In *Heaven Was Detroit: From Jazz to Hip-Hop and Beyond*, edited by M. L. Leibler, 222–225. Detroit: Wayne State University Press, 2016.

Singleton, Theresa A. "Facing the Challenges of a Public African-American Archaeology." *Historical Archaeology* 31, no. 3 (1997): 146–152.

Smith Laurajane, and Emma Waterton. *Heritage, Communities, and Archaeology.* London: Duckworth, 2009.

Smothers, David. "Visit to 12th Street." *Bryan Times*, May 1, 1970, 5.

Snell, Robert. "Feds Issue First Charges in Long-Running Detroit Demolition Probe." *Detroit News*, April 8, 2019.

Sojourner Truth Housing Project. Walter Reuther Library, Wayne State University. Accessed October, 24, 2019. https://projects.lib.wayne.edu/12thstreetdetroit.

Solis, Ben. "Childhood Memories from Detroit 1967: 'It Was War.'" *MLive*, July 20, 2017.

"Son Gets Life Sentence in Slaying of His Father." *Detroit Free Press*, March 8, 1938, 4.

"Son Shoots Father Who Beat Mother." *Chicago Defender*, November 20, 1937, 2.

Stafford, Kat. "Bribes, Bid-Rigging Alleged in Detroit Demolition Program Charges." *Detroit Free Press*, April 8, 2019.

———. "Detroit Mayor Mike Duggan Seeking Residential Blight Removal with $420M Price Tag." *Detroit Free Press*, September 16, 2019.

———. "Land Bank Will No Longer Oversee Beleaguered Detroit Demo Program." *Detroit Free Press*, March 7, 2019.

"Staff Record Company and Dessa Label." *Michigan Chronicle*, May 7, 1949, 21.

State Historic Preservation Office of Michigan. *Ransom Gillis House, Brush Park, Detroit, Michigan: Historic and Architectural Survey.* SHPO Form P56423, undated. On file at the State Historic Preservation Office, Lansing, Michigan.

Steinmetz, Pam. "Bianchini Family Oral History." Recorded by Krysta Ryzewski, January 22, 2019.

Stephens, Roy W. "Jazz in Detroit Is Terrific and 'Crazy'—But Someone Please Tell Us Where It Is!" *Michigan Chronicle*, May 29, 1948, 19.

———. Stemmin' with Steve. *Michigan Chronicle*, October 10, 1948, 10.

———. Stemmin' with Steve. *Michigan Chronicle*, October 30, 1948, 11.

Stoler, Ann Laura. Introduction to *Imperial Debris: On Ruins and Ruination*, edited by Ann Laura Stoler, 1–38. Durham, NC: Duke University Press, 2013.

Stone, Joel. *Detroit 1967: Origins, Impacts, Legacies.* Detroit: Wayne State University Press, 2017.

Stottman, Jay M., ed. *Archaeologists as Activists: Can Archaeologists Change the World?* Tuscaloosa: University of Alabama Press, 2010.

Stryker, Mark. "Detroit Rising: The DIA's $170 Million Challenge." *Detroit Free Press*, November 21, 2015.

———. *Jazz from Detroit.* Ann Arbor: University of Michigan Press, 2019.

———. "ReBop: Detroit's Blue Bird Inn Revives its Past Jazz Glories." *Detroit Free Press*, November 3, 1996, 1G + 7G.

Sugrue, Thomas J. *The Origins of the Urban Crisis: Race and Inequality in Postwar Detroit.* Princeton, NJ: Princeton University Press, 2014.

Surface-Evans, Sarah L. "A Landscape of Assimilation and Resistance: The Mount Pleasant Indian Industrial Boarding School." *International Journal of Historical Archaeology* 20, no. 3 (2016): 574–588.

Surface-Evans, Sarah, Amanda E. Garrison, and Kisha Supernant, eds. *Blurring Timescapes, Subverting Erasure: Remembering Ghosts on the Margins of History.* New York: Berghahn, 2020.

Tabb, William K. "If Detroit Is Dead, Some Things Need to Be Said at the Funeral." *Journal of Urban Affairs* 37, no. 1 (2015): 1–12.

"Third Street Matters." *Detroit Free Press*, May 27, 1892, 5.

"Thirsty Americans Drink 250,000,000 Gallons of Rum." *Detroit Free Press*, May 28, 1927, 1.

Thomas, June Manning. *Redevelopment and Race: Planning a Finer City in Postwar Detroit.* Baltimore: Johns Hopkins University Press, 1997.

"3 Killed by Gang: 5 Jailed." *Detroit Free Press*, September 17, 1931, 1.

Thurston, Chuck. "City's Nightlife Landmarks Escape Serious Damage." *Detroit Free Press*, July 29, 1967.

"Ticket Seller under Arrest." *Detroit Free Press*, October 11, 1907, 1.

Tilley, Christopher. "Archaeology as Socio-Political Action in the Present." In *Critical Traditions in Contemporary Archaeology: Essays in the Philosophy, History, and Socio-Politics of Archaeology*, edited by Valerie Pinsky and Alison Wylie, 104–116. Cambridge: Cambridge University Press, 1989.

Townley, Mary. "Memo: From Mary Townley, VP MHA, Hardest Hit Blight Elimination Program. Notice of Funding Availability." Lansing: Michigan State Housing Development Authority, June 2016.

"Trans-Love Evolves." *Detroit Fifth Estate*, August 15, 1967.

"20 Fined for Liquor Violations." *Detroit Free Press*, July 23, 1950, 6.

"Two Bars Cited after Dope Raids." *Detroit Free Press*, May 17, 1951, 13.

"2 Landlords in Slum Area Draw Big Fines." *Detroit Free Press*, January 8, 1955, 1.

Uhelszki, Jaan. "Twenty-Five Years of *Creem*—Kiss and Not Tell, or Confessions of One of the Film Foxes." In *Heaven Was Detroit: From Jazz to Hip-Hop and Beyond*, edited by M. L. Leibler, 289–290. Detroit: Wayne State University Press, 2016.

United States Census Bureau. "Detroit, Michigan. State and County Quick Facts." 2019. Accessed October 24, 2019. www.census.gov/quickfacts.

———. Detroit, Ward 1, Wayne, Michigan. Roll T624_679, 1910, 130.

———. Detroit, Ward 1, Wayne, Michigan. Roll T625_803, 1920, 9A.

———. Detroit, Ward 8, Wayne, Michigan. Roll T624_683, 1910, 10A.

———. Detroit, Ward 18, Wayne, Michigan. Roll T625_817, 1920, 45B.

———. Detroit, Wayne, Michigan. Population, III, 1910.

———. Detroit, Wayne, Michigan. Population, III, 1920.

———. Detroit, Wayne, Michigan. 1940, 7A.

———. Detroit, Wayne, Michigan. 1930, 8A.

———. Detroit, Wayne, Michigan. 1940, 10A.

———. Detroit, Wayne, Michigan. 1930, 16A.

United States Constitution, Amendment XVIII (repealed 1933).

United States Department of Labor. *Wage Chronology: General Motors Corporation, 1939–66*. Bulletin No. 1532. Washington, DC: US Department of Labor, October 1966.

United States Department of the Interior. *Mothballing Historic Buildings: Preservation Brief 31*. Washington, DC: National Park Service, Cultural Resources, Preservation Assistance, 1993.

United States National Advisory Commission on Civil Disorders and Otto Kerner. *Report of the National Advisory Commission on Civil Disorders*. Washington, DC: US Government Printing Office, March 1, 1968.

"U.S. Dry Agents Stage Raids." *Detroit Free Press*, September 26, 1926.

Uzzell, David, and Roy Ballantyne. "Heritage That Hurts: Interpretation in a Postmodern World." In *Contemporary Issues in Heritage and Environmental Interpretation*, edited by David Uzzell and Roy Ballantyne, 152–171. Norwich: Stationary Office, 1998.

Vachon, Paul. *Legendary Locals of Detroit*. Charleston, SC: Arcadia, 2013.

"Various Thefts Reported." *Detroit Free Press*, September 26, 1898, 5.

Vergara, Camilo José. *Tracking Time*. 2013. www.camilojosevergara.com.

"View of Riotous Scene." Acme News Service, Getty Images, June 22, 1943. www.gettyimages.com.

Vlach, John M. "Above Ground on the Underground Railroad: Places of Flight and Refuge." In *Passages to Freedom: The Underground Railroad in History and Memory*, edited by D. W. Blight, 95–115. Washington, DC: Smithsonian Institution Press, 2004.

Walker, George. "The Voice of the Budding Underground: A Careful Look at the Fifth Estate." *Detroit Magazine*, April 2, 1967.

Walsh, Todd A., and Leo Early. "Grande Ballroom." National Register of Historic Places Inventory/Nomination Form. Lansing: Michigan State Historic Preservation Office, Lansing, August 10, 2018.

Waltzer, Kenneth. "East European Jewish Detroit in the Early Twentieth Century." *Judaism* 49, no. 3 (2000): 291–309.

Ward, Jack A. "Detroit 1967 Sculpture: Email to Alejandra Salinas, 2008." Displayed as part of the *Monument to Rebellion* exhibit, by Aeron Bergman and Alejandra Salinas, 2015.

Ward, Stephen M. *In Love and Struggle: The Revolutionary Lives of James and Grace Lee Boggs.* Chapel Hill: University of North Carolina Press, 2016.

Wayne County Register of Deeds. Foreclosure Notice, 2038 Halleck Street, 2007.

———. Parcel 04003331, Sale History. 624 Third, Detroit, 48226, 2018.

———. Parcel 16001965, Sale History. 5021 Tireman, Detroit, 48204, 2018.

———. Sale of 2038 Halleck Street from Federal National Mortgage Association to Ali Said, August 21, 2007.

———. Sale of 2038 Halleck Street from Willie and Mary Johnson to Laschella Johnson, 2001.

WDET News. "Why Do Hamtramck and Highland Park Exist Inside the City of Detroit?" *CURIOSID*, September 19, 2014.

"Weitzman Loans." *Detroit Free Press*, September 18, 1916, 12.

White, Walter, and Thurgood Marshall. *What Caused the Detroit Riot? An Analysis.* New York: NAACP, 1943.

Whiteman, Andrew. "Weitzman Family Oral History." Recorded by Krysta Ryzewski, November 17, 2014.

Wikipedia. "1948 in Television." Accessed October 24, 2019. https://en.wikipedia.org/wiki/1948_in_television.

Wilkerson, Isabel. *The Warmth of Other Suns: The Epic Story of America's Great Migration.* New York: First Vintage Books, 2010.

Wilkie, Laurie A. *Creating Freedom: Constructions of African American Identity at a Louisiana Plantation, 1840–1950.* Baton Rouge: Louisiana State University Press, 2000.

———. "Documentary Archaeology." In *The Cambridge Companion to Historical Archaeology*, edited by Dan Hicks and Mary C. Beaudry, 13–33. Cambridge: Cambridge University Press, 2006.

———. "Heritage Inheritances." *Archaeological Papers of the American Anthropological Association* 31, no. 1 (2020): 146–154.

Wilkinson, Mike. "Detroit Police Improve Response Times: Not All Neighborhoods Are Equal." *Bridge*, October 3, 2017.

Williams, Candice. "Michigan Lawmakers Revive Push of Historic Tax Credit." *Detroit News*, April 22, 2019.

———. "Officials Celebrate the Opening of the Flats in Historic Brush Park." *Detroit News*, April 16, 2019.

Williams, Jeremy. *Detroit: The Black Bottom Community*. Charleston, SC: Arcadia, 2009.

Wilson, Sunnie, and John Cohassey. *Toast of the Town: The Life and Times of Sunnie Wilson*. Detroit: Wayne State University Press, 2005.

Wisely, John. "Historic Marker Unveiled at 1967 Detroit Riot Flash Point." *Detroit Free Press*, July 23, 2017.

Wurst, LouAnn. "Toward a Collective Historical Archaeology." *Reviews in Anthropology* 44, no. 2 (2015): 118–138.

Zimmerman, Larry, Courtney Singleton, and Jessica Welch. "Activism and Creating a Translational Archaeology of Homelessness." *World Archaeology* 42, no. 3 (2010): 443–454.

Zimmerman, Larry, Karen D. Vitelli, and Julie Hollowell-Zimmer. *Ethical Issues in Archaeology*. New York: AltaMira Press, 2003.

Zunz, Olivier. *The Changing Face of Inequality: Urbanization, Industrial Development, and Immigrants in Detroit, 1880–1920*. Chicago: University of Chicago Press, 1982.

INDEX